# SHOCK TO THE SYSTEM

# Shock to the System

## COUPS, ELECTIONS, AND WAR ON THE ROAD TO DEMOCRATIZATION

*Michael K. Miller*

PRINCETON UNIVERSITY PRESS

PRINCETON & OXFORD

Published by Princeton University Press
41 William Street, Princeton, New Jersey 08540
6 Oxford Street, Woodstock, Oxfordshire OX20 1TR

press.princeton.edu

Library of Congress Control Number 2021936957
ISBN 978-0-691-21759-8
ISBN (pbk.) 978-0-691-21700-0
ISBN (e-book) 978-0-691-21701-7

British Library Cataloging-in-Publication Data is available

Editorial: Bridget Flannery-McCoy and Alena Chekanov
Production Editorial: Jill Harris
Cover Design: Pamela L. Schnitter
Production: Brigid Ackerman
Publicity: Kate Hensley

Cover image: Thomas Cole (1801–1848), *The Course of Empire: Destruction,* 1836. Oil on canvas (39 1/4 × 63 1/2 in.). Gift of the New-York Gallery of the Fine Arts, New-York Historical Society, 1858.4. Digital image: Oppenheimer Editions

This book has been composed in Miller

10  9  8  7  6  5  4  3  2  1

For Laura and Rebecca, who I hope never need it

# CONTENTS

*Preface and Acknowledgments* · ix

CHAPTER 1    Introduction                                              1

*Overview of the Book's Theory*                                        3

*Contributions to Literature and Implications*                        12

*Methodology and Inference*                                           18

*Plan of the Book*                                                    23

CHAPTER 2    Two Paths to Democratization                             26

*Defining Democracy*                                                  26

*Defining the Paths*                                                  29

*Theory: No Disruption, No Democracy*                                 39

*A Two-Step Theory: Disruption and
Democratization*                                                      47

CHAPTER 3    Domestic Shocks                                          64

*Coups*                                                               66

*Civil Wars*                                                          96

*Assassinations*                                                     114

CHAPTER 4    International Shocks                                     122

*Defeat in Foreign War*                                              123

*Withdrawal of an Autocratic Hegemon*                                133

CHAPTER 5    Electoral Continuity                                    141

*Background*                                                         141

*Electoral Continuity Cases*                                         147

*Path to Democratization*                                            150

*Electoral Confidence and Democratization*                          159

CHAPTER 6      Other Autocracies                                          175

               *Outlier Transitions*                                      175

               *Negative Cases: Patterns of Non-Democratization*          182

CHAPTER 7      Direct Effects of the Paths                                188

               *Predictions*                                              188

               *Empirical Setup*                                          190

               *Empirical Results*                                        193

CHAPTER 8      Mediated Effects of the Paths                              208

               *Predictions*                                              209

               *Mediation, Moderation, and Democratization*               210

               *The Paths, Pro-Democratic Activity, and
               Democratization*                                           211

               *Structural Factors and Democratization:
               A New Empirical Framework*                                 215

               *The Paths' Predictive Power*                              227

CHAPTER 9      The Paths and Democratic Survival                          230

               *Legacies of Transition: Democratic Survival
               and Quality*                                               230

               *Empirical Results*                                        234

CHAPTER 10     Conclusion                                                 241

               *Theoretical Contributions*                                241

               *Implications*                                             244

               *The Future of Democracy*                                  249

               Appendix                                                   253

               *List of Democratic Transitions by Paths*                  253

               *Coding Details*                                           255

               *Case Narratives*                                          261

               *Citations · 311*

               *Index · 343*

IN 2011, I sat down with an opposition party leader on a bleak gray morning in Singapore. We talked about the great paradox that Singapore is among the best-educated countries in the world, full of democratic supporters, and yet autocracy remains entrenched. The Party holds fast like a concrete dam. He excused himself in a rush—he had to report to jail the next day for protesting in the wrong place.

Although the spread of democracy is among the greatest transformations in human history, its victory is far from complete. Around the world, we still find overwhelmingly democratic populations facing resilient dictatorships. Recently, major protest movements in the Arab Spring, Iran, Burma, Thailand, Hong Kong, and Venezuela achieved only scattershot democratic progress. Many argue autocracy is once again ascendant.

What are the missing pieces that allow these democratic demands to succeed? Why, in contrast, have we seen successful transitions in unexpected places like Zambia, Niger, and Nepal? Starting around 2013, I set out to study as many cases of successful democratization as possible, seeking out the anomalous and lesser-studied countries. This quickly revealed a significant gulf between existing theories on democratization and the way transitions actually play out.

Yet soon clear patterns jumped out at me, especially the surprising commonality of coups and civil and foreign wars prior to democratization. And nearly all the rest were ruling party autocracies distinguished by the parties' successes after democratization. The more I read, the more I convinced myself of an overarching logic connecting democratization to elite political violence and leaders' expectations about their political power. It meant that the existing literature was largely missing some key ingredients and that much of how global actors try to promote democracy is misdirected effort.

This book is my attempt to convince you of this logic of democratization. I hope it can provide useful knowledge for those on freedom's front lines.

⟨⁂⟩

I wrestled with the research and writing of this book off and on for about seven years, through a ten-thousand-mile move, two teaching jobs, tenure, the birth of a child, and a wedding. I've accumulated a lot of debts in that time.

Among academics, I'm indebted most of all to Carles Boix, my primary advisor during graduate school, an early coauthor, and a continuing mentor. He showed me the value of hard questions and clear, no-nonsense thinking divorced from easy assumptions. He has always been ready with ungilded advice and critiques without sparing any punches and I emerged better for it. I'm also thankful for other more senior academics who have helped and encouraged me along the way, including Grigore Pop-Eleches, Philip Pettit, Milan Svolik, Susan Hyde, Christian List, Torun Dewan, and Keith Dowding.

This book was improved immensely by a book workshop in August 2019 at George Washington University. I'm grateful to Milan Svolik, Seva Gunitsky, Rachel Riedl, Dan Slater, Adam Glynn, David Szakonyi, Bit Meehan, and Bruce Dickson for participating and offering comments. Special thanks to Bruce and staff for funding and organizing and Steven Schaaf for taking notes. Thanks as well to Carles Boix and his Princeton graduate class for reading the book draft and providing great feedback. I also thank Bridget Flannery-McCoy and the team at Princeton University Press for as smooth a publication process as can be imagined.

The book benefited from many comments on its summary paper version. Thanks especially to Michael McKoy, Lisel Hintz, Jennifer Gandhi, Erica Frantz, Jennifer Dresden, Michael Joseph, and audiences at UCSD, WUSTL, Penn State, American, George Washington, and the annual meetings of APSA and MPSA. The feedback was critical for not only crafting the argument but revealing genuine interest in the idea.

For keeping me sane and still unjaded about academia, I must thank my academic friends and colleagues, especially my Princeton friends (you know who you are), Yon Lupu, Eric Lawrence, Adam Dean, David Szakonyi, Michael Joseph, Lee Morgenbesser, Brinkley Milkman, and my coauthors Maggie Peters and Christian Houle.

This book would not have happened without support from three great universities: Princeton, where I did my PhD and got the first glimmers of the idea; Australian National, where I had my first teaching job and started the qualitative work; and George Washington, where I work now and wrote the book. I can't express enough gratitude to the faculty and graduate students at George Washington, a famously collegial department yet one that has always pushed me to be a better scholar and speak to the whole discipline. I'm also grateful to Alex Fisher and Stas Gorelik for serving as excellent research assistants, including independent verifications of some of the qualitative coding.

Thanks of course to my family, especially my mother, who has supported me at every step.

Finally, my deepest thanks to my wife, Laura, who put up with a lot of me isolating myself and distractedly thinking about democratization at all hours. You've been a constant source of strength and the best part of my life. Te amo. We were lucky enough to have a daughter, Rebecca, just before I finished. One of the early quotes in the book is from a Brazilian protest leader who describes the beginning of democracy as like witnessing "the birth of a child, a miracle of nature." And now we have to care for this funny, fragile creature, but what a joy it is.

# SHOCK TO THE SYSTEM

# CHAPTER ONE

# Introduction

AFTER FORTY-EIGHT YEARS of stable autocracy, Portugal suddenly exploded. Just past midnight, a banned song promising "It is the people who give the orders" played on Lisbon radio to launch the surprise junior officer coup of April 1974 (Raby 1988: 248). This event would both transform Portugal and inaugurate the greatest global expansion of democracy in history. Yet this was no coup by pro-democratic idealists. Military leaders soon split into bitterly opposed factions, with the dominant leftist group nearly transforming Portugal into a Marxist dictatorship. After his ouster, the first president shelled an artillery regiment in a failed comeback. Opposing citizen groups seized farms and factories, firebombed party offices, and mobilized for revolution (Hunt 1976; Ferreira and Marshall 1986; Bermeo 2007). Only after two years of "traumatic psychological, economic, and political shocks" (Maxwell 1995: 116) was a group of moderate officers able to countercoup and steer the country to democracy. As Huntington (1991: 3–4) writes, this was an "implausible beginning of a world-wide movement to democracy." In fact, Portugal is so discordant with current theories of democratization that it's the sole case of twenty-one transitions Ruth Collier (1999) was unable to classify. Yet I consider Portugal the ideal illustration of how democratization really happens.

Consider a very different transition: Taiwan. Rising isolation following its derecognition by the United States in favor of China convinced President Chiang Ching-kuo to liberalize the single-party regime in the mid-1980s (Dickson 1997; Rigger 2001). Central to this decision was the accurate belief that the ruling Kuomintang (KMT) party would continue to win elections, first under competitive authoritarianism and then in the first democratic elections of 1996 (Hood 1997; Cheng 2008: 130). In fact, as of 2020, the party has controlled both the presidency and legislature in most years since democratization. Instead of violent instability and weakness, we find strength, most importantly a confidence among leaders that democratic competition did not mortally threaten the ruling party's survival. The result was a strategic, ordered accession to democracy, albeit one first prompted by international change.

Portugal and Taiwan illustrate two distinct *paths* to democratization, one following violent *shocks* and the other with a ruling party confident it can win democratic elections. I call the latter the *electoral continuity* path. These cases are not anomalies; I show that more than 9 in 10 democratic transitions since 1800 fit one of these two paths. Put another way, democratization almost never happens without a country first experiencing a major violent shock (such as a coup or civil war) or having a ruling party capable of winning power in democracy. This presents a stark contrast with popular images of democratization, as it shows that the preservation of autocrats in power and violent events typically viewed as antithetical to democracy are instead central to its foundation.

Despite their evident differences, Portugal and Taiwan also share some surprising logical connections. Both transitions followed significant *disruptions* to the autocratic status quo, respectively the 1974 coup and the international turmoil that prompted liberalization. These disruptions radically changed leaders' power calculations. In particular, both regimes democratized from a distinctive political context that *minimized the shift in power implied by democratization*. In Portugal, the regime was sufficiently divided that no stable autocratic project was viable. As a result, little power was sacrificed by accepting democracy. If anything, the final military leaders under Colonel António Ramalho Eanes maximized their long-term power by securing a right to veto legislation until 1982 and winning Eanes the presidency from 1976 to 1986. In Taiwan, KMT leaders calculated the party would thrive in democracy, again making democratization a tolerable choice.

These similarities are not coincidences. Examining the many cases that fit the two paths reveals an overarching theory of democratization that emphasizes regime power and the pivotal role of disruptive events like coups, wars, and elections. Although rarely intended to lead to democratization, these events upend stable autocracies and provide openings for democratic actors. If autocrats calculate they have little to lose from democracy and face sufficient pro-democratic pressure, then they accede to democratization.

This theory is compatible with many existing perspectives on democratization—such as providing a needed bridge between structure- and agency-centered theories—while challenging others. For instance, it implies that outside the specific political contexts defined by the paths, high-profile factors like protest, international pressure, and economic conditions rarely matter. More generally, a neglect of context has led to poor predictions and misunderstood cases of successful and failed regime change. The theory also points to new strategies for how domestic and international actors can restore momentum to the global expansion of democracy.

Combining the broadest qualitative and quantitative examinations of democratic transitions to date, this book aims to revise our understanding of both the process and root causes of democratization. The book follows several years of qualitative study of all 139 democratic transitions from 1800 to 2014, covering thousands of sources and a diverse array of countries and actors. It spans the 1848 "spring of nations" and Greece's 1862 overthrow of its Bavarian king to the Bolivian military's ill-fated alliance with drug lords and ex-Nazis in the 1980s and Argentina's folly in the Falklands War, all the way to Fiji's post-coup democratization in 2014. In the process, it intertwines global events like the two world wars and the Soviet Union's fall with the story of democratization.

Quantitative testing confirms that the starting conditions for the paths strongly predict democratization. For instance, satisfying at least one path condition (a recent shock or durable ruling party) makes democratization more than *seven times* as likely compared to satisfying none. I also introduce a novel mediation framework for testing country characteristics like economic development, natural resources, and inequality that illuminates *why* they do or do not predict democratization, addressing several outstanding puzzles. Lastly, results show that electoral continuity produces more durable and higher-quality democracies, with major implications for democracy's future.

In this chapter, I overview the general logic and process of democratization, topics that are expanded upon in the following theory chapter. For clarity, I summarize the main arguments in six key theoretical claims and explain how they are empirically supported. I then discuss how the theory builds on the existing literature and the practical implications. In the methodology section, I discuss my approach to inference, including causation and alternative explanations. A plan of the book concludes.

## Overview of the Book's Theory

### AN ALTERNATIVE LOGIC OF DEMOCRATIZATION

When Brazil's military stepped down in 1985, a teary-eyed protest leader marveled that it was like witnessing "a miracle of nature" (Sun-Sentinel Wires 1985). He had a point. Since 1800, an autocracy's annual chance of democratizing barely clears 1%. Since the United States' founding, less than one in three country-years have been democratic,[1] and essentially none prior to this date.

From the beginning, it must be stressed that democracy itself is a political paradox. Democracy means equal electoral power for individuals with manifestly unequal economic and social resources. It means groups that could take power by force and rulers that could use their positions to dramatically

---

1. The figure is 33% using Boix, Miller, and Rosato 2013 and 28% using Polity (Marshall and Jaggers 2017) with a threshold of 6.

advantage themselves in future elections choose not to. This sharply conflicts with our image of political actors ruthlessly maximizing their power.

Further reinforcing the paradox, a popular premise of scholars and non-scholars alike is that transitions bring a major shift in power from the old regime to the new (e.g., Moore 1966; Acemoglu and Robinson 2006; Bunce and Wolchik 2006; Haggard and Kaufman 2016). Autocrats and their allies lose, newly empowered parties and pro-democratic citizens win. But why do the losers let this happen? Why not fight to retain power like most autocratic regimes? One might reply that elite or popular forces coercively wrest power from the regime, leaving volition out of it, but this almost always produces a new autocracy, if only temporarily (Levitsky and Way 2012, 2013). Revolutions, coups, and protests that oust autocrats do not automatically install democracy. Rather, virtually every democratic transition culminates with a decision maker in autocracy (either a single leader or a small set of junta or ruling party leaders) accepting democratization, albeit perhaps reluctantly and under pressure.

So how is this "miracle" possible? This book proposes that the popular premise is wrong. Instead, democratization is most likely when the resulting shift in power is as small as possible, because leaders either are already weak in autocracy or believe they will be strong in democracy. If autocratic leaders calculate they have *little to lose* from democracy in long-term power and personal security, they will be less determined to resist it. When this is combined with strong pro-democratic pressure, autocrats concede to democratization. This does not require that power is the *only* thing rulers care about, but it does place it front and center. As a result, the less power autocratic leaders sacrifice by accepting democracy, the more likely it becomes.

The first component in this calculation is the leader's current power in autocracy, with *power* defined as a combination of leader security and regime strength. Leaders want to survive in office and have the capacity to rule as they see fit. To be more precise, I define *leader insecurity* as the current likelihood that a regime's leadership will be coercively overthrown, by either mass or elite challenges. I define *regime strength* as the institutional and material characteristics—including coercive capacity, internal cohesion, state penetration, and popular legitimacy—that help regimes govern and survive challenges. Strong regimes typically have more secure leaders, although a weak regime may be temporarily secure because it doesn't face any organized challenges. Leader security is especially significant because autocrats face terrible personal consequences if they are coercively overthrown.

Unfortunately for democrats, autocratic equilibria—in which leaders and support coalitions combine to neutralize opponents—can be very hard to shake once locked into place. To sufficiently erode autocratic power, the status quo must first be *disrupted* through major violent events and crises. Especially when this includes leader turnover, the resulting instability yields highly insecure leaders, supporters uncertain about regime survival, and newly emboldened opponents. In fact, most democratic transitions since 1800 featured an irregular executive turnover in the five years prior to democratization, compared with less than one in four other autocracies.[2] In contrast, peaceful mass challenges (such as protests and strikes) by themselves tend not to seriously weaken regimes nor pose a mortal threat to strong ones. A cohesive autocratic government with military loyalty and a determination to retain power is extremely difficult to defeat from below (O'Donnell and Schmitter 1986: 21; Goodwin 2001; Bellin 2004). However, *after* autocratic regimes are disrupted, they become much more vulnerable to mass opposition, similar to the pattern for social revolution (Skocpol 1979; Goodwin 2001).

The second component in the "little to lose" calculation is autocratic leaders' expectations about their power in democracy. This is mainly driven by the likelihood of winning elections, with secondary factors including other governing positions (such as cabinet offices and regional control) and reserves of institutional power (such as control of the military). Dictators, ruling parties, and regime allies frequently prosper within democracy, yet the connection from this phenomenon to democratization is woefully understudied (Slater and Wong 2013; Albertus and Menaldo 2018; Miller 2021). Perhaps surprisingly, the final autocratic decision maker in accepting democracy subsequently won the executive or legislature after 48% of all transitions, mainly through a continuing ruling party.[3] When a party accedes to democratization, it has more than a three-fourths chance of winning democratic power. Thus, autocrats with strong electoral parties should be much more willing to tolerate a democratic outcome.

In sum, autocrats are most likely to democratize when they face little loss of power from democracy, especially when combined with pro-democratic pressure. In turn, this is most likely to be satisfied either after a violent rupture or when ruling party leaders believe they can prosper in democracy. What must be emphasized is that these violent events and ruling parties are almost never *intended* to lead to democracy. Rather, they're initially elite projects to grab or maintain autocratic power. In the aftermath, autocratic leaders (many of whom take power through the ruptures) face unanticipated consequences that contribute to democratization. We can thus summarize the central thesis as follows: Democratization typically results when an elite struggle for power unintentionally produces a political context in which regime leaders do not sacrifice significant power by accepting democratization.

2. Unless noted otherwise, all descriptive statistics use data described in the appendix.

3. After 65% of transitions, *some* ruler from the autocratic period gained democratic power.

| Path | Starting condition | Key motive for democracy | Popular opposition | Examples |
|------|--------------------|--------------------------|--------------------|----------|
| Shock | Recent violent shock (coup, civil war, assassination, foreign war defeat, hegemon withdrawal) | Leader insecurity in autocracy | Protests Violent threats | Italy 1946 Portugal 1976 Argentina 1983 Thailand 2011 |
| Electoral continuity | Established electoral ruling party | Positive electoral prospects in democracy | Protests Electoral mobilization | UK 1885 Taiwan 1996 Mexico 2000 |

FIGURE 1.1. Summary of the two paths to democratization.

## THE PATHS AND PROCESS OF DEMOCRATIZATION

Having laid out this general logic, what does the process of democratization look like? What are the observable sequences of events that show this theory in action? It's most illuminating to think in terms of two *paths*, concretely defined patterns of democratization that illustrate the logic of minimal power loss.

In the first and more common path, democratization follows one or more violent *shocks* that disrupt the autocratic equilibrium. In most cases, this shock causes turnover to a new autocrat, while in others the autocrat survives but is often so insecure that democracy becomes a salvation rather than a sacrifice. I limit shocks to five of the most significant violent events, divided into domestic elite conflicts (coups, civil wars, and assassinations) and foreign shocks (defeat in war and withdrawal of an autocratic hegemon). Relying on a specific list allows for a more concrete categorization than trying to subjectively judge disruption and weakness. It also draws attention to unique elements of the political environments following events like coups and civil wars (see chapters 3 and 4). I typically require democratization to occur within five years and in 88% of cases it's within three years. A total of 100 of 139 transitions since 1800 follow the shock path, including the most recent transitions in Portugal, Greece, Argentina, and Thailand.

In the second path, which I call *electoral continuity*, an established ruling party (in power for at least four years) democratizes through elections because party leaders expect to remain competitive within democracy. To proxy for these expectations, I conservatively include only those parties that regained executive or legislature power within the ensuing democracy.[4] As a result, leaders would need to have severely underestimated their chances to fail the confidence requirement. Chapter 5 overviews extensive supporting evidence that party

---

4. For quantitative testing predicting democratization, I instead use a simpler measure of whether a sufficiently durable electoral ruling party exists.

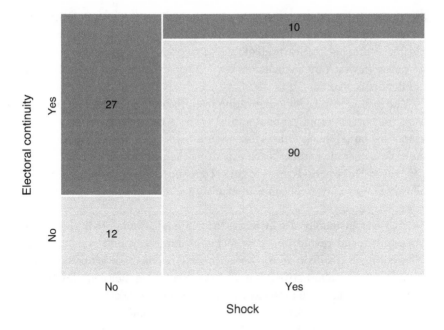

FIGURE 1.2. Two paths to democratization. Frequencies of all 139 democratic transitions since 1800 by the path taken. Over 90% of transitions fit either the shock or electoral continuity path.

leaders in these cases democratized with high confidence. To reduce subjectivity, however, my coding of electoral continuity relies solely on the concrete observables of party existence and later electoral success. In total, 37 of 139 transitions fit this path, encompassing older transitions in the UK and Sweden and more recent transitions in Taiwan, Mexico, Ghana, and South Korea. However, 10 of these also follow a shock that's considered more causally significant.

Of 139 democratic transitions since 1800, more than 9 in 10 fit one of these two paths. Thus, they combine to make up a *virtually necessary* condition for democratization. Figure 1.1 summarizes the key features of each path, namely the starting conditions, the central motives for leaders to democratize, and the most common sources of popular pressure. Figure 1.2 displays the number of democratic transitions that fit each path. Only 12 transitions fit neither, although several of these still satisfy the underlying logic well (see chapter 6).

Although clearly distinct paths, they share some important characteristics. For both paths, democratic transitions can be understood as involving two steps. First, an event dislodges the autocratic equilibrium and launches a *disruption period*. For the first path, these are of course the shocks. Many cases involve a series of shocks, but it's usually possible to identify an initial shock that sets off this instability. For electoral continuity, nearly all cases similarly involve a *trigger* that ushers in a more competitive electoral period. These are a mix of disruptions internal to electoral politics (e.g., party splits) and external (e.g., the Soviet Union's collapse) and are rarely as violent or desta-bilizing as the shocks. Nearly all of these disruptions flow from elite struggles for power in which the main actors see democracy as at most a possible, but unintended, outcome.

The second step is democratization from the disruption period. In some cases, this occurs rapidly: about a third of shock cases democratize within a year of the initial shock. Others take several years and follow chaotic cycles of multiple autocratic regimes, each exploiting their predecessor's weakness to win power. These periods provide critical openings for pro-democratic actors, allowing democracy to become an explicit goal that opposition and regime actors bargain over.

However, instability also increases the potential for other radical changes, including social revolution, new forms of autocracy, and state collapse (Skocpol 1979; Goodwin 2001; DeFronzo 2011). Democratic actors must win out against these alternatives, as well as the current regime's consolidation of power. Unfortunately, in most cases they fail. Although shocks and ruling par-ties combine to form a virtually necessary condition for democratization, they are not a *sufficient* one. Success still depends on autocrats deciding they have little to lose and actors maintaining sufficient pro-democratic pressure, with the latter strongly dependent on socioeconomic conditions.

Finally, I qualitatively coded how the final decision to democratize was made in each transition, tracking the specific actors and motives behind this choice. In brief, the decisions overwhelmingly fit into three patterns, corresponding to the mechanisms of high insecurity within autocracy, high expected power in democracy, and an elite-reformer pattern tied to regime weakness and pro-democratic sentiment. See Claim 5 below.

Figure 1.3 presents a visualization of the theory. In the shock path, a vio-lent disruption weakens regimes through effects on leaders, supporters, and the opposition. In the electoral continuity path, a ruling party believes it has strong prospects within democracy. In either context, autocrats believe they have little to lose from democracy. When also facing pro-democratic pressure, they become likely to accept democratization. Additional arrows could be added from opposition openings and ruling parties to pro-democratic pres-sure, as both provide greater room for democratic actors to organize.

## MAIN THEORETICAL CLAIMS

It's worth taking a breath here and summarizing six key theoretical claims. Each is expanded upon in the following chapter, but this provides a succinct overview and initial exploration of the implications. In chapters 7–9, I develop more specific empirical hypotheses for quantitative testing.

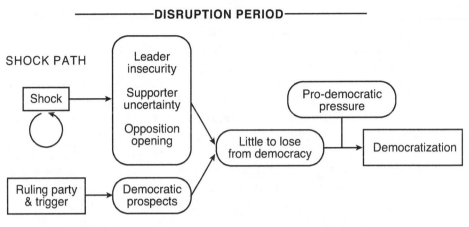

FIGURE 1.3. Summary of the book's theoretical argument, with the key mechanisms in rounded boxes. In the shock path, a violent disruption contributes to regime weakness through leader insecurity, uncertain allies, and openings for mass opposition. In the electoral continuity path, a ruling party believes it has strong prospects for winning democratic power. In either context, autocrats have little to lose by democratizing. When combined with strong pro-democratic pressure, autocrats are highly likely to accede to democratization.

I also indicate how each claim is empirically supported. Across the book, I employ three main types of evidence: case studies (chapters 3–6), cross-country quantitative testing (chapters 7–9), and qualitative measures. The latter—covering elements like the paths, motives for shocks, and the final decisions to democratize—function as "causal process observations," qualitative codings that provide evidence of causal mechanisms at work and help to discount alternative theories (Collier, Brady, and Seawright 2004).

> Claim 1: Democratization is most likely when autocratic leaders perceive they have little to lose from democracy in power and personal security, because of either existing weakness within autocracy or high expectations of power within democracy.

There are two main components to this claim: the locus of decision making and the motives for accepting democracy. First, we can source democratization to a decision made by a single autocrat or small set of regime leaders. This is a more innocuous statement than it may appear at first. Although coercive regime changes are common in autocracy, in and of themselves they can only begin a new (perhaps fleeting) non-democratic period. Ultimately, democracy requires an authority in autocracy to accept its installation. This decision may be highly reluctant and influenced by violent threats and protests. We may judge that the leaders were so vulnerable they had no "real" choice. However, it's still vital to recognize that a choice is made, rather than viewing democratization as somehow willed into being by societal preferences.

Second, leaders balance the expected benefits from struggling to retain autocracy versus acceding to democracy, with the implications for power and personal security paramount. Facing elite challenges, many autocrats determine that democracy is a tolerable outcome compared to risking violent overthrow. Alternatively, leaders may calculate that they will prosper within democracy.

The case studies and coding of decisions to democratize provide critical qualitative evidence for this claim. In addition, I directly test the mechanisms by showing that an autocrat's risk of coercive ouster and a ruling party's likelihood of regaining power in democracy both predict democratization (chapter 7).

> Claim 2: Democratization almost always occurs from specific political contexts defined by the aftermath of violent shocks or the presence of a confident electoral ruling party.

This claim posits that the conditions in Claim 1 will rarely be satisfied outside of two political contexts. Reaching sufficient weakness in autocracy requires disruption to the autocratic equilibrium in the form of violent instability. Alternatively, for regime leaders to have high confidence in their democratic chances, they typically need an existing ruling party. As a result, more than 9 in 10 democratic transitions closely follow one of five violent shocks or occur with an established ruling party that regains power in democracy.

The rarity of democratization outside these two paths reflects the solidity of autocracy without violent disruption or electoral change. Even challenges like protest movements, economic crises, and internal regime divides (that don't result in coups) are usually insufficient to dislodge these regimes. Thus, democratization is almost never driven by popular pressure from below or strategic choices to democratize independent of these political contexts.

The paths coding provides the clearest evidence for this claim. The case studies, which are organized around the individual shocks and electoral continuity, focus on how they contribute to regime weakness, electoral confidence, and ultimately democratization. Finally, empirical tests in chapter 7 show that shocks and durable ruling parties strongly predict democratization, whereas the likelihood outside these contexts is extremely low (around 1 success every 200 years).

> Claim 3: The initial shocks and events that disrupt stable autocracies are almost never intended to lead to democratization.

The events that produce the distinctive contexts leading to democratization are almost exclusively about elite contestation for power. In only six transitions (four coups and two foreign wars) did elites carry out an initial shock with the intention of causing democratization. In all other cases, autocrats or foreign powers hoped to establish a new autocratic regime or opposed the regime for other political reasons. In some, elite reformers took power intending to democratize, but within *existing* disruption periods. Similarly, in the electoral continuity cases, none of the ruling parties were founded with the goal of democratizing and nearly all of the events that triggered heightened competition were outside of any actor's control (e.g., economic crisis, Soviet collapse). Thus, democracy is usually an entirely unintended outcome of elite rivalries and autocratic failures. As evidence for this, I track the actors and motives behind the initial disruptive events and confirm that virtually none were motivated by democratization.

> Claim 4: Shocks and confident ruling parties create openings for pro-democratic activity and make this activity more effective at achieving democratization.

A consequence of autocratic disruption and weakness is greater opportunities for pro-democratic actors, including popular protest and international pressure. The same applies to competitive electoral regimes following disruption. In addition, these contexts add leverage to pro-democratic pressure since regimes are more vulnerable. Thus, pro-democratic activity takes on a pivotal importance in a way it usually doesn't in stable autocratic periods.

This has several implications. First, pro-democratic activity should be more common following shocks and with durable ruling parties. Second, democratization should be more likely in these contexts when combined with strong pro-democratic pressure. This helps to explain variation in democratic success from these contexts, as democracy always competes against autocratic reconsolidation and other forms of radical change. Third, country characteristics that predict pro-democratic sentiment should have a heightened importance following shocks and with durable parties. Chief among these are regional democracy and modernization variables like economic development and literacy.

A range of evidence supports this claim. I coded for the presence of significant pro-democratic protest, international pressure, and elite reformers—89% of transitions on the paths include at least one. The case studies bring close attention to how shocks and competitive elections increase openings for pro-democratic opposition. Lastly, empirical tests in chapter 8 confirm that protests and other pro-democratic activities are more common following shocks or with ruling parties and are more democratizing in combination with them. The same applies to structural factors like regional democracy and economic development, which have their strongest effects following shocks. In turn, this suggests a new framework for testing how structural factors flow through preceding events to predict democratization.

> Claim 5: Nearly all final decisions to democratize are made by either autocrats facing severe elite threats, reformers who grab power within

existing disruption periods, or rulers/parties that regain power in democracy.

Many democratization theories leave it unclear how the final decision to democratize is made. To validate the mechanisms, I qualitatively coded the specific actors and motives behind this decision.[5] These decisions overwhelmingly fall into three patterns. First, in the *Salvation* pattern, a leader accedes to democratization due to high insecurity stemming from elite challengers. This is a direct observation of the leader insecurity mechanism and is most common after domestic shocks. Second, in the *Reformer* pattern, a reform-minded elite takes power *within* a preexisting disruption period (i.e., not through an initial shock) and quickly and deliberately pushes the country to democracy. This is mutually exclusive from the Salvation pattern and is closely connected to regime weakness and pro-democratic sentiment. Third, in the *Regained Power* pattern, the final autocratic decision maker (either a leader or party) gains power in the ensuing democracy. This can overlap with the other two and is satisfied by all electoral continuity cases. Again, this identifies the autocrats who believed they could compete in democracy.

Seven in eight transitions overall and 94% of those on the paths fit one of these patterns. In contrast, it is rare to find decisions to democratize driven purely by protest threats, elite-driven strategies without a strong ruling party or insecure leaders, or pro-democratic actors who carry out the initial shock and then democratize.

> Claim 6: Despite some shared logical features, the two paths significantly differ on the circumstances of democratization and the chances of democratic success.

The existence of an overarching logic to democratization should not obscure the pronounced variation in how transitions play out. The shock and electoral continuity paths differ on the average level of disorder and violence, the opposition's mode of participation, the typical motives of the final autocrat, the displacement of autocratic elites, and their control of the transition. In turn, chapter 9 shows that electoral continuity leads to stabler and higher-quality democracies, although with larger roles for autocratic elites and greater institutional continuity.

## Contributions to Literature and Implications

How does this book relate to previous work on democratization? No attempt is made to comprehensively cover this literature, which might fill ten similarly sized books. Rather, I tackle three more modest aims. First, I explain how this

---

5. For more detail, see the next chapter and the appendix.

book's theory complements existing perspectives on democratization. Second, I discuss perspectives that my theory does challenge. Third, I explain how I advance related strands of the literature on regime power, critical events, and expectations about democracy. In addition, I overview some of the practical implications of the theory.

## INTEGRATION OF PAST WORK

At its core, this book concerns how the near-term political context shapes democratization. Because this is a relatively underexamined area, the framework is compatible with many existing theories and can help to integrate and contextualize them, such as by explaining under what conditions causal factors are most powerful. In particular, the political context provides a bridge between the structural- and actor-based approaches to democratization that have dominated past work.

The oldest segment of the literature, known as the *structural school*, focuses on country characteristics and broad socioeconomic forces like economic development, culture, and education (Lipset 1959, 1960; Moore 1966; Dahl 1971; Przeworski et al. 2000; Inglehart and Welzel 2005). Long-term, impersonal elements like average income are said to provide preconditions for democratization (Lipset 1959; de Schweinitz 1964; Burkhart and Lewis-Beck 1994; Barro 1999; Boix and Stokes 2003). Despite presenting clear predictions, this work often struggles to identify chains of causation that translate into actors' choices on regime change. As Huntington (1991: 107) reminds us, "A democratic regime is installed not by trends but by people."

This theoretical fuzziness produced a turn in the literature, often termed the *actor-based school*, that shifted attention to individuals, strategic choices, and sequences of events (Rustow 1970; O'Donnell and Schmitter 1986; Di Palma 1990; Colomer 1991, 2000; Przeworski 1991). This perspective sees democratization as possible almost anywhere if actors make the correct choices. Yet because transitions are buffeted by "unexpected events (*fortuna*), insufficient information, [and] hurried and audacious choices" (O'Donnell and Schmitter 1986: 4), luck and contingency also loom large. Critics contend that this approach problematically minimizes societal actors and the political context (Haggard and Kaufman 1995; R. Collier 1999; Carothers 1999; Way 2008, 2015). As Remmer (1991) argues, a focus on luck and individual initiative is effectively a retreat from generalizable theory. Causal claims, if any, tend to be specific to the actor and country, rendering democratization inexplicable and unpredictable prior to the moment of transition (Mahoney and Snyder 1999).

Instead of a long-term structural view or an exclusive focus on the moment of transition, this book's theory lies squarely in the middle and links the two approaches. As shown in chapter 8, structural characteristics strongly predict shocks and ruling parties and take on greater importance in their after-math. This provides critical connecting tissue from structure to the arena in which democratization decisions are made. Further, the theory complements the actor-based approach by incorporating individual strategic choices but improves generalizability by allowing the political context to influence these decisions.[6]

The same integrative logic applies to other causal factors for democ-ratization. Instead of challenging their causal impact, this book's framework indicates *when* these factors are most likely to matter. For instance, the theory certainly does not imply that popular protest is ineffectual. Rather, results show it is *most* effective following violent shocks and against electoral ruling parties. The mediation model introduced in chapter 8 provides researchers a method of testing variables that reveals not just whether they predict democ-ratization but *why*.

A useful analogy is that the theory works like a lens, through which causal factors pass to produce a final image. A lens can refract, dim, or color the incoming light, but the image is a product of both working together. When the light changes, so does the image. Similarly, various causal factors—from protest to economic development—can influence democratization through regime power, shocks, and parties, often with intricate patterns explicable by the theory.

## CHALLENGES TO PAST WORK

Although consistent with some theories, this book challenges many others, especially regarding the process and fundamental logic of democratization. Most obviously, it disputes a commonly held idea that violent events like coups and civil wars are detrimental to reaching democracy. As a theory about mini-mizing shifts in power, it challenges images of democratization as wholesale defeats for unified autocrats at the hands of the masses. It also clarifies the importance of tracking individual leaders and regimes to understand authori-tarian outcomes.

Yet the most significant challenge is to the neglect of *context* in theories of democratization. I argue that political context, especially how regime power is transformed by major ruptures like coups and wars, is a necessary element for understanding democratic transitions. Omitting it from theories has led to a proliferation of puzzles, misunderstood cases, and weak predictions. For instance, it has contributed to a presumption that protest-led democratization is always possible, so that if it fails the reason must lie within the protest

---

6. This follows past attempts to integrate structure and agency by allowing struc-ture to influence actors' preferences, choice sets, and resources (Karl 1990; Mahoney and Snyder 1999).

movement. To the contrary, political structure strongly predicts when protests succeed or fail (Schock 2005; Way 2008, 2015). This neglect of context extends to how scholars explain both the causes and process of democratization.

A widespread assumption is that democratization can be understood as a direct function of societal actors' preferences. In other words, democracy emerges if it has sufficient support in mass culture (Dahl 1971; Lipset 1994; Inglehart and Welzel 2005; Woodberry 2012) or among class representatives (Rueschemeyer, Stephens, and Stephens 1992), especially economic elites (Llavador and Oxoby 2005; Acemoglu and Robinson 2006; Ansell and Samuels 2014; Albertus and Gay 2017). Yet this view neglects the intervening role of regime power, as sufficiently strong regimes can nullify even the most widespread democratic sentiment. Instead, we should expect mass preferences to matter after the regime has been disrupted through shocks and crises. Overlooking such cataclysmic events is like trying to understand losses at sea by focusing on the sailors' desires to return home and ignoring the storms.

An instructive parallel is the modern literature on social revolutions. Skocpol (1979) criticized earlier work for seeing revolutions as products of popular dissatisfaction and the purposive organization of revolutionary movements. Although these elements are not irrelevant, revolutions depend first on the state facing a crisis that leaves it vulnerable. Revolutions require "politico-military crises of state and class domination" (Skocpol 1979: 17) that "both weaken[s] the state and embolden[s] the opposition" (Foran 2005: 22). Skocpol focused on international crises surrounding war, while more recent work encompasses various domestic and economic crises (Goodwin 2001; Foran 2005; DeFronzo 2011). Thus, the state must be front and center, with its leaders not reducible to dominant classes (Skocpol 1979: 29). I place a similar emphasis on regime vulnerability and crisis in reaching a different popular outcome. However, this outcome is usually reached more consensually, including through an electoral continuity path that has no parallel for revolutions.

The most common framework for describing the democratization process divides by the actors responsible for pushing along the transition (Karl 1990; Huntington 1991; Przeworski 1991; Haggard and Kaufman 2016). Huntington (1991), for instance, contrasts transitions directed *from below* by opposition movements, *from above* by regime insiders, and *from joint action*. Although a useful descriptive tool, reducing most transitions to a single protagonist overlooks strategic interaction and the political context. For instance, popular protest is most effective only *after* elites have electorally liberalized or weakened the regime through violent conflict. Indeed, nearly all transitions combine actions from above and below, with different actors taking the initiative at different times (Casper and Taylor 1996; Wood 2000). South Africa's democratization, for instance, was prefaced by years of protest and mass violence, then reform by ruling party elites, and finally extended bargaining (Jung and Shapiro 1995; Sparks 1996; Wood 2000).

Identifying *who* is driving democratization is ultimately a way of redefining the outcome to be explained. If from below, we need to identify what allowed popular actors to reach a dominant position and why regime leaders relented. If from above, we need to explain what motivated elites' choices. A gradually liberalizing ruling party and a coup leader retreating due to elite threats are both transitions from above, but radically dissimilar processes. Therefore, recognizing the constellations of power that shape transitions is indispensable to *how* and *why* they succeed.

Falling squarely on the "from above" side, O'Donnell and Schmitter's (1986) influential theory argues that democratic openings stem from splits between regime *soft-liners* and *hard-liners*, who are defined by their support for or opposition to liberalization. In fact, they claim that *all* transitions are "the consequence—direct or indirect—of important divisions within the authoritarian regime" (19). Successful transitions then require soft-liners to become dominant and ally with opposition moderates, often through an explicit pact (Colomer 1991; Przeworski 1991). This book agrees on several points, such as the centrality of the state, the rarity of transitions driven solely from below, and the common occurrence of openings prior to democratization. However, the shock path is otherwise only superficially similar. Although shocks often involve elite splits, these are violent ruptures that weaken or overthrow autocracies, not ideological divides within continuing regimes. In other cases, especially electoral continuity, the democratizing regime need not be internally divided, nor is there necessarily an accord with opposition actors. Thus, I don't find the O'Donnell and Schmitter (1986) pattern to fit many cases, although it does match some of the outliers.

## OTHER RELATED WORK

This book's theory intersects with several existing strands of literature. For starters, autocratic elections and the five shocks have each been linked to democratization, although in varying depth and without anyone integrating these events into a general theory. Further, the work on elections has emphasized their danger for autocrats, whereas I stress their contribution to long-term *security*. This research is discussed in chapters 3–5. Here, I address more general theoretical areas, specifically how regime power, violent events, and expectations about democracy have been treated in past work.

The democratization literature has only recently given close attention to the critical role of autocratic regime strength, including coercive capacity (Bellin 2004; Levitsky and Way 2010; Albertus and Menaldo 2012; Andersen et al. 2014; Way 2015) and institutional organization (Bratton and van de Walle 1997; Slater 2006, 2010; Levitsky and Way 2010; Svolik 2012). For instance, Way (2015) argues that rising political competition in post-Soviet countries often results from state weakness rather than pro-democratic sentiment or opposition strength. Given the importance of regime incapacity, many scholars recognize that democratization can be disordered and violent (Moore 1966; Wood 2000; Berman 2007; Klopp and Zuern 2007; Cervellati, Fortunato, and Sunde 2014; Varol 2017), "a story of narrow squeaks and unexpected twists" (Mazower 1998: xii) and "notoriously a chaotic affair" (Marks 1992: 397). Although O'Donnell and Schmitter (1986: 66) compare transitions to a "multilayered chess game," they also note that chaos coexists with strategy: behavior is "tumultuous and impulsive . . . with people challenging the rules on every move, pushing and shoving to get to the board, shouting out advice and threats from the sidelines, trying to cheat wherever they can."

This focus on autocratic weakness and disorder has brought attention to how disruptive events can provide democratic openings (Marks 1992; Casper and Taylor 1996; Colomer 2000; Higley and Burton 2006; Miller 2012). These can take the form of geopolitical shifts like the Soviet Union's collapse (Huntington 1991; Gunitsky 2017), economic crises (Haggard and Kaufman 1995; Aidt and Leon 2016; Houle, Kayser, and Xiang 2016), or scattered events like war and leader deaths (Marks 1992; Linz and Stepan 1996: 57–60; Boix 2003: 28–29; Treisman 2015). These events can form "critical junctures" that set regimes on divergent and often unanticipated trajectories (Paige 1997; Mahoney 2001; Capoccia and Ziblatt 2010).

For the most part, however, disruptive events in this literature are treated in passing as exogenous sources of regime crises that don't connect to a deeper theory of democratization.[7] Exceptions, like the work on coups and civil wars, are limited to specific events and struggle to account for how they translate to democratization, often mistaking the events as intentionally pro-democratic (see chapter 3). This book fills a need for a more expansive theory that encompasses a full range of shocks and explains the resulting process of regime change. Further, it draws attention to the interactive role of pro-democratic pressure following disruption.

A substantial literature touches on how elite expectations about democracy influence their resistance to democratization. This work has especially focused on fears of policy radicalism within democracy, including high levels of redistribution (Przeworski 1991; Wood 2000; Boix 2003; Lizzeri and Persico 2004; Acemoglu and Robinson 2006; Dunning 2008; McKoy and Miller 2012). Logically, leaders will also fiercely oppose democratization if it threatens them with prosecution (Huntington 1991; Krcmaric 2018) or economic ruin (Baturo 2017; Albertus 2019). As Przeworski (2015: 102) quotes a Polish communist reformer, "What matters is not *whether* we would win or lose but *what* we would lose." Despite leaving a bad taste in the mouth, amnesty and

---

7. For instance, O'Donnell and Schmitter (1986) note that elite splits can follow from protest or autocratic failure but treat this as external to their theory (R. Collier 1999: 5) and don't connect the idea to specific events (except for a fleeting mention of defeat in war).

other guarantees are therefore often necessary to reassure outgoing autocrats (Dahl 1971; Haggard and Kaufman 1995; Albertus and Menaldo 2018). The emphasis in this book is instead how expectations about political *power* influence autocratic decision makers, especially ruling parties. This expands on a growing body of work on the subject (e.g., R. Collier 1999; Slater and Wong 2013; Riedl 2014; Ziblatt 2017), which I argue in chapter 5 has been limited in scope and disconnected from wider patterns of democratization.

### PRACTICAL IMPLICATIONS

What are the theory's practical implications for promoting democracy? Although I provide greater detail in the book's conclusion, it's worth highlighting a few points here. To head off one common concern, the book does *not* suggest sponsoring coups, civil wars, or assassinations to trigger regime change, nor does it characterize them as desirable. These are bloody and destructive events that contribute to democracy precisely because of how destabilizing they are. The resulting cost in lives and long-term political disorder outweighs any temporary boost to democratization.

Instead, the book points to a superior route to democracy: electoral continuity. This is a smoother, often nonviolent path that produces more durable and higher-quality democracies, albeit at the cost of greater institutional persistence (see chapter 9). Although shocks are responsible for far more transitions, the recent trend has moved sharply toward electoral continuity. In turn, this attests to the value of supporting competitive elections and guided liberalization.

Another crucial implication is the importance of context in how protest and foreign pressure influence democratization. These actions are generally ineffectual without shocks or durable ruling parties, implying that much of democracy promotion is misdirected (or mistimed) effort. This helps to explain why so many large-scale protests fail, from the 1848 revolutions to Tiananmen Square to the Arab Spring. Simultaneously, it suggests that while violent events like coups and wars should not be encouraged, they should still be recognized as *opportunities* for democrats to strike.

## Methodology and Inference

In this section, I discuss the sample of democratic transitions, the general methodological approach focusing on the paths, threats to causal inference, and alternative explanations.

### THE SAMPLE

This book examines all 139 democratic transitions from 1800 to 2014, focusing on how shocks and ruling parties explain and predict democratization. I start with a case-based qualitative analysis of successful transitions, briefly discuss how the paths illuminate stable autocracies, and then move to quantitative testing predicting democratization in a full sample of autocracies. The next chapter describes how democracy is defined, as well as the consistency of findings using other democracy measures.

As a starting point for the qualitative analysis, I developed a detailed case history for each transition, covering the key actors and events leading up through democratization. These histories collectively draw on thousands of sources, including past case studies, news accounts, primary documents, and election results. Synopses of these histories are in the appendix.

Using these histories and event data, I qualitatively coded several features of each case. Most importantly, I determined which cases fit the two paths. Again, the shock path requires democratization to follow any of five violent events (coups, civil wars, assassinations, defeat in foreign war, and hegemonic withdrawal), generally within five years or less. The electoral continuity path requires a ruling party to democratize through elections and regain power in democracy. In total, 127 cases satisfy one of these strict criteria, leaving 12 outliers. In addition, I coded the final decision to democratize, the presence of pro-democratic protest and international pressure, and the motives for shocks. Further detail is in chapter 2 and the appendix.

By covering all cases since 1800 (including microstates), this is to my knowledge the most comprehensive qualitative analysis of democratization to date. This sacrifices depth on individual cases but greatly improves generalizability. A continual problem with the democratization literature is that theories are often built on a small number of cases in specific periods or regions (Remmer 1991; Bunce 2000, 2003; Munck 2001; Capoccia and Ziblatt 2010; Haggard and Kaufman 2016). For instance, O'Donnell and Schmitter's (1986) theory fit a pattern common in Latin America in the 1970s–1980s but less so elsewhere (McFaul 2002), whereas post–Cold War transitions shifted attention to mass protest (Bratton and van de Walle 1997; Bunce 2003). The literature has also focused on a few prominent cases like Brazil, Mexico, Poland, and South Africa. Significantly, several of this book's outliers have disproportionately influenced past theory, including the pacted transitions of Uruguay and Brazil and cases like South Africa with unusually large shifts in power. In this book, all cases are given equal weight in theory generation and descriptive statistics. As a result, wholly ignored, undertheorized, or "anomalous" cases like San Marino, Suriname, Cape Verde, and Portugal are given their proper due as equally informative examples of how and why democratization happens.

## GENERAL METHODOLOGY

Having already summarized the book's main theoretical claims and how they are tested, I focus here on my general methodological approach, particularly how the two paths structure the book's organization and empirics. According to the theory, a "little to lose" dynamic drives autocrats' choices to democratize, especially when combined with pro-democratic pressure. The paths describe *how* this is satisfied in successful transitions.

Following the general theory in the next chapter, I organize the case analysis in chapters 3–5 around the six path conditions (five shocks plus electoral continuity). For each, I develop specific theory on how they contribute to democratization. This is followed by case analysis, with two main purposes. First, I describe subpatterns within each category. For instance, I differentiate civil war cases by the war's outcome. This adds further explanatory power and depth to the patterns of democratization. Second, the cases lend support for the theory's key mechanisms. For shocks, these include leader insecurity, regime weakness, and openings for pro-democratic actors. For electoral continuity, I focus on leaders' confidence in their parties' democratic prospects. Where possible, I incorporate judgments in the secondary literature regarding motives and chains of causation. The most in-depth case studies cover Portugal, Bolivia, Nicaragua, the Philippines, Spain, Japan, Poland, the UK, Brazil, and Madagascar, providing global and temporal breadth.

To avoid focusing solely on successes, a common limitation of democratization studies, I next examine non-democratizing cases in chapter 6 and then a full sample of autocracies. In chapters 7–9, I quantitatively test the direct effects of shocks and ruling parties on democratization, their interactive effects with protest and economic structure, and the paths' effects on democratic survival. To ensure a comprehensive analysis, I developed an extensive global data set covering 1800–2014. For all variables, I carefully extended and merged existing data sources. For shocks and ruling parties, as well as other important political variables, I tried to ensure full global and temporal coverage by filling in the remaining country-years using historical sources. (See the appendix for further detail.) All data mentioned but not cited in the text are covered there.

Chapter 7 shows that shocks and ruling parties sharply raise the likelihood of democratization. The annual chance is magnified by 5 times with a shock in the previous five years and by 3.5 times with a durable ruling party (compared to neither). Yet despite their predictive power, most shocks and ruling parties fail to produce democratization. Coups, for instance, precede about half of all transitions, but 7 in 8 coups are not followed by democratization within five years, reflecting the rarity and difficulty of transition. Rather than being sufficient for democratization, the paths are facilitating conditions that require further elements to succeed.

Chapter 8 confirms that shocks and ruling parties more strongly predict democratization when combined with pro-democratic activity and structural elements that spread pro-democratic preferences. Similarly, pro-democratic activity is highly predictive in these contexts but has a virtually zero effect outside of them. Further, the interactive effect is so strong that with positive structural conditions, autocracies are much more likely than not to democratize within five years given shocks or ruling parties.

Organizing the book around the paths has several benefits. Distinguishing among the shocks and electoral continuity embraces distinct routes to democracy rather than a homogeneous, monocausal story. Using objective criteria, including a specific list of shocks, captures the mechanisms in a transparent and concrete manner. In addition, the paths bring attention to the specific political contexts in which democratization happens. No country's politics immediately following a coup or defeat in war can be understood without grappling with this context. Indeed, each type of shock contributes distinct features to the political environment that tie into democratization, such as sharply divided militaries following coups and coercive weakness during civil wars. A complete theory of democratization needs to recognize these features, while also binding the events into a unifying logic.

## CAUSAL INFERENCE AND ALTERNATIVE EXPLANATIONS

Nearly all democratic transitions occur through the paths, and empirical testing confirms that shocks and ruling parties strongly predict democratization. Before concluding that this confirms the main theory, to what degree can we infer that these are *causal* effects? Further, could alternative mechanisms explain the link?

This book presents abundant evidence for the causal effects of shocks and confident ruling parties. Causation here simply means that these conditions raise the ensuing likelihood of democratization compared to their absence.[8] For the shocks, causation played out in different ways, sometimes setting off a rapid chain of events with democracy as the final domino and other times selecting for insecure leaders who fumbled around for a bit before democratizing. Note that the shocks are intentionally limited to events with significant political effects. Plainly, experiencing a president's coercive ouster or defeat in war matters to a country's politics. Thus, it's highly plausible these events could affect democratization.

Yet shocks and ruling parties could still be endogenous to factors that also predict democracy. Leaning against this threat is that most major predictors of democratization are unlikely to also predict violent instability or the development of durable electoral ruling parties.[9] Chapter 8 provides strong support

8. In a handful of cases, a shock ends a prior democracy and the country redemocratizes soon after (e.g., Thailand 2011). Since I am predicting *democratization*, these are in fact exemplary cases of causation as the shock contributes to both the autocratic starting point and the democratic outcome.

9. For instance, Miller (2020b) finds that autocratic election adoption and democratization are predicted by entirely different factors.

for this, finding that most structural factors significantly predict shocks and democratization in *opposite* directions. Thus, it's at least as likely that omitted factors lead to an underestimate for shocks. Further, both shocks and ruling party creations are external to the democratization process since they are not a formal part of transitions and rarely result from actors intentionally aiming for democratization.

Regime weakness represents the most plausible confounder for shocks and democratization. I argue shocks produce weak regimes as a central theoretical mechanism, but what if shocks are symptoms as much as causes? Indeed, regime weakness can contribute to shocks by encouraging challenges and making regimes easier to overthrow. Despite this potential mutual causation, there are several reasons why this does not undermine the causal link from shocks to democratization. First, if regime weakness routinely caused democratization independently from shocks, then we should observe many transitions from weak regimes but prior to any shocks. In fact, this should be about as common as the shocks occurring first. Yet democratization absent a shock is very rare (excepting the stronger electoral continuity cases). Second, the causal effects of shocks, including through mechanisms outside of regime weakness, are strongly supported by case analysis in chapters 3 and 4.

Third, many of the shock cases were in fact highly durable prior to the initial shocks, including the regimes preceding democratization in Portugal 1976, Spain 1977, Nicaragua 1984, and the post-communist cases. In the Dominican Republic, Rafael Trujillo held power for 31 years prior to his assassination, which unleashed an extraordinarily unstable period. On average, before the initial shocks, autocratic regimes had continuously held power for 18.7 years and the countries had been autocratic for 53.0 years. Both figures are marginally *higher* than the average for all autocracies. Thus, these were not chronically unstable regimes. Rather, the shocks caused them to destabilize, setting them on the road to democratization.

Nevertheless, I employ several empirical techniques designed to address endogeneity threats, including a *difference-in-differences* model (that controls for country and year) and *placebo tests* (see chapter 7). I emphasize the findings' robustness to potential confounders, using a technique called *extreme bounds analysis* that explores several thousand control combinations. In particular, shocks' effects on democratization show little to no change when controlling for markers of regime weakness. I also contrast shocks with events predicted by similar factors (such as failed coups and revolutions) and find no effects on democratization.

Although there is strong evidence for causation, skeptical readers who doubt this should still find the analysis illuminating. Instead of seeing the shocks as independent causes, one could view them as *proxies* for regime weakness, with the implications for leader insecurity and democratization still following. Even if one thinks the shocks are masks for more fundamental causes—like regime strength, economic structure, or recalcitrant militaries—the fact remains that democratization proceeds in the unique contexts that follow these shocks.[10] The same applies to electoral continuity, where the electoral confidence logic holds even if the presence of ruling parties is endogenous to other factors.

Finally, suppose we believe in the causal effects. What are the most plausible *alternative explanations* for why the path conditions predict democratization and how do I counter them? For shocks, the simplest alternative (and a presumption of some scholars) is that the shocks are carried out by pro-democratic actors. Thus, democratization results from a deliberate plan and not weakness or unintended consequences. In response, I show that the initial shocks that disrupt autocracies are almost never pro-democratic.[11] For electoral continuity, an alternative is that ruling parties are forced to liberalize, with their expectations about democracy playing no role. After this, some parties later gain power by happenstance, accounting for the pattern. To counter this, chapter 5 furnishes extensive evidence of party agency and the causal importance of electoral confidence.

## Plan of the Book

This book presents a revisionist theory that counterintuitively claims that violent ruptures and continuations of autocratic party dominance are integral to democratization. When autocratic leaders face pro-democratic pressure and believe they have little to lose from democracy, because of either existing weakness in autocracy or prospective strength in democracy, they are likely to accept democratization. This corresponds to two main paths to democracy, which account for more than 9 in 10 transitions since 1800. Among many implications, the theory clarifies the interactive roles of elites and masses, showing that popular movements need to grasp opportunities unintentionally pried open by elite conflict. As the theory is based around concrete events, it improves predictions of democratization, while suggesting a new framework for testing structural factors.

Chapter 2 covers key definitions and the theory. It begins by defining the set of 139 democratic transitions and the six conditions (five shocks plus electoral continuity) that delineate the two paths. To open the theory section, I explain why the primary motives for democratization are lacking absent shocks or confident ruling parties, making transition very rare. I then elaborate on the two-step theory of the democratization process. First, a shock or trigger disrupts the autocratic regime, shifting to a period of leader insecurity,

10. After all, masks matter—they block sight, frighten children, heighten drama.
11. Even including later shocks (following existing disruption), fewer than one-sixth of shock cases include a pro-democratic shock.

supporter uncertainty, and openings for opposition actors. Second, facing this challenging environment, dictators abandon repression and accede to democratization.

Chapter 3 begins the qualitative analysis with the democratic transitions following three types of domestic shocks: coups, civil wars, and assassinations. For each, I review the related literature and develop specific theory connecting the events to the mechanisms, especially leader insecurity. For the coup cases, the largest category, I show that democratization centers around military factionalism, failed autocratic projects, and chaotic cycles of violence, rather than pro-democratic coup plots. I contrast cases with single versus multiple coups, as well as by the initial motives of the single coups. Bolivia 1979–82 and Portugal 1976 are the most detailed cases. For civil wars, I argue that ongoing wars (e.g., the Philippines 1986) and stalemates (e.g., Mozambique 1994) should predict democratization more than rebel or government victories, unless the winners are unusually divided or weak. Lastly, I show that assassinations can predict democratization either by creating power vacuums (e.g., Pakistan 1988) or by shifting power to reformist leaders (e.g., Spain 1977).

Chapter 4 examines two international shocks: defeat in international war and withdrawal of an autocratic hegemon. I argue that *defeat* in war has a special relationship to democratization, matching an earlier pattern for liberalization in medieval Europe. I divide the cases by whether the victor intentionally democratized the country or not. The former include the defeated Axis powers after World War II. More surprisingly, democratization can also result if the victor is indifferent or even hostile to democracy (e.g., Prussia for France 1870). For hegemonic withdrawal, I focus on nine cases of post-communist transition after the Soviet collapse, particularly Poland 1989. I also briefly discuss Nazi Germany's withdrawal in several transitions that are primarily attributed to war.

Chapter 5 covers the electoral continuity cases. I elaborate on the triggers that initially shift ruling parties to heightened competition, as well as the sources of pro-democratic pressure. The chapter's second half presents case evidence that party elites democratized because of positive electoral expectations. I divide between older cases like UK 1885 (involving suffrage extension) and newer cases like Taiwan 1996 (involving increased competition), as well as between parties that kept power through democratization versus winning power later. I also discuss near-misses for the electoral continuity path (e.g., Brazil 1985) and autocrats that *resisted* democratization because they were not confident (e.g., Central African Republic 1993).

Chapter 6 overviews all other autocracies. I first discuss the twelve outliers outside the two paths, arguing that several fit the logic (if not the letter) of specific path conditions and noting some commonalities, such as the roles of protest and autocratic elections. I then examine how the paths framework can help explain autocratic *stability*. In fact, a majority of non-democratizing autocracies are well explained by the theory as they neither follow shocks nor have a sufficiently durable ruling party.

Chapter 7 begins the quantitative analysis, focusing on direct effects of the shocks and durable ruling parties. Using a range of controls and empirical techniques, I show that these path conditions strongly predict democratization, whereas events like revolutions, coup attempts, and victories in war do not. I also compare subtypes within the shocks (such as civil war outcomes) that test expectations drawn from the case studies. Lastly, I use country- and party-level characteristics to estimate propensities for irregular turnover and party victories in democracy, proxying for leader insecurity and party confidence. Both estimated propensities are shown to predict democratization.

Chapter 8 shows that pro-democratic activity and structural characteristics like economic development have stronger democratizing effects in combination with shocks and durable ruling parties. In fact, given positive structural conditions in either context, it is much more likely than not that countries democratize within five years. I then develop a novel mediation framework for testing how structural variables predict democratization. Country-level factors can predict shocks or ruling parties, as well as interact with them in predicting democratization. This illuminates *why* certain characteristics predict democratization and allows for other nuanced predictions like the type of democratization. I first apply this mediation framework to economic development, then summarize the patterns for a range of other variables, only a hint of the potential applications.

Chapter 9 relates the paths to ensuing democratic performance. I argue that electoral continuity should produce more durable and higher-quality democracies compared to post-shock cases. Empirical analysis confirms that countries that democratize with durable ruling parties produce healthier democracies, especially compared to transitions following domestic shocks.

Chapter 10 summarizes the findings and draws out further implications, such as what the findings recommend for international democracy promotion and opposition strategy. I also offer ideas for work building on this book and explore what the theory suggests for the future of global democracy.

CHAPTER TWO

# Two Paths to Democratization

THIS CHAPTER EXPLAINS how shocks and ruling parties shape regime power and produce political contexts favorable to democratization. It begins by introducing the measure of democracy, with the resulting 139 transitions. I then define the two paths to democratization, as captured by six concrete conditions: five shocks and electoral continuity. More than 9 in 10 democratic transitions satisfy at least one of these six conditions. I also present initial evidence that they predict a higher likelihood of democratization.

The book's theory of democratization follows. I begin by outlining how stable autocracy rests on an equilibrium in which leaders rely on elite supporters to restrain opponents. I then argue the key motives for democratization— leader insecurity within autocracy and expectations about democracy—are muted without prior shocks or a strong ruling party. This explains why the two paths collectively form close to a necessary condition for democratization. Next, I flesh out the two-step process of democratization through the paths. First, a disruptive event breaks the autocratic equilibrium, producing an unstable period with insecure leaders, uncertain elite supporters, and openings for the opposition. Second, autocratic leaders accede to democratization when they perceive they have little to lose from democracy and face sufficient pro-democratic pressure. I place special emphasis on describing these disruptive contexts and autocrats' calculations regarding democratization.

## Defining Democracy

Scholars have debated the proper measure of democracy for decades. Although I focus on a specific measure to reach a well-defined set of cases, I confirm my findings on the paths with two other popular measures. Throughout the book, I use the binary democracy measure of Boix, Miller, and Rosato (2013; hereafter BMR) to identify democratic transitions, as well as samples of democracies and autocracies.[1] In its current update, the measure covers 1800–2015 and is globally comprehensive, including microstates. BMR follows Dahl 1971 in conceptualizing democracy along two dimensions: contestation (the fairness and competitiveness of elections) and inclusiveness (who is allowed to participate). Specifically, a democracy in BMR must allow free and fair elections with a suffrage threshold of half of adult men.[2] This is a relatively minimal democracy coding, without a requirement of electoral turnover or subjective facets of democratic quality.[3]

I make two minor restrictions to the democratization cases. First, I limit transitions to 1800–2014. In BMR, two countries (Tunisia, Nigeria) democratize in 2015, but this is too recent to determine if they satisfy the electoral continuity path. Second, four countries democratized within a few years of independence but without fully formed autocratic regimes. Since my concern is democratization from autocracy, these are omitted (but see below on how they fit the paths).[4] Following normal practice, I also don't count the 69 countries that were democratic at independence.[5]

As one of the BMR authors, I was involved in the coding, mainly for 1990 onward. However, except for the 2011–14 period, which includes only three transitions, the coding was completed before this book was conceived. While writing the book, I identified a small number of recommended changes to

1. There is ongoing debate as to whether continuous measures of democracy are preferable given the rise of "hybrid regimes" (Cheibub, Gandhi, and Vreeland 2010; Boix, Miller, and Rosato 2013). However, increases on a continuous measure lump together disparate events like autocratic liberalization and democratic deepening alongside democratization. Further, for theory development, it's advantageous to focus on a manageable number of fundamental cases.

2. The focus on male suffrage, which follows R. Collier 1999 and Rueschemeyer, Stephens, and Stephens 1992, is due to the historical contingency of men getting enfranchised first. Requiring female suffrage would almost entirely omit the nineteenth century's political development along class lines. However, BMR now includes a democracy measure requiring female suffrage. Using this instead does not dramatically change the set of cases: it introduces 9 new transitions (including the United States), eliminates 12, and shifts the dates for 9. Nearly all of the new and shifted transitions fit the electoral continuity path. On the essential subject of female enfranchisement, see Paxton et al. 2003; Przeworski 2009a; and Teele 2018.

3. Note that BMR codes countries under foreign occupation as continuations of the previous regime type. This avoids counting the restoration of elected government in, say, the Netherlands after World War II as democratization. Counting these cases would only bolster my theory, as they all followed defeat in war. Countries like Vichy France that had functioning domestic governments despite foreign domination are considered autocracies.

4. Post-Soviet transitions in Latvia and Lithuania are included despite brief autocratic spells since they were previously independent and had semiautonomous regimes under Soviet rule.

5. What determines regime type at independence is an interesting question but a fundamentally different one than democratization from an independent autocracy.

the data, which are described in the appendix.[6] Since the changes are minor and don't meaningfully affect the theory, I keep the original data to avoid any perception of my "rigging" the measure.

The result is 139 democratic transitions between 1800 and 2014, with the first in France in 1848 and the most recent in Fiji in 2014. A full list of these transitions is in the appendix, along with case histories and categorizations. Throughout, I use "France 1848" to stand for "the democratic transition in France in 1848" and often omit the year when this is clear from the context. For empirical testing and some descriptive statistics, I use a slightly smaller sample that omits the microstates but still includes 132 democratic transitions and 11,489 autocratic country-years.

This list of democratic transitions corresponds well with other popular measures. For comparison, consider the transitions in Cheibub, Gandhi, and Vreeland 2010 (hereafter CGV) and the Polity data set, using a threshold of 6 on the cumulative democracy score (Marshall and Jaggers 2017). Both are widely used data sets that differ somewhat on the criteria for democracy. For instance, CGV requires at least two electoral alternations in power and Polity omits a suffrage requirement. I consider transitions to match if they disagree on timing by two years or less or if there's a clear shift on Polity to just below the 6 threshold. Using these criteria, 124 of 139 transitions (89.2%) in BMR match one or both of these data sets, are missed by Polity because they correspond to suffrage extensions (five cases), or both data sets are missing data (one case). For 1946–2008, CGV's date range, 103 of 108 BMR transitions (95.4%) match.[7] Below, I discuss how additional democratic transitions in Polity and CGV fit the paths.

For 1800–2014, Figure 2.1 shows the annual fraction of independent countries that are democratic according to BMR, as well as global averages for Polity and V-Dem's polyarchy index (Coppedge et al. 2018). The three waves of democratization identified in Huntington 1991 are easy to see, especially for BMR. In the First Wave from roughly 1848 to 1920, competitive electoral regimes in Europe and Latin America democratized by extending suffrage to previously excluded groups. Polity exceeds BMR during this period because it ignores suffrage limitations. After a reverse wave punctuated by the rise of fascism, the Second Wave from about 1945 to 1955 followed the Allied victory in World War II, again centered in Europe and Latin America. The percentage of democracies subsequently declined due to Cold War tensions and a host of new countries in Africa and Asia that became autocratic, although the absolute

6. I make seven recommendations. Five slightly shift the democratization date without affecting the path coding. One adds a postwar case (Denmark 1945) and one consolidates two post-coup cases (Panama 1950, 1952) into one (in 1956). Thus, the total number of transitions and number that fit the paths are unchanged.

7. For democracy itself (rather than transitions), BMR agrees with CGV in 95.5% of country-years and with Polity in 93.8%.

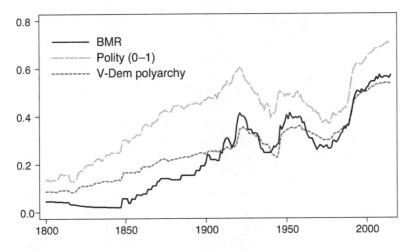

FIGURE 2.1. Global average of democracy over time. Global yearly averages of three democracy measures: BMR (the main measure), Polity (normalized to 0–1), and V-Dem's Polyarchy Index for 1800–2014 (N=11,489).

number of democracies increased (Doorenspleet 2000). Lastly, the Third Wave, often dated as beginning with Portugal's coup in 1974, was the most dramatic and globally inclusive, encompassing the fall of the Soviet Union and the democratization of much of Eastern Europe, Latin America, and sub-Saharan Africa. Although some count us as still in the Third Wave, democracy has stagnated globally since about 2000.[8]

## Defining the Paths

I now rigorously define the two paths and how the transitions are categorized. The first path consists of five shocks (three domestic, two international) that precede democratization, all major disruptions surrounding elite contestation for power. In every case, autocracy continues after the shock, but a (possibly new) leader eventually relents to democratization. The second path is electoral continuity, with requirements both before and after democratization. I first describe my qualitative coding of the paths, then explain why this categorization was chosen and some of its advantages. Finally, aided by quantitative proxies for the six path conditions, I overview descriptive statistics on the paths, the timing of events, and how the conditions predict democratization. Significantly, democratization is extremely rare when none of the six conditions are satisfied.

8. For more on waves, see Huntington 1991; Doorenspleet 2000; Weyland 2014; and Gunitsky 2017.

## DEFINITIONS OF SHOCKS AND
## ELECTORAL CONTINUITY

Starting with the five shocks, I define the six conditions and indicate the number of corresponding transitions. Lists of transitions that satisfy each condition are in chapters 3–5.

For each transition, I used the detailed case history summarized in the appendix to determine which of the conditions it satisfies. Importantly, each condition is defined concretely, whereas most existing categorizations of democratization depend on subjective judgments like the degree of redistributive pressure. The definitions do not entirely eliminate subjectivity but reduce it by revolving around specific events. I discuss some nuances in these judgments below. In particular, the shock conditions all require democratization *after* a specific event. I generally focused on the five years before democratization but counted three cases that took longer because of a clear causal link from the event to democratization. Most cases took much less than five years.

Several transitions satisfy multiple conditions, with a sequence of events leading up to democratization. For these cases, I judged which condition was most significant, with a preference for events earlier on the causal chain. The transition is considered a *primary case* for the most significant condition and a *secondary case* for any others. For instance, Argentina democratized shortly after defeat in the Falklands War, but the war followed (temporally and causally) coups in 1976 and 1981. Hence, Argentina 1983 is a primary coup case and secondary postwar case. This designation is just for categorization purposes and does not affect the quantitative testing. The transition numbers below are for primary cases, with secondary cases discussed in the descriptive statistics.

### DOMESTIC SHOCKS

#### *Coup (55 transitions)*

Democratization occurs after a successful coup that forcibly removes the executive or changes the system of government.

The 55 post-coup transitions make up the most common type of democratization, reflecting both the frequency and disruptive impact of coups. A coup is defined as a coercive change in leadership or regime orchestrated by government elites. By far, the most common coup initiators are military actors, with a mix of generals and more junior officers. A handful of cases involve other state security forces (such as the national police chief in Panama 1950 and 1952) or government elites (such as the king and fascist council in Italy 1946, a secondary case). The definition also includes foreign-supported coups and self-coups, in which an executive unconstitutionally changes the system of government and consolidates power. However, only two cases qualify solely through self-coups. As we will see, nearly all post-coup cases are characterized by violent instability, factionalism, and regime weakness.

### Civil War (18 transitions)

Democratization occurs during or after a civil war or major insurgency.

- The conflict must involve at least 1,000 deaths or more than 1 in 1,000 citizens.
- The principal aim of the anti-government side is not democracy.

These transitions can proceed after a civil war's resolution or while it's still ongoing, which occurred in 6 of 18 primary cases. Internationalized civil wars and both peripheral and center-seeking conflicts are counted. However, governments involved in other states' civil wars are not. There are two further requirements. First, the civil war must be sufficiently destructive, with all but one exceeding 1,000 total deaths. The "1 in 1,000 citizens" clause allows in Suriname 1988, which followed a civil war with about 500 deaths out of a population of 400,000. I judged this conflict to be significant enough to the country to merit inclusion. Second, conflicts fought over democracy are not counted. This is to avoid including cases of mass violence that were internal to the transitions themselves, such as the disordered fighting leading up to Romania 1991 and Indonesia 1999. The civil wars triggered high regime instability and coercive incapacity, with transitions especially likely after negotiated settlements or during ongoing wars. Significantly, only two primary cases (Nicaragua 1984, Liberia 2006) involved revolutionary takeovers of the state.

### Assassination (2 transitions)

Democratization occurs after the assassination of the head of state or head of government.

The final domestic shock category is by far the smallest, with only two primary cases. An assassination involves the killing of the head of state or head of government, but not during an organized takeover of the state. Thus, an executive getting killed during a successful coup is not counted. By abruptly changing leaders, assassinations disrupt power relations and increase uncertainty, while potentially shifting control to a pro-democratic leader.

## INTERNATIONAL SHOCKS

### Defeat in War (16 transitions)

Democratization occurs after an external warring power produces government collapse by removing the executive or conquering substantial state territory.

These cases followed defeat in an international war. In 12 cases, the victor fully conquered the state or coercively removed the leader. In another 4 cases, an external power took over significant state territory and the government collapsed in the aftermath. In some cases, democratization followed through deliberate imposition by the external powers (as in Italy and Japan post–World War II), while in others the victor was indifferent or hostile to democracy. Even without full conquest, defeat in war shatters regime legitimacy and coercive capacity, creating an opening for pro-democratic actors.

## *Withdrawal of Hegemon (9 transitions)*

Democratization occurs after an external autocratic hegemon withdraws coercive control.

The final shock category involves the withdrawal of an autocratic hegemon from coercively dominating the state, best typified by the end of Soviet control of Eastern Europe in the late 1980s. This does not count states following independence or military occupation without functioning domestic governments. Rather, each state must have had nominal independence but with the hegemon in sufficient control that it prevented any democratizing moves. This control ends when the hegemon is unable or unwilling to enforce such a veto. Concurring with Gunitsky (2017), I define the set of autocratic hegemons during this period as the Soviet Union and Nazi Germany. The primary cases are all post-Soviet transitions, with secondary cases following liberation from the Nazis.

## ELECTORAL CONTINUITY

### *Electoral Continuity (27 transitions)*

Democratization occurs when an established ruling party (or party leader) democratizes through elections and then wins power in the ensuing democracy.

- The ruling party must have continuously controlled government without a coup or revolution for at least one election cycle and at least four years.
- By two electoral cycles after transition, the party (or party leader) must either (a) win executive power, (b) win a legislative plurality, or (c) win at least 40% of legislative seats (and later win a legislative plurality).

The core logic of the electoral continuity path is an established ruling party democratizing through elections due to confidence in its democratic prospects. Capturing this necessitates the most involved definition, with requirements both before and after democratization. It must be emphasized that this does *not* include all transitions through elections. For instance, El Salvador 1984 fails despite the military party later winning power because it was created too close to democratization. Brazil 1985 fails because the ruling party never regained power.

Let's go through each element of the definition. First, a ruling party must democratize through elections, by either winning a founding democratic election or accepting a loss. If the regime is overthrown before elections, it's disqualified. Second, the ruling party must have continuously controlled government for at least four years before democratization and won a prior national election.[9] Surprisingly, only 37.5% of autocracies with elections meet this party durability condition. There is no requirement of prior *multiparty* elections, allowing in nine single-party cases. Third, the party (or party leader) must then win executive or legislative power within democracy, in either the founding democratic election or the following two elections. Parties in power solely through power-sharing agreements or transitional governments are not counted. Alternatively, the party can gain at least 40% of seats and later win power—this allows in Guyana 1992, in which the former ruling party consistently exceeded this threshold but did not regain power until 2015. Including the party leader as sufficient allows in Benin 1991, where the ruling party disintegrated but the party leader and president regained power as an independent.

The requirement of a post-democratization victory proxies for party confidence before democratization. Directly measuring these expectations is inherently subjective, whereas post-transition outcomes can concretely identify parties that should have anticipated democratic success. In fact, all we need to assume is that party elites did not drastically underestimate their chances. However, this conservatively omits a number of parties that were electorally confident but miscalculated, a point elaborated upon in chapter 5. Another limitation of using post-transition events is that cases cannot be categorized immediately after democratization (as already seen for Nigeria and Tunisia) nor can the events predict democratization. Therefore, for empirical testing, I only use the initial requirement of a durable electoral ruling party, of which about three-quarters regain power if they accede to democracy.

### Why This Set of Events

Why use these specific events to define the paths to democratization? Initially, I derived the two paths concept inductively, by examining case histories and recognizing a consistent pattern of either violent contestation among elites or an electoral continuity path preceding democracy. I then specified what I regard as the most politically significant events related to elite competition for

9. For older constitutional monarchies, parties with a lower-house majority are counted as controlling government since they could effectively control legislation. This is only relevant to Denmark 1901.

autocratic power, whether against domestic rivals (coups, civil wars, assassi-nations) or foreign adversaries (international war, hegemonic withdrawals).[10] In particular, all disrupt autocratic regimes and contribute to political flux. Similarly, electoral continuity springs from the ruling party's consolidation and maintenance of power. In several cases, the conditions were pared down to avoid applying to too many autocracies. For instance, electoral continu-ity only includes a carefully defined subset of transitions through elections. Finally, two conditions were slightly altered to include three transitions that fit the condition's logic while missing on a technicality.[11]

One advantage of this set of shocks is that none can be part of the democ-ratization process itself. No planned transition process culminates with a coup or assassination, although they may shift power to actors who begin such a process. For electoral continuity, because of the four-year durability require-ment, none of the parties were created solely for democratization.

To be clear, I don't claim these are the only events relevant to autocratic power or regime change, only that they form a parsimonious and theoretically coherent set of events that strongly predict democratization. In chapter 6, I consider whether other events should be added as shocks, including natural leader deaths, economic crises, natural disasters, and other elite splits. Most have little explanatory power, especially for the twelve path outliers. Further, economic crises and elite splits are best thought of as mechanisms for the existing shocks.

## DESCRIPTIVE STATISTICS

The coding described above is a *qualitative* paths coding based on my evalua-tion of events (e.g., what constitutes a coup) and their links to democratization. This categorization structures the theory and case discussion. For empirical testing, I use a *quantitative* coding that captures each condition using cross-country data. These alternative measures provide an external check on my evaluations and a way to test in the full autocratic sample. In about 90% of cases, my coding and the external measures agree.

### Frequency of Shocks and Durable Ruling Parties
The five shocks and the requirement of a durable electoral ruling party rep-resent six *path conditions* that predict democratization. Comprehensively testing this requires measures of each condition across the full sample of autocracies, supplementing my coding of successful transitions. For each

10. For this reason, protest-led ousters of autocrats are not counted as shocks but as mechanisms following shocks. Considering them independent shocks would explain four further transitions (see chapter 6).

11. These are Suriname 1988, Benin 1991, and Guyana 1992.

shock, I track whether such an event occurred in the previous five years.[12] As described in the appendix, I extended existing data sets on coups, civil wars, assassinations, and defeats in war to cover 1800–2014 and to be globally comprehensive. Hegemonic withdrawal is counted for Nazi-dominated countries in 1944 and for Soviet-dominated countries in 1989. Lastly, electoral continuity is proxied for by the presence of an electoral ruling party in uninterrupted power for 4+ years. Measuring this again required extending existing data and checking for party turnovers. These measures are used throughout the book, especially in the quantitative testing in chapters 7–9.

Using these measures, a shock occurred in 11.6% of autocratic country-years. If we omit ongoing civil wars, this drops to 5.5%, mostly representing coups. In total, 29.4% of autocracies faced a shock in the previous five years and 24.5% had a sufficiently durable electoral ruling party. Just under half of autocracies satisfy one of these two. Thus, the path conditions are neither so rare nor so common that we cannot get empirical leverage.

### Relationship to Democratization

As already highlighted, 91% of democratic transitions (127 of 139, to be precise) qualify for one of the two paths by my coding.[13] In addition, 45 transitions qualify for multiple conditions, including 17 secondary civil war cases and 10 secondary electoral continuity cases. Five transitions qualify for three conditions.[14] Further, 80 of the 127 transitions that fit the paths followed multiple violent events, such as countercoups and insurgencies. Again, a narrow *majority* of autocratic country-years lack a shock in the previous five years or a sufficiently durable ruling party.

At minimum, this shows that democratization almost always occurs in contexts defined by violent shocks or confident parties. Even if one doubts the rest of the theory, this fact by itself is of great significance for understanding the democratization process and autocratic stability.

Figure 2.2 presents an initial demonstration of how well the path conditions predict democratization, comparing the annual likelihood of democratization by how many conditions are satisfied (using the quantitative measures). What is most illuminating is the extremely low likelihood of democratization absent any of the conditions: a 0.28% annual probability (or one case every 357 years).[15] Thus, the paths together form a virtually necessary condition for democratization. With one condition satisfied, the probability jumps to 1.81%. With two or more satisfied, it jumps again to 3.01%. In total,

12. Thus, if a transition occurs in 2000, this measure looks for shocks from 1995 to 1999.
13. Using the quantitative coding, 88% of the 132 transitions for which data are available qualify.
14. These are Italy 1946, Cyprus 1977, Nigeria 1979, Argentina 1983, and Nepal 2008.
15. Even this is a slight overestimate as it ignores events the same year as democratization, such as Zia's assassination in Pakistan 1988.

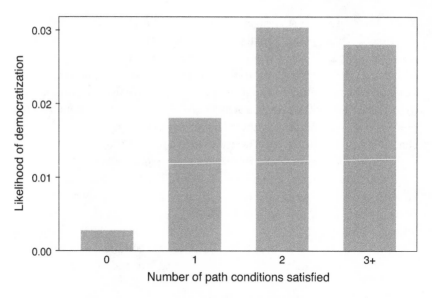

FIGURE 2.2. Path conditions and democratization. The likelihood of democratization by the number of path conditions satisfied. The conditions include coups, civil wars, assassinations, defeat in foreign war, and hegemonic withdrawal in the previous five years, as well as the presence of an electoral ruling party for four continuous years. The sample includes all autocracies, 1800–2014 (N = 11,489).

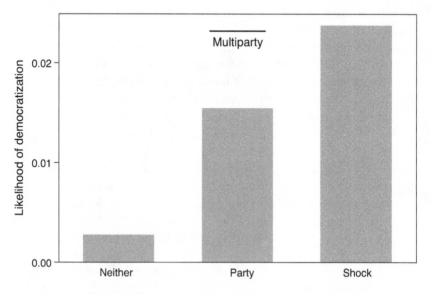

FIGURE 2.3. The two paths and democratization. The likelihood of democratization by whether there has been a qualifying shock in the previous five years, an electoral ruling party for four continuous years, or neither. The sample includes all autocracies, 1800–2014 (N = 11,489).

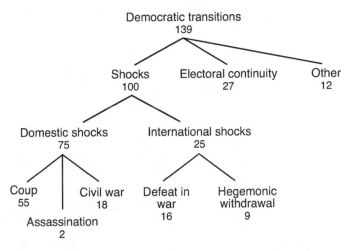

FIGURE 2.4. Frequency of specific routes to democratization for all transitions since 1800, broken down by the two paths and specific shocks.

the likelihood of democratization increases by a factor of *seven* when at least one condition is satisfied, a remarkably strong effect.

Figure 2.3 presents a slightly different cut of the data, comparing the likelihood of democratization after any shock, with a durable ruling party but without a shock, and with neither. The line above Party indicates the likelihood with the added requirement of 4+ years of multiparty competition, arguably a better proxy for the disruption periods. Shocks are the most predictive, but ruling parties (especially those allowing competition) also sharply increase the chances for democratization.

The figures also reveal that most shocks and ruling parties do not lead to democratization. Again, the paths are close to *necessary* but are not *sufficient*. Democratic success requires the opening to be grasped by pro-democratic actors. If they're absent or ineffective, democratization is often elusive. In turn, this implies that pro-democratic activity and its structural predictors will have heightened importance in these contexts.

### Distribution of Types

Figure 2.4 displays the distribution of transition types by my coding. The predominance of domestic shocks is striking, with 75 total transitions as primary coup, civil war, or assassination cases, and another 5 as secondary cases. The largest category by far is coups, with 64 total cases. Electoral continuity is the next most common, with 27 primary cases and 37 total. Foreign shocks account for 25 primary cases and 29 total. This leaves 12 outliers, although several are near-misses for the paths (see chapter 6).

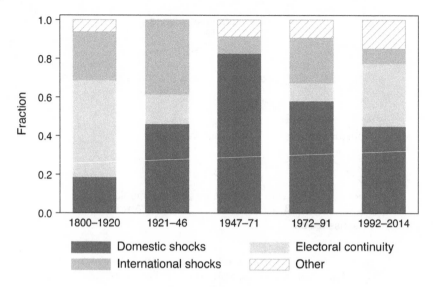

FIGURE 2.5. The distribution of types of democratization by time period.

Figure 2.5 shows how this distribution has shifted over time, dividing by five periods: democracy's First Wave, the First Reverse and Second Waves, the Second Reverse Wave, the early Third Wave, and post–Cold War. Domestic shocks were uncommon through World War I but peaked in the early Cold War periods. Despite a relative decline since then, they represent a plurality in every post–World War I period. Electoral continuity has the opposite pattern, appearing mainly pre–World War I and post–Cold War, with only three cases between 1920 and 1990. These old and new periods represent distinct types of electoral transition, with the former involving suffrage extensions and the latter improvements in contestation (R. Collier 1999; Miller 2015a). The international shocks cluster around the two world wars and Soviet collapse, with only six cases not a direct result of these events. In part, these patterns reflect general changes in autocratic governance, namely a decline in coups and an increase in electoral authoritarianism.

*Timing*

This book deliberately focuses on the near-term political context of democratization. As such, the shocks are almost all very recent events, with the window between the final shock and democratization only 1.6 years on average. In only 12 of 100 cases is this window longer than three years and in only three cases longer than five years.[16] The qualifier of *final* shock is needed as many cases involve a sequence of violent events. Most often, one can clearly identify an

16. One longer window is for Japan 1952, due to the lengthy American occupation after its 1945 defeat. Windows of six (Cuba 1940) and nine years (Bangladesh 1991)

*initial shock* that set off the disruption period. The window between this initial shock and democratization averages 3.7 years and is 2 years or less in about half the cases.[17] Thus, the disruption periods occur over fairly short time spans.

### Paths of Additional Transitions

As shown above, nearly all BMR transitions correspond to transitions in Polity or CGV. We can also flip this and look for additional transitions in either data set as a useful out-of-sample test of this book's theory. Perhaps the best comparison group is the set of 19 transitions that are not in BMR but are in Polity or CGV and are not clearly contradicted by the other data set (e.g., no shift on Polity for a CGV transition). Of these, 16 of 19 fit one of the paths. We can go further and look at any transition that appears in Polity or CGV—this adds 23 Polity cases (22 of which fit) and 8 CGV cases (6 of which fit). Lastly, we can include potential transitions omitted from this book's sample: the two post-2014 transitions, the four cases that quickly democratized after independence (Luxembourg 1890, Ireland 1922, Pakistan 1950, Gambia 1972), and three cases where democracy was installed in a new country closely associated with an autocratic predecessor (West Germany 1945, Pakistan 1972, Russia 1991).

In total, 51 of 59 (86.4%) of these shadow cases fit one of the paths, about the same success rate as the main BMR cases. Details are in the appendix. Thus, the fit of the main sample with the paths does not depend on the BMR sample of transitions.

## Theory: No Disruption, No Democracy

I now turn to this book's theory of democratization, which is divided into two sections. The current section explains the rarity of democratization *absent* shocks or durable ruling parties. I outline how an autocratic equilibrium operates in stable regimes and limits the major incentives for democratization: threats within autocracy (push factors) and the expected benefits of democracy (pull factors). In particular, protest pressure is rarely sufficient to incentivize democratization without a prior disruptive event, while democratic expectations are usually weak without a confident ruling party. Although elite challengers can coercively grab power in this context, I discuss why coercive democratization is extremely rare. Autocratic persistence is thus the default, explaining why regimes so rarely transition outside the paths.

To borrow from Barrington Moore: No disruption, no democracy.

The next section describes how shocks and ruling party crises break the autocratic equilibrium. Autocrats must then decide whether to accept democracy

---

followed coups that produced prolonged disruption periods but led in a clear causal path to democratization.

17. Excluding civil wars, 84% of disruption periods are five years or less.

or risk trying to reconsolidate control. When democracy presents little loss of power and pro-democratic sentiment is widespread, accession to democracy becomes likely.

## THE AUTOCRATIC EQUILIBRIUM: LEADERS, SUPPORTERS, AND OPPONENTS

To understand regime stability, we need to consider the autocratic equilibrium formed among three sets of actors: the regime leadership, elite allies, and opponents. The latter two are potential threats, yet it's possible to construct interlocking relationships of control that powerfully reinforce the autocratic status quo. As long as elite supporters remain loyal, it becomes very difficult for opponents to challenge the regime.

The leadership is typically a single autocrat or small group of party or military junta leaders who make key political decisions, including the choice to allow democratization.[18] I make the common and well-founded assumption that long-term power and personal security are primary concerns for any autocrat.[19] Maximizing power has a special allure; as historian Shelby Foote argues, "Power doesn't so much corrupt; that's too simple. It fragments, closes options, mesmerizes" (quoted in Varol 2017: 160). Thus, decisions to democratize require leaders to believe they are not sacrificing too much power, because of either existing insecurity within autocracy or prospects of power within democracy.

Autocrats face two main sources of danger within autocracy: threats from other government elites and popular opposition (Casper and Taylor 1996; Svolik 2012). To maintain power, all leaders rely on a support coalition. Although the most critical are security forces, other key supporters include governing elites, local leaders, party members (if applicable), and loyal citizens. Defections within the elite coalition threaten dictators either by directly challenging them or by withdrawing support and leaving them vulnerable (Hale 2005; Higley and Burton 2006; Way 2015). Traditionally, autocrats have faced their chief threat from fellow elites: in autocracies since 1800, coups are about three times as common as ousters from below (through protests or revolutions).[20] Elite defections can also magnify electoral challenges if defectors form or join opposition parties, as occurred in Mexico, Kenya, Brazil, and Georgia (Magaloni 2006; Brownlee 2007; Langston 2017).

---

18. For simplicity, I'll refer to the leadership as a single actor.

19. Although it's worth remembering, "the motives of political leaders are varied and variable, mixed and mysterious, and often unclear to themselves" (Huntington 1991: 107).

20. However, since the end of the Cold War, the two threats are about as likely (Kendall-Taylor and Frantz 2014).

Contentious popular action, a major focus of democratization theory for decades, can also undermine autocratic stability (Sharp 1973; Bermeo 1997; R. Collier 1999; Bunce and Wolchik 2011). Many scholars focus on threats of violent unrest and revolution as a way of forcing liberalization (Wood 2000; Acemoglu and Robinson 2006; Klopp and Zuern 2007; Aidt and Franck 2015; Aidt and Leon 2016). Increasingly, others counter that nonviolent opposition is more effective at achieving political reform, as it attracts wider participation and discourages repression (Sharp 1973; Ackerman and Duvall 2000; Schock 2005; Chenoweth and Stephan 2011; Celestino and Gleditsch 2013; Bayer, Bethke, and Lambach 2016).[21] Yet pro-democratic activists are not always the chief opponents: social revolutionaries, religious fundamentalists, and other anti-democratic forces may take the lead and compete with democrats over regime change.

Critically, these two threats are linked as mass opposition both encourages and benefits from elite defections, especially in security (Wood 2000; Schock 2005; Schmitter 2010; Chenoweth and Stephan 2011). As Hale (2013: 346) explains, "Mass protest is often not what it appears on the surface and is often tied somehow to tensions or competition within the elite." For instance, the opposition movement in the Philippines 1986 spurred a dissident army faction to break from the regime, then triumphed when security forces refused to fire on protesters (Ackerman and Duvall 2000: 386–88). Similar elite fissures eroded state security in Bangladesh 1991, Serbia 2000, Georgia 2004, and Tunisia. This link helps to explain why exactly protests are dangerous for autocrats. In contrast to revolutionary violence or strikes, mass marches are not damaging in and of themselves. Rather, the dramatic signal of noncompliance spurs on more tangible threats like coups, revolutions, and electoral opposition (Sharp 1973; Tilly 1978; Goodwin 2001; Johnson and Thyne 2018).

A stable autocratic equilibrium therefore requires leaders to maintain elite loyalty and mobilize allies against popular threats. To minimize opposition, the support coalition implements some combination of favorable policies, propaganda, and repression. When opponents actively challenge the regime, supporters neutralize the threat, often through coercion. Similarly, loyal supporters help to deter elite challengers. Because elites gravitate toward the side they believe will remain in power, this quickly becomes a self-reinforcing equilibrium in stable times (Svolik 2012; Singh 2014). To organize this system of control and reward supporters, leaders often rely on durable institutions like ruling parties, legislatures, and military hierarchies (Gandhi 2008; Slater 2010; Svolik 2012).

---

21. Popular activism is said to be especially effective when the opposition forms broad coalitions (Howard and Roessler 2006; Chenoweth and Stephan 2011) or attracts international support (Levitsky and Way 2010; Beaulieu 2014).

In this section, I assume such an equilibrium has held without recent disruption from major shocks or crises, such as coups or elite defections. The aim is to explain why democratization is so unlikely in this context. I first discuss why the leader's primary motives for accepting democratization—threats within autocracy and prospects of power within democracy—are so limited. This challenges the commonly held view that successful pro-democratic protests and strategic top-down democratization are feasible regardless of political context.

## LIMITS TO THREATS WITHIN AUTOCRACY

Democratization offers weak autocrats an escape from elite and popular threats. Yet these threats are rarely strong enough to incentivize democratization without recent disruption, even with widespread pro-democratic popular sentiment. What gives autocratic persistence in this context such an advantage? In particular, why is pro-democratic protest unlikely to provide a sufficient push?

Most importantly, cohesive regimes have coercive and financial resources that impede organized opposition and can usually defeat large popular movements even if they do form. Regimes with loyal security forces that can direct their full weight against popular challenges are virtually impregnable. As O'Donnell and Schmitter (1986: 21) write, transitions cannot "be forced purely by opponents against a regime which maintains the cohesion, capacity, and disposition to apply repression." Bellin (2004: 143) concurs: "Democratic transition can be carried out successfully only when the state's coercive apparatus lacks the will or capacity to crush it." Although proponents of the effectiveness of nonviolence, Schock (2005) and Chenoweth and Stephan (2011) agree that protest is unlikely to succeed if the regime maintains a united front and is willing to repress.[22]

Cohesive regimes have repeatedly proven capable of violently suppressing large protest movements, as in China in 1989 (Schock 2005; Pei 2013) and Zimbabwe through the 2000s (Levitsky and Way 2013). In Armenia, a war-hardened security state managed to "consistently fend off external challenges," including a 120,000-strong rally protesting the stolen 1996 election (Levitsky and Way 2010: 207; also Way 2015: 149–51). Mass repression defeated Operation Ghost Town, a 1991 general strike and tax revolt by two million Cameroonians (Levitsky and Way 2010: 260). Simultaneously in Zaire, co-ethnic loyalists in the army propped up Joseph Mobutu's government by freely shooting protesters and "bombarding the home of the leader of the

---

22. The same holds for violent challenges: "fiscally and militarily sound states that enjoy the support of united elites are largely invulnerable to revolution from below" (Goldstone 2001: 146).

opposition with rocket-propelled grenades" (Baker 1998: 122–23). Similarly, Burma's pro-democratic movement persevered through several thousand deaths in August 1988 and an annulled 1990 election victory but was finally dismantled by a military government willing "to hold onto power by whatever means necessary" (Casper and Taylor 1996: 69; also Chenoweth and Stephan 2011; Morgenbesser 2016).[23]

It follows that successful oppositions need to peel away regime supporters, ideally within the security apparatus, or cause sufficient economic damage that they imperil the state's maintenance of patronage and paychecks. Fernando Cardoso, a leader of Brazil 1985's democratic movement and later president, explains that oppositions must convince factions to "break away from the government to join the opposition. It will not be the opposition alone" (interview, Bitar and Lowenthal 2015: 17). Yet this is a significant challenge without existing elite divisions or a shock that weakens the regime's coercive and fiscal capacity. Supporting elites are wary of breaking from the regime unless it is unlikely it will survive. Indeed, among autocracies without a shock in the prior five years, the annual likelihood of a coup is less than 2% and an executive ouster through protest or revolution less than 0.8%.

Beyond raw coercion, there are significant psychological barriers to change that solidify the autocratic equilibrium. Citizens and elites who have not seen the regime seriously challenged in decades will naturally hesitate to believe it can be defeated tomorrow. In many cases, this goes beyond calculations about regime strength and is embedded in a "social and moral universe" that dictatorships construct to make change unthinkable (Derby 2009: 231).

Many totalitarian regimes enforce public behavior that displays obedience and thus communicates the futility of opposition (Wedeen 1999; Marquez 2016). Havel (1991: 143) points to the grocer in Communist Czechoslovakia who places Party slogans in his window and thus signals that he conforms and will "treat any non-involvement as an abnormality, as arrogance." This explains why dictatorships pass on absurd myths, such as Kim Jong-il shooting 38 under par in his first round of golf (Longman 2011), and compel dramatic rituals like Turkmenbashi's annual Walk of Health, in which all government officials had to complete a twenty-three-mile circuit of the capital in sweltering heat (Morton 2014). Submission does not signal belief in the myth but recognition of regime control.

This mentality extends to other durable, but non-totalitarian, regimes. In Indonesia, even citizens hostile to Suharto's New Order dictatorship "found it hard to imagine any way to challenge the regime, let alone replace it" (Aspinall and Mietzner 2013: 149). Pointing to Mexican voters' support for the ruling

---

23. Schock (2005) concurs that the Burmese regime's triumph can be understood as a "function of the context" (109), as "no elite divisions within the military command manifested" during the 1980s (110).

PRI from "fear of the unknown and tradition," Casar (1995: 17) notes how stability rests on the stickiness of "embedded habits and routines." Ultimately, successful protest movements require a "cognitive liberation" (Schock 2005: 27). However, this shift can be elusive without elite shocks or electoral surprises that signal vulnerability.

Lastly, major shocks are usually needed to sufficiently transform power relations and eliminate pivotal *blockers* to democratization. I define blockers as the hard-liners within the support coalition (including military factions and party rivals) that will resist any democratizing move as long as they believe autocracy is viable. Although leaders have the authority to begin democratization, blockers can still attempt to coup and reestablish autocracy.

Thus, even when protests oust individual leaders, they often produce little change or ephemeral liberalization. In El Salvador in 1944, for instance, the long-ruling military dictator Maximiliano Hernández Martínez resigned in the face of a massive general strike joined by shopkeepers, teachers, and doctors (Ackerman and Duvall 2000: 252–63; Mahoney 2001: 205–16). However, with fundamental power relations unchanged, the regime failed to democratize: "The military was unwilling to follow the general out of the corridors of power, and the coffee growers refused to expose their interests to the vagaries of democratic politics" (Ackerman and Duvall 2000: 263). A hard-liner coup forestalled democratic elections and established institutional military rule that prevailed for another forty years. Similar failures followed popular uprisings in 1848 and the Arab Spring, both of which flowed from protest contagion rather than domestic shocks.

## LIMITS TO BENEFITS FROM DEMOCRACY

Democracy is not one-size-fits-all. It implies different things to different actors at different times. Autocratic elites contemplating regime change will therefore consider what democracy means for their political, material, and ideological interests, then adjust their degree of resistance in response. Although democracy presents some attractions, I argue these are relatively meager compared to stable autocratic power. An exception is when leaders control a ruling party likely to prosper within democracy. Even then, the risks outweigh the benefits unless the party faces heightened competition within autocracy. Thus, without prior disruption, strategic top-down democratization is very rare.

Democracy often brings general benefits to a country like increased international aid, business investment, and legitimacy (Alesina and Dollar 2000; Jakobsen and De Soysa 2006; Jensen 2008). Acceding to democracy also allows outgoing leaders to control the transition process, securing personal benefits like amnesty and manipulating the political and economic design of the new democracy through constitutions and pacts (Karl 1990; Huntington 1991; Przeworski 1991; Albertus and Menaldo 2018; Albertus 2019).

In particular, military rulers have a democratic option of "returning to the barracks" and retaining influence over security affairs (Geddes 1999; Albertus 2019).

Although these are real advantages, they are rarely sufficiently attractive if regime leaders believe they are permanently sacrificing power by democratizing. Fallback positions in business offer pale compensation for the prestige of leadership. General benefits like increased foreign aid or regime legitimacy carry little weight if leaders won't be in office to enjoy them, while theories on democracy's value in achieving economic goals (e.g., Lizzeri and Persico 2004; Llavador and Oxoby 2005) are limited since regimes rarely function purely as representatives of elite economic actors. These benefits may appeal to specific regime allies but rarely enough to take the extreme risk of breaking with the regime.

Democracy also looms as a dangerous prospect for many autocrats and supporters, who will fight democratization if it threatens prosecution, mass redistribution, or economic decay (Boix 2003; Mainwaring and Pérez-Liñán 2013; Miller 2016; Gunitsky 2017). Acceding to democracy allows outgoing autocrats to bargain for personal protections and favorable rules. However, promises to protect autocrats' interests can be broken (Huntington 1991; Przeworski 1991; Albertus 2019), as in the early collapse of South Africa's power-sharing agreement and the prosecution of military leaders in South Korea 1988 and Argentina 1983. This is especially likely when autocratic groups lose their vestiges of power (Albertus 2019). Further, engineering political rules is mainly valuable when autocrats have a party they hope to return to office.

Thus, democratic benefits are limited without a viable route back to power. Such morsels may satisfy autocrats who are already highly vulnerable after shocks, but more secure leaders require better democratic prospects. In turn, this depends on whether dictators and party leaders believe they can compete for electoral power in democracy (Slater and Wong 2013; Loxton 2018).

Critically, the likelihood of returning to power is much greater with a preexisting party that continues into the democratic period. After 67 transitions, the autocratic leader or party that acceded to democracy regained power, yet in only one (nominal) case did this occur without a preexisting party or recent shock.[24] Of the 67 cases, 37 qualify for electoral continuity and another 10 had ruling parties, but with insufficient durability. Another 3 were engineered by established parties not yet in full control of the state. Thus, about 3 in 4 cases of resurrected power involved preexisting parties, and essentially all of the remainder followed shocks. Outside of the paths, democracy therefore offers little attraction for secure autocrats.

---

24. The sole case (Peru 1956) only nominally qualifies because the former autocrat, Manuel Odría, reached an agreement to take power but a military coup prevented him from sitting.

## VIOLENT REGIME CHANGE AND DEMOCRATIZATION

Of course, autocratic regimes do not survive forever. Without prior shocks or crises, the likelihood of a coercive ouster from a coup or revolution is low, but not zero. We will explore the motives and predictors of these challenges in chapter 3. The final issue to address here is why these coercive ousters are almost never in pursuit of *democracy*.

There are two primary reasons why coercive democratization against stable autocracy is unlikely. First, there is an important asymmetry between autocratic and democratic aims. An elite faction or insurgent group takes a significant risk by challenging the regime. Failure is a near-guarantee of imprisonment or death. Yet the allure of power and ambitions to satisfy radical ideological or identity-based aims can overwhelm this risk (Goodwin 2001). However, the calculation is very different if the goal is democracy. Now, coercive entrepreneurs take the same risk but face a low (often negligible) likelihood of keeping power *even if successful*. Similarly, given democracy's unpredictability, specific political aims are far from guaranteed. Although some actors may value democracy enough to take the gamble, the population will be much smaller than power-hungry challengers.

Second, pro-democratic actors are the least likely to have the coercive resources and will to challenge stable regimes. Military factions and violent revolutionary movements tend not to coalesce around democratic aims (Levitsky and Way 2012, 2013; Yukawa, Kushima, and Hidaka 2019). Further, successful revolution selects for coercively ruthless and internally cohesive movements that can establish highly stable autocracies (Levitsky and Way 2012, 2013; Lyons 2016). As discussed below, some pro-democratic *reformers* successfully used violence to take power and followed through on democratization. However, they almost exclusively struck against weak regimes following shocks, when the risk of failure is much lower. There are only four cases of pro-democratic domestic elites coercively taking power without recent shocks and two of these were against exceptionally weak regimes (see chapter 3).

## SUMMARY

The stopping power of stable autocracy is significant. Without prior disruption and elite defections, popular challenges are much less likely to succeed. Even if they do, democratization is not guaranteed given the continued resistance of blockers. As long as the elite coalition holds, autocratic leaders enjoy relatively high security within autocracy and the benefits of democracy will appear slim in comparison, especially without a strong ruling party. Thus, a calculated choice by autocrats to democratize is improbable. A coercive ouster that implants democracy is also unlikely given potential challengers' risks when facing a stable regime and the limited payoff. The result is a virtual absence of democratic transitions without a prior shock or a durable ruling party capable of winning power in democracy.

## A Two-Step Theory: Disruption and Democratization

This section explores how disruptions through shocks and ruling party crises fundamentally transform a country's politics. With the autocratic equilibrium broken, leaders face high insecurity in autocracy (especially in the shock cases) and relatively brighter prospects within democracy (especially in electoral continuity cases). If autocrats perceive they have little to lose in power and security from democracy, democratization becomes a possibility. When combined with sufficiently strong pro-democratic pressure, democratization becomes a probability. Because chapter 5 is dedicated to electoral continuity, I place more emphasis here on shocks but draw out several parallels between the paths.

We can think of democratization proceeding on the paths in *two steps*. First, an event disrupts autocracy, with most shocks producing new autocratic regimes and leaders. Electoral continuity cases also typically face triggers to heightened electoral competition. I place special emphasis on describing the resulting political contexts faced by autocrats, characterized by leader insecurity, supporter uncertainty, and openings for opponents. In turn, repression and reconsolidation of autocratic power become risky and uncertain options.

Second, regime leaders accede to democratization from these disruption periods. I describe the leader's decision-making process and why pro-democratic pressure makes this choice more likely. A qualitative coding of the final decisions to democratize adds further support for the mechanisms. Finally, I consider what sets apart the autocrats who successfully reconsolidate power after shocks.

### DISRUPTIONS TO AUTOCRACY

#### Shocks

Autocracy is often undermined by "some critical event" (Colomer 2000: 11) or a "triggering crisis" (Higley and Burton 2006: 64). The five shocks are indeed major events that disrupt regime power and frequently set the stage for democratic transition. Coups and defeat in war generally bring regime change, while assassinations imply leader turnover. Civil wars and hegemonic withdrawal are similarly cataclysmic events that erode coercive resources. In most cases, a new leader and support coalition face the aftermath of these shocks and must decide how to survive.

Although a few regimes quickly reassert control, the norm after shocks is a period of vulnerability to further elite and popular challenges. Given a shock, there is a 65.8% chance of another shock in autocracy within five years,[25] as well as a 31.3% chance of autocratic regime change. In comparison, the 10.5% chance of democratization is modest, but still a big jump from the chances otherwise. Democratization competes with many possible trajectories, including renewed autocracy, state collapse, and revolution.

Again, I count only six cases in which the initial shock was intended to democratize: four coups and two international wars. In fact, 22% of the initial shocks ended democracy. Because of this lack of purposive democratization and cycles of instability, the disruption periods vary in length from roughly one to five years, with time for countershocks, popular mobilization, fraught decision making, and high-stakes elections.[26]

### Electoral Continuity Triggers

Electoral continuity is defined by the presence of an established ruling party that gains power in democracy. Nevertheless, nearly all these cases also fit the pattern of a disruptive trigger shifting the regime into a period of heightened vulnerability and electoral competition. Although the parties retained confidence in their democratic prospects, they also faced challenges to maintaining autocratic power.

In 16 of 18 modern (post-1940) cases, this trigger was *external* to electoral politics. The most common was the Soviet Union's fall, which destabilized Marxist regimes like Cape Verde and Guinea-Bissau. Other frequent triggers include economic crises and natural deaths of dictators. In 2 modern cases and all 9 pre-1940 cases, the trigger was instead *internal* to electoral politics, most commonly from party splits and electoral protests. Although less disruptive than the shocks, these events still undermined party control (see chapter 5).

Many characteristics of disruption periods discussed below apply to any autocracy with meaningful electoral competition but especially fit periods of vulnerability after triggers. However, the match to the shock cases is not exact. The degree of leader insecurity and coup threat is typically much lower, for instance. Nevertheless, there are instructive parallels despite the different power calculations at the climax.

### Divergence between the Paths

What determines which path a country follows? The key point of divergence is the development of a strong ruling party, which can have many possible origins (Smith 2005; Miller 2020a). In turn, ruling parties shield regimes from shocks, with more entrenched parties even more secure (Huntington 1968; Ziblatt 2017; Miller 2020a). Having any electoral ruling party lowers

---

25. Note that this includes continuing civil wars. If we omit these, the chance is 42.7%.

26. In contrast, the six shocks intending to democratize all led to founding democratic elections within eighteen months.

the relative risk of a shock to 72% that of other autocracies. With the same party in place for 4+years, this declines to 58%. At 10+years, it's down to 46%. Conversely, shocks disrupt and prevent party control, although some civil wars produce strong parties. Thus, the establishment of state power through either coercion or ruling party dominance tends to be self-reinforcing. Chapter 8 examines the structural factors that predict shocks and durable parties and how this helps to explain democratization.

## WHAT AUTOCRATS FACE AFTER DISRUPTION

Following disruption, a new or significantly weakened autocratic leader faces a fundamentally different political context, with high uncertainty about regime persistence, eroding elite support, and openings for opposition actors. Post-shock periods are especially marked by leader insecurity and violent instability. The autocratic equilibrium lies in shambles, with each fraying thread weakening the whole. As autocrats consider how to reestablish power, they find that supporter unreliability and opposition mobilization makes repression more dangerous, further closing their options. After describing this political environment, I turn to the autocrat's decision on whether to fight to reconsolidate power or accept democratization.

### Leader Insecurity

Disruption periods following shocks are usually highly unstable, with multiple violent challenges and shifts in power, including continuing civil wars, coups, assassinations, and soldiers' rebellions. Dominican Republic 1966, for instance, began with the assassination of Rafael Trujillo, then continued with an aborted takeover by Trujillo's brothers, two military coups bracketing an election, a revolution by the ousted election winner, and an American invasion (Wells 1966; Hartlyn 1998). As the saying goes, violence begets violence. As a result, about 3 in 4 post-shock cases feature a violent executive turnover in the five years before democratization, three times the rate of other autocracies. Given the dire consequences of being ousted from office, this insecurity dramatically lowers the value of struggling to retain autocratic power. A heavy crown may feel grand, but not when one is treading water.

How do shocks contribute to leader insecurity? Most directly, shocks damage the regime's coercive and economic capacity, as detailed below. Yet the most significant effect is the dismantling of the autocratic equilibrium. Especially when they change the leader, shocks fracture the previous coalition and alienate regime allies, putting the regime support base in a state of flux and uncertainty. Reacting to the new leadership, previously pro-regime actors within the military, government, and business may now prefer democratization or seek power themselves rather than submit. This lack of cohesion also facilitates opposition mobilization, further damaging leader security.

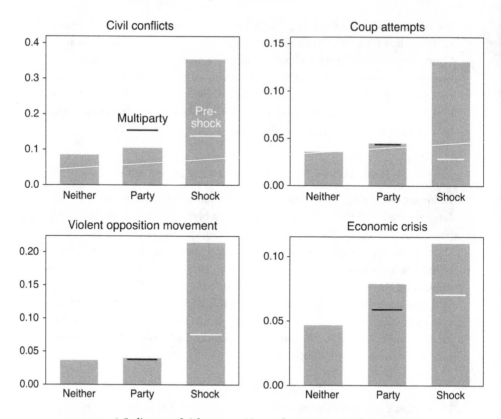

FIGURE 2.6. Indicators of violent opposition and economic crisis by whether there has been a qualifying shock in the previous five years, an electoral ruling party for four continuous years, or neither. The lines above Party show the averages with the additional requirement of multiparty competition. The lines above Shock show the averages for the five years prior to shocks. The sample includes all autocracies, with varying years defined by the data.

Figure 2.6 illustrates the increase in violent challenges after shocks. Similar to Figure 2.3, it compares several measures of violence across three conditions: autocracies within five years of a shock, autocracies without a shock but with an electoral ruling party in power for 4+ years, and all remaining autocracies. The lines above Party show the averages given 4+ years of multiparty competition. In addition, each panel shows the average for the five years *prior* to a shock (and without any in the previous five years) to illustrate the forward causal effects of the shocks. Shown at the top left, over one-third of post-shock years feature a violent civil conflict, about four times the rate for other autocracies (using a threshold of 25 annual battle deaths, from UCDP 2017). To the right, 13.1% of post-shock autocracies face a coup attempt each year, again nearly four times the rate for other autocracies (using Marshall and Marshall 2018). Lastly, at the bottom left, a violent opposition movement seeking regime change is about six times as common after shocks (using Chenoweth and Lewis 2013). In every case, the risk is more than double that pre-shock.

The result of this dissent is dramatically lower leader security. Following a coup earlier in the year or the previous five years, the annual chance of a coup rises from 2.3% to 11.5%, a fivefold increase (see Londregan and Poole 1990; Powell 2012). More broadly, after any shock in the same window, the annual chance of violent turnover rises from 4.6% to 14.3%.[27] Put another way, following a shock, an autocrat has a *less than even* chance of avoiding a coercive ouster for five years.

When assessing these threats, a key motivator for autocrats is that their fates depend a great deal on *how* they leave office. When autocratic leaders leave through regular constitutional channels, 2% are imprisoned or killed in the following year, with another 4.3% exiled (using Goemans, Gleditsch, and Chiozza 2016). In contrast, when they leave through irregular means (from coups, rebellions, or protests, but not foreign intervention), 36.6% are imprisoned or killed and another 43.7% exiled.[28] Therefore, it is highly advantageous to lose power through regular elections or by accepting a transitional government rather than waiting to be overthrown. Being a dictator is a dangerous, high-stakes game where, much like global thermonuclear war, sometimes the only winning move is not to play.

Besides leader-specific insecurity, shocks also erode regimes' coercive capacity. This is especially likely after civil war, defeat in foreign war, and hegemonic withdrawal, which divert coercive capabilities. For instance, in the Philippines 1986, Ferdinand Marcos's struggle to defeat a Communist insurgency diverted tens of thousands of security forces and contributed to the breakaway military faction that helped topple the regime (Brown 1987: 313; Bitar and Lowenthal 2015: 417). Following coups and assassinations, a different problem arises: weakened cohesion makes security forces less willing to repress and may even induce them to support the opposition. In turn, coercive weakness limits the tools available to autocrats, leaving them vulnerable to popular and elite challenges (Bellin 2004; Albertus and Menaldo 2012; Way 2015).

A final effect of shocks is their contribution to economic crisis, further limiting the regime's resources (Remmer 1995; Haggard and Kaufman 1995, 2016; Zak and Feng 2003). Figure 2.6 shows that autocracies following shocks are more than twice as likely to face a serious economic crisis (defined as a 5% economic decline or 50% inflation rate averaged over two years). Roughly one in three post-shock autocracies feature a negative growth rate each year.[29]

27. The chance of *any* turnover roughly doubles from 12.9% to 24.4%.

28. Just under half of autocratic turnovers are irregular, with the majority of these coups.

29. Among the post-shock *transitions*, 43% faced a serious economic crisis and 76% faced negative growth in the prior five years.

Civil and international wars also erode fiscal health by draining vast sums of money and interfering in taxation and trade (P. Collier 1999; Bayer and Rupert 2004). At minimum, economic crises inflame opposition and regime defections (Ulfelder 2005; Reuter and Gandhi 2010; Brancati 2014). Crises also make regimes vulnerable to pro-democratic pressure from business groups and international actors, as occurred in several Marxist regimes after the Soviet Union's collapse. At the extreme, crises threaten the ability to pay security services, which contributed to democratization in cases like Serbia, Nicaragua, and Mali.

An important cautionary note is that *too much* state weakness can compromise democratization. Even if leaders are willing to concede, democracy still requires a "usable state" (Linz and Stepan 1996: xiv) capable of maintaining territorial integrity, holding elections, and establishing a national government. In some cases, such as following a civil war settlement, minimal state capacity can be restored alongside democratization, although this considerably ramps up the difficulty (Wantchekon 2004). However, continuing state collapse is essentially incompatible with democratization, with only one case of state collapse through the democratizing year (Dominican Republic 1966). The lesson is that regime weakness is conducive to democratization but must not be so extreme that sufficient state capacity cannot be restored.

### Supporter Uncertainty and Changed Beliefs

Shocks and competitive elections also influence regime trajectories through actors' beliefs, especially in the closed information environments of repressive autocracies (Ackerman and Duvall 2000; Colomer 2000: 11; Pop-Eleches and Robertson 2015; Przeworski 2015). Where once a regime looked impregnable, critical events puncture "the web of self-fulfilling expectations about the stability of the regime" (Marks 1992: 404) and demonstrate the possibility of further change. In turn, regime allies' uncertainty and opponents' beliefs in regime vulnerability tear at dictatorship's roots in compliance and fear.

By removing dictators, coups and assassinations demonstrate that leaders can be changed through concerted action. Even without turnover, defeat in war, hegemonic withdrawal, and persistent civil conflict all reveal the regime is not invincible. Competitive elections can also expose regime unpopularity while providing an outlet for change (Magaloni 2006; Pop-Eleches and Robertson 2015; Przeworski 2015). Sometimes idiosyncratic events shift beliefs: in Nicaragua, President Somoza's heart attack and long recovery abroad in 1977 dented "the pervasive myth of his regime's invincibility and the popular 'fear of fear'" (Lawton 1987: 139).

For elite supporters, changes in leadership and signs of weakness question the regime's durability and the credibility of its promises. This inevitably erodes loyalty and the willingness to take risks in exchange for long-term rewards (Albertus and Gay 2017). In particular, it "plants doubt in the minds of police and military cadres about how long the rulers whom they serve can last," reducing their incentives to follow orders to repress (Ackerman and Duvall 2000: 487). The result is an opening for both mass actors and dissenting elites to challenge the regime, with the noted rise in coups and civil conflict.

Significantly for democracy, regime insecurity has opposite effects on two key groups of elites. Blockers who would otherwise resist democratization are less likely to intervene. The same insecurity that pushes the current regime to give in also discourages rivals to the crown when autocracy is no longer viable.[30] In contrast, elite reformers who favor democratization are *more* likely to grab power since the coercive challenge is more likely to succeed and they do not intend to reestablish autocratic rule. This shift in elite threats further encourages the leader's preemptive choice to democratize.

### Political Openings for the Opposition

Disruptions to the autocratic equilibrium, whether through violent shocks or rising electoral competition, act like cracks in the dam through which long-repressed opposition can flood. Although the initial shocks are almost always about competing for autocratic power, in the aftermath enlivened popular movements enjoy a sudden opportunity to actively push for democratization. Significantly, disruptions both facilitate organized pro-democratic pressure *and* increase the regime's vulnerability to this pressure. However, regime weakness simultaneously creates openings for various mass and elite actors, who compete with democrats over desired regime change.

For citizens, just as with elite supporters, disruption reveals the regime's coercive weakness and shakes the routines of loyalty so critical to autocratic stability. In Uganda 1980, citizens recognized Idi Amin's rebel ouster in 1979 as "a major precedent. Ugandans had fought against their own national army— and won. . . . If Amin could be overthrown, why couldn't [his successor]?" (Kokole and Mazrui 1988: 278). The possibility of change can also awaken long-buried opposition. Lewis (2002: 192) describes the mood at the end of military rule in Argentina 1983: "Strikes and demonstrations were almost daily events as, after six years of conformity and fear, Argentine civil society was expressing its pent-up revulsion for the military." As de Tocqueville wrote on the French Revolution, "a grievance comes to appear intolerable once the possibility of removing it crosses men's minds."

Disruptive events can also coordinate collective action. By publicizing vulnerability, "incumbent regime instability is a potential signal to nonviolent

---

30. Fidel Ramos, a Filipino military leader who broke with the Marcos dictatorship, recalled his thought process when fellow generals advised him to coup: "I said no. I might seize the presidency and keep it for maybe three years, but I would not be able to hold it any longer than that because the people of the Philippines would not allow it" (interview, Bitar and Lowenthal 2015: 223).

activists that the time is right to go on the offensive" (Chenoweth and Ulfelder 2017: 309). Mass protest movements swelled into life following diverse events like the NATO bombing of Serbia (Levitsky and Way 2010: 55), insurgencies in El Salvador (Dunkerley 1988: 380) and Nicaragua (Booth 1990), Germany's defeat in World War I (R. Collier 1999: 101–8), the 1974 Portuguese coup with its resulting "disintegration of coercive power" (Ramos Pinto 2013: 12), and the 1979 Bolivian coup that lasted sixteen days before the leader relented (Dunkerley 1984).

Similarly, shocks galvanize international attention and pressure. Many states have policies of shutting off aid after coups and pressuring juntas to restore democracy, a pivotal catalyst in Ecuador 2003, Honduras 2010, and Niger 2011 (Shannon et al. 2015; von Soest and Wahman 2015; Wobig 2015). International actors are also frequently involved in civil war resolutions through settlement mediation and peacekeeping (Kumar 1998). Most obviously, international shocks allow global powers to push for democracy after war or in their rivals' former client states.

The result is a rise in pro-democratic pressure following disruption. As in Figure 2.6, Figure 2.7 captures this pressure in autocracies after shocks or with ruling parties. The panels show the annual likelihood of an anti-government protest (using Banks and Wilson 2017), a count of nonviolent movements seeking regime change (using Chenoweth and Lewis 2013), a 0–1 rating of civil society strength (using Coppedge et al. 2018), and a count of international sanctions aimed at regime change or human rights (using Morgan, Bapat, and Kobayashi 2014). In each case, opposition activity is greatest under multiparty competition but is also consistently higher with any ruling party or after shocks.

In addition, popular movements and international actors enjoy greater leverage when facing weak, divided regimes (R. Collier 1999; Trinkunas 2011: 80–81). Pro-democratic actors can strategically target wavering elite supporters. In Venezuela 1959, for instance, the opposition exploited a stalemate between military factions in "a strategy of 'divide and conquer' to create regime leverage and to impose institutional reforms" (Trinkunas 2011: 85). Civil and international wars also increase the leverage of citizens, who can threaten to disrupt the war effort or support the enemy, a critical factor in Nicaragua, El Salvador, and the Philippines 1986. Naturally, this increased leverage only encourages further popular organization.

The claim that disruptions provide openings for pro-democratic activity closely parallels the modern literature on social revolutions (Skocpol 1979; Goodwin 2001; Goldstone 2001; Foran 2005; DeFronzo 2011). As with democratization, regimes with loyal security forces and without preexisting economic or military crises are largely immune to revolution (Arendt 1963; Goldstone 2001: 146). Even Lenin (1920/1966: 84–85) concurs that "revolution is impossible without a nation-wide crisis [that] . . . weakens the government, and

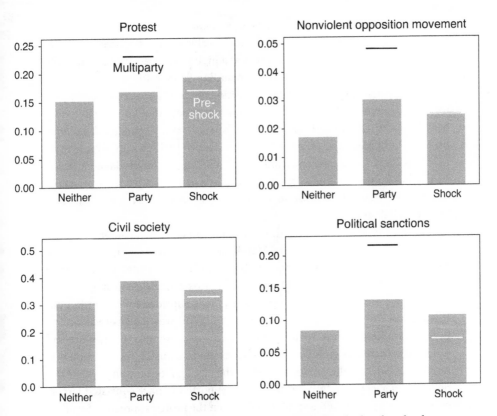

FIGURE 2.7. Indicators of protest and international sanctions by whether there has been a qualifying shock in the prior five years, an electoral ruling party for four continuous years, or neither. The sample includes all autocracies, with varying years defined by the data.

makes it possible for the revolutionaries to rapidly overthrow it." As discussed, Skocpol (1979: 23) contends that international crises from war and colonial competition spark revolutionary openings by undermining "existing political authorities and state controls." More recent authors concur that revolutions depend on a crisis "that both weakens the state and emboldens the opposition" (Foran 2005: 22) and paralyzes "administrative and coercive capabilities of the state" (DeFronzo 2011: 13). This crisis is often but not always the result of an international shock like war (Goldstone 2001, 2014).

Thus, disruptions provide openings for actors to seek their preferred regime outcomes, whether they're rival elites, revolutionaries, or democrats. Democratization thus often hinges on the presence of a critical mass of pro-democratic actors capable of seizing the opening (Linz and Stepan 1996: 57). This implies that pro-democratic activity and structural factors that predict mass and elite preferences for democracy should have a heightened importance following shocks or ruling party crises. This idea is tested in chapter 8.

*Limits to Repression*

It's tempting to believe that autocratic leaders always have a repressive option to restore control. Yet repression comes at a high risk, especially for internally fractured regimes. Maximal violence, including firing into crowds and mass arrests, threatens to provoke wider opposition, international punishment, and military defections (Lichbach 1987; Goldstone 2001: 160–62; Schock 2005; Martin 2007; Chenoweth and Stephan 2011).[31] State-sponsored violence backfired and alienated regime allies, including the military, in diverse cases like Venezuela 1959, Czechoslovakia 1990, Mali 1992, and Madagascar 1993. In Thailand 1992, the king's personal reprimand of military leaders over a protest crackdown was broadcast on national television and led the incumbent to resign (Callahan 1998).

Perhaps no case illustrates the catalyzing effect of government violence better than South Korea 1960. In March, rioting in Masan erupted over the rigged election of President Syngman Rhee, continuing in total darkness after a government fire truck accidentally crashed into an electric pole and blacked out the city (Kim 1996: 1188). Opposition activity subsided for a month, until the body of a sixteen-year-old named Kim Ju-yul was discovered floating in the Masan harbor on April 11. When a crowd broke into the morgue and discovered he had been killed by a police tear-gas canister, the reaction was immediate. That night, students torched the city's police buildings, while the police chief's jeep was "burned by a group reported to have consisted largely of infuriated mothers" (Trumbull 1960). When the protests spread to Seoul on April 19, police fired on a crowd of fifty thousand, transforming "the protest movement into a major violent rebellion" and giving the movement the symbolic name of the "4-19 Revolt" (Kim 1996: 1189). Outraged by state repression, crowds grew to several hundred thousand by April 26, destroying the ruling party's national headquarters and ransacking politicians' homes (Kim 1996: 1190). Rhee resigned the following morning.

In some cases, autocrats resort to innovative tactics to obscure their responsibility. A common technique is the use of regime-allied paramilitaries to coerce opponents, although this can create tensions with the military (Schock 2005; Greitens 2016). For instance, the Malawi Young Pioneers served as an aggressive paramilitary force until attacked and disbanded by the military in 1993 (Phiri 2000; Roessler 2005). More crudely, Bangladesh's Hussain Ershad dealt with student protests by releasing several prisoners and "allowing them to go armed into the university campus to break up the student front," which prompted military defections and his 1990 downfall (Crosette 1990). Not to be outdone, members of Brazil's ruling military party let loose

---

31. Croissant, Kuehn, and Eschenauer (2018) examine forty autocracies that faced nonviolent protest and responded with repression. The military remained loyal and repressed just under half the time.

"an angry bull [to] break up an opposition Democratic Movement Party election rally" in 1982 (Fraser 1982).

Regardless of autocrats' techniques, regimes with already tenuous support from prior shocks are particularly vulnerable to missteps and incapacity in the dark arts of repression. Security forces ordered to shoot protesters or coerce opposition leaders need to either believe the regime is likely to survive or feel a high degree of cohesion with it (Poe 2004; Pion-Berlin, Esparza, and Grisham 2014; Dragu and Lupu 2018). Yet shocks produce uncertainty over the regime's staying power, and coups and defeats in war damage cohesion. The frequent result is the military refusing to follow repressive orders, as in Bangladesh, or actively joining the opposition, as in the Philippines.

For ruling parties, the parallel threat is that coercion will erode the veneer of electoral legitimacy and popular support needed for future elections. This long-term calculation encourages restraint once competitive elections are ongoing, even in regimes that previously employed large-scale violence like in Mexico, Taiwan, Brazil, and South Korea. Parties that do resort to repression to maintain control often find themselves unable to continue with contested elections (Burma, Algeria) or thrust from power once elections resume, either temporarily (Madagascar, Indonesia 1999) or permanently (Romania, Bangladesh 1991).

## AUTOCRATIC DECISION MAKING AFTER DISRUPTION

To sum up the preceding argument, disruptions through shocks and ruling party crises have cascading effects as each component of the autocratic equilibrium collapses. Alienated and uncertain elite supporters become more likely to challenge the leadership, while also more reticent to repress opponents. The opposition is galvanized by signs of regime weakness from disruptive events and wobbly supporters, while thriving in the face of coercive incapacity. As former elite supporters and opponents defect, remaining actors in each group are reassured they can follow.

We now consider the autocrat's decision-making process in the face of this crisis. Autocrats have two main options: accede to democracy or attempt to reconsolidate power.[32] If the latter, they may succeed in reconstructing an autocratic equilibrium, as discussed below. However, most fail and are replaced by another autocrat, returning us to the starting point. A series of coercive turnovers is thus possible—Ecuador 1948, Guatemala 1958, Dominican Republic 1966, and Bolivia 1982 all had at least five in the five years before democratization. The cycle ends when a successor either accepts democratization or reconsolidates power.

---

32. In theory, they could voluntarily cede power to another autocrat, but then they are locked out of power anyway and still face high risk of punishment.

This section explains why autocrats have power-centered motives to embrace democratization in this chaotic context. However, disruption does not guarantee such a choice by any specific autocrat. Many leaders are short-sighted and self-deluded. Given the allure of power, numerous autocrats ignore their vulnerability and try to maintain control. But there is a corrective to this stubbornness: they get overthrown, by either pro-democratic forces or a new autocrat. The result is akin to a natural selection toward autocratic leaders who correctly evaluate their vulnerability and either democratize or weather the storm and reconsolidate power.

### When Autocrats Have Little to Lose from Democracy

Why do autocratic leaders often concede to democratization after disruption, especially when combined with pro-democratic activity like protests and strikes? The first concern is whether leaders are *able* to successfully democratize. Besides minimal state capacity, this requires the unwillingness of blockers to interfere or countercoup, which is more likely with existing autocratic insecurity and pro-democratic activity, as explained below. The second concern is whether leaders *want* to democratize.

Assuming democratization is possible, autocrats will compare the costs and benefits of fighting to preserve autocracy versus accepting democratization. The former choice holds onto supreme power for today but risks overthrow tomorrow. Further, when leaders are removed within autocracy, the consequences are dire; it is highly likely they will be put to death, imprisoned, or permanently excluded from power. Democracy instead minimizes the concentration of power and promises constant competition for high office but offers a peaceful method of exchanging power that ensures losers can keep competing in the future.

When autocratic leaders and supporters believe the democratic option sacrifices a sizable share of power, they are likely to resist. Alternatively, there are two circumstances in which autocrats have *little to lose* from democracy. Following shocks, new or surviving autocrats are often highly insecure and have limited room to repress and reconsolidate. This weakened hold on power means that accepting democracy is a lesser sacrifice and maybe even a salvation. With a durable ruling party that can compete in democracy and faces weakening control within autocracy, leaders also face a low cost from democratization. For both paths, nothing requires that autocrats particularly like democracy, only that it's an acceptable option that outweighs struggling to retain autocracy.

A preference for democracy might still not lead to accession if it makes sense to stall until overthrown by protests or elite reformers. However, if democratization will happen regardless, there are major advantages to being the first mover rather than getting thrust from power. Liberalizing autocrats can control the transition process and maximize their electoral chances in democracy (Slater and Wong 2013; Miller 2021). They are also more likely to be remembered as reformers and enjoy lucrative positions in business, government, and international organizations (Albertus and Menaldo 2018; Albertus 2019).[33] For instance, after securing a democratic bargain, F. W. de Klerk, South Africa's last autocratic president and a decades-long supporter of apartheid, was showered with prestigious awards and positions, including a Nobel Prize, university fellowships, and board memberships on international foundations (Keller 2011). Despite a less bloody transition, ousted Tunisian President Ben Ali was rewarded with exile in Saudi Arabia and multiple life sentences from trials held in absentia (BBC News 2012).

Pro-democratic activity is also critical to securing democratization in these contexts. Besides contributing to regime fragility, its most significant role is communicating the spread and intensity of pro-democratic preferences in the population. This often comes as a revelation to autocrats (and even fellow citizens) habituated to quiet obedience, as in Portugal 1976, Poland 1989, and Indonesia 1999. In turn, this has several effects on the autocrat's calculations. It implies greater long-term difficulty in consolidating autocratic power. Unless there's a stark divide between elites and masses, it raises the threat of elite reformers and lowers that of blockers, who should be more reticent to coup against strong pro-democratic opposition. In addition, wider pro-democratic sentiment and international incentives promise greater rewards for transforming into the pioneering liberalizer who founded democracy. Finally, democratic mobilization helps to steer weak autocracies to democracy rather than social revolution or other regime change, an especially significant factor following shocks.

The little-to-lose condition and the benefits of proactively pursuing democratization may be sufficient to persuade autocrats to democratize but can also yield indifference and hesitance. Rapturous pro-democratic crowds and international pressure provide a further push, even an overriding momentum, that can overpower autocrats' natural caution. Of transitions on the paths, 68% featured widespread pro-democratic protests, 35% featured targeted international pressure for democracy, 40% had a pro-democratic elite reformer take power after disruption, and 89% experienced at least one of these (my coding). As explored in chapter 8, pro-democratic activity and civil society strength predict democratization much more strongly following shocks or with durable ruling parties.

33. Simple esteem can also be influential. In Guatemala 1986, Óscar Mejía pushed for democracy because "he want[ed] to leave a good name in the history books" and democratic leaders in Spain "impressed upon him what a historic responsibility he had" (Kinzer 1985).

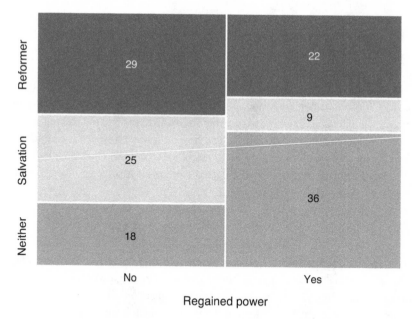

FIGURE 2.8. Frequency of types of final decisions to democratize. The Salvation and Reformer patterns are mutually exclusive, but both can coexist with the final autocratic decision maker regaining power within democracy.

### The Final Decision to Democratize

We come at last to how the fateful decision to democratize is made.[34] Using the case histories, I qualitatively coded this decision in each transition, focusing on the final autocratic ruler (see the appendix). Although this is pivoting toward evidence rather than theory, this coding is worth discussing here as it directly links to the preceding discussion on autocrats' motives. In particular, the coding furnishes causal process observations that validate the key theoretical mechanisms of leader insecurity, positive democratic prospects, and openings for pro-democratic elites.

The final decisions to democratize overwhelmingly correspond to three patterns, with the first two defined to be mutually exclusive:

*Salvation*: In the Salvation pattern, autocrats accept democracy because they face internal elite threats and calculate they are unlikely to maintain power. Note the threats cannot be exclusively protest-based. In essence, autocrats recognize democracy as their salvation from a violent ouster. For instance, after a period of intense military infighting, Argentina's junta accepted democratic elections in 1958 as "more of an escape for the dictatorship than a

---

34. The process of democratization *following* this decision can take different forms—including installing a caretaker executive, a formal pact, and fair elections—but the concern here is the decision itself.

triumph" (Lewis 2014: 114). History repeated itself fifteen years later when a coup leader, Alejandro Lanusse, conceded because "he saw no escape from the chaos without a political transition" (Krause and Pereira 2003: 8). Salvation cases overwhelmingly follow coups and civil wars, including Greece 1974, Bolivia 1979 and 1982, Argentina 1983, and the Philippines 1986. In total, 31% of post-shock cases fit this pattern (and 24% of all transitions).

*Reformer*: In the Reformer pattern, a pro-democratic elite actor who is not responsible for an initial shock takes power *within* the disruption period and successfully ushers in democracy.[35] This does not count leaders who take power in democratic elections or who are appointed as caretakers to install democracy. It does count foreign powers who install democracy and, for electoral continuity, reformers who take power through autocratic elections. Of course, deciding who is genuinely pro-democratic deep in their souls is impossible, so this coding primarily hinges on evidence they took power intending to introduce democracy and followed through. Thus, they may be "pro-democratic" for instrumental reasons. Classic reformers include Spain's King Juan Carlos I, Indonesia's B. J. Habibie, and Portugal's António Eanes.

Most commonly, reformers rose to power without violence on their part, such as through succession (following an assassination, natural death, or resignation), appointment, or election. In 11 cases, a domestic reformer took power violently (always after prior coups), in addition to 6 cases where the reformer was a conquering foreign power. In total, 37% of all transitions fit the Reformer pattern, including one-third of electoral continuity cases and 42% of post-shock cases. If we omit foreign powers, 32% of post-shock cases qualify.

Reformers face similar incentives as other autocrats after disruption but are distinguished by not intending to keep autocratic power. In particular, the reformers who rose through violence are as much a product of regime weakness as the insecure leaders in the Salvation pattern. Grabbing power to install democracy is always risky, but much less so when the regime has already been disrupted, other pro-democratic actors have emerged, and potential blockers are held at bay. Since reformers don't intend to hold on to autocratic power, they are not deterred by regime weakness the way that blockers are. This dependence on existing disruption explains why the Reformer pattern is about nine times as common as a pro-democratic *initial* shock.

*Regained Power*: The final pattern is where the autocrat or ruling party that accedes to democratization regains power in the following democratic spell.[36] This occurred in 52% of on-path transitions. In 69%, *some* leader from the autocratic period (not necessarily last) regained power in democracy. By

---

35. Reformers *may* be soft-liners in the sense of O'Donnell and Schmitter 1986 and Przeworski 1991 but are not necessarily within the regime leadership before rising to power.

36. This counts senior members of ruling juntas and three cases with power regained in a democratic spell divided from the immediately following one by a single year.

definition, all electoral continuity cases satisfy this, as do 38% of post-shock cases. Note that this can overlap with either the Salvation or Reformer pattern. However, it's much more common with the latter. Omitting the postwar cases (where reformers are mostly foreign powers), 56% of reformers gained power in democracy, compared to 26% of autocrats in the Salvation cases.

As shown in Figure 2.8, 94% of transitions on the paths fit one of these three patterns, as well as 87% of all transitions.[37] These patterns correspond well to the two paths, with Salvation and Reformer combining for 73% of post-shock transitions and Regained Power accounting for all electoral continuity transitions. Thus, in nearly every transition, either the final autocrat cedes power due to elite-driven insecurity, an autocratic successor intentionally installs democracy, or the final autocratic authority regains power in democracy. To best understand the implications of this, consider what is *not* included among the three patterns. Specifically, it's extremely rare for an autocrat to install democracy due purely to protest threats (even after disruption), to strategically democratize without regaining power or facing a prior shock, or to overthrow a stable regime and then introduce democracy.

### Autocrats Who Successfully Reconsolidate Power

Finally, what explains the autocratic leaders who are able to reestablish stable autocracy? Within a few years, most leaders following disruption either democratize or are overthrown, but a significant share restore durable autocratic rule. Following a shock in autocracy, just over one in three leaders survive as autocrats for the ensuing five years.

We've discussed several conditions that make this outcome more likely: the leader's belief they will sacrifice power by democratizing (either from perceived security in autocracy or fear of democracy), insufficient pro-democratic pressure, and the dominance of blockers. These conditions can in turn have several sources. For instance, structural factors like economic development and regional democracy make wide-scale pro-democratic activity more likely, while also affecting autocrats' long-term security. By nature, some shocks will lead to more secure leaders, such as successful revolutions (Levitsky and Way 2012, 2013; Lyons 2016) and institutional military coups (O'Donnell 1973; Singh 2014). We also shouldn't discount individual initiative and leadership among both autocrats and the opposition. Many dictators are wily and ruthless and not even democratization can tear them from power. I return to these issues in chapter 6, where I overview cases of non-democratization.

Lastly, we must keep in mind the daunting challenge and rarity of democratization. No mix of conditions can *guarantee* such a transformation. However,

---

37. Of the nine on-path outliers, five occurred after guardian coups (see chapter 3). One followed a pro-democratic initial shock (Portugal 1911). The three remaining cases are Czechoslovakia 1990, Senegal 2000, and Pakistan 2008.

we will see in chapter 8 that the interaction of shocks and favorable structure can make it much more likely than not a country democratizes within five years.

## Summary

To borrow from Barrington Moore once again: No disruption, no democracy. Stable autocratic equilibria, in which support coalitions control and repress the opposition, are very difficult to defeat from below. Without recent shocks, autocracies can typically nullify popular pressure and elite threats, whereas autocracies without strong ruling parties are unlikely to regain power in democracy. The result is the rarity of democratization outside of these contexts, even with the assistance of much-discussed factors like popular protest, international pressure, and favorable economic structure.

To create an opening for democratization, a disruption must break the autocratic equilibrium and make democracy a more tolerable outcome. As a result, 91% of democratic transitions fit one of two paths, either following a violent shock or occurring with a durable ruling party that wins power in democracy.

Transitions proceed in two steps. Without intending to produce democracy, an event disrupts autocracy and ushers in a period characterized by leader vulnerability, uncertainty about regime survival, and openings for pro-democratic activity. Autocrats then democratize when they have little to lose—either because of high insecurity within autocracy or confidence in their prospects in democracy—and face sufficient pro-democratic pressure. Validating the mechanisms, the final decision to democratize overwhelmingly corresponds to either insecure dictators facing elite threats (Salvation), reformers who take power after disruption and quickly give up power (Reformer), or a ruling party or leader who regains power in democracy (Regained Power).

The following chapters detail the routes from individual shocks and electoral continuity to democracy. I provide case evidence for the theoretical claims laid out above, including the motives for the initial shocks, how they shape regime power, and autocratic leaders' decision making. For electoral continuity, I focus on ruling party leaders' expectations about democratic competition. Lastly, I discuss the outliers that do not fit the paths and cases of non-democratization.

# CHAPTER THREE

# Domestic Shocks

ROMANTICS MAY BELIEVE that if democracy was ever founded through shared enlightenment and deliberation rather than disorder and violence, it would surely be ancient Athens.[1] Yet the true story of Athenian democracy's birth starts with a revenge killing and ends in war. From 527 BCE, Athens was ruled by the co-tyrant brothers Hipparchus and Hippias. After being rejected romantically by Harmodius, Hipparchus insulted Harmodius's sister by publicly declaring she was no longer a virgin (Everitt 2016: 89). In revenge, Harmodius and his lover assassinated Hipparchus in 514, leading an enraged Hippias to rule more repressively (Cartledge 2016: 58; Everitt 2016: 90). In 510, Athenian exiles from the tyranny bribed the Delphic oracle to convince the Spartan king to invade and free Athens, sending Hippias in flight abroad (Cartledge 2016: 59).[2] A power struggle resulted between two of the returning exiles, Isagoras and Cleisthenes. When the former tried to take power with Spartan assistance, he was overthrown by a popular revolt (Ober 1993; Cartledge 2016: 59–65). Facing high instability, Cleisthenes shrewdly calculated how to maintain order while still retaining power: "Acting from the most self-interested of motives, Cleisthenes invented democracy," allowing him to "continue to play a leading role in the affairs of a grateful polis" (Everitt 2016: 97). As expected, we see violence not only disrupting authoritarianism but providing an opening for popular contestation and strategic elite acceptance of democracy.

Athens does not stand alone. In Western European history, early democratic institutions and constrained government did not evolve seamlessly but lurched forward through a series of violent cataclysms (Moore 1966; Tilly

---

1. In truth, Athens departed from modern democratic standards, as it was a slaveholding society and sharply restricted participation. Nevertheless, it was a highly influential innovator in popular governance (Everitt 2016).

2. Hippias fled to Persia, where he was instrumental in planning Darius I's ill-fated invasion of Greece at Marathon (Thucydides; Cartledge 2016: 59).

2004; Berman 2007; Capoccia and Ziblatt 2010).[3] In England, liberal advances followed medieval defeats in war (see the next chapter), the English Civil War, and the Glorious Revolution of 1688, a coup/invasion in which William III secured victory in exchange for accepting the Declaration of Rights and the annual meeting of parliament (North and Weingast 1989; Higley and Burton 2006: 55–60; Varol 2017: 67–70). In France, democratic experiments followed the French Revolution, defeat in the Napoleonic Wars (the Charter of 1814), the 1848 revolution, and defeat in the Franco-Prussian War (Zeldin 1958; R. Collier 1999: 40–44). In Portugal, advances followed a military revolt in 1821, the Portuguese Civil War of 1828–34, popularly supported military revolts in 1836 and 1851, and the republican coup/revolution of 1910 (Atkinson 1960; Wheeler 1978; Collier 1999: 46–51). Lastly, in Spain, liberal openings followed the Napoleonic Wars, the 1830s Carlista War, and the 1868 Glorious Revolution.[4]

This close communion between violence and liberalization continues to the present day. Since 1800, major violent shocks preceded 100 of 139 democratic transitions. Domestic shocks in the form of coups, civil wars, and assassinations preceded 80 (75 as primary causes), thus representing the predominant path to democracy in the modern era. The current chapter covers these domestic events, with the following chapter addressing international shocks. For each type of shock, I discuss how they influence democratization, overview the cases and patterns among them, and delve into details on specific cases. The goal is both to add depth to the descriptive analysis and to provide evidence for the general theory.

It's worth restating what the theory predicts for this case evidence. First, very few of the initiating shocks should be motivated by democratization. To confirm this, I devote particular attention to identifying the actors and motives behind each shock. Second, we should see significant roles played by regime weakness and leader insecurity, with shocks exacerbating this vulnerability. In addition, shocks should widen opportunities for regime opponents, with pro-democratic actors ultimately grasping these openings. Building on the general theory, I discuss how each shock contributes to regime weakness and pro-democratic openings, then illustrate these dynamics in the case studies. Third, autocrats' final decisions to democratize should primarily follow

3. Similarly, although the Roman Republic's origins are shrouded in myth, the story goes that it was founded by an aristocratic revolt triggered by the king's son's abduction and rape of Lucretia, the wife of an aristocrat who became one of the first elected consuls (Beard 2015).

4. In the latter, the military overthrew Queen Isabella and searched for a less repressive successor, with the coup leader Juan Prim complaining that "looking for a democratic monarch in Europe is like trying to find an atheist in heaven" (Atkinson 1960: 299). Prim was assassinated the very day their choice, an Italian prince, landed in Spain, a harbinger of years of violence that chased the prince back to Italy and ushered in the First Republic in 1873 (Atkinson 1960; Phillips and Phillips 2015).

from leader insecurity, pro-democratic elites who grab power after earlier shocks, or anticipation of regaining power in democracy. I confirm this by noting how many cases fit the Salvation, Reformer, and Regained Power patterns discussed in the last chapter.

## Coups

Many scholars view coups as the antithesis of democracy and naturally resist the idea they could positively influence democratic development. Indeed, coups are behind virtually all democratic breakdowns and are almost always led by anti-democratic forces. Yet coups are also the most common disrupters of the autocratic status quo, frequently transforming solid dictatorships into disordered, vulnerable regimes ripe for pro-democratic upheaval. As a result, coups are by far the most common triggers for democratization, preceding nearly half of all transitions. How do these coercive takeovers of the state end up paving the way to democracy?

### OVERVIEW

#### Cases

There are 55 primary coup cases, which are overwhelmingly marked by violent instability: 32 had multiple coups and 21 also qualify for another path condition (13 civil war, 4 assassination, 2 postwar, and 2 multiple). Another 9 transitions are secondary coup cases (5 primary postwar, 4 primary civil war), meaning that 46% of all 139 democratic transitions closely follow coups. The cases are listed in Table 3.1, with a * indicating multiple coups.

Unsurprisingly, military actors were central to these coups. In 47 of 55 primary cases, military actors organized the initial coup, 37 by senior leaders and 10 by junior officers. In another 4 initial coups, military actors were closely involved in support. In another 2 cases, military actors led later coups in the disruption period.[5] In the final 2 cases (Panama 1950, 1952), the leader of Panama's National Police, the country's sole armed force and closest equivalent to the military, orchestrated a coup. Thus, every primary case involves a segment of the military (or National Police) as a significant actor.

More surprisingly, only in seven cases was the military *as an institution* the relevant actor leading to democratization. Even when senior leaders were involved, most coups were by generals representing a specific faction rather than a united military.[6] Specifically, only in seven cases did senior military

5. For the initial coups, one was by the vice president while the president was ailing abroad (Honduras 1957) and one was a presidential self-coup (Niger 2011).

6. Of course, the rarity of unified militaries is partly due to their higher likelihood of restoring stable dictatorship.

**Table 3.1.** Coup Cases, 1800–2014

**Primary Cases**

| | | |
|---|---|---|
| Greece 1864 | Cuba 1909 | Portugal 1911 |
| Greece 1926* | Spain 1931* | Chile 1934* |
| Cuba 1940* | Guatemala 1945* | Brazil 1946 |
| Ecuador 1948* | Costa Rica 1949 | Panama 1950 |
| Panama 1952* | Honduras 1957* | Argentina 1958* |
| Colombia 1958* | Guatemala 1958* | Venezuela 1959* |
| Burma 1960 | Turkey 1961 | Argentina 1963 |
| Peru 1963* | Dom. Rep. 1966* | Guatemala 1966 |
| Ghana 1970 | Argentina 1973* | Greece 1974* |
| Thailand 1975 | Portugal 1976* | Bolivia 1979* |
| Ecuador 1979* | Ghana 1979* | Nigeria 1979 |
| Peru 1980 | Bolivia 1982* | Honduras 1982* |
| Argentina 1983* | Thailand 1983* | Turkey 1983 |
| El Salvador 1984* | Guatemala 1986* | Sudan 1986 |
| Bangladesh 1991 | Suriname 1991 | Mali 1992 |
| Thailand 1992 | Niger 1999* | Lesotho 2002* |
| Ecuador 2003* | Comoros 2006* | Bangladesh 2009 |
| Honduras 2010 | Niger 2011* | Thailand 2011 |
| Fiji 2014* | | |

**Secondary Cases**

| | | |
|---|---|---|
| Italy 1946 | Sudan 1965 | Honduras 1971 |
| Cyprus 1977 | Uganda 1980 | Grenada 1984* |
| Suriname 1988 | Sierra Leone 2002* | Nepal 2008 |

*Note:* Years shown are for democratization, not the coups. * = multiple coups

leaders coup, retain hierarchical control, and face no countercoups prior to democratization.[7] Thus, these are primarily cases of sharply divided militaries, with the resulting implications for regime stability.

Two special categories of coups are worth noting. First, six primary cases involve *foreign-supported* coups, but only in one (Guatemala 1958) was a coup initiated and led by a foreign power.[8] In the others, foreign powers either gave implicit support or intervened to restore order following a coup (e.g., U.S. intervention in Cuba 1909). Hence, the coups are overwhelmingly domestic

---

7. These are Greece 1864, Brazil 1946, Turkey 1983, Suriname 1991, Bangladesh 2009, Honduras 2010, and Thailand 2011.

8. This also occurred in Cyprus 1977, a secondary case.

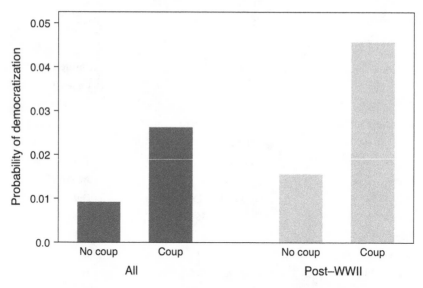

FIGURE 3.1. Coups and democratization. The likelihood of democratization by whether there has been a successful coup in the previous five years, for all autocracies (1800–2014) and post-1945 autocracies (N = 11,489/5,375).

affairs. Second, six cases feature *self-coups*, in which already empowered leaders extraconstitutionally transform the regime and consolidate their rule. In four, the self-coup was followed or preceded by a military coup, leaving two that only included self-coups. In Costa Rica 1949, a self-coup was met with a bloody elite-driven civil war that ousted the dictator. In Thailand 1975, a 1971 self-coup by the military leader Thanom Kittikachorn inspired mass protests that led the king to remove Thanom and install a reformist prime minister (Girling 1981; Slater 2010: 250–51). Thus, with the partial exception of Thailand 1975, all coup cases feature elite-led irregular leader change prior to democratization.

Figure 3.1 shows the likelihood of democratization dividing by whether autocracies are within five years of a successful coup, both for the full period and post-1945. Overall, a recent coup roughly triples the annual chance of democratization, from 0.92% to 2.62%. After 1945, the annual probability following a coup is 4.57%, or roughly a one-in-four chance within five years. This is tested more rigorously in chapter 7.

### Past Work

Scholars have only recently connected coups to democratization, but the literature has grown rapidly.[9] To my knowledge, the earliest empirical analysis was in Miller 2012, which examines how irregular turnovers (and coups

9. Earlier authors noted that military coups offer an escape from the worst despots, potentially improving governance and allowing for elections (Snyder 1992; Bratton and

specifically) predict democratization. Since then, several authors have argued that coups increase the likelihood of democratization, marshaling quantitative (Powell 2014; Chin 2015; Miller 2016; Thyne and Powell 2016) and qualitative evidence (Varol 2012, 2017; Albertus and Gay 2017). Research also shows the effect may differ by economic development (Miller 2012), foreign linkage (Trithart 2013; Tansey 2016; Chacha and Powell 2017), coup type (Chin 2015; Varol 2017), and the prior regime (Thyne and Powell 2016).[10]

Despite this burgeoning empirical work, existing theories on *why* coups lead to democratization are problematic.[11] Previous authors mainly characterize democratization as an intentional project of coup plotters, who hope to improve the country's political legitimacy or attract economic benefits from abroad (Varol 2012, 2017; Thyne and Powell 2016; Chacha and Powell 2017). Varol (2017: 39) refers to these as "democratic coups," in which the military serves as a "relatively neutral caretaker" for free and fair elections. According to Thyne and Powell (2016: 197), most of these coup leaders have a "lack of ambition for continued [autocratic] rule" and instead coup because democracy looks sufficiently attractive. However, as this section will argue, this does not fit how most coups lead to democratization. By my count, in only 14 of 55 primary cases was a coup launched with the purpose of democratizing. Of these, 4 were the initial coups and 10 were Reformer coups that followed earlier coups. In the remaining cases, the decision to democratize was made under extreme threat (the Salvation pattern), it was not made by a coup leader at all, or the initial coup *overturned* democracy. Thus, far from smoothly planned transitional processes, the post-coup cases are dominated by unintended consequences and insecurity.

Several authors correctly note that outgoing coup leaders often bargain for favorable democratic rules in exchange for democratization, such as amnesty, military control, and legislative vetoes (Miller 2011; Tansey 2016; Albertus and Gay 2017; Varol 2017). However, these limited concessions do not explain why coup leaders take the risk of launching a coup nor why they give up power. Significantly, coup leaders rarely retain governing power in democracy: in only nine cases did the final coup leader or a key ally keep power through

---

van de Walle 1997; Anene 2000; Collier 2009). On coups and election adoption, also see Marinov and Goemans 2014 and Grewal and Kureshi 2019.

10. The link has also attracted critics (Derpanopoulos et al. 2015; Croissant, Kuehn, and Eschenauer 2018), but the only quantitative critique (Derpanopoulos et al. 2015) was shown to be the result of a biased empirical design in Miller 2016. Andrew Miller (2011) and Tansey (2016) instead argue that democratic shifts following coups tend to be shallow and short-lived. Although post-coup cases are not the most durable (see chapter 9), half survive as democracies for 10+years.

11. One simple explanation is that coups are generally followed by military regimes, which are especially fragile and democratization-prone (Geddes 1999; Alemán and Yang 2011). Since military dynamics are central to my theory, this is really a *mechanism* for the coup effect rather than an alternative explanation.

democratization.[12] In another seven cases, a coup leader or military party regained power later in democracy. Thus, in nearly three in four cases, coup leaders permanently lost governing power by democratizing, meaning the economic or legitimacy gains accrued from democracy mainly benefited a different leader.

Coups stem from a diverse range of motives (Huntington 1968; Belkin and Schofer 2003; Powell 2012; Yukawa, Kushima, and Hidaka 2019), including military grievances surrounding pay or security affairs (Stepan 1971; Jackman 1978; Powell 2012; Singh 2014), economic or political crises (Finer 1962; Huntington 1968; Stepan 1971; O'Donnell 1973; Johnson and Thyne 2018), and ideological disagreements triggered by policy change or elections (O'Donnell 1973; Wig and Rød 2016). However, what matters for democratization is less the specific motives animating each coup than the *intentions* of the coup plotters for the incipient regime. Do they plan to quickly democratize, found an enduring autocracy, or something else? Naturally, these intentions flow from their political and economic aims, which differ in how quickly they can be secured and whether they are threatened by democratization.

I find that the coups preceding democratization are overwhelmingly organized either to establish a new autocratic regime or for a political goal like ousting an unsatisfactory leader or resolving a crisis, with the duration of rule left open. Democratization then results from either a failure to establish control or as an unintended consequence of these elite contests for power. Thus, coups often facilitate democratization without themselves being "democratic" in any sense. In the remainder of this section, I discuss how post-coup instability stems from coups' effects on leader insecurity and opposition openings. I then examine several coup cases in greater detail, contrasting cases with multiple versus single coups and comparing across coup plotters' intentions.

## EFFECTS OF COUPS

Post-coup democratization is most directly connected to the regime instability that follows coups. Initially concerned with establishing permanent rule or resolving political crises, coup leaders often find themselves unable to securely retain power. This opens up the possibility of leaders accepting democratization due to severe elite threats (the Salvation pattern, 21 primary cases) or losing power to pro-democratic leaders (the Reformer pattern, 18 primary cases), which together account for 71% of primary coup cases.[13] Still

12. Two cases involved "key allies." In Colombia 1958, the military partnered with a party that kept power in democracy. In Burma 1960, the civilian prime minister U Nu asked military head Ne Win to coup and purge the Communists, then won democratic power (Silverstein 1966).

13. Of the remaining 16 cases, 4 were pro-democratic initial coups, 7 involved coup leaders who regained power in democracy (4 immediately), and 5 followed the guardian coup pattern in which military leaders topple democracy and later give up power.

others democratized to head off increasing instability or were overwhelmed by protest movements that took advantage of regime incapacity. The centrality of military actors is especially significant here, as military regimes are more fragile than other autocracies (Geddes 1999; Alemán and Yang 2011; Geddes, Wright, and Frantz 2018) and the threat of military infighting adds urgency to restoring stability.

Above anything, these cases were beset by violent disorder, with cycles of coups and countercoups, insurgencies and assassinations, protests and strikes. Of the 55 primary cases, 32 (58%) featured multiple coups and 44 (80%) featured multiple significant violent events, including 15 with civil wars. In Guatemala, a 1963 coup preceded elections overshadowed by a major insurgency (a legacy of a failed 1960 coup), "a rise in urban revolutionary violence" (Grandin 2004: 96), and the "mysterious suicide" of the main opposition party's presidential candidate (Schlewitz 1999: 471). In Dominican Republic 1966, the 1961 assassination of Rafael Trujillo and a 1962 coup were followed by scholar Juan Bosch winning an election, falling to a coup the next year, then launching a revolution that took over the capital in 1965 (Kantor 1969a; Sanchez 1992; Blum 2003: 175–83). Despite a major U.S. military intervention to restore order, violence remained so endemic during the 1966 election that Bosch only twice left his house to campaign (Kryzanek 1977: 120; Yates 1988).

The remainder of this section explains what underlies post-coup instability and how it translates to democratization. First, disrupting the previous elite coalition produces insecure and illegitimate leaders, pushing both dictators and pivotal elites concerned about military splits to support democratization. Second, coups provide openings for pro-democratic protest and international electoral pressure. Like all shocks, coups can lead to change in many directions, from greater repression to liberal democracy. Democratization therefore hinges in large part on the strength and agency of pro-democratic actors.

### Leader Insecurity

Launching a coup is not a move for those who want to sleep well at night. As the literature on "coup traps" shows, successful coups dramatically raise the likelihood of future coups and coup attempts (Londregan and Poole 1990; Powell 2012; Singh 2014). Although some establish durable autocratic rule (e.g., South Korea in 1961, Indonesia in 1966, Egypt in 2013), the norm is for coup leaders to face high insecurity and short tenures.

Figure 3.2 examines the fates of all coup leaders from 1875 to 2015 (using Goemans, Gleditsch, and Chiozza 2016).[14] Of those not still in office, fewer than half exited through a regular, constitutional process. Just under one-third

---

14. This uses a sample of 286 leaders identified as entering through irregular means and following a leader ousted by a coup.

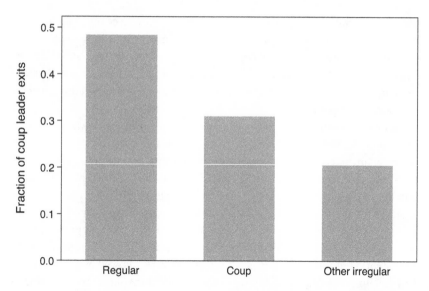

FIGURE 3.2. Frequency of types of exit for all coup leaders in Goemans, Gleditsch, and Chiozza 2016 (N = 277).

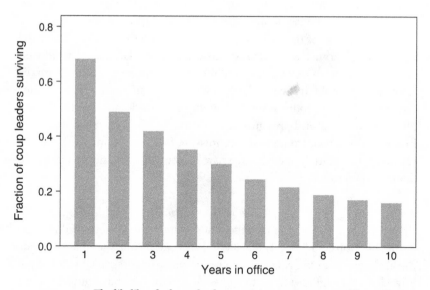

FIGURE 3.3. The likelihood of coup leaders surviving to given tenure (N = 286).

fell to another coup and about one-fifth were ousted through other irregular means (such as rebellion, foreign removal, or assassination). Similarly, their fates one year after losing office are grim: 31.5% are exiled, 13.9% are in jail, and 12.5% are dead, leaving barely two in five unharmed. Figure 3.3 shows the survival rate to a given tenure of all coup leaders, including the seven still in office. Incredibly, only 68.2% of coup leaders make it to the following calendar year, less than half survive for two years, and less than one in four make it to six.

Why do coups yield such insecure leaders? First, coups tend to fragment power and generate strong rivals opposing the regime. Coups imply leadership change and a fundamental transformation of authority, even when shifting among military coalitions.[15] As noted, only seven coup cases involved cohesive militaries that retained hierarchical control through democratization. Thus, after nearly all coups preceding democratization, one segment of the military is empowered and others are left out. Coups therefore produce hostile out-groups that may temporarily obey but form a natural breeding ground for countercoups (Anene 2000; Singh 2014). Most obviously, coups alienate supporters of the preceding regime, including senior military leaders. Other factions may be dissatisfied with the new regime's political direction or simply eager for personal power. In addition, there are ample opportunities to grasp power, as military factions control coercive resources and typically have equal claims to legitimacy. Countercoup plotters can also appeal to post-coup instability and leaders' missteps or pretend to be restorers of constitutional government.

A common result is the fracturing of military power into bitterly opposed factions (Geddes 1999; Anene 2000; Barracca 2007). The resulting cycles of violence not only damage military prestige but threaten to spiral into virtual civil war, as occurred in Cuba 1909, Venezuela 1959, Dominican Republic 1966, Guatemala 1966, and Lesotho 2002. After a 1978 coup, "Bolivia plunged into political chaos," with five presidents over the next two years and a "cluster of coups under almost constant preparation" (Dunkerley 1984: 249). Even after civilian rule returned, the military remained sharply divided, with one side "refusing to accept orders from the new commanders . . . [and] both military factions publishing angry advertisements in the press and impeding each other's representatives from entering their offices" (Dunkerley 1984: 271).

Besides making coup leaders less secure, factional conflict generates paralysis within the regime, eroding its ability to institutionalize dictatorial rule or respond effectively to pro-democratic movements. In Venezuela 1959, the army's fragmentation following a 1958 coup "prevented any military leader from unifying the institution or using the threat of force to limit the democratization process. . . . Any move by one faction leader to seize power could and would have been opposed by other factions in the military" (Trinkunas 2011: 85). Similarly, a Guatemalan junta's plan to retain power for three years following a 1957 coup was scuttled by opposition from fellow officers (Schlewitz 1999: 302).

Second, besides encouraging strong factional rivals, coups produce weak supporting coalitions. The sudden political change and the presence of military rivals magnify uncertainty about the leader's survival, weakening elite buy-in (Singh 2014; Wig and Rød 2016; Albertus and Gay 2017). Coup leaders also typically lack institutions, such as durable ruling parties, that could solidify

15. Some count consensual turnovers of leadership within a junta as "regime-shuffling" coups, but I ignore them for the coup categorization.

their coalitions.[16] A related source of weakness stems from the organizing basis of coup plots, which usually determines the new regime's leadership. Although military factions sometimes grow from ideological agreements, in other cases they derive from shared experiences or social groups, such as cohorts in officer training schools (Singh 2014: 109), fraternal organizations (e.g., the Black Eagles in Bolivia; Dunkerley 1984: 338–39), and service in war (e.g., the Armed Forces Movement [MFA] in Portugal 1976). Although these links provide social capital, they do not necessarily yield a shared vision on how to actually govern, leading to intracoalition splits and fragile coalitions held together by graft.

Third, given the coercive takeover, coup leaders often score very low in legitimacy, which invites both popular and elite challenges. Coup leaders themselves recognize this and routinely present reasons for their power grabs. Yukawa, Kushima, and Hidaka (2019) examine the public justifications offered by all coup leaders from 1975 to 2014, of which 93.4% present something. Although they have shifted over time, the most common justifications are democracy, governance problems, domestic instability, and economic issues, with very few citing ideology or military rivalry. Each justification presents significant quandaries for long-term legitimacy. If appealing to democracy (usually insincerely), audiences will expect concrete moves in that direction. Although many dictators introduce controlled elections to allay democratic demands, insecure and party-less coup leaders are among the least capable of managing this. The remaining justifications appeal to crisis resolution, yet lose relevance if the crisis is resolved. Further, coup periods, often beset by uncertain leadership and violent instability, tend to negatively impact governance and economic growth (Fosu 2002; Chacha and Powell 2017; Albertus and Gay 2017).

As stressed throughout the book, insecurity pushes leaders toward accepting democratization. If clinging to power means a coin flip to survive in office another two years, then democracy becomes much more attractive, especially when military leaders can bargain out favorable terms and return to the barracks. Of course, this is contingent on coup leaders discerning they are not among the lucky few able to consolidate power. It also depends on hard-liner rivals allowing democratization, but military leaders are strongly motivated to limit internecine splits within the armed forces (Geddes 1999; Singh 2014). Actors who are initially indifferent or hostile to democracy may therefore support it to repair persistent military divides. Thus, if no single military faction proves capable of establishing order, both military leaders and pivotal elites can shift to supporting democratization as an escape.

16. Although the military hierarchy can sometimes serve this purpose, it's more often upended and fragmented through coup activity.

## Pro-Democratic Openings

Despite the repression unleashed in their immediate aftermath, coups frequently trigger rising popular opposition. Thirty-six primary cases included major pro-democratic protests after the initial coups, with particular effect in Colombia 1958, Venezuela 1959, Thailand 1975, Bangladesh 1991, Mali 1992, and Thailand 1992. Brancati (2014: 1520) concurs that "coups d'état are associated with a significantly higher likelihood of pro-democracy protests." Post-coup regimes are also more sensitive to protest (Fukuoka 2015; Thyne et al. 2018), as elite divisions "open up political space for mass preferences to matter" (Hale 2005: 141).

Coups are dramatic moments of change that coordinate opposition movements and signal that the reigning powers are not invincible. In Thailand, a 1991 hard-liner coup "had the effect of galvanizing mass opposition" (Haggard and Kaufman 2012: 511), especially when coup leader Suchinda Kraprayoon was appointed prime minister. Despite violent repression that killed hundreds, a series of hunger strikes and marches grew to at least 500,000 by May 1992 (Schock 2005: 129), convincing the king to push out Suchinda and accept democratic elections (Callahan 1998). Post-coup regimes also present ideal environments in which to organize mass protest, as they suffer from low legitimacy and problems maintaining order. For instance, the success of democratic activists in Venezuela 1959 "was substantially enhanced by the rapid factionalization of the Venezuelan armed forces" (Trinkunas 2011: 80–81).

By challenging fractured regimes and further undermining regime legitimacy, protest movements have particular leverage following coups. Thyne et al. (2018) find that protests lower post-coup regime durability, with two protests reducing expected autocratic tenure by ten months. Given the danger of this opposition, "the military considers public opinion and mobilisation in both its decision to seize power and in whether to hold on to power" (Barracca 2007: 140). Indeed, numerous coup leaders have conceded to protests. In Guatemala, after invading with U.S. assistance in 1954, Carlos Castillo Armas hoped to rule unimpeded for several years but soon faced "pressure from a variety of middle class groups [that] forced the government to make a full 180 degree turn and call for congressional elections" (Ebel 1998: 46). Similar opposition convinced the generals behind a 1962 Peruvian coup that "it was impossible to go back to the old ways, and they promised to permit another election" (Kantor 1969b: 477).

Yet the most common route for protests to defeat post-coup regimes is by spurring military defections or reform-minded countercoups. Opposition is thus most effective when it appeals to regime soft-liners or rival military factions (Schock 2005; Trinkunas 2011; Fukuoka 2015; Chenoweth and Ulfelder 2017). In Bangladesh 1991, after police fired on a student demonstration opposing Gen. H. M. Ershad, protesters carried the dead body of a fellow student to the main campus and "swore an oath of unity over it" (Crosette 1990). Unable to quickly defeat such determined opposition, Ershad asked the army head to take control, but he declined, saying he "was not prepared to confront the combined might of the students, opposition groups and masses" and was therefore "in favour of the restoration of democracy" (Ali 2010: 95–96). In Ecuador, popular opposition to a 2000 junior officer coup, clearly revealed by a survey conducted the night of the coup, "almost certainly influenced the decision of senior military officials to oppose the putsch led by junior officers and to opt for restoring the constitutional order" (Barracca 2007: 145).

Coups also attract negative international attention, with diplomatic and economic pressure frequently aimed at restoring elected government. Following the Cold War, several states and international organizations, including the EU and regional organizations in Latin America (OAS) and Africa (AU), instituted policies of pressuring and shutting off aid to post-coup regimes (Shannon et al. 2015; von Soest and Wahman 2015; Wobig 2015). In the United States, this was codified in a 1997 extension to the U.S. Foreign Assistance Act, which restricts aid to "any country whose duly elected head of government is deposed by military coup or decree." The international reaction to the 2009 coup in Honduras was especially swift: within a week, "the OAS voted unanimously to suspend Honduras, the World Bank froze economic aid, France and Spain recalled their ambassadors, and Venezuela put its military on alert for a potential invasion" (Thyne and Powell 2016: 193). About one-third of the coup cases featured significant pro-democratic international pressure. In turn, several authors find that coup leaders are especially sensitive to pressure from abroad (Trithart 2013; Marinov and Goemans 2014; Thyne and Powell 2016; Chacha and Powell 2017; Thyne et al. 2018).

However, the democratizing role of international pressure should not be exaggerated. For one, the timing doesn't fit well, as 42 of 55 primary coup cases democratized before 1987, compared with only 43% of other transitions. In part, this reflects a general decline in coups, which were about twice as common in autocracies before 1987. Nevertheless, most post-coup democratization occurred in an era without strong international norms on democracy.[17] Further, empirical testing doesn't show any measurable increase in the likelihood of post-coup democratization with the Cold War's end (see chapter 7). Although international pressure can contribute to post-coup democratization, in practice it's often blunted by weak sanctioning of powerful states (Tansey 2016; Thyne et al. 2018; von Borzyskowski and Vabulas 2019). For instance, Egypt's 2013 military coup was simply not called a coup by the United States and received little pushback. International pressure also focuses more on encouraging contested elections than full democracy, since judging the latter is more subjective (Carothers 1999; Brown 2011). As a result, a country's

17. Yukawa, Kushima, and Hidaka (2019) confirm that only a small fraction of coups received international criticism before 1990. In my coding, a majority of post-1987 cases featured such pressure compared to about one in four earlier cases.

dependence on external democracies predicts its adoption of multiparty elections but not democratization (Miller 2020b). This suggests that international pressure following coups should play a modest and contingent role.

## PATTERNS FROM COUPS TO DEMOCRATIZATION

We can now examine the coup cases and their paths to democratization in more detail. Although there are many patterns across the 55 cases, it's useful to think in terms of four groups. First, I distinguish cases with a single coup prior to democratization (23) versus multiple coups (32). Second, for the single coups, I identify the cases where coup leaders intended to keep power by founding an enduring autocratic regime (7). Third, I distinguish the remaining single coups by whether the motivating purpose was transitioning to democracy (4) versus some other political or economic goal (12). In the latter group, coup leaders may have foreseen democratization as a possibility but did not organize around this goal.

Categorizing the single-coup cases requires judging coup leaders' actions and intentions, which was based on an inspection of primary and secondary literature surrounding each case.[18] The large majority were easy to judge, particularly regarding coup leaders' attempts to found an enduring regime. Of the remaining 16, 7 were clearly not motivated by democracy because they toppled one. For the remainder, I focused on the organizing basis of the coup plot and the speed of transition. Less attention was given to public justifications for the coup, which are typically specious and self-serving. However, since coup leaders often pretend to be pro-democratic to mollify observers, *not* doing so was considered telling.[19] Besides this categorization, I discuss how many cases fit the Salvation, Reformer, and Regained Power patterns, as well as how leader instability and protest contributed to post-coup democratization.

### *Pro-Democratic Initial Coups*

Only four cases involved pro-democratic coup leaders that initiated the disruption period and followed through with democratization: Portugal 1911, Brazil 1946, Turkey 1961, and Mali 1992.[20] This is distinct from the Reformer pattern, in which a pro-democratic leader takes power *after* a prior shock. Here, I discuss the rarer pattern in which coup plotters topple a durable

18. I thank my research assistant, Alex Fisher, for conducting a parallel study of these cases that independently validated the categorizations.

19. Democracy is far from a universal justification among coup leaders. According to Yukawa, Kushima, and Hidaka (2019), a majority publicly appealed to democracy only in the 1990–2009 period, whereas fewer than one-third did so during 1975–89 and 2010–14.

20. Among the cases with multiple coups, it's possible some initial coups were pro-democratic but got blocked by countercoups. Although they're more difficult to judge given their curtailed periods of control, examining these cases reveals few if any likely examples.

autocracy intending to democratize. Since there are so few cases, each can be briefly recounted.

In Brazil, Getúlio Vargas established the neo-fascist Estado Novo regime in 1937, outlawing the legislature, parties, and unions (Hilton 1987). Under military pressure, Vargas announced a major liberalization in February 1945, legalizing multiple parties and promising elections in December. In a surprise move, War Minister Eurico Dutra, the presidential nominee of the new pro-government party, couped in October, ostensibly to ensure a fair election and prevent Vargas from reneging.[21] Dutra proceeded to win democratic elections in December (Fausto and Fausto 2014: 193–272; Dulles 2014).[22] In Turkey, a 1960 military coup against the increasingly repressive Democratic Party was initially plotted by Colonel Alparslan Türkes, but military necessity handed control to General Cemal Gürsel. After marginalizing Türkes and engineering a pro-democratic turn, Gürsel retained the presidency following 1961 elections (Harris 1970; Ahmad 1977; Pope and Pope 2000).[23]

In Mali, multiple sources of strain weakened Moussa Traoré's single-party regime in the early 1990s. First, a secessionist insurgency by ethnic Tuaregs erupted in 1990, costing roughly 1,000 lives. Although the Tamanrasset peace accord was signed in early 1991, it was never implemented due to factional Tuareg resistance (Keita 1998; Florquin and Pézard 2005). Second, rising popular pressure for democratic reform was met with limited concessions (Reyntjens 1991: 50; Bratton and van de Walle 1997: 212). Alongside economic problems, this produced deep divisions within the state and army (Levitsky and Way 2010: 297). Political tensions culminated in March 1991, when the government fired on a disordered protest in Bamako, killing at least 150 civilians (Reyntjens 1991: 50). A few days later, with a general strike looming and the military balking at further repression, Colonel Amadou Touré, head of the presidential guard, ousted Traoré (Bratton and van de Walle 1997: 213). Touré immediately promised the army was "just passing by" (Reyntjens 1991: 50) and made rapid strides toward democracy, with a national conference in July, a constitutional referendum in January 1992, and elections completed by April (Nzouankeu 1993; Clark 1995). Surprisingly, Touré decided not to run in 1992 but was later elected president in 2002 (before being removed in a coup in 2012).

As a hybrid of factional military coup and mass social revolution, Portugal 1911 stands in stark contrast to these ordered routes to democratization. Prior to the coup, Portugal was a highly unstable constitutional monarchy,

21. Contributing to Dutra's paranoia, Vargas installed his younger brother as the capital city's chief of police just before the coup (Hilton 1987).

22. Vargas rebounded to win the 1950 presidential election, but his support plummeted and he committed suicide in 1954 (Dulles 2014).

23. Türkes would later emerge as a major right-wing nationalist figure, founding the infamous Grey Wolves paramilitary and serving as deputy prime minister in the 1970s.

with a fragmented parliament and at least six coup plots from 1896 to 1908 (Atkinson 1960; Wheeler 1972, 1978; R. Collier 1999: 46–51). From the 1870s, the Portuguese Republican Party (PRP) plotted to end the monarchy, recruiting within the urban middle class and military (Wheeler 1978: 34; Gallagher 1983: 12–37). Despite wide support, rigged elections limited the PRP's legislative power (Wheeler 1978: 35–37). Facing economic and political crises, King Carlos I dissolved the parliament in 1907 and gave Premier João Franco decree powers, followed by a crackdown of the press and opposition (Wheeler 1978: 43–44). In response, when they couldn't find Franco, radical Republicans assassinated Carlos and his eldest son in 1908, sending Franco fleeing abroad. With political support disintegrating, desperate monarchists searched for allies, with the queen even beseeching Spain to militarily intervene (Wheeler 1978: 45). An August 1910 election again produced a chaotic legislature with the PRP underrepresented. This unleashed a wave of working-class strikes and riots that the PRP feared almost as much as the monarchy, contributing to an "atmosphere of growing violence, passion, and confusion" (Wheeler 1978: 46).

In the dawn hours of October 4, 1910, the Republicans finally struck, with cannon fire from a ship in Lisbon harbor the signal for military rebels to take the capital (Wheeler 1972, 1978: 48).[24] Despite their initiative, Republican military forces were badly outnumbered in Lisbon and virtually nonexistent outside the capital. Their rapid victory hinged on the unwillingness of other military units to defend the faltering monarchy, as well as an explosion of popular violence among the poor (Wheeler 1972). An observer in Lisbon reported seeing masses of "barefoot women, little boys and ragged men [with] pitchforks and rifles at the ready" (quoted in Wheeler 1978: 53). Lisbon was taken on October 5, followed by autonomous declarations of republican support in towns across Portugal (Wheeler 1978: 55). The PRP dominated the May 1911 assembly election, leading to a new republican constitution and an assembly-selected legislature in September. To secure its continued electoral power, the PRP resorted to electoral manipulation and suffrage limitations (Bermeo 2010b: 1126).[25] This coexisted with a rocky democratic period, with failed royalist coup plots in 1912 and 1913, fleeting military coups in 1915 and 1917, and a more permanent coup in 1926 (R. Collier 1999: 46–51; Bermeo 2010b).

A striking feature of these cases is how varied they are, complicating the lessons we can draw from them. The cases differ in prior regime fragility (high in Mali and Portugal), the depth of planning and organization (highest in

24. The coup was planned for later that month but was suddenly triggered when a Republican leader was randomly assassinated by his medical patient. In a tragic irony, another Republican leader didn't hear the cannonade and, thinking the rebellion had failed, committed suicide (Wheeler 1978: 48–49).

25. The PRP fractured in 1911–12, with the main bloc (and dominant party until 1926) informally calling itself the Democratic Party (Wheeler 1978: 82–85).

Portugal, lowest in Brazil and Mali), and the significance of protest (high in Mali and Portugal). Of course, individual agency was of paramount importance in each, especially in Turkey and Mali. Further, in every case, a coup leader subsequently gained power within democracy, as compared to one-fifth of other coup cases. However, this plausibly motivated the coups only in Portugal and Brazil. In Turkey, the initial coup plotter was anti-democratic and ousted from the junta, whereas in Mali the coup leader bowed out from politics for ten years. More likely, this commonality resulted from voters rewarding the coup leaders for their roles in founding democracy. Perhaps the most salient conclusion to be drawn here is how rare and idiosyncratic this specific path is, affirming that pro-democratic intentions are not the driving force in post-coup democratization.

## Power-Seeking Coups

In seven cases, a coup leader attempted to found a new, enduring autocratic regime, but the project failed and democratization resulted without another coup: Costa Rica 1949, Panama 1950, Guatemala 1966, Thailand 1975, Peru 1980, Bangladesh 1991, and Thailand 1992. The average gap between coup and democratization was 3.4 years. These cases provide clear counters to the idea that coups lead to democratization because of the intentions and preferences of coup leaders. To the contrary, each coup leader hoped to retain power and forestall democracy. Their projects instead foundered in the face of elite fragmentation and popular opposition, with large pro-democratic protests in six cases and a populist civil war in Costa Rica. The relatively small number of cases reflects the fact that most failed power-seeking coups were met with countercoups and so ended up in the multiple coups category.

Although none of these coup leaders were ousted in later coups, three were replaced by reformers prior to democratization. In Costa Rica, this occurred through a rapid civil war (see civil war section). The Thai cases both involved a fractured military coup, the violent repression of student protests, and the king's intercession in favor of democratic leaders. Each of these initial coups was fiercely anti-democratic—overturning an election in Costa Rica, organized against liberalization in the Thai cases—and resulted in bloody confrontations with pro-democratic groups (Likhit 1992; Callahan 1998). Ultimately, the combination of determined popular resistance with elite opposition led to regime collapse.

Another three cases follow the Salvation pattern (Panama, Peru, Bangladesh).[26] Peru and Bangladesh both involved military coups that produced unstable, but relatively long-lasting, dictatorships that succumbed to

---

26. A final case, Guatemala 1966, follows the Regained Power pattern. Enrique Peralta couped in 1963, founded the ruling party PID, democratized amid a major insurgency, and the PID won back power in 1970 (Ebel 1998; Schlewitz 1999).

protests and military defections. In Peru, Francisco Bermúdez focused on economic reforms after grabbing power in 1975, but protests in 1977 triggered
his acceptance of a slow democratic transition in exchange for keeping the
reforms intact (Dietz 1992; McClintock 1999; McClintock and Vallas 2003). In
part, this concession resulted from "divisions within the officer corps" (Masterson 1991: 264) and Bermúdez's recognition that continued rule would further
demoralize and politicize the military (Dietz 1992; Hunefeldt 2004). In Bangladesh, H. M. Ershad couped in 1982 shortly after another military dictator's
assassination but failed to fully consolidate power. Mass strikes and the opposition's "decisive support of the army" (Crosette 1990) led Ershad to resign in
1990 (Crosette 1991; Ali 2010).[27]

Panama proceeded very differently, with its brief return to civilian rule
in 1950 a consequence of National Police Chief José "Chichi" Remón's failed
attempts to install a friendly president. Remón's initial motive was to over-
rule the 1948 electoral victory of pro-Axis nationalist Arnulfo Arias, who had
earlier fallen to a 1941 coup (LaFeber 1989; Leonard 1998; Pearcy 1998;
Robinson 2012). Swaying the Elections Board, Remón installed the runner-
up Díaz Arosemena, but he died of a heart attack in August 1949. Remón then
couped against his successor, Daniel Chanís, when he refused to countermand
a Supreme Court decision invalidating a slaughterhouse contract Remón was
involved in. After Remón's cousin briefly took over, Chanís rescinded his resignation, delivering a "blistering attack on Remón" in the National Assembly
and winning the Supreme Court's support (LaFeber 1989: 86). Attacked on
multiple sides, Remón relented, declaring, "If they want legality, I'll give them
legality. I'll give them Arnulfo!" ("Arnulfo again" 1949). Remón struck a deal
in which Arias became president in return for not interfering with the police
(Leonard 1998: 97), believing "he could handle Arnulfo" and win the presidency in 1952 (LaFeber 1989: 87). The Elections Board dutifully discovered
some new Arias votes and the likely winner of the 1948 election became president (AP 1949).

It's worth continuing with the chaotic aftermath, which included a quick
democratic breakdown and a restoration of elected government, even though
the Panama 1952 transition falls in the multiple coups category. Upon assuming power, Arias "ruled in a dictatorial fashion" (Lentz 2013: 617), censoring
newspapers and unleashing his secret police on political opponents, including
former presidents (Calhoun 1951; LaFeber 1989; Robinson 2012). On May 7,
1951, Arias formalized a self-coup, abrogating the constitution and dismissing
the National Assembly and Supreme Court (LaFeber 1989; Major 1993: 274;
Robinson 2012). Politicians and protesters implored Remón to intervene, but
he failed to convince Arias to back down (Calhoun 1951). Finally choosing to

27. Despite being in and out of jail since 1990, Ershad has remained influential as head
of the Jatiya Party and became the leader of parliament's opposition in 2019.

abandon Arias, Remón sent two aides to evict him from the presidential palace. After Arias supporters "killed both in cold blood" (LaFeber 1989: 89), a police contingent "armed with machine guns, rifles and grenades" stormed the palace and arrested the president following a four-hour firefight (INS 1951). Crying "We will return!" while being dragged from the palace, Arias served a brief prison sentence and won the 1968 presidential election, although he was removed in a coup after eleven days in office (Ropp 1982; Robinson 2012).[28] In 1952, Remón won the presidency over his cousin but was assassinated at a racetrack in 1955, with his vice president jailed in connection with the hit (Ropp 1982; Harding 2006).[29]

### Other-Motivated Coups

In twelve cases, a single coup preceded democracy with neither an attempt to consolidate power nor democracy as a motive. Rather, the coups were inspired by motley political crises and rivalries. After resolving these issues, the coup plotters calculated that installing democracy was preferable to struggling to found a new autocratic regime. Because of the relatively stable and controlled transitions, these coup leaders often bargained for favorable political arrangements in democracy, including policy constraints. For instance, in 1983, Turkey's military kept its major political reforms (including a new constitution with onerous party restrictions) and retained broad veto powers over electoral candidates and policy, ultimately banning nearly seven hundred candidates from the 1983 election (Casper and Taylor 1996: 125; Aydin-Düzgit and Gürsoy 2013: 290). The 1980 coup leader was also guaranteed the presidency until 1989.

If not power or democracy, what motivated these coups? The most common motive was opposition to the current leadership, including both democratic leaders (Argentina 1963, Honduras 2010, Thailand 2011) and dictators (Greece 1864, Cuba 1909, Ghana 1970, Nigeria 1979, Sudan 1986). Of course, these personal conflicts drew on deeper political divides, including ideological disagreements in Argentina (against Juan Perón) and Thailand (against Thaksin Shinawatra), abuses of power in Greece, Cuba, Nigeria, and Honduras, a corruption scandal in Ghana, and opposition to civil war policy in Sudan. In other cases, the coups were aimed at solving political crises within democracy, namely rising Communist influence (Burma 1960), widespread political violence (Turkey 1983), an unsatisfactory civil war settlement (Suriname 1991), and political disorder surrounding an election (Bangladesh 2009). Most importantly, none of these coups were motivated by pro-democratic impulses.

28. Remarkably, Arias likely won the 1984 presidential election, but the vote was manipulated by Manuel Noriega, then head of the successor force to Remón's National Police (Lentz 2013).

29. As noted in the appendix, 1956 is a better date for democratization in Panama, qualifying it as a secondary assassination case.

In fact, 7 of the 12 coups overturned democracy (compared to 28% of other initial coups).[30]

Several of these cases involved forward-thinking coup leaders who chose to accede to democracy before major threats could develop. However, not all the roads to democracy were so smooth. Three cases fit the Reformer pattern: in Greece 1864 (R. Collier 1999: 38–40; Dawson 1922: 107) and Cuba 1909 (Millett 1968; Aguilar 1993), the reformers were foreign powers to which the coup leaders ceded control; in Nigeria 1979, a reformer took over following the initial coup leader's assassination (see assassinations section).

Two cases (Ghana 1970, Sudan 1986) fit the Salvation pattern. In Ghana, the military couped in 1966 while Kwame Nkrumah was abroad, justifying it "as a 'last resort' to combat [Nkrumah's] authoritarian entrenchment" (Powell 2014: 214). The junta violently split over ethnic politics, the timing of democratization, and a bribery scandal involving the junta's leader, eventually allowing a constitutional assembly and elections in 1969 (Pinkney 1972; Hutchful 1973). In Sudan, a political crisis triggered by civil war and economic collapse culminated in an April 1985 popular uprising while the dictator Jaafar Nimeiri was abroad for medical treatment (El-Affendi 2012; de Waal 2013: 216–18). Hoping to prevent further unrest and a looming junior officer coup, senior military leaders under Abdel al-Dahab couped the same month ("U.S. aides" 1985; Holt and Daly 2014). Compared to immediate security concerns, democracy was a distant consideration (Anderson 1999; Collins 2008), leading the military to initially hedge on elections (Schumacher 1985; Holt and Daly 2014). However, intense popular pressure (Schumacher 1985; Woodward 1990) and the fact the army was "riven by factions" (Holt and Daly 2014: 142) convinced al-Dahab, "an unambitious man who did not desire a long term in political office" (Berridge 2015: 53; also UPI 1985), to accept democratization. A former prime minister won the 1986 election but fell to a 1989 coup by Omar al-Bashir.

The remaining seven cases (Burma 1960, Argentina 1963, Turkey 1983, Suriname 1991, Bangladesh 2009, Honduras 2010, Thailand 2011) conform to a *guardian coup* pattern, in which senior military leaders coup against democracy, resolve some political issue to their satisfaction, and return to democracy. In all but Thailand, this occurred within three years. This guardian coup pattern represents the most common alternative to the Salvation, Reformer, and Regained Power patterns, although in Burma and Suriname a coup plotter regained power in democracy. The remainder represent five of the nine on-path cases that do not fit any of these three patterns. Democratization in these cases was generally not driven by major protests or elite insecurity. Rather,

---

30. Of the remaining five, only in Sudan 1986 was the turn to democracy especially swift, and scholars agree the Sudanese coup was not motivated by democracy (Anderson 1999; Collins 2008; Yukawa, Kushima, and Hidaka 2019).

military leaders couped for specific political goals and then determined ceding power was preferable to waiting for major threats to develop. Most often, this was aimed at preventing political rifts within the military itself. In fact, these cases include five of the seven total cases with a united military hierarchy through the transition.

Turkey 1983 is an emblematic case. Endemic political violence between right-wing nationalists and Communists, which was killing twenty per day in the late 1970s (Pevsner 1984; Aydin-Düzgit and Gürsoy 2013: 292), led to a 1980 coup that military chief Kenan Evren justified to "protect the unity of the nation [and] prevent a possible civil war" (Varol 2017: 184). A massive military crackdown, including the prosecution of nearly a quarter million Turks and the dissolution of all existing political parties and unions, successfully tamped down the violence (Sunar and Sayari 1986; Aydin-Düzgit and Gürsoy 2013). Believing that permanent rule would tarnish its legitimacy, the military instituted a tightly controlled democratic opening, with two of the three legal political parties created by the junta. Surprisingly, the opposition Motherland Party won the 1983 election and was allowed to take power after its leader, Turgut Özal (who had served as deputy prime minister under the junta), signaled deference to the military's continued influence (Huntington 1991: 176; Casper and Taylor 1996: 127; Pope and Pope 2000).

*Multiple Coups*

The final category is cases with multiple coups preceding democratization (listed with a * in Table 3.1). With 32 transitions, this not only comprises the majority of coup cases but outweighs any other primary path category.

These cases perfectly illustrate how regime weakness and internal divisions contribute to democratization. Democratization was overwhelmingly driven by "push" factors from autocracy, particularly elite insecurity and pro-democratic protest. On average, the cases featured 2.7 coups leading up to democratization, with 3 or more in 15 cases and 4 or more in 6. Nine cases qualify as secondary civil war or assassination cases, including Colombia, Argentina 1983, El Salvador, and the Comoros. Three in four featured major pro-democracy protests after the initial coup, with particular effect in Guatemala 1945, Greece 1974, Portugal 1976, Argentina 1983, and Ecuador 2003. The transitions also coincided with difficult economic times: 22 cases featured a two-year period of negative economic growth in the five years before democratization.

The greatest contributing factor to this instability was conflict within the military: in 29 of 32 cases, the multiple coups were by rival military factions. Further, the three exceptions (Panama 1952, Niger 2011, Fiji 2014) involved self-coups before or after military coups, with resulting divides between executive-aligned security forces and the military. These internal conflicts had many sources. In Spain 1931, Greece 1974, and Argentina 1983, hard-liners and soft-liners clashed over liberalization.[31] Relatedly, in Guatemala 1958 and Fiji, the conflict partly revolved around the incorporation of excluded ethnic groups. In Ecuador 1948, Argentina 1958, Portugal 1976, and El Salvador, the divide was between left and right. In still other cases, such as Honduras 1957, Venezuela 1959, Guatemala 1986, and Ecuador 2003, rivals fought to preserve personal advantage, safeguard military integrity, or oppose corruption. Finally, some countries faced a chaotic blend of conflicts. In Peru 1963, the "military was certainly divided, with several factions, including some who weren't keen on elections" and a partly overlapping left-right divide, according to Cynthia McClintock.[32] "The key to understanding Peru is everything is precarious."

With multiple military factions fighting and each faction's hold on power tenuous, a long cycle of damaging coups and countercoups was an ever-present threat. In the Salvation pattern, an insecure dictator democratized to escape this cycle (16 of 32 multiple-coup cases).[33] Alternatively, a pro-democratic Reformer took power and quickly democratized (12 cases). In 10 cases, this resulted from a reformer-led coup, of which 5 followed multiple earlier coups.

*ILLUSTRATIVE CASES.* To capture the instability in these cases, and in particular the role of leader insecurity, I overview some illustrative cases, beginning with Colombia 1958 (a Reformer case), Argentina 1983 (Salvation), and Comoros 2006 (Regained Power). I then turn to more detailed accounts of Bolivia 1979 and 1982 (Salvation cases) and Portugal 1976 (Reformer), the latter long considered historically significant (given its timing setting off democracy's Third Wave) and a puzzling theoretical outlier (O'Donnell and Schmitter 1986; R. Collier 1999: 161–65; Bunce 2000; Fishman 2018). As I explain, Portugal is an ideal case for this book's theory.

Colombia 1958 illustrates how actors can push for democratization when they cannot secure power themselves yet are unwilling to accept any other autocrat. Despite one of the most ideologically polarized environments of any transition, it culminated in a surprisingly broad coup plot, with the two major parties, students, the Church, and military elements combining to oust General Gustavo Rojas Pinilla (Dix 1987: 37; Higley and Burton 2006: 76–77). The starting point was the 1949 eruption of La Violencia, a brutal civil war between insurgencies allied with the Liberal and Conservative parties that

---

31. In Greece, a hard-liner that couped to prevent a liberal opening proclaimed, "We are not playing. We shall have a dictatorship, send all our opponents to exile on the islands and stay in power for thirty years!" (quoted in Tzortzis 2003: 10). The country democratized a year later.

32. Personal interview, May 6, 2019.

33. In some cases, an insecure leader *attempted* to democratize but was stopped by blockers. In Greece 1974, a failed naval coup in 1973 convinced an "alarmed [Georgios] Papadopoulos to speed up the pace of the transition" (Tzortzis 2003: 5), but this was (temporarily) countered by a right-wing coup (Diamandouros 1986; R. Collier 1999: 157–59).

ultimately cost 160,000 lives (Oquist 1980; Roldán 2002; Bermeo 2010a: 80). With political order disintegrating, the Conservative president Laureano Gómez Castro attempted to consolidate personal power though a new constitution, triggering a bipartisan coup in 1953 that empowered Rojas (Peeler 1977: 11; Hartlyn 1984: 249).

Although initially viewed as apolitical, Rojas transformed into a Frankenstein's monster of runaway ambition, rapidly consolidating political power and founding the Third Force populist movement "to support his increasingly personalistic regime and to challenge the dominance of the traditional Colombian parties" (Mauceri 1989: 210; also Peeler 1977; Dugas 2000: 86). This generated opposition from both parties and military leaders averse to permanent military rule (Mauceri 1989: 210). The result was a 1956 meeting in Spain between bitter rivals Gómez and Liberal leader Alberto Lleras Camargo, who crafted the Pact of Benidorm committing both to Rojas's ouster (Mauceri 1989: 209). After Rojas extended his rule through a farcical constitutional convention, the elite conspiracy forced him out in May 1957, aided by military factions, a general strike, and mass protests (Payne 1968: 151; Dix 1987: 37).[34] During a provisional military junta, the parties bargained out the Declaration of Sitges (approved by referendum in December) that guaranteed equal legislative representation and a presidential rotation until 1974 (Dix 1987; Dugas 2000; Bermeo 2010a). Following the preemptive arrest of military conspirators plotting to disrupt the election, Lleras was confirmed as president in May 1958 (Hartlyn 1984: 263).

Argentina 1983 is an exemplar of the Salvation pattern, with the military's acceptance of democratization stemming from its internal implosion and widespread popular mobilization. Although some accounts source this to the regime's defeat in the Falklands War, the military's fragmentation began much earlier and was really the cause of the foolhardy war rather than an outcome. Following Juan Perón's death in 1974, his widow, Isabel, was unable to manage rising leftist violence and a break with labor, falling to a right-wing military coup in 1976. Under Jorge Videla, the hard-liner junta unleashed a brutal wave of violence against the left in the Dirty War, including some thirty thousand "disappearances" and thousands more tortured and imprisoned (Ackerman and Duvall 2000: 270; Lewis 2002). In 1981, army head Roberto Viola pushed for a gradual democratic opening, envisioning "a graceful exit for the armed forces" (Schlaudeman 1987: 236). However, economic problems and Viola's personal health provided pretexts for another hard-liner coup under Leopoldo Galtieri, who explained that prior Argentinean dictators "took the wrong path

34. Rojas refused to fade away, leading a failed countercoup in 1963 and losing a possibly stolen presidential election in 1970, which in turn inspired the M-19 guerrilla movement (Hanratty and Meditz 1988).

and thought elections were the solution to the political problem. . . . We must not make the same mistake" (quoted in Stohl 1987: 229).

Facing a sharply divided military and renewed protest from Perónists, Galtieri recognized his precarious hold on power and decided on "a desperation move to preserve a regime already in trouble" (R. Collier 1999: 125). By seizing the Falklands from Great Britain, Galtieri hoped to ride the military victory and resulting wave of nationalism to an elected presidency (Schlaudeman 1987: 237; Potash 1996: 509). Unfortunately, the 1982 invasion was a disaster, leading to Galtieri's ouster four days after the surrender and producing "a dramatic collapse in the regime's legitimacy and an internal crisis in the armed forces" (Mainwaring and Viola 1985: 207). A retired army general, Reynaldo Bignone, was installed as leader in July 1982, triggering a defection of air force and navy leaders. Although the military initially hoped to prolong its grip on power (Casper and Taylor 1996: 137; Lewis 2002: 192), internal coup threats and rising protests, strikes, and tax boycotts convinced Bignone to relent (Mainwaring and Viola 1985: 207; Rock 1987: 383; Munck 1998; Veigel 2010: 99–100). In fact, the military was so divided, disgraced, and "preoccupied with covering up crimes and failures during the previous six years" (Veigel 2010: 107) that it was unable to create an allied party for the 1983 elections (Mainwaring and Viola 1985: 208). Instead, leaders signed an amnesty deal with the Perónists in exchange for their legalization and control of the unions (Casper and Taylor 1996: 160–61). When Raúl Alfonsín's UCR won instead, military leaders (including Videla, Viola, and Galtieri) were prosecuted, although military revolts led Alfonsín to back off and they were pardoned in 1990 (Rock 1987; Munck 1998).

The Comoros 2006 is a case of endemic political weakness, with more than a dozen coup attempts and six irregular turnovers of power from independence in 1975 through 2000. A key engine of this instability was the remarkable career of Bob Denard, a French mercenary-turned-strongman who carried out a 1975 coup, returned the ousted leader to power in 1978 (assassinating the president), ruled as de facto leader for eleven years, and supported another presidential assassination and coup in 1989 (Weinberg 1994; AP 1995). Although he was exiled by French forces in 1989, he returned to kidnap the new president in a 1995 coup that was quickly overturned by another French intervention (Keaten 2007). Incredibly, Denard managed to coup against every non-provisional president in the country's first twenty-one years. After his final removal, the Comoros descended into political crisis over the degree of centralization in its island federation, with two islands (Anjouan and Mohéli) seceding in 1997, a national military coup over the issue in 1999, and a coup in Anjouan in 2001 (AP 1997; Ayangafa 2008). Although a power-sharing deal secured sufficient peace for democratic elections in 2006, an international force invaded Anjouan in 2008 and removed the leader (Ayangafa 2008). Meanwhile, the 1999 coup leader, Azali Assoumani, won a flawed presidential election in 2002 and a democratic election in 2016. The contrast with Denard, who had little hope of winning in democracy, is telling.

BOLIVIA 1979 AND 1982. The Bolivian transitions combine elements of the last two cases, with a "notoriously weak" state (Levitsky and Way 2010: 179) and an even greater disintegration of the military than in Argentina (Dunkerley 1984; Hudson and Hanratty 1989; R. Collier 1999: 143–49). With deep internal divides over liberalization, ideology, the U.S. alliance, and the drug trade, Bolivia ricocheted between seven military juntas and two civilian governments from 1978 to 1982, in "one of the darkest and most unstable periods in Bolivian history" (Hudson and Hanratty 1989: 183). At the core of this instability was an intractable conflict between a dominant conservative anti-democratic faction in Bolivia's military and the popular forces unleashed during the 1952 National Revolution (Dunkerley 1984; Klein 2003/2011: 222). These forces were personified by the worker-centric and nationalist MNR party, which led the revolution and whose leaders won all but one contested election not overturned for fraud from 1951 to 1993.[35] Knowing its consequences, the military resisted democratization yet repeatedly proved unable to establish stable autocracy.

Following twelve years under MNR rule, a 1964 coup restored military supremacy, but ideologically motivated coups whipsawed the country from left to right and back in 1969, 1970, three days later in 1970, and 1971 (Dunkerley 1984: 1–200; Klein 2003/2011: 212–29; Albertus and Gay 2017: 637). Colonel Hugo Banzer, the right-wing 1971 coup leader, held that "democratic rule ultimately led to social chaos" (Klein 2003/2011: 230) and self-couped in 1974, outlawing all parties and dissolving his own civilian front. However, economic problems and military and U.S. opposition caused him to return to elections in 1978 (Dunkerley 1984: 238–48; Malloy and Gamarra 1987: 108; Hudson and Hanratty 1989: 45). Forced by the military to abandon his plan to run himself, Banzer chose Gen. Juan Pereda as his successor, believing he could control and govern through him (Casper and Taylor 1996: 72; Klein 2003/2011: 234). Pereda's subsequent election in July 1978 was so obviously fraudulent, with some villages recording vote totals at ten times the population and whole boxes of ballots simply thrown into a lake, that Pereda himself requested the courts annul it (Dunkerley 1984: 244–48; Casper and Taylor 1996: 73). Fearing Banzer's next move and believing a resurgent left couldn't be defeated electorally, Pereda couped and withdrew his support for elections. However, this was reversed four months later by a general who wanted the military out of politics (Whitehead 1986; Malloy and Gamarra 1987: 110).

---

35. This counts the victories of Hernán Siles Zuazo, an MNR cofounder who split from the party. To be clear, MNR's leaders were hardly ardent democrats, with Siles and others supporting military coups when it served their purposes (Dunkerley 1984: 117–18, 266).

The instability was far from over, with "Bolivia plunged into political chaos . . . [and a] cluster of coups under almost constant preparation" (Dunkerley 1984: 249). Although free elections proceeded in July 1979, the results were fragmented and congress was unable to agree on a presidential winner. With an interim president installed awaiting new elections, Banzerist general Alberto Natusch launched a bloody coup in November, triggering mass protests and military and U.S. opposition (Hudson and Hanratty 1989). Relying on a colonel nicknamed the "Marshal of Death" for capital security, the Natusch regime machine-gunned protesters and bombed a labor group's headquarters but collapsed after only sixteen days in power (de Onis 1979; Dunkerley 1984: 267; Klein 2003/2011). Natusch stepped down in exchange for the removal of the former interim president, thereby empowering the head of the lower house (Alexander 1982; Whitehead 1986).[36] With civilian government restored and elections allowed the following year, this is considered the first democratization date, albeit a temporary reprieve.

The June 1980 elections were more decisive, with MNR cofounder Hernán Siles Zuazo defeating his fellow cofounder and Banzer for the presidency.[37] Yet two weeks later, before the election winners could take power, General Luis García Meza couped, pointing to political dysfunction and threats of military prosecutions. Proclaiming he would "stay in power for twenty years, until Bolivia is reconstructed" (quoted in Dunkerley 1984: 292), García Meza unleashed a repressive turn that "sought to make the entire society tremble" (Malloy and Gamarra 1987: 114), killing hundreds of union leaders, miners, journalists, and political opponents in the first few months (Panama City ACAN 1980). However, García Meza would gain the greatest infamy by employing exiled fascists as enforcers—including ex-Nazi Klaus Barbie, who organized a mercenary force called "the fiancés of death"—and partnering with cocaine traffickers to accrue money for bribes and security (Dunkerley 1984: 292–335; Hudson and Hanratty 1989: 185; Klein 2003/2011: 237). So valuable was this partnership for Bolivia's drug lords that income from cocaine rose to four times that of traditional exports (Dunkerley 1984: 293). Despite his ruthlessness, García Meza's regime was weak and isolated, "debilitated by dissent" within an embarrassed military and from rising pro-democratic opposition (Dunkerley 1984: 292). When a military rebellion organized by Natusch finally ousted García Meza in August 1981, the regime "ended as virtually a purely parasitic government openly looting a cowed and frightened nation" (Malloy and Gamarra 1987: 114).

36. To oppose the deal, the interim president snuck into congress "disguised in a wig and sport clothes," gave a fiery speech, and fled through the pantry (Dunkerley 1984: 268).

37. In democracy, the indefatigable Banzer was finally elected president in 1997 (his sixth try).

Despite being wholly discredited and demoralized, the military empowered another conservative general, Celso Torrelio, who opposed elections and continued many of García Meza's policies (Dunkerley 1984: 338). Yet the status quo was untenable—military divisions, economic crisis, and domestic and international opposition forced the military to accept a liberal opening under Guido Vildoso in July 1982. When Vildoso proposed delaying elections for a year, a massive popular movement erupted in September, complete with students blocking the capital's streets, the ransacking of public buildings, a mass march of over 100,000, and a promised general strike (Dunkerley 1984: 343; Hudson and Hanratty 1989: 184–85). Military leaders capitulated, allowing the 1980 congress to re-select Siles as president in October (Dunkerley 1984: 343–44; Malloy and Gamarra 1987: 114). Ultimately, democracy was an escape for the divided and besieged military. As Malloy and Gamarra (1987: 114) write, "Bolivia turned to democracy because it was the only choice. In those circumstances, there was no capacity to mount an authoritarian government."

PORTUGAL 1976. Portugal's stunning transformation from neo-fascist dictatorship to democracy between 1974 and 1976 is rightly recognized as a legacy of the April 1974 junior officer coup that upended a forty-one-year-old regime. However, a common misconception is that the coup itself was pro-democratic and led rather seamlessly to democracy (Pace 1999; Varol 2012, 2017: 7; Kuehn 2017; Ginsburg and Huq 2018: 43). The truth is nearer the polar opposite: the anti-democratic seizure of power prefigured several failed attempts at a radical Communist-aligned autocracy, alongside a "general climate of instability and crisis" (R. Collier 1999: 163) and "bewildering reversals and turmoil" (Maxwell 1995: 94). Ideological divisions within the military produced cycles of regime volatility, in turn creating openings for pro-democratic mobilization and a virtual social revolution that surprised even the most ardent leftists in the junta (Raby 1988; Maxwell 1995: 61; Linz and Stepan 1996: 118; Fishman 2018). Only after "a turbulent breakdown of authority" (Maxwell 1995: 208), with the state in "a period of near-anarchy" (Chilcote 2010: 103), were moderates able to launch a reformer coup and steer the country to democracy.

An unassuming economics professor, António de Oliveira Salazar, installed the neo-fascist Estado Novo regime in 1933 and was succeeded by Marcello Caetano in 1968.[38] After an aborted feint toward liberalization, Caetano faced rising economic problems and labor protests in the early 1970s (Hunt 1976;

---

38. Despite its durability, the Salazar regime did not go unchallenged (Ferreira and Marshall 1986; Raby 1988; Accornero 2013). Its greatest threat was the 1958 presidential candidacy of a dissident general, Humberto Delgado, who attracted joyous crowds while fearlessly campaigning for liberal democracy. After the election was stolen, Delgado failed to inspire a mass uprising, although significant allied coup plots continued until 1962 (Raby 1988: 177–213; Maxwell 1995: 49–51).

Maxwell 1995: 55). Yet the regime's greatest challenge was its endless colonial wars in Angola, Mozambique, and Guinea-Bissau, grinding conflicts that consumed 46% of the national budget in 1971 and led around 100,000 young men to emigrate to avoid conscription (Hunt 1976: 20; Raby 1988: 244). A desire to end the unsustainable wars inspired a faction of junior military officers to plot the regime's overthrow (Ferreira and Marshall 1986: 29; Raby 1988: 244). Fuel was added to the fire by a 1973 change in military promotion policy that particularly disadvantaged captains (Maxwell 1995: 35–38; Raby 1988: 245), a rank already divided from more senior officers by ideology and class (Ferreira and Marshall 1986: 14–15). Although the roughly 200 officers in the emerging Armed Forces Movement (MFA) had a leftist tilt, in part from their exposure to African revolutionary doctrines (Maxwell 1995: 60; Bermeo 2007: 399), the group was ideologically diverse and mainly united by a "convergence of resentments" (Maxwell 1995: 38–39). In the words of the chief coup organizer, Otelo Saraiva de Carvalho, "Initially, the Movement of Captains had nothing to do with politics. The Movement was formed to defend the privileges of the professional army officers" (quoted in Ferreira and Marshall 1986: 115). In particular, the leading officers were not motivated by democracy (Huntington 1991: 4) and "did not appeal to democratic values at all" (Yukawa, Kushima, and Hidaka 2019: 5). Instead, many would come "to see themselves as a revolutionary vanguard" for a quite different outcome (Maxwell 1995: 60).

Just past midnight on April 25, 1974, an allied DJ broadcast a banned song containing the prophetic line, "It is the people who give the orders" (Raby 1988: 248). This was the final signal to launch the MFA's coup.[39] As in 1911, the coup was surprisingly easy, finished within hours, and almost bloodless (Hunt 1976; Maxwell 1995: 42). Although led by Carvalho, the MFA opted to make António de Spínola, a right-leaning senior officer fired by Caetano for writing a book critical of the regime's colonial policy, the figurehead leader and first president (Hunt 1976; Maxwell 1995: 32–35; R. Collier 1999: 163). Further signaling a broad coalition, the MFA established a ruling junta nominally separate from the MFA and a cabinet with strong civilian representation. Most significantly, Mário Soares, a long-time dissident who had established the moderate Socialist party while in exile, was brought in as foreign minister and began negotiating an end to the colonial wars (Maxwell 1995: 73).

Harbingers of two future sources of state disintegration—mass mobilization and elite fragmentation—arose immediately. First, the coup was met by rapturous popular support, with crowds placing carnations in the barrels of the soldiers' guns (giving rise to the name Carnation Revolution). Against the

---

39. The immediate trigger was a mass arrest of officers following a failed coup in March, which threatened to close the window on the main MFA plot (Raby 1988: 247; Maxwell 1995: 44).

MFA's wishes, this evolved into mass activism, with two million mobilized in May and as many strikes in the two months post-coup as in the previous five years (Fernandes and Branco 2017: 413). Second, the MFA rapidly divided into five rough factions: Spínola supporters on the right, pro-democratic moderates who were large in number but disorganized, a socialist group opposed to Communist influence, a Marxist group typified by Vasco Gonçalves that allied with the Portuguese Communist Party (PCP), and an even-farther-left group under Carvalho opposed to parties (Hunt 1976; Maxwell 1995: 86–89; Bermeo 2007: 399–400). The first of the period's many intense ideological fights arose between Spínola and the leftist MFA leaders, with Spínola resisting significant economic changes and an immediate end to the colonial wars (Ferreira and Marshall 1986: 90; Raby 1988: 248; Maxwell 1995: 77). Spínola worked to enhance his power, demanding the right to arrest strikers and attempting to dissolve the MFA (Hunt 1976; Ferreira and Marshall 1986: 37; Maxwell 1995: 63–64). In return, the MFA asserted its control by vetoing Spínola's choice for prime minister and installing Gonçalves, who declared that freedom required "collective ownership of the principal means of production" (quoted in Ferreira and Marshall 1986: 95). As early as August, the CIA's deputy director grimly reported "Portugal was as good as lost to the communists" (Maxwell 1995: 91).

In September 1974, Spínola was ousted after he organized a supportive mass demonstration that was blocked by leftists and army units (Ferreira and Marshall 1986: 40–41; Maxwell 1995: 79–80). Stepping down, Spínola decried the regime's accelerating radicalism, ominously warning, "Under the false flag of liberty, there are being prepared new forms of slavery" (quoted in Maxwell 1995: 66). Indeed, the hard left now dominated the government, with Francisco da Costa Gomes (a former armed forces chief fired with Spínola) in the presidency, Gonçalves consolidating power, and Carvalho heading a new special forces command (COPCON) charged with safeguarding the MFA's revolutionary mission (Maxwell 1995: 79–80). The MFA closely allied with the PCP, a disciplined group that received about $45 million from the Soviets to help organize (Hunt 1976: 117; Maxwell 1995: 72; Bermeo 2007: 401). When Communists marched for a single state-controlled union in January, MFA leaders supported them, although the plan was narrowly quashed by moderates (Maxwell 1986: 121; Maxwell 1995: 109).

In March 1975, a failed countercoup by Spínola bombed an artillery regiment before collapsing, handing Gonçalves an opening to push further left and centralize control under the new Council of the Revolution (Hunt 1976: 6; Ferreira and Marshall 1986: 33; Maxwell 1986: 121). At this point, the country veered very close to becoming a Marxist dictatorship (Graham 1992: 291; Casper and Taylor 1996: 142; Linz and Stepan 1996: 126). Most of the general officer corps was jailed and there were soon more political prisoners than before the coup (Maxwell 1995: 89, 110–11). Communists were put in charge of state radio and television (Hunt 1976). Starting in March, the regime nationalized the banking, insurance, energy, and transportation industries (Hunt 1976: 7; Ferreira and Marshall 1986: 45–46; Maxwell 1995: 112), with the fixed capital formation of the public sector rising from 10% to 47% of GDP (Solsten 1993). In rural areas, an upper limit was placed on landholdings, while the MFA's Cultural Dynamization Campaign instructed 1.5 million rural workers about the MFA's mission and how to vote in coming elections (Bermeo 1986: 39). In July, the regime debuted a plan to link the central Council to workers' committees in charge of economic production and local government, which Soares warned was "only one step short of outlawing all democratic rights and creating a dictatorship" (quoted in Hunt 1976: 102).

Despite these radical aims, the regime remained poorly organized and sharply divided below the top level, with the MFA beset by "internal contradictions . . . [and] political naivete" (Raby 1988: 249). The result was a "political vacuum" after decades of stifling conservative rule, triggering an eruption of mass activism that approached a social revolution (Bermeo 1986; Maxwell 1986, 1987: 198). As Ramos Pinto (2013: 12) writes, "There is no doubt that the disintegration of coercive power of the state that followed the 25 April coup allowed the emergence of popular movements of the period." Or as the American ambassador later put it, "Total chaos prevailed and there was no leadership" (Binnendijk 1987: 209). About a quarter of the nation's farmland was spontaneously seized by rural workers (Bermeo 1986, 1997; Maxwell 1995). Urban laborers took over homes and factories and established ruling neighborhood committees (Ferreira and Marshall 1986: 186; Maxwell 1995: 118–19; Linz and Stepan 1996: 118; Ramos Pinto 2013). Along with the regime's nationalizations, this represented the "most massive seizures of property in Europe since the Russian Revolution" (Bermeo 1997: 308). The economic maelstrom occurred alongside a diffuse cultural revolution, overturning "hierarchies in all sorts of settings: schools and universities, government ministries, private firms, urban neighborhoods, and at least to some degree in gender relations" (Fishman 2018: 617). Although MFA leaders attempted to harness this revolutionary zeal, they were surprised and alarmed by its strength (Ferreira and Marshall 1986: 91, 183; Maxwell 1995: 61).

The political vacuum also provided space for parties, democratic activists, and right-wing groups (Hunt 1976: 5; Maxwell 1995: 75). The key pivot point for this countermobilization was the April 1975 constitutional assembly election. Although MFA leaders agreed to elections after the coup, they subsequently regretted this and forced the parties to sign a pact guaranteeing that military control and the MFA's leftist program would persist for at least three years regardless of the result (Hunt 1976: 97; Ferreira and Marshall 1986: 46; Maxwell 1995: 112–13). According to Costa Gomes, this was necessary because the "Portuguese people are not sufficiently enlightened politically to reject the elitist parties or pseudo-democrats" (quoted in Maxwell 1995: 111). The MFA's left-most faction campaigned for voters to return blank ballots to signal opposition to elections, but only 7% of voters complied (Hunt 1976: 98; Maxwell 1995: 113; Linz and Stepan 1996: 124). Instead, the election was a triumph for Soares's Socialists (with 38% of the vote) and moderate pro-democratic parties in general (72%), fatefully revealing the MFA to be less popular and the population more pro-democratic than previously thought (Pimlott 1977; Maxwell 1995: 115; Linz and Stepan 1996: 121). Although the MFA and PCP shrugged off the election as insignificant,[40] the results spurred on both moderate and reactionary mobilization. In July, Catholics and farmers protested and began to reclaim expropriated land (Maxwell 1995: 138). Right-wing armed groups joined with farmers to bomb 49 PCP offices, storm the PCP headquarters with 5,000 men, and burn the Spanish embassy (Hunt 1976; Ferreira and Marshall 1986: 50; Maxwell 1995: 147, 155). Throughout the "hot summer" of 1975, a reinvigorated coalition of democratic moderates and conservatives "blocked the momentum of revolution" (Maxwell 1986: 124).

The April election and rising social disorder brought the MFA's factional strife to a crisis point (Raby 1988: 260; Linz and Stepan 1996: 122; Chilcote 2010: 104). The MFA was "carved up into as many different factions as there are generals, colonels, and captains," an Italian journalist explained, with slight exaggeration. "Even the state no longer exists" (quoted in Chilcote 2010: 122). In particular, the MFA's rank and file grew alarmed over the radical political program, economic problems, instability, and threatened isolation from the West (Hunt 1976: 108; Maxwell 1995). In August 1975, the clandestine Group of Nine within the MFA released a pro-democratic manifesto called the Document of the Nine, which was left-leaning but rejected the "Eastern European model of a socialist society, to which we will be fatally led" (quoted in Ferreira and Marshall 1986: 271; also Maxwell 1995: 149; Bermeo 2007). Gonçalves declared this "an act of treason against the revolution" and the MFA's left released a rival manifesto that concluded with "LONG LIVE THE ALLIANCE BETWEEN THE WORKERS AND THE PEASANTS! . . . LONG LIVE THE SOCIALIST REVOLUTION!" (quoted in Ferreira and Marshall 1986: 92–93, 282). Yet the Group of Nine's claim that 80% of officers had signed their document could not be ignored; Gonçalves was forced out in September and the government reorganized under moderate socialists and a civilian-heavy cabinet (Hunt 1976: 9; Bermeo 2007). The eclipse of the left brought an influx of foreign aid, but the danger had hardly passed. Instead, "The crisis had split

---

40. After the election, Gonçalves promised the vote would not "decisively influence the revolutionary process" (quoted in Hunt 1976: 99). PCP head Álvaro Cunhal insisted that "elections have nothing or very little to do with the dynamics of a revolution. . . . I promise you there will be no parliament in Portugal" (quoted in Linz and Stepan 1996: 121).

the MFA wide open . . . [and] the specter of civil strife became real" (Maxwell 1995: 152).

The left did not take its downfall well. An assassination attempt against the new prime minister failed in September 1975, followed by Marxist bombings in Lisbon and Oporto and widespread protests by leftist soldiers (Hunt 1976). The prime minister openly admitted he lacked the "authority or the capacity to govern" (Hunt 1976: 120). A period of "terrorism and anarchy" (Chilcote 2010: 104) reigned, during which "Portugal came very close to civil war" (Maxwell 1987: 200). In a final bid for power, leftist paratroopers supported by Carvalho attacked several air force bases in November (Ferreira and Marshall 1986: 57; Maxwell 1995: 156–57). The uprising was crushed by Group of Nine member António Ramalho Eanes, a "taciturn prodemocracy colonel" (Huntington 1991: 5) who launched a countercoup in response that "decisively changed the course of the revolution" (Graham 1992: 289). This was a classic Reformer coup, with the MFA subsequently "purged of its radical officers and dominated by those sympathetic to social democracy" (Graham 1992: 288). As Eanes's co-conspirator explained, "We brought about the coup in order to achieve a western parliamentary democracy" (quoted in Ferreira and Marshall 1986: 166). But there was a catch: a February 1976 pact and the April constitution established the military's Council of the Revolution as a de facto constitutional court that could veto legislation, which held until 1982 (Maxwell 1995: 159; Linz and Stepan 1996: 123). The Socialists won the April 1976 legislative election and formed a minority government under Soares. In June, Eanes won the presidency over Carvalho, who was later imprisoned for involvement with a far-left terror group called Popular Forces 25 April (Huntington 1991: 237). In 1986, Soares succeeded Eanes as president.

Instead of a puzzling outlier, Portugal 1976 perfectly fits this book's theory: the 1974 coup upended a durable autocracy, yielding a divided, insecure regime and an opening for mass mobilization and pro-democratic pressure. In turn, this provided an opportunity for a pro-democratic countercoup, with Eanes fulfilling both the Reformer and Regained Power patterns. The case also fits the logic of defeat in war, with the deteriorating colonial wars contributing to elite divisions and state incapacity (Raby 1988; Bermeo 2007). Echoing this book's theory, Raby (1988: 13) explains that the lesson from Portugal is that once fascism is implanted, "its overthrow becomes extremely difficult in the absence of external war or political reorientation within the regime itself." A remaining question is why the pro-democratic side prevailed over the Marxist revolution pushed by MFA leaders, the PCP, and many citizens. Despite the radical left's initial advantage in organization, there was widespread democratic support in Portugal, especially among military officers. Although Portugal in 1974 was underdeveloped relative to Europe, it was still in the top quarter of all countries in average income, a facilitating condition for democratic values. Further, more than one-sixth of the population was working abroad,

mostly in Western Europe, with the resulting exposure to democracy influencing both returnees and family back home (Binnendijk 1987: 203–4; Bermeo
2007, 2010a). Similarly, many military officers, including Eanes, had extensive
exposure to fellow NATO members in Europe (Maxwell 1995: 107). Despite
multiple reversals, the result was a belated triumph for a long-submerged
coalition of democrats.

## Civil Wars

Civil wars are among the most destructive political events in history. Sudan's
two separatist civil wars killed about 2.5 million people and so devastated the
economy that the country's per capita income at independence in 1956 wasn't
exceeded until 2001. In Sierra Leone, the civil war created millions of refugees
and shrunk the economy by more than half during the 1990s. Despite this
chaos, Sudan 1965, Sudan 1986, and Sierra Leone 2002 all democratized during or immediately after their civil wars. How does civil war in cases like these
pave the way to democracy?

### OVERVIEW

#### Cases

There are 18 primary civil war cases, of which 9 also qualify for another path
condition (3 coup, 1 coup/assassination, 1 postwar, and 4 electoral continuity).
Another 17 are secondary civil war cases, of which 15 are primary coup cases,
1 assassination, and 1 postwar. Thus, about one in four democratic transitions
occur during or shortly after a civil war. The cases are listed in Table 3.2.

Note that 5 in 6 primary cases are from 1984 onward, suggesting the
importance of the increasingly pro-democratic international environment as
the Cold War wound down. Most are in Africa (6 primary, 10 total) or Latin
America (2 primary, 10 total), but there are multiple cases in Europe and
Asia. As discussed below, some involved rebel or government victories prior
to transition, others negotiated settlements, and still others had ongoing wars
at democratization. Civil war duration also varied greatly among the primary
cases, ranging from Albania, where the war started and ended the same year,
to Mozambique, where the war lasted 15 years. The average duration (up to
democratization) is 7.0 years for the primary cases and 6.7 years for all cases.

Figure 3.4 shows the likelihood of democratization dividing by whether
countries are within five years of civil war, both in the whole sample and post-
1945 (the observed period of post–civil war democratization). A recent civil
war predicts a significantly higher chance of democratization, especially in
the modern era, when a civil war proportionally raises the chance of democratization by 46%.

**Table 3.2.** Civil War Cases, 1800–2014

**Primary Cases**

| | | |
|---|---|---|
| Indonesia 1955 | Sudan 1965 | Lebanon 1971 |
| Nicaragua 1984 | The Philippines 1986 | Suriname 1988 |
| Sri Lanka 1991 | Mozambique 1994 | Albania 1997 |
| Croatia 2000 | Senegal 2000 | Serbia 2000 |
| Sierra Leone 2002 | Burundi 2005 | Liberia 2006 |
| Solomon Islands 2006 | Nepal 2008 | Pakistan 2008 |

**Secondary Cases**

| | | |
|---|---|---|
| Costa Rica 1949 | Colombia 1958 | Burma 1960 |
| Guatemala 1966 | Argentina 1973 | Cyprus 1977 |
| Spain 1977 | Nigeria 1979 | Argentina 1983 |
| Turkey 1983 | El Salvador 1984 | Guatemala 1986 |
| Sudan 1986 | Suriname 1991 | Mali 1992 |
| Comoros 2006 | Thailand 2011 | |

*Note:* Years shown are for democratization, not the civil wars.

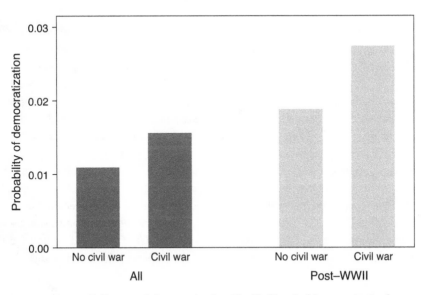

FIGURE 3.4. Civil wars and democratization. The likelihood of democratization by whether there has been a civil war in the previous five years, for all autocracies (1800–2014) and post-1945 autocracies (N = 11,489/5,375).

*Motives for Civil Wars*

The civil wars in Table 3.2 were motivated by a diverse range of political and cultural issues, but democracy was never the primary goal. Warring groups often ended up strategically opting for democratization, but this does not imply democracy was a sincere preference and even less so the initial purpose of the war. In Nepal, for instance, militarily ascendant Maoist rebels accepted democratization in a 2006 peace settlement and won the first democratic elections. However, as Huang (2016: 116) quotes a senior government official, "Democracy is a byproduct of the war. It wasn't a goal of the Maoists. The Maoists had launched a war against a democracy system."

For most conflicts, the motivation was clear. Among the rebels instigating conflict were religious extremists (Indonesia, Lebanon, Pakistan), Communists (the Philippines, Nepal), extreme leftists (El Salvador, Nicaragua), ethnic separatists (Sudan 1965 and 1986, Spain, Nigeria, Sri Lanka, Mali, Croatia, Senegal, Serbia, Solomon Islands), failed coup leaders (Guatemala 1966, 1986), and combinations of these (Burma, Thailand). Other conflicts were initiated over ethnic exclusion (Suriname 1988 and 1991, Burundi), left-right political divisions (Costa Rica, Colombia, Argentina 1973 and 1983, Turkey, Mozambique), secession (Comoros), and desire for unification with another state (Cyprus). Albania's conflict was triggered by the collapse of several government-sponsored pyramid schemes, which led to rioting and a takeover of the south by opposition-allied rebels (Levitsky and Way 2010: 119–24; Abrahams 2015; Pike 2017).

The remaining two cases present more ambiguous motives but still not primarily democratic ones. Liberia's civil war was galvanized by ethnic exclusion and the intended overthrow of Charles Taylor's repressive government. Although these goals are consistent with democracy and the two main rebel groups had "democracy" in their names, both groups developed from irregular forces defending neighboring autocracies against Taylor. Further, they displayed little political agreement between them outside of opposition to Taylor (Sawyer 2005; Dennis 2006). The most ideologically ambiguous rebel movement was Sierra Leone's Revolutionary United Front (RUF), organized in 1991 to overthrow a military dictatorship and later fueled by diamond plunder. The RUF was clearly not motivated by democracy, however, as it displayed little taste for political liberalization in settlement talks or the brief power-sharing arrangement and was infamous for mass atrocities like the use of child soldiers and the mutilation of suspected opponents (Hirsch 2001; Gberie 2005; Harris 2012).

*Past Work*

At first glance, civil wars present an unlikely starting point for democratization given the extent of violence and difficulty of compromise in such polarized contexts. Yet several scholars argue that civil war can provide a democratic opening by creating a power balance between the state and rebels (Wantchekon and Neeman 2002; Wantchekon 2004; Gurses and Mason 2008; Bermeo 2010a; Joshi 2010), or at least sufficiently threatening elites that they prefer conceding to democracy (Wood 2000; Acemoglu and Robinson 2006; Alemán and Yang 2011). From there, the warring parties can agree to a mutually satisfactory democratic bargain. As Gurses and Mason (2008: 319) argue, fighting provides information about the balance of power and "lays the groundwork for reaching an equilibrium from which democracy can emerge." However, this requires that the warring parties each believe they will have sufficient power in democracy and that the arrangement is credible, which often requires an international mediator (Wantchekon and Neeman 2002; Wantchekon 2004; Joshi 2010).[41]

Although a few scholars suggest that civil conflict positively predicts democratization (Wood 2000; Wantchekon 2004; Alemán and Yang 2011), most emphasize conditional effects that depend on war characteristics or economic structure (e.g., Gurses and Mason 2008; Fortna and Huang 2012; Colgan 2015). Fortna and Huang (2012) note that the array of empirical strategies makes arriving at conclusions difficult. For instance, there is widespread disagreement as to whether civil war outcomes relate to democratization, with different scholars claiming that rebel victories are positive for democratization (Toft 2010), negative (Gurses and Mason 2008; Levitsky and Way 2012, 2013; Lyons 2016), or unrelated (Fortna and Huang 2012). There is some agreement that negotiated peace settlements are positive for democracy (Gurses and Mason 2008; Bermeo 2010a; Joshi 2010; Nilsson 2012), but Fortna and Huang (2012) find the effect fades quickly.

Post–civil war research has largely focused on conflict renewal and later democratic survival, producing a range of recommended institutional rules (Ardón 1999; Lijphart 2002; Roeder and Rothchild 2005; Harris 2012; Graham, Miller, and Strøm 2017). Chief among these stabilizing strategies is the multivaried concept called *power-sharing*, a set of institutions that diffuse power across groups and limit majority dominance. Key examples include ethnic quotas in the legislature and military; group vetoes over sensitive issues like language policy; territorial decentralization; and internal constraints like strong independent judiciaries (Lijphart 2002; Binningsbø 2013; Gates et al. 2016; Graham, Miller, and Strøm 2017). When implemented well, power-sharing guarantees enough power to warring groups, particularly minorities, that democracy becomes preferable to continued conflict. As a result, power-sharing has become a near-universal post-conflict strategy, with 37 of the 38 negotiated settlements to civil wars from 1945 to 1998 containing some form of power-sharing (Hartzell and Hoddie 2003). Although the focus has been on conflict renewal (Hartzell and Hoddie 2003; Roeder and Rothchild 2005;

41. This logic resembles Rustow's (1970: 352) argument that democratization occurs from compromise after a "prolonged and inconclusive political struggle."

Gates et al. 2016), Hartzell and Hoddie (2015) argue that post-conflict power-sharing also predicts democratization.

## EFFECTS OF CIVIL WARS

The logic of democracy as a bargain between deadlocked warring parties coheres well with this book's theory on autocratic weakness and expectations of power within democracy. This perspective is especially useful for understanding democratization after negotiated settlements, which help to ensure that each side anticipates sufficient power in democracy to give up arms. Besides power-sharing, a key provision of many peace agreements is the guarantee that rebel groups can become political parties, as occurred in Mozambique, Burundi, Nepal, and El Salvador (Lyons 2016; Wittig 2016). In turn, they often become stronger and more cohesive parties than those formed from broad nonviolent movements, such as Poland's Solidarity and Czechoslovakia's Civic Forum (Bermeo 2010a). Although not all win, this guarantee provides a critical share of expected power within democracy. In total, 16 of 35 civil war cases featured the last autocratic party or executive gaining power within democracy, in addition to rebel party wins in Burundi, Nepal, and El Salvador.

Settlements frequently have two other attributes that facilitate democratization: pro-democratic stipulations and international involvement (Fortna 2004; Joshi 2010; Toft 2010). Of the 13 civil war cases with peace agreements, 7 had explicit pro-democratic guarantees and 10 involved international mediation (including 8 with international peacekeepers). The influence of (mostly democratic) international actors helps to orient peace resolutions around democratic goals, including quick multiparty elections (Kumar 1998; Reilly 2008).

However, negotiated settlements are not the only route from civil war to democracy, as many theoretical accounts assume (Joshi 2010: 830). In fact, less than half of the primary cases and about one-third of all cases democratized after a negotiated peace agreement. Similarly, only one-third of the primary cases and one-fourth of all cases democratized after a stalemate in the war—the remainder featured one side's victory or the war was ongoing.

How can civil war contribute to democratization without an explicit democratic bargain? I stress two additional mechanisms: regime weakness and openings for pro-democratic actors. Civil wars contribute to both, particularly while the war is ongoing, whereas their effects fade quickly after one side has won. After this theoretical discussion, I turn to a detailed overview of the cases, dividing by war outcome.

### Regime Weakness

Civil war has the immediate effect of weakening the autocratic regime by diverting coercive resources and compromising state control over territory and population. Civil war also has devastating economic consequences by shifting public spending to security, destroying infrastructure, and disrupting economic production and trade (P. Collier 1999; Bayer and Rupert 2004). Across all civil wars in autocracies, the growth rate averages −0.47% and inflation averages 146%. The resulting economic problems impair state services, at the extreme impacting funding for security personnel. In turn, serious rebel challenges foster uncertainty and fear among economic elites, encouraging them to favor democracy as a lesser evil if this can secure peace or reduce the rebels' appeal (Wood 2000; Acemoglu and Robinson 2006; Alemán and Yang 2011). Analyzing El Salvador and South Africa, Wood (2000: 198) argues that insurgencies reshaped economic elite interests and "eventually persuaded elites that the costs of repression were too high."

Due to mass violence, economic crisis, and repression, civil wars frequently inflame citizen opposition beyond the insurgency itself, further weakening the regime. In Pakistan, a bloody standoff in 2007 between the army and Islamists at the Red Mosque in Islamabad unleashed a wave of urban terrorist attacks, increasing frustration with Pervez Musharaff's counterinsurgency efforts and contributing to his electoral defeat in 2008 (Goodson 2008: 8). In 1970s Philippines, the regime's declaration of martial law and widespread repression "drove hundreds of educated youth into the countryside," expanding the ranks of the Communist insurgency (Schock 2005: 70). As citizen support dwindles, autocracies face added pressure to reduce repression and concede on liberalization.

Ongoing civil war can also generate dissent within the regime itself, especially after setbacks. Indeed, coups are more likely during civil conflict (Powell 2012; Singh 2014), with many of these coups motivated by the war's conduct. For some dictators, this threat is sufficient to trigger reform: 11 of 35 civil war cases followed the Salvation pattern, with the majority of these during ongoing civil wars. In addition, 10 of 35 cases followed the Reformer pattern, frequently after coups (Colombia, Guatemala 1986).

Thus, civil wars weaken regimes materially and by alienating key supporters. However, state weakness can also go too far. As Wantchekon (2004) emphasizes, a central challenge with post–civil war democratization is that political order and liberalization must be established simultaneously. A prerequisite for democracy is the creation of a "usable state," which in some cases requires extensive international aid and security support (Linz and Stepan 1996). Cases like Libya, Iraq, and Afghanistan demonstrate how the challenge of establishing order can impede democratic efforts, even with strong international influence.

### Pro-Democratic Openings

Besides weakening regimes, civil wars provide openings and greater leverage for pro-democratic actors. Serbia 2000 is an emblematic case. Prior to Kosovo's separatist civil war starting in 1998, the Serbian opposition was active but effectively managed by the Milošević regime (Thomas 1999). As Levitsky and Way (2010: 55) note, "Opposition forces were mobilized throughout the 1990s, but autocratic breakdown occurred only after military defeat and a severe economic crisis had weakened the state." The civil war and an eleven-week NATO bombing campaign devastated the economy and disrupted public services, which "crystallized widespread anger at a number of worsening social and economic ills . . . [and] helped to reanimate the regime's opposition" (Jennings 2013: 105). Just as significantly, financial shortfalls from the war caused defections from the army and police just as the regime began to over-rely on repression (Levitsky and Way 2010: 110; Jennings 2013: 94–95). This provided an ideal opening for the student-led Otpor! ("Resistance!") movement, which mastered humorous, attention-getting tactics like waving baby rattles to mock Milošević (Ackerman and Duvall 2000: 488). After a stolen election in 2000, mass protests and a storming of parliament went unchallenged by state security and Milošević was forced to resign (Cohen 2001; Levitsky and Way 2010: 111).

As Serbia demonstrates, regime opponents can take advantage of economic crisis and coercive incapacity caused by civil war. In Sudan, strikers angry about the separatist civil war with the south allied with dissident military factions to overthrow the government in the (mostly peaceful) October Revolution of 1964 (Eprile 1974; El-Affendi 2012; Berridge 2015). In El Salvador in 1979, "the momentum of demonstrations, strikes, occupations, guerrilla attacks and almost ritual burning of buses . . . brought the regime to the verge of collapse" (Dunkerley 1988: 380).

Protesters also have increased leverage during civil war because of the potential for citizens to disrupt the war effort or actively support the rebels. This was a major concern of regime elites, and in turn a spur to liberalization, in El Salvador, Nicaragua, the Philippines, Sudan 1986, and Nepal.[42] The same applies to international actors, who can use the provision of aid and weapons as political leverage. This was pivotal in the Philippines (from U.S. pressure), Suriname 1988 (from Dutch aid pressure), and Mozambique (from South African influence on the rebels). International mediators also frequently police democratic peace settlements (Wantchekon and Neeman 2002; Wantchekon 2004; Joshi 2010). Finally, state weakness provided an opening for international actors to intervene militarily in Sri Lanka, Sierra Leone, and Albania.

In contrast, when one side wins the civil war, the window of opportunity for democratization can close rapidly. Victory establishes coercive control

42. According to Huang (2016: 130), insurgencies that rely on civilian support are especially likely to generate politically active, pro-democratic populations. In Nepal, the Maoist insurgency "informed the population about political alternatives and incited them to actively seek them."

of the state, with an enemy eliminated or seriously weakened. This frees up coercive resources—including an enlarged internal security apparatus with experience killing their fellow citizens—to maintain control in a new regime. Further, the victory often generates strong elite cohesion by fusing the regime leadership and armed forces, forming tight bonds among the war victors, and neutralizing prior political opponents (Levitsky and Way 2012, 2013). After winning power through great sacrifice, the victorious side is also "more likely to adopt exclusionary policies backed up by its military dominance rather than seek cooperation with the defeated side in the form of democratization" (Joshi 2010: 834). As a result, successful revolutionary parties tend to produce highly durable autocracies (Levitsky and Way 2012, 2013; Lyons 2016). A similar effect should hold for autocratic *government* victories, which also produce cohesive, coercively experienced regimes facing minimal opposition and without the instability wrought by regime change.[43]

In sum, countries following a stalemate and negotiated settlement or experiencing ongoing civil war should be most likely to democratize. Democratization should be least likely after one side has won, unless the victor emerges from war especially weak or dependent on external democracies.

## CIVIL WAR OUTCOMES AND DEMOCRATIZATION

The civil war cases can be divided into four main categories: those following rebel victories, government victories, and stalemates, plus those with civil wars still ongoing. As predicted, across the 35 cases (18 primary, 17 secondary), relatively few followed one side winning: only 3 (2 primary) followed rebel victories and 5 (2 primary) followed government victories. In contrast, 16 cases (6 primary) had ongoing civil wars and 9 (6 primary) followed stalemates. There are also two unique cases: one following a region seceding (Serbia) and one following its own secession (Croatia). To put these numbers into perspective, there were 65 rebel victories, 138 government victories, and 37 stalemates in autocratic civil wars from 1800 to 2013 (see the appendix on coding). Thus, approximately 1 in 22 rebel victories, 1 in 28 government victories, and 1 in 4 stalemates were followed by democratization, a marked difference across outcomes. Figure 3.5 shows this visually, with the dark bars indicating the fraction of democratization cases and the light bars the fraction of all civil war resolutions.

I now examine illustrative cases in each category, focusing first on the roles of division and regime weakness in the exceptional cases that democratized after rebel or government victory. I then discuss how parities in power and expectations about democracy underlie bargains after stalemates. Finally, I

---

43. Slater (2010) and Slater and Smith (2016) similarly argue that successful elite counterrevolutionary pacts help to strengthen autocracy.

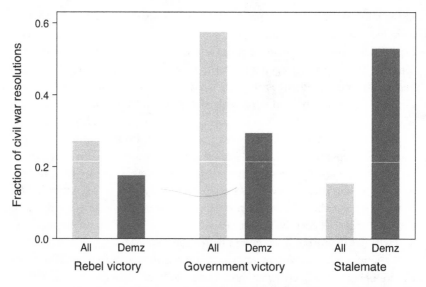

FIGURE 3.5. Fraction of civil war resolutions for all civil wars in autocracies (light bars) and democratic transitions following civil war resolutions (dark bars) (N = 240/17).

emphasize instability and popular openings in democratization during ongoing civil wars.

### Rebel Victories

How can we explain the rare instances where rebel victories led to democratization? As noted, there are only three qualifying transitions: Nicaragua 1984, Liberia 2006, and Costa Rica 1949 (a primary coup case). We can also consider a near-qualifier, Nepal 2008, where rebels almost won but accepted a peace agreement. I argue that democratization in these cases stemmed from the unusually fragmented character of their rebel movements. Unlike most successful rebellions, they emerged from victory without a unified movement assured of consolidating dictatorship. Combined with pro-democratic domestic and international pressure, this weakness ultimately translated into acceptance of democracy.

*NICARAGUA 1984.* In Nicaragua, the main rebel organization (the FSLN, or Sandinistas) briefly contemplated single-party rule after the revolution but backtracked and accepted democracy. This reversal is primarily explained by the severe security and economic crises the FSLN faced after taking power, exacerbated by furious U.S. opposition. In particular, the FSLN faced a new civil war that can be partly sourced to the fractured nature of the initial insurgency and broader revolutionary movement.

The leftist FSLN formed in 1961 to oppose the Somoza family regime, a repressive multigenerational kleptocracy that had ruled Nicaragua since

1936 (Booth 1990). The FSLN gained notoriety for audacious schemes like a 1974 raid on a Christmas party that captured several political leaders and the storming of the National Palace in August 1978, which led to a successful trade of 1,500 hostages (including most of the country's parliament) for political prisoners and ransom (Meiselas 1978; Stahler-Sholk 1987: 74; DeFronzo 2011: 261). However, the FSLN initially commanded a relatively small fighting force, with only 150 full-time soldiers in the early 1970s and around 3,000 in early 1979 (DeFronzo 2011). Before 1977, the FSLN "had been little more than a nuisance" (Close 1985: 153) that "the national guard easily controlled" (Booth 1990: 471).

Opposition to Anastasio Somoza's regime grew in the late 1970s due to economic problems, corruption, and uncertainty about the dictator's health,[44] which punctured "the pervasive myth of his regime's invincibility and . . . convinced [Nicaraguans] finally that they could act" (Lawton 1987: 139). The regime further undermined itself with extreme repression, which "drove thousands, especially young people, to join the FSLN" (Booth 1990: 473). Opposition accelerated when business allies of Somoza killed journalist Pedro Chamorro in 1978 after he exposed a scheme involving illegal blood exports to the United States (Meiselas 1978; DeFronzo 2011: 260). Facing widespread protests, violence, and rising international pressure, the Somoza regime reached a crisis point.

The FSLN was far from the sole opposition in 1978 and in fact was internally fractured over a disagreement about tactics (Booth 1990). Outside the FSLN, moderate party leaders formed the FAO to pressure Somoza into a political resolution, although there was little popular appetite for anything but a sharp break (Gorman 1984: 60). Not until the spring of 1979 did the FSLN unite itself and several independent rebel groups into a cohesive insurgency, focusing on urban combat and a general strike in June (Close 1985; Booth 1990). It also announced an alternative government with several non-FSLN members, including Violeta Chamorro, Pedro's widow. The FSLN's victory critically depended on "a strategy of alliances with all anti-Somoza sectors [which] gave them new life and a new outlook" (Close 1985: 153). With elite support collapsing, Somoza fled to Miami in July 1979.[45] After his successor's two-day attempt to keep power, the rebels marched into Managua, ending a civil war that left fifty thousand Nicaraguans dead (Stahler-Sholk 1987: 76; Goodsell 1983: 475).

Although the FSLN certainly dominated the resulting transitional government, it attempted to maintain a coalitional governing base (Gorman 1984; Isbester 2001; Close, Puig, and McConnell 2012). The five-person ruling junta

44. Somoza spent seven weeks in Miami recovering from a heart attack in mid-1977 (Lawton 1987).

45. He should have stayed; he was assassinated in Paraguay the following year.

kept two opposition members, while a Council of State established in May 1980 included opposition parties and various mass organizations (Williams 1994). However, concerned with the FSLN's moves to consolidate power, conservative elements left the Council in November, followed by mass protests and a shutoff of U.S. aid (Close 1985: 153). Having benefited from cross-party and cross-class partnerships up to that point, the FSLN faced a dilemma regarding whether it was strong enough to secure hegemonic rule. Divorced from other factors that now asserted themselves, it may have been, but a combination of security, economic, and international pressure would prove decisive.

The FSLN soon faced its own violent rebellion from the Contras, a collection of U.S.-supported rebel groups that began operating in the early 1980s (Booth 1990; LaFeber 1993; Isbester 2001). Although often characterized as uniformly right wing, the Contras included former anti-Somoza allies of the FSLN who splintered off following the revolution, especially in rural areas (Gelb 1983; Riding 1984). This included a group under Edén Pastora ("Commander Zero"), a former FSLN leader who masterminded the 1978 National Palace takeover (Riding 1984). Ultimately killing more than 20,000, the insurgency gradually eroded the regime's popular support and diverted half the national budget to defense spending (DeFronzo 2011: 272), sapping the FSLN's resources. The FSLN also inherited a country in economic freefall, with 29% of GDP and about a third of the country's industrial capacity destroyed in the 1979 revolution (Goodsell 1983: 475). Unemployment quickly reached 30% and inflation soared to 33,000% by 1988 (Foran 2005: 194; DeFronzo 2011). Simply put, the "status quo became unsustainable" (Levitsky and Way 2010: 141).

Facing numerous internal challenges and a real threat of U.S. invasion, the FSLN was forced into an abrupt about-face in its political plans. After proposing and scrapping a law that would make it the sole governing party, the FSLN instead passed the 1983 Law of Political Parties that allowed multiparty competition, independent electoral oversight, and presidential term limits (Close 1985: 154; Walker 2000). Opposition pressure even forced them to push elections up a year to 1984 (Stahler-Sholk 1987: 81), as "the Sandinistas hoped that a competitive election with heavy turnout would deter a U.S. military intervention and reassure the FSLN's defenders" (Cornelius 1986: 62). Huntington (1991: 193) concurs that vulnerability from the Contra war "induced the Sandinista regime to call elections."

Although partly boycotted by the opposition, "the November 1984 elections signaled the formal adoption of liberal democratic institutions" (Williams 1994: 178). Judged a reasonably fair election by most international observers (Close 1985), this is considered the moment of democratization. However, given that the election was won by the FSLN and its leader, Daniel Ortega, Nicaragua's new democracy remained imperiled. Not until 1990 did a large coalition led by Violeta Chamorro oust the FSLN in "elections that U.S.

pressure (via sanctions, a blockade, and millions of dollars in aid for the opposition party) ensured they lost" (Gunitsky 2017: 202).[46] Reminiscent of the electoral continuity path, the FSLN ceded power with employment guarantees for Sandinistas in the military and bureaucracy (Williams 1994: 180). Further, "the FSLN remained the country's largest, best-organized, and most popular individual political party" (DeFronzo 2011: 275), paving the way for Ortega's electoral comeback in 2006.

*OTHER REBEL VICTORIES.* Liberia's democratization followed a brutal 1999–2003 civil war that killed as many as 150,000 before dictator Charles Taylor (himself a former rebel leader) was ousted (Sawyer 2005; Dennis 2006). The successful rebellion consisted of two main groups. The northern LURD rebels formed a loose coalition around opposition to Taylor and were supported by Guinea. The southern MODEL rebels emerged in 2003 and were supported by the Ivory Coast. After the rebels collaborated to remove Taylor in 2003, the Accra peace agreement (under strong international mediation) established a power-sharing arrangement and transitional government, followed by the disbanding of both rebel groups (Dennis 2006; Harris 2012; Spatz and Thaler 2018).

The secondary civil war case, Costa Rica 1949, is a hybrid of self-coup and successful rebellion in response. The rebels were initially organized by José Figueres Ferrer to oppose the government's conservative turn, then ideologically broadened in reaction to a stolen election (Bell 1971; Lehoucq 1991; Yashar 1997). Significantly, Ferrer shared the mantle of legitimate rule with the rightful election winner, Otilio Ulate Blanco. After the brief but bloody war ended with American and Guatemalan involvement, Figueres made a deal with Ulate to rule provisionally for eighteen months, during which he rewrote the constitution, established universal suffrage, and abolished the national army (Bell 1971; Peeler 1985). During this period, "the democratic norms that had governed Costa Rica over the previous half-century reasserted themselves" (Mauceri 1989: 206) and Figueres relinquished power after losing the 1949 election, although he would later twice be elected president.

After Nicaragua, the closest case to a cohesive rebel movement winning state power is Nepal 2008. Starting in 1996, a strong Maoist insurgency took control of most of the country's territory in a conflict that killed more than 18,000 Nepalis (Chadda 2000; Sengupta 2005; Huang 2016). Critically, however, the rebels did not fully conquer the country; rather, the war ended in a Comprehensive Peace Accord in 2006 that included the abolition of the monarchy, the creation of a republic, and the merger of armed forces (UN 2006). Although the rebels were militarily ascendant, they were joined in opposition to the government by the Nepali Congress, a nonviolent

46. Note that if democratization is dated to 1990 (as in Polity), this remains a civil war case (now post-stalemate) and would also qualify for electoral continuity.

movement-turned-party that engineered the 1991 democratic transition, and an increasingly mobilized and pro-democratic populace (Raeper and Hoftun 1992; Chadda 2000; Parajulee 2000; Huang 2016). Thus, the opposition as a whole was again divided.

These fragmented rebel groups can be contrasted with the unified and disciplined revolutionary movements in China, Vietnam, and Zimbabwe, which then produced strong single-party dictatorships.[47] However, the goal here is not to posit a general theory of revolutionary outcomes. Rather, what matters for the theory of democratization is that only a small share of successful rebels accepted democracy. Of those that did, they were conspicuously divided, suggesting weakness and fragmentation as central drivers of democratization.

### Government Victories

Government victories are even less likely to produce democratization, given that they involve victory in war without the instability of regime change. The few exceptions represent unusual cases of weakness and instability despite this victory.[48]

The first primary case, Indonesia 1955, involved an unconsolidated state that won its independence from the Netherlands in 1949 after a bloody revolution (Cribb 1986; Goodwin 2001). Although ultimately commandeered by Sukarno, the revolution was "a splintered struggle" that failed to unify the state (Slater 2010: 107). Even before independence, the state faced secessionist conflicts and a Communist rebellion starting in 1948. This was followed by the formation of breakaway Islamic regions in South Maluku in 1950 and Aceh in 1953, a serious attempted coup in 1950, and a military shakeup after dissident officers protested the regime in 1952. Sukarno's PNI narrowly won the first legislative and constituent elections in 1955, with twenty-eight total parties gaining seats, but the resulting chaos led Sukarno to overthrow the republic in 1959 (Ghoshal 1982).

The remaining primary case, Sierra Leone 2002, had perhaps the weakest state of any case of democratization. After an attempted multiparty opening, a devastating civil war began in 1991 between Joseph Momoh's military government and the RUF, an ideologically ambiguous rebel group supported by Liberia's Charles Taylor (Gberie 2005; Hirsch 2001; Cheeseman 2010; Harris

---

47. Russia is a more complex case; although the revolutionaries of 1917 were divided, the Bolsheviks unified control during the resulting civil war. Revolutionaries in France were perhaps too highly fragmented, producing an aborted parliamentary opening and a succession of dictatorships. Revolutions ousting *foreign* powers have had several democratic successes, including the United States, Ireland, Israel, and East Timor (all new states). An important distinction is that the state is usually left with multiple domestic organizations and interests, providing the basis for competitive politics.

48. Among the three secondary cases, two followed guardian coups (Burma, Turkey) and a third (Nigeria) followed a coup and an assassination during a later coup attempt.

2012). Disaffection with Momoh's leadership of the war inspired a 1992 junior officer coup led by a twenty-five-year-old captain named Valentine Strasser (Bratton and van de Walle 1997: 212). Another coup then yielded to an elected civilian government under Ahmad Kabbah in 1996. Meanwhile, government forces—supported by British and South African mercenaries and a West African multilateral force—retook the capital and began pushing the RUF back. After another coup in 1997, the ruling junta chose to share power with the RUF, but Nigerian forces invaded and reinstated Kabbah. With UN involvement, the Lomé Peace Accord was signed in 1999, with highly favorable terms for the RUF: the group was given amnesty and control of the country's diamond mines, as well as the vice presidency for the RUF's leader, Foday Sankoh (Gberie 2005; Harris 2012). Nevertheless, splinter groups (including the West Side Boys, who kidnapped several UN and British peacekeepers) undermined the agreement and reignited the war. With UN, British, and Guinean assistance, the war was finally ended in 2002, at the cost of over fifty thousand lives and millions displaced. Kabbah was reelected in a landslide in 2002 elections, while the RUF transformed into a (powerless) political party.

Needless to say, Indonesia and Sierra Leone suffered from significant state and regime weakness at the point of democratization. Although victors in war, both had recently survived roiling, multisided conflicts with high chances of reigniting. This made democratic elections a valuable inducement to peaceful contestation for the RUF in Sierra Leone and disaffected regions in Indonesia. Sierra Leone was also heavily influenced by international actors, who twice intervened militarily to protect its elected governments.

### Stalemate

Stalemates occur when a civil war ends without a definitive victor, usually accompanied by a formal peace agreement. Six primary cases and 3 secondary cases are counted as stalemates, of which 8 had peace agreements.[49] This compares with less than 1 in 5 remaining civil war cases. As noted above, peace agreements have two common features that aid democratization: explicit pro-democratic guarantees and international involvement. Of the 8 peace agreements, 5 had democratic guarantees (Colombia, Mozambique, Burundi, Comoros, Nepal) and 7 had international mediation, including 5 with peacekeeping troops. In contrast, only about 1 in 4 non-stalemate cases had international mediation and 1 in 6 had peacekeepers.

By definition, stalemates involve warring sides that are too weak to establish political rule over the entire country, making them prime candidates for accepting democracy to escape insecurity. However, their expectations of

---

49. The exception is Albania 1997, where a disordered civil conflict fueled by economic collapse ended with a UN peacekeeping force and snap elections (Levitsky and Way 2010: 119–24).

power within democracy must also be aligned with this choice, particularly given high-stakes violent conflicts. Democracy is no salvation if it simply means continually losing elections to one's mortal enemy. Further, electoral losers must trust that victors will not abuse their powers (Graham, Miller, and Strøm 2017). This makes the transition from stalemate to democratization not just about democracy itself but a careful calibration of expected power and effective safeguards. The cases of Mozambique 1994 and Burundi 2005 illustrate the point.

Mozambique's civil war was a Cold War proxy conflict that ultimately cost around one million lives from war or famine (Cabrita 2000; Alden 2001; Manning 2002; Levitsky and Way 2010: 246–51; Huang 2016). After winning independence from Portugal in 1975, the Frelimo movement established a single-party Marxist state. Supported by Rhodesia and South Africa's apartheid government, the anti-communist Renamo rebels triggered war in 1977. With the Cold War waning, international funding froze up for both sides and momentum for peace grew (Cabrita 2000; Newitt 2002). After peace talks got underway in 1990, Frelimo passed a new constitution allowing opposition parties and expanded civil liberties. The Rome General Peace Accords followed in 1992 under UN mediation. Among the provisions was a guarantee of "a multi-party democracy in which the parties would freely cooperate in shaping and expressing the will of the people" and a requirement that all parties "must accept democratic methods for the pursuit of their aims" (UN 1992: 8–9). Further, the accord recognized Renamo as a political party, with associated privileges and protections (UN 1992: 11).[50]

The mutual understanding that both sides would continue as political parties was critical to the agreement's success, as it offered an expected share of power that outweighed the insecurity of continued war (Cabrita 2000; Manning 2002). The parties have since dominated the country's politics, combining for 97.3% of assembly seats in the five elections from 1994 to 2014 (Nunley 2012). However, Frelimo has perpetually won both the presidency and assembly and governed in an increasingly autocratic manner, contributing to Renamo's alienation. In 2013, Renamo claimed to be abandoning the Rome agreement and renewed its insurgency, accusing Frelimo of "monopolizing political and economic power through a one-sided electoral system" (Reuters 2013). This captures the delicate balance that is needed to secure warring parties' loyalty to democracy.

Perfecting this balance was even more critical to ending the ethnic conflict in Burundi. The civil war between the majority Hutus and minority Tutsis erupted in 1994 after a plane crash killed the presidents of Burundi

---

50. Several other safeguards, including equal representation in the army and full demobilization before the first elections, were based on lessons learned from failure in Angola (Bermeo 2010a: 81).

and Rwanda, although it was preceded by a Tutsi coup in 1987, a massacre of Hutus in 1988, an assassination of a Hutu leader in 1993, and a massacre of Tutsis in response (Falch and Becker 2008; Reyntjens 2005; Vandeginste 2009). The ethnic war, which killed about 300,000 in a country of barely 6 million in 1994, proved difficult to resolve. The 2000 Arusha Accords provided a key step with a guarantee of democracy but failed to achieve a cease-fire as it left the precise dimensions of ethnic and military power-sharing unclear (Arusha Accords 2000; Falch and Becker 2008). Only in 2003 was a cease-fire negotiated with the main Hutu rebel group, the CNDD-FDD, followed by a power-sharing deal in 2004 and army integration and elections in 2005. The agreements established strict ethnic power-sharing in the army and government, with a 60% Hutu/40% Tutsi breakdown mandated for the cabinet and legislature (Falch and Becker 2008; Vandeginste 2009). As in Mozambique, they allowed the CNDD-FDD rebels to become a political party (Wittig 2016). Unlike in Mozambique, the CNDD-FDD has subsequently dominated post-democratization politics, with its elected president Pierre Nkurunziza controversially winning a third term in 2015 at the cost of mass protests, an attempted coup, and a serious erosion of democracy.

### Ongoing Civil Wars

The final category consists of cases where civil wars were still ongoing at democratization, corresponding to one-third of the 18 primary cases and just under half of all cases. The civil wars varied greatly in longevity. For the 6 primary cases, the conflicts had been ongoing between 2 and 14 years. In Guatemala 1986 (a secondary case), the conflict—started by leftist military officers after a failed coup—had lasted 24 years, spanning two democratic transitions. Because many of these civil wars didn't formally relate to democratization processes, they are frequently passed over in case studies, especially on Spain, the Philippines, Mali, Senegal, and Pakistan. Yet these wars powerfully shaped the political contexts leading to democracy, both by destabilizing autocratic regimes and by facilitating mass opposition.

One sign of the instability wrought by these civil wars is the predominance of further triggers preceding democratization. Across the 16 total cases, 9 had coups during the civil war and before democratization. Several coups opposed the war's conduct, including those in Burma, Guatemala 1966 and 1986, El Salvador, and Mali. In Suriname 1991, the ex-dictator Dési Bouterse instead couped (over the telephone) to oppose a peace deal with the rebels (Singh 2008: 82). A further two cases experienced assassinations carried out by rebel groups,[51] two had mass protests oust the executive (Sudan 1965, the

---

51. These are Spain and Sri Lanka 1991. In the latter, the assassination occurred during the war, but in 1993 after the coded date of democratization. However, 1994 is a better date for transition (see the appendix).

Philippines), and two involved ruling parties losing through elections.[52] In the sole remaining case, Suriname 1988, Bouterse acceded to democracy but remained head of the military and couped two years later.

By inflaming citizen grievances and weakening regimes, ongoing civil wars supplied motives and opportunities for nonviolent opposition. Fourteen of 16 cases experienced major pro-democracy protests, compared to just under half of completed civil war cases. Moreover, the two exceptions were the cases that democratized through elections, meaning that opposition was present but channeled differently. An important dynamic at play in these cases is that the public often viewed democratization as a way to resolve the conflict, either by assuaging the rebels or by producing a democratic government better able to defeat or negotiate with them.[53] This was a significant motivation, for instance, in El Salvador, Guatemala 1986, and the Philippines. However, democratization did not prove especially effective in this regard: cease-fires followed democratization (with mixed success) in the Philippines, Suriname 1988, Senegal, and Mali but ground on for years in other cases.

THE PHILIPPINES 1986. The Philippines illustrates several of the contextual effects of civil wars that contribute to democratization. The case is usually and appropriately characterized as driven by a strong popular movement that overwhelmed the decaying regime of Ferdinand Marcos (Brown 1987; Wurfel 1988; Franco 2001; Thompson 2002). The role of military defections also gets due attention—the climactic two-million-strong EDSA demonstration in February 1986 was organized in defense of a coup plot—as does the U.S. choice to pressure and finally abandon its ally Marcos (Manglapus 1987; McKoy and Miller 2012). What is often neglected as a causal factor is the civil war's role in exacerbating regime weakness, military and popular disaffection, and even U.S. disengagement.

The Philippines faced a serious Muslim separatist challenge in Mindanao in the early 1970s, resulting in around 100,000 deaths, but the insurgency had declined by 1980. By then, the more serious challenge came from the New People's Army (NPA), the armed wing of the Communist Party of the Philippines, which commanded a force of roughly 25,000 insurgents concentrated south of Luzon (International Crisis Group 2011: 4). With active fighters in every Filipino province and control of large swathes of territory, the NPA at its peak threatened an armed takeover of the state (Lohr 1985; Wurfel 1988; Bermeo 1997; Schock 2005). As Defense Minister Juan Enrile acknowledged in 1985, the NPA rebels "constitute the most formidable threat to our national

52. In both cases (Senegal, Pakistan), the parties declined precipitously after democratization, an unusual outcome for ruling parties acceding to democracy through elections.
53. The same idea can occur to dictators. In Argentina 1973, facing constant bombings, bank robberies, and hostage-taking by rural guerrillas, the military dictator Alejandro Lanusse believed democratization "would lead to the disappearance of social tension and the end of guerrilla terrorism" (Krause and Pereira 2003: 8).

security today," citing their uses of terrorism and infiltration of student and labor groups (Lohr 1985). Even more worrisome, by the mid-1980s, the NPA "had been increasing in effectiveness while the competence of the Philippine military had been declining" (Schock 2005: 57; also Lohr 1984).

The direct costs of combating the NPA, as well as perceptions of Marcos's ineffectiveness, significantly weakened the regime and contributed to the transition (Brown 1987; Wurfel 1988: 220–31; Huntington 1991: 54; Schock 2005). Damage to the state's coercive apparatus was substantial, with 1,282 military or police deaths in 1985 alone (International Crisis Group 2011: 4). The NPA threat also eroded support for Marcos within the military (Brown 1987: 313), contributing "to the weakening of the Marcos regime and to the Reform the Armed Forces Movement (RAM), which helped topple Marcos" (Bitar and Lowenthal 2015: 417). Critics argued that the regime's corruption and repression "represented a boon to the NPA" (Brown 1987: 314). Even business leaders, a group long allied with Marcos, began to favor democratic elections to "offer an alternative to armed rebellion . . . [as] they were concerned that as long as [Marcos] stayed, the communist NPA would keep attracting followers" (Ackerman and Duvall 2000: 378). Conservative elements further expressed alarm that Filipinos were becoming sympathetic to the NPA as a means of combating inequality (Bonner 1986). As a result, the NPA provided "a context that increased the leverage of the democratic opposition" as a less threatening alternative (Schock 2005: 158).

Marcos's inability to handle the insurgency, especially while facing other domestic opposition, also influenced U.S. decision making. According to Brown (1987: 314–15), "It was only when Marcos's grip began to slip, when he was judged by many analysts to be incapable of handling the NPA threat that the United States began to change its attitude toward Marcos and another pillar of the transition was put in place." As Casper (2000b: 152) notes, "By 1985, senior officers in the State Department publicly acknowledged their fear that Marcos was losing control of his regime and would be overthrown by the NPA." This led to a split between State Department officials, who were "apprehensive of the growing communist insurgency" (Schock 2005: 72), and stalwarts in the Reagan White House and Pentagon who favored sticking by Marcos until the very end. Believing that democratic elections could reduce the NPA's appeal, "the anti-Marcos faction in the U.S. government provided key support to both the reformist elements of the people power movement and the reform movement within the military" (Schock 2005: 88).

The democratic opposition, dissidents in the military, and the United States combined to fatally undermine the regime. Already inflamed due to economic problems and the NPA, opposition accelerated in 1983 after political leader Benigno Aquino was assassinated on the airport tarmac while returning from exile. Over 2 million gathered for his funeral procession and the opposition rallied behind his widow, Corazon Aquino. In 1985, anti-Marcos military officers organized RAM and began plotting a coup, but delayed until after planned elections (Casper 2000b: 151; Fukuoka 2015). Facing U.S. pressure, Marcos agreed to hold snap elections in February 1986, miscalculating that the opposition was too divided to challenge him (Armacost 1987; Schock 2005: 76). When the election was blatantly stolen, Aquino organized mass protests and support for Marcos collapsed. The denouement was a brief standoff in which crowds surrounded a military base to protect RAM members from being apprehended. To prevent a violent crackdown, the opposition shrewdly positioned nuns kneeling with rosaries in front of tanks and sent grandmothers and pregnant women to give water to soldiers (Ackerman and Duvall 2000: 386–88; Casper 2000b: 154; Goldstone 2014: 106–9). With military units refusing orders to fire and the United States signaling withdrawal of support, Marcos fled into exile (McKoy and Miller 2012). The new Aquino regime was vulnerable—it defeated major coup attempts by RAM members in 1986 and pro-Marcos business elements in 1989 thanks to U.S. support—but it survived, and power was handed to a RAM general in 1992.

## Assassinations

Assassinations can be highly traumatic and disruptive events. Like virtually all coups but unlike other shocks, they imply a change of leadership, often with significant long-term implications. Yet they also represent the "smallest" events in the sense of the larger political structure, as they can sometimes be sourced to single individuals and do not directly entail regime change. How can assassinations nevertheless contribute to democratization?

### OVERVIEW

#### Cases

Assassinations represent the least-populated category in this book, comprising only two primary cases and six secondary cases.[54] The rarity of these events (82 assassinations of an autocratic head of state or government from 1800 to 2014) complicates theory and empirical testing. Nevertheless, assassinations are politically significant shocks that can upend the autocratic status quo.

The cases are listed in Table 3.3. Some assassinations removed long-ruling dictators (Portugal 1911, Dominican Republic 1966, Pakistan 1988, Nepal 2008), while others further destabilized politics in periods following coups (Guatemala 1958, Nigeria 1979, Niger 1999). In Spain 1977, the assassinated

---

54. The suggested date corrections in the appendix add two cases: Panama 1956 and Sri Lanka 1994. Ireland 1922 would qualify if counted as democratization. A slightly more distant assassination (in 1979) preceded South Korea 1988. Finally, Benito Mussolini was executed in 1945 while head of the northern "Italian Social Republic," but this was a German puppet state and Mussolini a desiccated figurehead.

**Table 3.3.** Assassination Cases, 1800–2014

| Primary Cases | | |
| --- | --- | --- |
| Spain 1977 | Pakistan 1988 | |

| Secondary Cases | | |
| --- | --- | --- |
| Portugal 1911 | Guatemala 1958 | Dom. Rep. 1966 |
| Nigeria 1979 | Niger 1999 | Nepal 2008 |

*Note:* Years shown are for democratization, not the assassinations.

figure was Prime Minister Luis Carrero Blanco, the head of government and de facto leader during Francisco Franco's decline in health.

The motives for the assassinations are generally well understood and only pro-democratic in one case. The assassinations were carried out by military or state security elements in Guatemala, the Dominican Republic, Nigeria, and Niger. Except for Guatemala, where a member of the presidential guard opposed the government's rightward turn (Weaver 1994: 140; Streeter 2000: 54), these were all during attempted coups. Other assassinations were by ethnic separatists (Spain) and a member of the royal family (Nepal). The culprit in Pakistan is unknown; in fact, this is the one case where the death may have been accidental (see below). Lastly, the one case where the assassination was by pro-democratic elements was in Portugal, where two republicans killed King Carlos I in 1908.[55]

Figure 3.6 shows the probability of democratization with and without an assassination in the previous five years. As seen, there is a very small and non-significant positive effect on democratization, but this is complicated by the small number of cases (only 3.4% of autocratic country-years) and the fact that two cases (Pakistan 1988, Niger 1999) experienced an assassination early in the year of democratization. The lighter bar shows the probability following assassination if the year of democratization is counted, which is now meaningfully higher than without assassination.

### Past Work

Perhaps because of their rarity, assassinations are a neglected subject of political study, with a few recent exceptions.[56] The most relevant study is that of Jones and Olken (2009), who exploit quasi-random variation in the success of assassination attempts to argue that assassinations raise the next-year

55. Together with the pro-democratic coup of 1910, this is one of the rare pro-democratic shocks.

56. Iqbal and Zorn (2006) predict assassinations, finding them more common with a confluence of repression, concentration of power, and lack of elections, as well as existing political unrest. Also see Patterson 1971 and Lentz 1988.

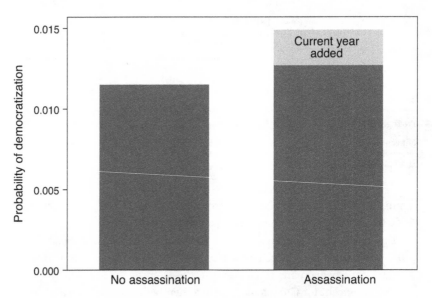

FIGURE 3.6. Assassinations and democratization. The likelihood of democratization
by whether there has been an executive assassination in the prior five years
(dark bars), as well as the likelihood when also including the current year (light bar),
1800–2014 (N = 11,489).

likelihood of democratization by 13% relative to unsuccessful attempts.[57] Iqbal
and Zorn (2008: 385) instead find that assassinations predict further political
unrest and even civil war, especially where "leadership succession is informal
and unregulated." Although the two studies may seem in tension, both reveal
how assassinations disrupt autocratic power. Further, as readers are now
familiar, political unrest can contribute to democratization.

## EFFECTS OF ASSASSINATIONS

The immediate effect of an assassination, of course, is that it suddenly removes
a political leader, increasing uncertainty and upending regime politics (Iqbal
and Zorn 2008; Jones and Olken 2009). Particularly when eliminating an
entrenched dictator, such as the Dominican Republic's Rafael Trujillo or
Nepal's King Birendra, assassinations "shock the political system of a country"
(Iqbal and Zorn 2006: 490). This leader instability is conducive to the main
post-shock patterns: five cases follow the Reformer pattern (Spain, Nigeria,

57. A questionable choice in this study is the too-low threshold of 0 on Polity to define
democracy, which includes dubious cases like modern Algeria and Cambodia. I find 6 cases
in their sample of countries shifting from ≤ 0 the year before assassination to above 0 the
year after. Of these, only 2 meet the more common Polity threshold of 6. Looking 10 years
out post-assassination, 6 of their 11 cases meet this threshold.

Pakistan, Niger, Nepal) and two the Salvation pattern (Guatemala, Dominican Republic). In contrast, the final autocratic leader or party gained power in democracy in only two of eight cases, half the average.

Assassinations also show both citizens and elites that the regime is not invincible, representing the sort of "critical event" that "modifies the expectations of actors concerning the existing regime and induces them to develop new strategies and decisions" (Colomer 2000: 11). For instance, Trujillo's death in 1961 was experienced by Dominicans "not only as the end of an era but as the end of a social and moral universe as three generations had come to know it" (Derby 2009: 231). As a result, assassinations can "embolden dissatisfied groups to push for greater political change, in extreme cases leading to coups, revolution, and even civil war" (Iqbal and Zorn 2008: 387).

A possible negative effect is where assassinations rally citizens around the regime and inflame anger at the culprits, who (fairly or not) can be connected to political movements or ethnic minorities. This in turn can justify heightened repression. Certainly the most significant example is the assassination of Archduke Franz Ferdinand by Serbian nationalists, which spurred Austrian repression against the Serbs and triggered World War I. However, the assassinations considered here rarely presented a useful target to solidify pro-regime sentiment as they were carried out by regime elites or unknown culprits in six of eight cases.

Moving beyond general effects, two patterns emerge in the immediate aftermath of assassinations that contribute to democratization. The first is where removing the dictator creates a power vacuum, in which leadership is highly unstable and uncertain. In particular, the prior dictator's strategy for control is suddenly cast into doubt. I place five cases into this category (Portugal, Guatemala, Dominican Republic, Pakistan, Niger). The second pattern is where a new leader is more firmly in control but pursues a new strategy, either to intentionally liberalize (Spain, Nigeria) or to consolidate power (Nepal).

### Power Vacuums

Assassinations can produce a sudden lack of order and cohesion, especially in personalist dictatorships and regimes without a designated successor. Succession struggles inflamed instability most notably in Guatemala and the Dominican Republic. In some cases, assassinations rapidly extinguished strategies for retaining power that elites took for granted for decades, opening windows for opposition action. For instance, in Portugal, Carlos I's assassination in 1908 (along with his eldest son) left the monarchy in the hands of eighteen-year-old Manuel II. Understandably, he was unable to fend off challenges from the Portuguese Republican Party and dissidents in the military and bureaucracy, finally falling to a coup-turned-revolution in 1910 (Wheeler 1978; R. Collier 1999: 46–51).

Pakistan 1988 exemplifies how the removal of a leader can produce a power vacuum that critically undermines the regime's strategy for preservation

(Crosette 1988; Hyman, Ghayur, and Kaushik 1989; McGrath 1996; Chadda 2000). The U.S.-allied military dictator Muhammad Zia-ul-Haq died in a plane crash in August 1988, along with senior military officials and the American ambassador. Controversy remains over whether this resulted from sabotage or mechanical failure, but a Pakistani investigation found in favor of sabotage, claiming to find traces of explosive on some mango seeds (AP 1988; Kaplan 1989). Zia's death immediately "altered the political landscape" (Crosette 1988), with the military unexpectedly ceding the presidency to the civilian head of the Senate. In October, the Supreme Court reversed Zia's mandate that planned elections be held on a no-party basis (Chadda 2000). With courts reasserting themselves and the military endorsing free elections, opposition politicians "scrambling to fill the vacuum [were] surprised by the latitude allowed them" (Crosette 1988). Elections in November were won by the PPP under Benazir Bhutto, the daughter of the president Zia overthrew to gain power. Zia's death was likely pivotal for this outcome given his plan for controlled elections and widespread "fears that the voting would not have gone unhindered had [Zia] survived" (Crosette 1988).

The extraordinary instability that followed Trujillo's assassination in the Dominican Republic has already been summarized. Yet it's worth focusing on the immediate aftermath, a period of "profound political and social (not just economic) stress" from the "death of a dictator who had governed through total personal control" (Derby 2009: 231). Almost immediately, as if a spell had been broken, the regime leadership proved unable "to wield the power or exert the authority that Trujillo had for thirty-one years" (Wiarda and Kryzanek 1992: 39). Intricate systems of personal control and fear evaporated. Within weeks, the former puppet president Joaquín Balaguer and Trujillo's son Ramfis, the head of the military, began pivoting toward liberal reforms (Hartlyn 1998: 73). As Wells (1966: 15) argues, "Balaguer seems to have recognized that the Trujillo system of personal autocracy could not survive its founder and that his own continuance in office depended on a democratizing of the new regime." The result was a fracturing of power as "the country was quickly overcome by factions battling to take control of the vacant political space" (Derby 2009: 231), a harbinger of five years of chaos and conflict.

### New Leaders and Political Change

Leaders' identities, preferences, and skills matter. As a result, who rises to power after an assassination can have a dramatic effect on regime change (Jones and Olken 2009). In three cases, regimes did not immediately fracture after the leadership shock, making the resulting path a product of a new leader's choices. In most cases of autocratic stability, such as Egypt after Sadat's assassination, this choice was to preserve the autocratic status quo. In the successful democratization cases, the leader instead forged a new path.

Spain 1977 is among the best examples of the significance of individual leadership, not to mention one of the most impressive secret plots in history.

Following the end of the Spanish Civil War in 1939, Francisco Franco ruled as caudillo of Spain, heading the neo-fascist Movimiento superstructure with its sole ruling party, the Falange (Grugel and Rees 1997). By the late 1960s, Franco began contemplating a succession plan that would ensure the survival of Francoism (Gunther, Sani, and Shabad 1988; Grugel and Rees 1997; Preston 2004). First, he sought a symbol of national unity to succeed him as head of state, for which he chose the son of the rightful heir to the abolished Spanish monarchy. Juan Carlos, born in exile in Italy, had been raised by Francoists in Spain from age ten (effectively as a hostage) and groomed by Franco as a key supporter from the early 1960s (Preston 2004: 187). Second, Franco wanted a loyal Francoist to serve as prime minister, ultimately choosing Admiral Luis Carrero Blanco, a personal confidante and "guarantee of untrammelled Francoism" (Preston 2004: 212). By his final days, Franco's "plans for the continuity of the regime were built around" Carrero Blanco (Preston 2004: 280), who became prime minister in June 1973 and ruled during Franco's worsening illness.

This dual strategy was shrewd, as unbeknownst to Franco, Juan Carlos harbored a secret desire to democratize Spain (Grugel and Rees 1997; Preston 2004). Although the origins of this motive are somewhat mysterious given his royalist background and cloistered upbringing, Juan Carlos became a dedicated conspirator who fooled several key members of the regime (Maravall and Santamaría 1986; Foweraker 1989; Grugel and Rees 1997). At the 1969 ceremony officially making him successor, Franco praised Juan Carlos as having "given a clear demonstration of loyalty to the principles and institutions of the Regime" (quoted in Preston 2004: 241). Juan Carlos then solemnly swore to uphold Francoism, with "considerable anxiety" given his secret plans (Preston 2004: 242). Later warned by a journalist that Juan Carlos was plotting a democratic push, future prime minister Carlos Arias Navarro angrily replied, "The Prince has pledged himself to Spain. He has sworn an oath of fidelity to the values of 18 July [the date of Franco's coup in 1936] and he has to fulfill that oath" (quoted in Preston 2004: 275). Juan Carlos's collaboration even "earned the suspicion and contempt of the majority of the democratic opposition" (Preston 2004: 249).

Driving home from Catholic Mass in December 1973, Carrero Blanco was killed by Basque separatists, who packed a tunnel under the street with so much explosive that his car launched into the air and cleared a five-story building (Foweraker 1989; Sullivan 2015). After the assassination, Franco was "completely overwhelmed" and his plans for regime continuity "shattered" (Preston 2004: 278–79).[58] Carrero Blanco's elimination may have been pivotal for the success of Juan Carlos's plans, which proved difficult enough without such an experienced defender to rally opposition. This was by design, as "it had always been clear that Franco expected [Carrero Blanco] to watch over Juan

---

58. Leadership was further destabilized by the death of the Movimiento general secretary in June 1975.

Carlos and ensure that he would not betray the principles of the *Movimiento*" (Preston 2004: 254). In fact, Carrero Blanco had been planning a repressive turn to root out "enemies of the regime," making it "difficult to imagine him standing by passively while Juan Carlos endeavoured to liberalize the regime" (Preston 2004: 278). Instead, the assassination shifted the prime minister position to a relatively moderate Francoist, Arias Navarro, who attempted to marginalize Juan Carlos.

Long seriously ailing, Franco died in November 1975, officially making Juan Carlos king of Spain and commander of a repressive system he was intent on destroying. An initial attempt at moderate reform under Arias Navarro failed, leading Juan Carlos to appoint Adolfo Suárez as prime minister in 1976. Although a regime insider, Suárez proved to be a genuine proponent of democracy and adept at mixing security guarantees and threats to convince the Francoist legislature to accept reforms in November (Maravall and Santamaría 1986; Colomer 1991; Linz and Stepan 1996: 87–115). A popular referendum gave 94% support to the opening, a momentum-building signal that rapidly led to the legalization of opposition parties, the disbanding of the Movimiento, and democratic elections in June 1977. Although much of this political activity was top-down, extensive violence, protests, and strikes from 1974 onward further propelled change (Gunther, Sani, and Shabad 1988; Bermeo 1997; R. Collier 1999: 126–32; Powell 2015: 348). As Colomer (1991: 1283) stresses, however, significant pacts did not occur until after the election, when Suárez's new UCD party was unable to form a majority coalition without agreeing to a major economic reform package (the Moncloa Pact) and a fundamental break with Francoism, including a new constitution in 1978 (Gunther, Sani, and Shabad 1988; Bermeo 1994. This broke a promise to old-guard Francoists, who attempted unsuccessful coups in late 1978 ("Operation Galaxia") and 1981 ("the 23-F plot"), the latter defeated with a key intervention by Juan Carlos (Colomer 1991: 1294; Geddes 1999; Preston 2004). The finale occurred in 1982 with electoral turnover to democratic activist Felipe González and the leftist PSOE.

Like Spain, Nigeria 1979 demonstrates how a reformist leader can quickly steer his country to democracy. In 1976, the recently installed military dictator Murtala Mohammed was killed during an attempted coup, shifting power to Gen. Olusegun Obasanjo. Although Mohammed had proposed a gradual return to democracy, the coup placing him in power was organized around clientelist demands and he likely envisioned a managed democracy with the military remaining in control (Falola and Ihonvbere 1985; Casper and Taylor 1996: 106). Obasanjo instead immediately pursued substantive democratic reforms, with a constitutional assembly in 1977 and the legalization of political activity in 1978. Finally, after 1979 elections, he became the first Nigerian military leader to hand power to a civilian president, Shehu Shagari (Falola and Ihonvbere 1985; Peters 1987). Drawing on this history, Obasanjo later won flawed presidential elections in 1999 and 2003.

Nepal 2008 shows how a new leader can influence the transition path through a very different set of choices. In Nepal, the civil war settlement discussed above was preceded by a remarkable episode in 2001 in which Crown Prince Dipendra went on a shooting spree during a family party, murdering several members of the royal family (including King Birendra) and then himself (BBC News 2001; Sengupta 2008).[59] Upon rising to power, the deceased king's brother Gyanendra illegally dissolved the government in a self-coup and harshly repressed the media and opposition figures, with the army "unleashed against the Nepalese people for the first time in history" (Sengupta 2008). Subsequently weakened by civil war, mass protests, and a general strike, Gyanendra was forced to reinstate parliament and accept a curtailment of his powers in 2006 (Sengupta 2005, 2008; Huang 2016). Following the peace accord with the Maoists, the monarchy was abolished entirely.

## Summary

As paradoxical as it may seem, most democratic transitions since 1800 closely followed major violent shocks. Although the initial shocks were almost never *intended* to produce democracy, they nevertheless propelled transition forward. In different ways, shocks ruptured the previous autocratic equilibrium, yielding insecure leaders unable to consolidate power against military rivals, rebels, and other hostile groups. The coup cases revolved around factional militaries and failed autocratic projects, with most featuring multiple coups. Among all transitions, these represent the most internally divided regimes. Civil wars were most conducive to democratization after stalemates or while the war was ongoing, contexts with the most balanced power relations between the warring sides. The exceptional cases following victory in war featured conspicuously weak or divided winners. Assassinations, by nature the most limited shocks, illustrate the significance of individual leadership for sustaining autocracy.

After rupturing autocratic regimes, shocks provided openings for previously excluded actors. When this opening was effectively seized by democrats, including protesters, opposition parties, and international actors, the result was democratization. Several cases—such as Portugal 1976, Spain 1977, Nicaragua 1984, Sudan 1986, and Ecuador 2003—reveal how easily the outcome could have been different with weaker pro-democratic sentiment, poorer structural conditions, or alternative choices of key actors. Regardless of how autocracy fell, democracy still needed to be built up.

---

59. Bizarrely, Dipendra was crowned while in a coma from the self-inflicted gunshot wound and reigned as king for three days (Sengupta 2008).

CHAPTER FOUR

# International Shocks

NO COUNTRY EXISTS in isolation from the wider world. By most accounts, international factors have risen in importance over time in explaining democratization (Huntington 1991; Boix 2011), with some scholars claiming they are now better predictors than states' domestic characteristics (Gleditsch and Ward 2006: 912; Boix, Miller, and Rosato 2013). International influence has many sources, including regional contagion, democracy promotion, international election monitoring, and aid conditionality (e.g., Schmitter 1996; Whitehead 1996; Carothers 1999; Pevehouse 2005; Wejnert 2005; Finkel, Pérez-Liñán, and Seligson 2007; Kelley 2012; Bush 2015). External powers can also have more direct, coercive effects on democratization through war, foreign-imposed regime change, occupation, and hegemonic control. Including colonial influence, Whitehead (1996: 9) claims that "approaching two-thirds of the democracies existing in 1990 owed their origins, at least in part, to deliberate acts of imposition or intervention from without."

This chapter focuses on the violent international events that most dramatically upend the autocratic status quo: defeat in foreign war and the withdrawal of an autocratic hegemon. These are cataclysmic events that clearly weaken autocratic regimes and provide openings for democratization. Further, in only two cases was the shock initiated with a democratizing aim, although some actors drawn into war later developed such an intention.

Despite tearing down autocratic regimes, these shocks could not by themselves implant democracy. Similar international shocks—from the Napoleonic Wars to Japan's occupation of Vietnam during World War II to the Soviet invasion of Afghanistan—instead birthed armed revolution or state collapse (Skocpol 1979; Goodwin 2001; Goldstone 2014). Moreover, outcomes were only partly determined by external powers' intentions: pro-democratic designs succeeded in postwar Japan and Germany but failed in Iraq and Afghanistan. Similarly, autocratic powers unintentionally produced democracy in France 1870 and Honduras 1971 but triggered social revolutions in France, Russia, and China (Skocpol 1979). As with other shocks, the resulting openings were shaped by actors' choices and structural conditions (Linz and Stepan 1996; Mansfield and Snyder 2010; Gunitsky 2017). When autocratic disruption combined with effective pro-democratic pressure, democracy could arise from the rubble.

## Defeat in Foreign War

Aside from revolution, no event disrupts the political and social order as completely as defeat in foreign war. Not only is an external power given room to transform a country's politics and economy, the defeat is often experienced as an emotional shock that discredits the political system and even a people's way of life. After Japan's crushing loss in World War II, for instance, "people behaved differently, thought differently. . . . People were acutely aware of the need to reinvent their own lives" (Dower 1999: 121). This section traces these often traumatic paths to democracy. Throughout, I stress that *defeat* in war is key—there is no democratizing effect from success in war or ongoing international conflict, nor does either explain any individual cases.

### OVERVIEW

#### Cases

To qualify, a country must democratize after a defeat in foreign war, with the external power either removing the leader or triggering government collapse. Thus, these are major defeats that directly produce political change. A total of 20 transitions (listed in Table 4.1) qualify, of which 16 are primary cases. Three followed World War I (Italy, Germany, Austria)[1] and 7 followed World War II (Greece, San Marino, Austria, France, Italy, the Philippines, Japan).[2] In another 4 cases (France 1870, Uganda, Grenada, Panama), the leader was removed by a hostile power, while in Honduras and Cyprus the government collapsed without the country being conquered.[3]

As discussed below, victors intentionally democratized the vanquished in nine cases. However, this aim was mostly formulated *after* they were drawn

1. I include post–World War I Italy, which allied with the winning side, for two reasons. First, it suffered a humiliating loss to Austria at the Battle of Caporetto, causing the parliamentary government to fall in 1917. Second, despite later gaining territory from Austria, it lost these acquisitions in the highly unfavorable Treaty of Versailles. This "mutilated victory" (as it was termed by Italians) produced bitter mass resentment, leading to the new prime minister's resignation in 1919 and fueling the birth of the fascist movement. For this reason, Paxton (2004: 31) also groups Italy among the "vengeful loser states" of the war.

2. West Germany is not included as it was a new state. Occupied democracies like the Netherlands and Norway are not counted as autocratic in defining democratization.

3. The secondary cases include three primary coup cases (Greece, Ecuador, Argentina) and one civil war (Serbia).

**Table 4.1.** Defeat in War Cases, 1800–2014

**Primary Cases**

| | | |
|---|---|---|
| France 1870 | Germany 1919 | Italy 1919 |
| Austria 1920 | Greece 1944 | San Marino 1945 |
| Austria 1946 | Italy 1946 | The Philippines 1946 |
| France 1946 | Japan 1952 | Honduras 1971 |
| Cyprus 1977 | Uganda 1980 | Grenada 1984 |
| Panama 1991 | | |

**Secondary Cases**

| | | |
|---|---|---|
| Greece 1926 | Ecuador 1948 | Argentina 1983 |
| Serbia 2000 | | |

*Note:* Years shown are for democratization, not the wars.

into war. In only two cases (Grenada, Panama) was the war itself motivated in part by spreading democracy. Certainly, neither world war was initiated for this reason. The eventual losers provoked war to preserve autocratic power in Uganda (Kokole and Mazrui 1988), Argentina (Potash 1996: 509; R. Collier 1999: 125), and France 1870 (Mansfield and Snyder 2010: 42). In other cases, autocracies fought each other over diverse issues but clearly without a democratizing aim (Honduras, Greece 1926, Ecuador). In Serbia and Cyprus, the external powers (NATO in Serbia, Turkey in Cyprus) were democratic but intervened over human rights and co-ethnic protection, respectively.

What about democratization proximate to war, but without defeat? Remarkably, I find only one example of democratization during war or within five years of a war's end without defeat.[4] This is Brazil 1946, which fought with the Allies on the ground in Italy and in the Battle of the Atlantic, suffering about 2,500 dead.[5] However, this was a minor factor in Brazil's democratization. Much like victorious governments in civil war, countries following foreign military victory lack the regime weakness and illegitimacy that are key to regime change after defeat. During foreign wars, countries lack sufficient regime divisions and weakened control (especially compared to ongoing civil wars)

4. France 1870 arguably occurred during war, but I consider this a defeat with the fall of the Second French Empire and Napoleon III's capture in 1870, although fighting continued under a new government through January 1871. Germany 1919 also remained at war through minor involvement in Latvian liberation fighting.

5. An amusing aside: The shoulder insignia for the Brazilian ground troops was a snake coyly smoking a pipe. This came from a Brazilian idiom that a snake would smoke (i.e., pigs would fly) sooner than Brazil would enter the war. After Brazil was thrust into the war by German naval aggression, soldiers adopted it as their symbol (Thompson 2016).

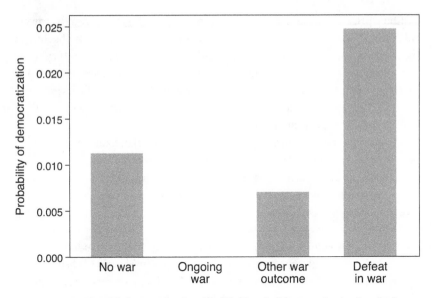

FIGURE 4.1. War and democratization. The likelihood of democratization by whether there has been a defeat in war in the prior five years, another war outcome, an ongoing war, or no recent war, 1800–2014 (N = 11,489).

and tend to benefit from rally-round-the-flag effects and lulls in opposition pressure.

Figure 4.1 shows the likelihood of democratization within five years of a defeat in foreign war, within five years of a different war outcome, during an ongoing war, and without recent war. As later empirics confirm, defeat in war more than doubles the chance of democratization, whereas success in war and ongoing war make it less likely.

### War and Liberalization in the Medieval Era

"Liberty was born in England of the quarrels of tyrants," Voltaire wrote in 1733. Indeed, war played an important role in the birth of parliamentary rule, a subject worth a brief digression from democratization. A prominent historical argument, focused on medieval Europe, claims that war helped to constrain royal power (North and Weingast 1989; Ertman 1997; Ferejohn and Rosenbluth 2016). In the feudal era, kings depended on nobles for soldiers and tax revenue yet had weak powers to induce compliance. Using their leverage during periods of conflict, nobles could thus force kings to accept institutions, such as ruling councils and parliaments, that enhanced noble influence and protected them from royal abuses of war powers. For instance, in 1225, England's Henry III reaffirmed the Magna Carta in exchange for a war tax, beginning "a process by which military expeditions would be financed at the expense of detailed concessions of political liberties" (Jones 2012: 196). However, while

military pressure certainly encouraged (or selected for) increasingly powerful states (Gurr 1988; Tilly 1990), the outcome was as likely to be absolutism
as liberalization (Anderson 1974; Downing 1993). In sixteenth-century western Europe, for instance, war threats produced royal-noble bargains oriented
around state power, bureaucracy, and militarism. Rather than fostering a liberal opening, this was "designed to clamp the peasant masses back into their
traditional social position" (Anderson 1974: 18).

Examining the early parliamentary histories of England and France instead
shows a special role played by *defeat* in war on the power and prestige of the
king. Military defeat directly weakened royal power and legitimacy, characteristic of an era when battlefield outcomes were considered ordained by God.
Nobles, and to a lesser extent early merchant classes, were then able to grasp
these moments of weakness to establish fledgling parliamentary institutions.[6]

Starting in the thirteenth century, England tentatively expanded basic liberties and parliamentary power in several sudden upheavals (Ackroyd 2011;
Jones 2012, 2015). In each case, nobles established temporary supremacy over
the king after defeat in war, then quickly lost their institutional gains. Most
famously, a disastrous defeat to France in the Battle of Bouvines left King John
Lackland "discredited" and "dangerously vulnerable" (Jones 2012: 181), leading
to a baronial rebellion calling itself the "Army of God" that captured London
and forced him to parley. John agreed to the Magna Carta, establishing limits
on royal authority and a permanent council of barons to ensure compliance
but immediately reneged, prompting the First Barons' War (Jones 2015).[7] In
1258, after losing territory in France and getting embroiled in a war in Sicily,
Henry III (John's son) faced a revolt by a group of powerful barons led by his
brother-in-law, Simon de Montfort. Henry was forced to sign the Provisions
of Oxford, expanding common law and creating the first regular parliament.
In 1261, aided by a papal bull, Henry reneged, triggering the Second Barons'
War. Lastly, reacting to corruption and royal failures in yet another French
war, the "Good Parliament" of 1376 insisted on annual parliamentary representation and administrative reforms. Although Edward III initially buckled
due to financial pressures, the agreement was rejected by his successor's regent
in 1377 (Tuchman 1978; Jones 2012: 435–41).[8]

6. Another similar case is Sweden, where elites deposed Gustav IV in 1809 after a
defeat to Russia, then established a much freer constitutional monarchy (Higley and Burton 2006: 68).

7. Not until 1297, following several expensive military campaigns and a defeat to the
Scots under William Wallace, did Edward I reaffirm the Magna Carta and place it firmly
into statute law (Ackroyd 2011: 220–21).

8. Many years later, King Charles I's embarrassing defeat to the Scots in the Bishops'
Wars of 1639–40 forced him to summon parliament, which directly led to the English Civil
War and his execution (Ackroyd 2014).

The same pattern occurred in another early political opening, the little-noted Merchants' Revolt of 1350s France (Funk 1944; Tuchman 1978; Cohn 2006). In 1356, France's King John II was captured by the English at Poitiers and imprisoned in London. Weakened by war and the king's absence, the teen-age dauphin (the future Charles V) was compelled to call the Estates General. Taking advantage of the power vacuum, the leader of Paris's merchants, Etienne Marcel, demanded political reforms in exchange for taxes. The dauphin initially refused, prompting Marcel to organize riots and strikes in the capital (Tuchman 1978). Facing financial ruin, the dauphin relented and agreed to the Great Ordinance of 1357, which limited the king's tax powers, established financial oversight by a permanent council, and allowed the Estates General to form at will (Funk 1944: 477; Tuchman 1978). This was the potential birth of parliamentary rule. However, a few months later, the imprisoned king spurned the reform. Marcel quickly turned violent, breaking from jail Charles the Bad, a rival to the crown, and supporting a mob that murdered two royal councillors in front of the dauphin. Unwisely, Marcel then tried to commandeer a major peasant uprising (the *jacquerie*) that developed in northern France in 1358, which lost him his remaining noble support (Tuchman 1978; Cohn 2006: 162–64). Marcel was assassinated and the *jacquerie* brutally suppressed by Charles the Bad (Funk 1944: 486). Although no more stable than the Magna Carta, the Great Ordinance again illustrates how regime weakness stemming from defeat in war can produce a liberal opening.

### Past Work on Modern War and Democratization

For the modern era, theories on war and democratization shift focus from nobles to the regime's relationship with the masses. In large part, this reflects the changing dynamics of warfare. Whereas medieval kings required noble support for soldiers and taxes, modern states rely on mass conscription and economic power. To mobilize a mass army and a workforce willing to sacrifice for war, the argument goes, states must offer something in return, with some choosing progressive taxation or social spending (Lindert 2004; Scheve and Stasavage 2010) and others suffrage expansion and democracy (Keyssar 2000; Ticchi and Vindigni 2008; Ferejohn and Rosenbluth 2016; Gunitsky 2017). However, the evidence that war by itself promotes democratization is weak (Bermeo 2003b), with different scholars finding a positive (Mitchell, Gates, and Hegre 1999; Gunitsky 2017), negative (Gleditsch 2000; Reiter 2001), or no relationship (Mousseau and Shi 1999; Mansfield and Snyder 2010). To partly reconcile this, Linz and Stepan (1996) and Grimm (2008) argue war's effect is conditional on social structure and economic conditions.

Several prominent works mention, usually in passing, that *defeat* in war can promote democratization (e.g., O'Donnell and Schmitter 1986; Linz and Stepan 1996; Schmitter 1996; Boix 2003; Higley and Burton 2006). To my knowledge, Reiter 2001 is the only prior study that tests this proposition at the country level. Although he finds weak support, the study only covers 1960–92 and so misses the critical cases following World War I and World War II (Ticchi and Vindigni 2008; Gunitsky 2017).

Foreign-imposed regime change (FIRC) comprises a final category worth noting. Although FIRCs include both wars and foreign-sponsored coups, they are particularly relevant here since the postwar cases all experienced government collapse. As with wars, the literature sharply disagrees as to whether FIRCs promote democratization (e.g., Peceny 1999; Kinzer 2006; Coyne 2008; Easterly, Satyanath, and Berger 2008; Downes and Monten 2013; Nomikos, Downes, and Monten 2014), with many studies showing they encourage greater instability (Blum 2003; Teorell 2010) or at best electoral autocracy (Kegley and Hermann 1997; Goldsmith 2008). Easterly, Satyanath, and Berger (2008), for instance, find equally bad democratic consequences from American and Soviet interventions during the Cold War. However, the evidence is more positive if the target country has good structural conditions (Grimm 2008; Downes and Monten 2013) or the intervenor intends to promote democracy (Nomikos, Downes, and Monten 2014).

In sum, the evidence on war and democratization points to a special role for *defeat* in war and an interactive effect with domestic structure. Both claims are supported qualitatively in this chapter and quantitatively in chapters 7 and 8. In addition, I find supportive evidence that the intentions of the foreign intervenor matter for democratization, but not the intervenor's regime type in and of itself.

## PATHS TO DEMOCRATIZATION

We can now examine cases of postwar democratization in more detail. Of the 16 primary cases, 9 featured an external combatant that intentionally sought to democratize the country. However, in only 2 cases was the conflict started partly for this reason. In 7 cases, the war victor lacked a liberalizing aim, but the country still democratized after the regime collapsed and democratic opponents grabbed the opening.

The postwar cases are dominated by the Reformer pattern (12 of 16), counting the external pro-democratic powers as reformers. Surprisingly, only three cases fit the Salvation pattern (San Marino, Honduras, Uganda), largely because the major security threats had passed before the moment of transition. Further, in only two cases did the final autocratic leader or party gain power in democracy (one-fourth the average rate), as defeat in war is harshly punished by future voters (Miller 2021). If anything, the shock of defeat and unfavorable peace terms produced overly strong reactions against prior regimes, especially in post–World War I Germany and Italy.

*Intentional Democratization after War*

In nine cases, an external democracy conquered a country and intentionally pushed it to democratize, although with varying degrees of control. Seven of these followed World War II, which also helped inspire several other transitions, especially in Latin America (Huntington 1991). After being drawn into the conflict, the Allies decided to secure democracy in the Axis powers and the conquered countries of France, Greece, and the Philippines. This included lengthy occupations of Austria and Japan, compared to more covert influence in Italy, France, and Greece (Kawai 1979; Pasquino 1986; Keyserlingk 1988).

Grenada and Panama are the only postwar cases in which the war itself was partly motivated by democratization. Grenada 1984 followed a Marxist revolution in 1979 by the New Jewel Movement, which established single-party rule (Payne, Sutton, and Thorndike 1984; Schoenhals and Melanson 1985; Foran 2005: 163–67). A hard-liner coup in 1983 ousted dictator Maurice Bishop, who escaped confinement but was quickly captured and executed during a second coup (Schoenhals and Melanson 1985). Responding to the instability and motivated to transform a nearby Marxist state, the United States invaded in October 1983, restored the pre-1979 constitution, and oversaw 1984 elections (Payne, Sutton, and Thorndike 1984; Schoenhals and Melanson 1985; Kinzer 2006: 219–38).

Panama 1991 followed the clandestine rise to power of National Guard leader Manuel Noriega, who forced out three presidents from 1984 to 1988 (Scranton 1991; Zimbalist and Weeks 1991). Noriega wore many hats: CIA informant, Cuban double agent, U.S. ally in the drug wars, and major operator in drugs, weapons, and money laundering (Scranton 1991; Andrew 1995: 513–15). In 1988, the United States indicted Noriega for drug trafficking, with additional threats if Noriega remained in power. After the opposition won the May 1989 election, Noriega annulled the result, declared himself supreme leader, and had the winning presidential candidate beaten by paramilitary forces (Scranton 1991; Furlong 1993). In an even bolder move, he declared war on the United States in December 1989. Within five days, the United States invaded, and within nine, Noriega had fled to the Vatican embassy, after which he soon surrendered (Ropp 2000; Harding 2006). The 1989 election winner, Guillermo Endara, was installed and a new legislative election held in 1991.

These nine cases represent the most straightforward route to democratization—an external power takes over and implants democracy. However, not all cases of intended democratization are successful. As Grimm (2008) discusses, nearly all post–World War II era attempts to implant democracy after civil or international war failed, with the only clear successes in Grenada, Panama, and El Salvador. The most significant failures, of course, were in Iraq and Afghanistan, wars partly justified by the successes in Japan and Germany.

To explain this divergence, we need to look beyond the war itself to the interaction with economic and political conditions (Grimm 2008; Mansfield and Snyder 2010; Downes and Monten 2013), as well as the choices of domestic actors and foreign occupiers (Kawai 1979; Linz and Stepan 1996; Nomikos, Downes, and Monten 2014). Even with the prior regime defeated and discarded, democracy still requires that "representatives of democratic forces in civil and political society are available and demand an electoral path" (Linz and Stepan 1996: 57). This in turn is more likely with "the basic facilitating conditions of democracy—economic development, literacy, an urban middle class," write Mansfield and Snyder (2010: 43). "Without well-laid tracks, war is a streetcar to nowhere."

Another supporting factor in the nine postwar transitions is that six had previously been democracies, and thus transition could be seen as a return to their own history. Among the exceptions, San Marino had a long republican tradition and was heavily dependent on Italy (which simultaneously democratized), while the Philippines and Japan experienced transformational occupations by the United States. Thus, a potential lesson is that externally imposed democratization requires either facilitating conditions or a lengthy occupation that can develop them (Grimm 2008). Japan's experience illustrates this well.

Of the many democratic successes following World War II, none exceeds Japan in the level of investment and control by the victors. After Japan's surrender in 1945, an occupation government under Douglas MacArthur—and, unlike in Europe, run almost exclusively by the United States—ruled Japan until sovereignty was restored in 1952 (Dore 1959/2013; Kawai 1979). Quickly growing to more than three hundred thousand personnel, the occupiers wrote a new constitution, liquidated the empire, abolished Shintoism as the national religion, and molded Japan into a liberal democracy with a New Deal policy base (Kawai 1979; Dower 1999; Coyne 2008). Japan's total defeat in war played a special role in this process (besides the obvious in leading to occupation) by aiding the country's receptivity to sweeping changes. The shock of defeat discredited the old Japan (Kawai 1979; Ikenberry and Kupchan 1990; Dower 1999; Toland 2003) and produced an openness "to consider personal and social change and a break from the past" (Coyne 2008: 123).

Demonstrating the perceived importance of social structure for democratic success, the occupation openly aimed both to institutionally democratize Japan (Kawai 1979; Dower 1999; Coyne 2008; Bermeo 2010a) and to transform its economy and culture (Dore 1959/2013; Kawai 1979; Ikenberry and Kupchan 1990; Dower 1999). To remake the state and bureaucracy, the occupiers went far beyond constitutional revision: they surveyed millions of Japanese and disqualified nearly a quarter million from public office for links to the military regime (Kawai 1979: 92–98). On the economic side, a major land redistribution program (reselling about 40% of national farmland) was designed to promote individualism and, in MacArthur's eyes, would "surely tear from the soils of the Japanese countryside the blight of feudal landlordism" (quoted in Dore 1959/2013: 137). For a glimpse of the cultural outreach, pamphlets were circulated among rural youth asking, "The wife takes a bath before her husband! But why this strict order? Is it not feudal and irrational? Let us stop such nonsense" (Dore 1959/2013: 486). Although often hamhanded and inattentive to local culture, the occupation oversaw extensive political and cultural change (Dore 1959/2013; Kawai 1979), which in turn smoothed Japan's transformation from fascist military dictatorship to successful democracy.

### Unintentional Democratization after War

In seven cases, the external power was indifferent or even hostile to democracy, but the defeated country nevertheless democratized from the resulting opening. This includes the three cases after World War I, which were strongly shaped by the war and democratic ideas but included little direct pro-democratic intervention (Barker 1973; Gunitsky 2017).[9] Of the remaining four cases, the victorious side was autocratic in France 1870 (Prussia), Honduras (El Salvador), and Uganda (Tanzania). In the latter, the war began when Uganda's (and more debatably, Scotland's) dictator Idi Amin invaded Tanzania to attack Ugandan rebels holed up there after a failed mutiny (Berg-Schlosser and Siegler 1990). Tanzania's counterinvasion ousted Amin in 1979. In Cyprus, democratic Turkey invaded in 1974 after a pro-Greek coup to protect co-ethnics and lay claim to territory (Hitchens 1997; Borowiec 2000).

These cases perfectly illustrate how transitions can result from shocks that are not intended to produce democracy. Military defeat demoralizes and divides regime elites, triggers economic crises, and erodes popular legitimacy (Jennings 2013). This legitimacy crisis was especially severe in military governments, such as in Honduras and Argentina, that justified their rule based on security expertise (Mainwaring and Viola 1985: 207; Dunkerley and Sieder 1996: 71). In each case considered here, the autocratic leader was also removed due to the war or its aftermath, further fueling instability and succession crises.

Military defeat is also corrosive to regime coercive capacity and popular control, creating openings for change from below. In many cases of defeat, "war temporarily broke down forces of authoritarian control, created opportunities for mass forces to mobilize, and induced elites to bargain with masses" (Mansfield and Snyder 2010: 43). This disruption in domestic power can be captured by the frequency of postwar attempts at social revolution. Besides prominent successes like France (1789), Russia, and China (Skocpol 1979),

---

9. The victors did intercede to prevent Austria from merging with Germany, so were pivotal to it remaining independent (Barker 1973).

there were failed revolutions in France 1870 (the Paris Commune), Germany 1919 (the November Revolution), and Italy 1919 (d'Annunzio's takeover of Fiume). Uganda's transition was also immediately followed by the Ugandan Bush War, a rebellion triggered by the first democratic election (Kokole and Mazrui 1988; Tripp 2010). As with intentional democratization, actors' choices and country characteristics shape what arises from postwar openings.

France 1870 demonstrates how quickly both democratic and radical actors can grasp openings from war. In 1870, six weeks into the Franco-Prussian War, France's dictator Napoleon III was captured at the disastrous Battle of Sedan (Zeldin 1958; Howard 2013). Two days later, a republican government was declared by Louis-Jules Trochu and Léon Gambetta in Paris, which was then surrounded by the Prussians. Escaping in a hydrogen balloon, Gambetta fled to Tours to lead the war effort, but Paris surrendered in January 1871 (Horne 2007; Howard 2013). Subsequent elections were won by supporters of constitutional monarchy led by Adolphe Thiers, who bargained out an unpopular treaty to end the war. Widespread anger combined with the state's coercive incapacity to create "an opportunity for popular forces to mobilize against the Prussian invaders and against the French elite" (Mansfield and Snyder 2010: 42). Threatening a very different postwar outcome, socialists and National Guard troops organized the Paris Commune in March and took over the capital. However, it was violently suppressed in May by Thiers at the cost of around twenty thousand lives (Tilly 2004; Horne 2007). Republicans gradually gained strength in the new government and secured a new democratic constitution in 1875, with Gambetta becoming prime minister in 1881 (R. Collier 1999: 40–44).

Honduras 1971 represents a less complete defeat but still an opening firmly grasped by pro-democratic actors. The war was preceded by a bloody 1963 coup by Air Force head Oswaldo López Arellano, who allied with the National Party of Honduras (PNH) to win fraudulent elections in 1965 and 1968, complete with thugs roaming rural areas and intimidating opposition voters (Anderson 1981: 62; Ruhl 1996: 36). Beginning in 1967, tensions mounted with El Salvador over a swelling refugee community that grew to about one-eighth of Honduras's population and competed for land with native Hondurans (Durham 1979; Schulz and Schulz 1994: 35). With Honduras ramping up migrant expulsions, a combustible situation was ignited by rioting over three World Cup qualifying matches in June 1969, leading El Salvador to invade in July. Despite much deeper roots, this context sufficed to "confuse the outside world into believing temporarily that the conflict was some kind of comic-opera battle over soccer," hence its nickname, the Soccer War (Anderson 1981: 95). Initial successes by El Salvador bogged down and the war ended within 100 hours thanks to OAS intervention, although it left several thousand dead and 100,000 without homes (Durham 1979: 1).

Despite the brief war, "the Honduran army was humiliated on the ground . . . [which] brought in its wake further disenchantment with the government" (Anderson 1988: 134). In particular, "López Arellano was largely discredited, for if El Salvador had not really won the war, Honduras clearly appeared to have lost it" (Anderson 1981: 157). With regime legitimacy cratering, pressure for leadership change came most emphatically from organized labor (Schulz and Schulz 1994: 39; Ruhl 1996: 36) and reformist factions in the military (Anderson 1981: 157; Dunkerley and Sieder 1996: 71). López was thus forced to accept elections won by a PNH-led coalition in March 1971.[10] In both France and Honduras, we again see the pattern of shattered regimes buffeted by mass opposition that eventually secures democracy.

## Withdrawal of an Autocratic Hegemon

The fall of the Soviet Union and Germany's defeat in World War II mark two of the most significant global events since 1800. Both events unleashed a wave of democratic transitions, as well as fundamental changes in how international actors promote democracy (Huntington 1991; Gunitsky 2017). In this section, I overview the democratic transitions that arose most directly from their downfalls, namely the transitions in the client states that these hegemons coercively dominated. The withdrawal of this control freed reformist elites and popular movements to push for democratization, liberating the post-Soviet cases after forty years of subjugation.

### OVERVIEW

#### Cases

Following Gunitsky (2017), I count two autocratic hegemons in the sample period: the Soviet Union and Nazi Germany. Both developed dominant relationships over client states in their immediate vicinity. Both also suffered quick downfalls, preceded by an inability or unwillingness to block political change in their clients. For the Soviet Union, this resulted from a deliberate policy shift in the mid-1980s, after which nine countries in the Soviet orbit democratized. These are the primary cases listed in Table 4.2, including six nominally independent countries in Eastern Europe, two new countries that democratized after a brief autocratic spell (Latvia, Lithuania), and Mongolia. New countries that were democratic at birth (e.g., Slovenia, Ukraine) are not included. The related effects on Marxist countries not under Soviet coercive control (e.g., Madagascar, Benin) are covered in the next chapter.

---

10. The democratic experiment survived a mere twenty months, as López couped again in December 1972 (Anderson 1988: 135).

**Table 4.2.** Hegemonic Withdrawal Cases, 1800–2014

**Primary Cases (Post-Soviet)**

| | | |
|---|---|---|
| Poland 1989 | Bulgaria 1990 | Hungary 1990 |
| Czechoslovakia 1990 | Mongolia 1990 | Romania 1991 |
| Albania 1992 | Lithuania 1992 | Latvia 1993 |

**Secondary Cases (Post–Nazi Germany)**

| | | |
|---|---|---|
| San Marino 1945 | Austria 1946 | France 1946 |
| Italy 1946 | | |

*Note:* Years shown are for democratization, not the withdrawals.

Four countries that democratized after liberation from Nazi control are considered secondary cases, with the war (and resulting external intervention) the primary cause. These are Italy, San Marino, Austria, and France.[11] A significant contrast with the post-Soviet cases is that none of these featured the final autocratic leader or party regaining power in democracy, whereas 7 of 9 Communist parties did. This democratic potential was crucial to the latter's peaceful acceptance of democracy (Orenstein 1998; Grzymala-Busse 2002; Ishiyama 2008).

Figure 4.2 shows the likelihood of democratization for the Soviet and Nazi client states within five years of each hegemon's downfall. Unsurprisingly, there is a very strong positive effect on democratic transition. In fact, the only client states to survive as autocracies were Hungary, Bulgaria, and Romania after World War II, each becoming a client to the new hegemon.

*Past Work*

A vast literature covers the fall of the Soviet Union and the democratic transitions in Eastern Europe and Mongolia (e.g., Ash 1990; Remnick 1993; Sebestyen 2009; DeFronzo 2011: 66–76; Stoner and McFaul 2013). Although many accounts understandably focus on popular movements in these countries, there is little doubt that the regional democratic wave ultimately originated from the common shock of Soviet withdrawal and not purely spontaneous diffusion (Huntington 1991; Goodwin 2001; Sebestyen 2009; Hale 2013; Gunitsky 2017). In fact, prior attempts at de novo liberalization (East Germany 1953, Hungary 1956, Czechoslovakia 1968, Poland 1980) had been ruthlessly crushed by the Soviets.

Several authors argue the regime types of major powers influence the spread of democracy through a mixture of coercion, incentives, and emulation

---

11. Again, countries purely under military occupation are not classified as autocratic. Judging Denmark to be sufficiently collaborationist from 1940 to 1942 to be autocratic (see appendix) would add another secondary case.

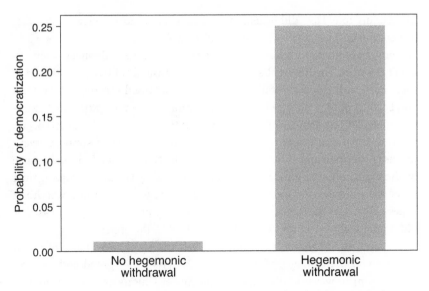

FIGURE 4.2. Hegemons and democratization. The likelihood of democratization by whether there has been a withdrawal of an autocratic hegemon in the previous five years, 1800–2014 (N = 11,489).

(Whitehead 1996; Owen 2010; Boix 2011; Gunitsky 2017). For instance, Boix (2011) finds that democracy spreads more when major powers are democratic, especially in countries at higher average incomes. Besides controlling regional client states, major powers shape international institutions and spread supporting ideologies (Owen 2010; Gunitsky 2017). In turn, this implies that the downfall of an autocratic major power presents a global opening for democracy. These hegemonic shocks represent "structural sources of regime change" (Gunitsky 2017: 7) that allow rising foreign powers to "exogenously shift the capabilities and institutional preferences of many domestic actors and coalitions at once" (17) and thereby "dramatically alter the balance of power among dominant and subordinate classes" (58).

## WITHDRAWAL AND DEMOCRATIZATION

Although the effects were global in reach, I focus here on how the downfall of autocratic hegemons freed their regional client states to democratize. This consequence is hardly surprising, but it was far from automatic—the crackdowns in China and Burma in 1989–90 capture the alternative path these regimes could have taken. Indeed, Eastern European Communist regimes retained formidable coercive resources and had effectively silenced popular movements for years, making these movements' subsequent organization a major challenge. Numerous regime hard-liners remained intent on maintaining power, while soft-liners generally favored modest reforms with the Party in a leading role. How did hegemonic withdrawal produce such a sudden disintegration of these domestic systems of control?

First, hegemonic withdrawal weakened the coercive and financial resources of client states. The Soviets had hundreds of thousands of troops stationed in their Eastern European satellites and Mongolia (Goodwyn 1991; Ackerman and Duvall 2000), with the explicit threat (prior to the mid-1980s) of intervention to defeat pro-democratic movements. In the late 1980s, the troops began to draw down and the Soviets signaled an unwillingness to support crackdowns (Ackerman and Duvall 2000). Among the Nazi clients, Italy and France by the war's end were almost exclusively defended by German troops against domestic and foreign opponents. Although the hegemon's withdrawal didn't necessarily leave the states defenseless, especially in the post-Soviet cases, it did dramatically lower the coercive threat faced by the opposition.

Second, the hegemon's downfall eroded the ideological basis of allied regimes and their images of invincibility. Whereas the spread and survival of communism was initially "aided by the Soviet Union's apparent economic progress" (Mueller 1999: 220), its reputation was in ashes by the late 1980s. With vivid signs of decline and division in the Soviet Union, elites across the Communist bloc began to question and push at previously immovable forces. In Poland, a U.S. embassy cable described how "the glue that has held the ruling coalition together—the permanence and inevitability of [Communist Party] rule—has been eliminated," opening a path for elite reform (quoted in Domber 2013: 69). In fact, the Polish leadership abruptly realized in 1988 that the opposition was the "only group that could provide the legitimacy the government needed" for economic reforms (Domber 2013: 63). Similarly, Soviet decline and early successes in Poland and Hungary encouraged *popular* forces to rethink the inevitability of Communist rule.

Hegemonic withdrawal provided an opening for pro-democratic pressure from multiple directions: domestic elites, foreign rivals, and popular movements. Uncertainty and policy divisions gnawed at regime solidarity, while dramatic events in the region effectively coordinated popular organization. We can now examine the aftermath of Soviet and Nazi withdrawal in more detail.

### Soviet Withdrawal

Following World War II, the Soviet Union forcibly imposed Communist regimes throughout Eastern Europe after brief attempts at electoral routes to power (Applebaum 2012), while Latvia, Lithuania, and Estonia were instead absorbed into the Soviet Union.[12] In Winston Churchill's phrasing, an "iron curtain" was drawn down the center of Europe, with the understanding that Eastern Europe was the Soviet sphere of influence. This was further codified

12. Mongolia was a Soviet client state from about 1924, following a Soviet-supported revolution.

in a mutual defense treaty called the Warsaw Pact in 1955. The so-called Brezhnev Doctrine, which called for Soviet interference in any faltering socialist country, was explicitly formulated in 1968 (to justify Soviet intervention in the Prague Spring) but was already implicit given the bloody Soviet crackdown in Hungary in 1956 (Ash 1990; Remnick 1993; Sebestyen 2009). As a result, the Soviets maintained hegemonic control of their client states into the late 1980s.[13]

In 1985, Mikhail Gorbachev rose to become General Secretary of the Communist Party of the Soviet Union. Disenchanted with Soviet economic failures and the disastrous invasion of Afghanistan in 1979, Gorbachev initiated a series of economic and political reforms collectively labeled perestroika ("restructuring"), including a changed attitude toward reform in Soviet client states (Remnick 1993; Domber 2013; Stoner and McFaul 2013). As early as 1985, at his predecessor's funeral, Gorbachev warned Eastern European leaders to no longer expect Soviet interference (Gunitsky 2017: 206). "A genuine turning point in the entire system of collaboration with our allies is needed," Gorbachev explained the following year (quoted in Domber 2013: 72). "We should hold more firmly to the principle of each communist party being responsible for what happens in its country." Despite the final result, Gorbachev almost certainly intended these reforms to merely liberalize and ultimately strengthen communism, not to trigger its collapse (Remnick 1993; Ackerman and Duvall 2000; Sebestyen 2009; Stoner and McFaul 2013).

Regardless of Gorbachev's intentions, Soviet withdrawal unleashed a wave of democratic transitions, starting in its Eastern European client states (Ash 1990; Sebestyen 2009; Gunitsky 2017). Simmering discontent and economic failure, long blocked from generating change, suddenly translated into both elite and popular political action. Anticipation of Soviet decline led Communist early-movers to open the political space and begin negotiating prior to 1989, most notably in Poland (Bernhard 1993; Domber 2013), Hungary (Ash 1990; Linz and Stepan 1996: 293–316), and Mongolia (Ackerman and Duvall 2000: 443–49). When popular movements exploited these opportunities without a coercive response, the floodgates opened. One East German recalled, "We saw what Poland and Hungary were doing; we heard Gorbachev. Everyone felt, Why are we being left behind?" (quoted in Huntington 1991: 104). In many cases, Communist elites became the most proactive in pushing reform, aiming to control the transition and forestall revolution (Ash 1990; Ackerman and Duvall 2000; Goodwin 2001; Gunitsky 2017). In Bulgaria and Romania, for instance, reformers ousted recalcitrant leaders, making their move "before the people could make a move against them" (Ackerman and Duvall 2000:

---

13. Of the democratizing cases, all except Albania were Warsaw Pact members (in Mongolia's case, only as an "observer" to mollify China). Albania withdrew in 1968 as part of a wider split with the Soviets but remained within the larger security umbrella (Biberaj 1999).

432). Soviet withdrawal also provided an opening for Western powers to apply significant democratizing pressure in Eastern Europe (Levitsky and Way 2010; Owen 2010). The result from 1989 to 1992 was the democratization of Mongolia and every Eastern European Communist regime except Yugoslavia, plus independence and democracy in another ten states.

The role of Soviet withdrawal was especially clear in the Polish transition. In 1980, Poland's regime faced a severe threat after a Gdansk shipyard strike, initially organized to protest the firing of a crane driver a few months before she could retire with her pension, spread to hundreds of factories within a week (Ackerman and Duvall 2000: 136). Led by Lech Wałęsa, a former electrician at the shipyard, the strike developed into the Solidarity movement, combining economic and political demands (Goodwyn 1991; Bernhard 1993; Walesa 1994). The movement succeeded in reversing planned price hikes and gaining recognition as an independent union, rapidly spreading to a membership of 10 million Poles (Goodwyn 1991). After a leadership change, the new Communist head negotiated with Solidarity and contemplated further concessions. But this opening was reversed under intense Soviet pressure and a threat of Soviet "invasion" if leaders didn't crack down. This threat was realistic given the brutal Soviet repression of the Prague Spring in 1968 and the presence of 200,000 Soviet troops already stationed on Polish soil (Goodwyn 1991; Ackerman and Duvall 2000). Instead of a political opening, Solidarity was crushed and a ruling military council led by Wojciech Jaruzelski placed Poland under martial law until 1983.

Economic conditions worsened in Poland through the 1980s. Political dissatisfaction rose in parallel, with many elites comparing Poland unfavorably against the West.[14] Once perestroika began in the Soviet Union, Gorbachev gave Jaruzelski the "green light" in 1986 for political reform and negotiations (Bitar and Lowenthal 2015: 254). Solidarity leaders were given amnesty that year and, following nationwide protests and strikes, clandestine negotiations began in 1988, with the Catholic Church acting as intermediary (Goodwyn 1991; Bernhard 1993; Domber 2013). Official talks were accepted by Communist hard-liners only when Jaruzelski and allies threatened to resign otherwise (Ackerman and Duvall 2000: 171). Finally, the famous Round Table talks in early 1989 culminated in Solidarity's legalization, increased freedoms, and limited multiparty elections in June that Solidarity won resoundingly (Ash 1990; Goodwyn 1991; Przeworski 1991). Unexpectedly, the Communists failed to win a single one of the 161 lower house and 100 Senate seats up for grabs. Although the Communists had kept 65% of the lower house removed

14. Aleksander Kwaśniewski, Poland's later president, remarked of his experiences abroad as a student: "For me it was quite easy to understand what it looked like to compare Communism and the Soviet Union with the West. . . . And it was absolutely a disappointing observation and an extremely frustrating situation" (Bitar and Lowenthal 2015: 257).

from competition, the message was unmistakable and Poland's first non-Communist prime minister since 1946, Tadeusz Mazowiecki, was inaugurated in August 1989.

Not for nothing did Mazowiecki call the Soviet Union "big brother," overruling the potential opening in 1981, monitoring the Polish leadership's posture, and then signaling its acceptance of reform from 1986 onward (Bitar and Lowenthal 2015: 287). If anything, the opposition was better organized in 1980–81 but prevailed in 1989 due to the changed international picture and closely related economic decline. The Soviet shift under Gorbachev and later collapse "opened the doors for previously unimaginable changes" (Bitar and Lowenthal 2015: 249; also Goodwin 2001: 272; Domber 2013). Yet this opening did not produce democratization by itself—it was seized by a renewed Solidarity movement, as well as reformers within the regime who believed the old system was unsustainable. In turn, these reformers transformed the Communist Party into the social-democratic SdRP, which led the winning coalition in the 1993 legislative election and defeated Wałęsa for the presidency in 1995 (Grzymala-Busse 2002).

### Nazi Withdrawal

Starting in 1943, Nazi Germany's European empire began to crumble, freeing several occupied states and four nominally independent client states that soon democratized. Since each of the four is a primary postwar case, their stories will only briefly be recounted. In France and Austria, the Allies liberated the countries and oversaw democratization. Italy and San Marino are more complex cases, in which the decline of fascist coercive power first allowed domestic forces to topple their governments. Democratic change was then secured through Allied intervention and German defeat.

With the Allied invasion of Sicily in July 1943, Italy's Benito Mussolini was ousted from power and arrested by the king and opponents in the fascist council. After being rescued in a daring mountaintop raid by Nazi paratroopers, Mussolini established the puppet Italian Social Republic in northern Italy, dividing Italian forces and triggering extended guerrilla warfare (Pasquino 1986; Paxton 2004). Germany took over Italy's defenses but lost Rome in June 1944. Meanwhile, Italy's new government, led by the disloyal fascist Pietro Badoglio, sought to end the German alliance but "harshly resisted" any turn toward democracy and "hoped to stalemate the process" (Pasquino 1986: 69). However, due to Allied pressure, anti-fascist Ivanoe Bonomi became prime minister following Rome's fall (Pasquino 1986). After Germany's defeat and Mussolini's capture and execution alongside his mistress, Italy's democratization was secured with fair elections in 1946 and a referendum abolishing the monarchy (Miller 1983; Pasquino 1986).

Tucked inside Italy's Apennine Mountains, San Marino—a nation about the size of Manhattan with only 12,000 citizens in the 1940s—was politically subordinate to Italy and held a low strategic priority for the warring parties (Sundhaussen 2003). Yet San Marino is noteworthy as the only fascist government to be overthrown by a popular movement. Aided by Italian coercion, the Sammarinese Fascist Party established control in 1923, eventually outlawing all opposition parties (Ring 1995: 611–16). With an anti-fascist movement secretly growing from 1942, a mass demonstration toppled the government in July 1943, three days after Mussolini's arrest (AP 1943; Veenendaal 2015: 70–101). September elections and a grand coalition government followed. In September 1944, Germans invaded the territory, but British troops sent the Germans into retreat after a three-day battle. The Fascist Party dissolved under British occupation, followed by 1945 elections won by a Socialist/Communist coalition, the world's first democratically elected Communist government (Ring 1995: 611–16; Sundhaussen 2003; Veenendaal 2015: 70–101).

## Summary

This chapter overviewed democratic transitions following the most disruptive coercive international events: defeat in foreign war and the collapse of an autocratic hegemon. I argued that *defeat* in war is distinct and, as with the withdrawal of hegemonic control, produces weak, illegitimate regimes unable to stifle opposition. Overwhelmingly, the initiators of these shocks were autocracies that did not intend to spread democracy. Yet as with many civil wars, they provided critical openings for international actors to apply pro-democratic pressure, most clearly in the post–World War II cases of Japan and Austria and the post-Soviet cases in Eastern Europe. However, the victorious foreign powers in several postwar cases remained indifferent or hostile to democracy. Domestic actors—including regime elites and mass organizations—were critical in deciding whether to steer the openings toward liberal democracy, social revolution, or reestablished autocracy. International or not, the logic of shocks remains the same—once the shock disrupts the autocratic status quo, the opening is what actors and structural conditions make of it.

CHAPTER FIVE

# Electoral Continuity

AFTER SIXTY-SEVEN DEMOCRATIC TRANSITIONS, just under half the total, the final autocratic executive or ruling party won power within democracy. This surprising resilience shapes autocratic leaders' attitudes about democratization, since transition does not necessarily imply a full sacrifice of power and thus need not be met with determined resistance. In the electoral continuity path to democracy, leaders of an established ruling party accede to democratization because they correctly anticipate that they can compete and win in democracy. However, as in the shock cases, this almost always requires a further push from autocracy, in the form of disruptive events and pro-democratic activism. With autocratic stability undermined, ruling party leaders calculate that liberalization is a safer bet for long-term power.

Before introducing the electoral continuity cases, I overview autocratic elections and parties, including prior work on democratization and the success of autocratic parties post-democratization. The theory on parties' paths to democratization follows, beginning with the triggers that disrupt electoral autocracies and amplify competition, then turning to why parties decide to liberalize. The final section details case evidence showing the causal role of high electoral confidence in successful democratization and the contrasting effect of low confidence for democratic resisters.

## *Background*

### OVERVIEW OF AUTOCRATIC ELECTIONS AND PARTIES

Although often considered a new phenomenon, autocratic elections have a long history (Posada-Carbó 1996; Przeworski 2009b; Miller 2015a). Forty-four dictatorships held elections by 1900, including eighteen in Latin America, Japan,

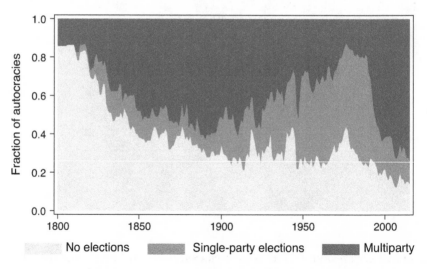

FIGURE 5.1. Elections in autocracies. The fraction of autocracies with no elections, single- or no-party elections, and multiparty elections by year, 1800–2015 (N = 11,626).

Liberia, Haiti, and Turkey, although many allowed no legal competition.[1] Figure 5.1 shows the annual fraction of autocracies that allowed no legislative elections, only no- or single-party elections, and multiparty elections. As early as the 1850s, a majority held multiparty elections (mostly legislative only), but they spread especially widely following the Cold War.

A further distinction concerns *how* electoral competition is restricted. Dahl (1971) famously categorized elections along two dimensions: contestation (the fairness and competitiveness of elections) and inclusiveness (primarily captured by suffrage). Authentic democracies require high values on both: fair competition decided by a large fraction of the population. Autocracies have embraced elections scoring low on one or both dimensions, with a global shift in strategies occurring around 1940 (Miller 2015a). Earlier cases allowed genuine party competition with restricted suffrage, a regime type commonly termed *competitive oligarchy*. For modern cases, in an era when suffrage limitations are widely condemned, inclusiveness is high but contestation is tightly controlled.

Autocratic ruling parties have historically been much less common. Although competitive oligarchies had well-defined parties, the first *hegemonic* ruling party—one effectively fused with the state and either the sole legal party or clearly preeminent—was arguably the Communist Party under Lenin. Since

1. See the appendix. Looking further back, we can add the popular assemblies and plebiscites in the medieval Italian city-states, medieval Germany and Scandinavia, and ancient Athens, Sparta, Syracuse, and Rome (Miller 2015a; Cartledge 2016).

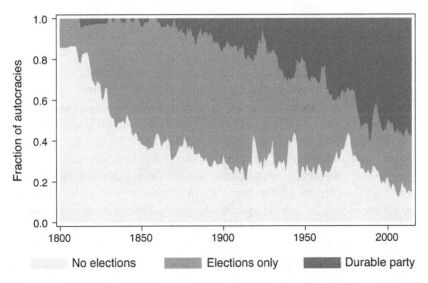

FIGURE 5.2. Durable parties and elections in autocracies. The fraction of autocracies with an electoral ruling party with 4+ years of control, others with elections, and no elections by year, 1800–2015 (N = 11,633).

then, about 60% of autocracies have had an identifiable ruling party, although few as dominant as Lenin's innovation. To qualify for electoral continuity, autocracies must have had elections and the same ruling party in power for at least four years prior to democratization. Figure 5.2 shows the annual fraction of autocracies that meet this requirement, plus those with legislative elections and no such party, and those without elections. There has been a steady rise in durable electoral ruling parties since World War I, although they did not become the majority form of autocracy until the past few decades.

Scholars generally agree that parties and elections are not adopted to produce democracy but rather to bolster autocratic power. Strategic purposes of elections and parties include co-opting and monitoring elites, increasing popular and international legitimacy, gathering information on popular demands, and signaling dominance through overwhelming electoral victories (Hermet, Rose, and Rouquié 1978; Geddes 1999; Lust-Okar 2006; Magaloni 2006; Schedler 2006; Brownlee 2007; Gandhi 2008; Gandhi and Lust-Okar 2009; Blaydes 2011; Svolik 2012; Morgenbesser 2016). Yet we cannot assume that these institutions' uses explain their origins (Gandhi and Lust-Okar 2009; Pepinsky 2014). Autocratic parties have widely varying histories and initial purposes, from revolution to colonial-era elections. Although there is little empirical work on election adoption, Miller (2020b) finds that shifts to multiparty electoral autocracy are explained by economic and security dependence on external democracies, as well as economic conditions that make elections easier to control.

## DO AUTOCRATIC ELECTIONS PREDICT
## DEMOCRATIZATION?

Despite frequently being dismissed as facades, elections can be dangerous for autocrats. Dictators employ various techniques to control elections, including vote-buying, punishing opposition voters, restricting rivals' funding and media access, and outright ballot-stuffing (Lust-Okar 2006; Magaloni 2006; Gandhi and Lust-Okar 2009; Levitsky and Way 2010; Blaydes 2011). Nevertheless, autocratic elections often get freer and fairer over time as the opposition gains experience, electoral bodies become more independent, and citizens increasingly demand a meaningful vote (Lindberg 2006, 2009; Magaloni 2006). Elections also provide openings for protest and international pressure, especially if they're stolen (Howard and Roessler 2006; Tucker 2007; Bunce and Wolchik 2010, 2011). As a result, autocrats frequently lose power due to elections: from 1800 to 2015, about 1 in 4 autocratic elections led to executive turnover or the ruling party losing its legislative majority (using Coppedge et al. 2018).[2] In turn, electoral defeats often usher in democratization, while in other cases they trigger civil wars or coups (Cederman, Gleditsch, and Hug 2013; Knutsen, Nygård, and Wig 2017; Wig and Rød 2016).

This danger must be balanced against the stabilizing potential of elections and parties (Knutsen, Nygård, and Wig 2017). Many autocracies have survived with multiparty elections for decades, including Singapore, Jordan, Tanzania, and Russia. In particular, several scholars argue that party-based autocracies are the most durable, primarily due to advantages in elite recruitment and power-sharing (Geddes 1999; Smith 2005; Slater 2006; Brownlee 2007; Svolik 2012).

Despite a robust debate, there is no consensus as to whether elections predict democratization, with some scholars finding a positive relationship (Bratton and van de Walle 1997; Lindberg 2006; Teorell and Hadenius 2009) and others none (Lust-Okar 2006; Blaydes 2011; Case 2011; Kaya and Bernhard 2013).[3] Other findings are highly contingent, differing by region (Lindberg 2009; Edgell et al. 2018), time period (Edgell et al. 2018), electoral characteristics (Miller 2015a), state strength (Levitsky and Way 2010; Seeberg 2014, 2018; Way 2015), and actor behavior (Howard and Roessler 2006; Cheeseman 2010; Bunce and Wolchik 2010).

The perspective taken here (and supported empirically in chapter 7) is that elections predict democratization *only* when combined with a ruling

---

2. From 1945 to 2015, 18.7% of autocratic elections resulted in the incumbent or ruling party being replaced, including related protests (using Hyde and Marinov 2012).

3. For case studies on democratization through elections, see Greene 2002; Magaloni 2006; Levitsky and Way 2010; Way 2015; Morgenbesser 2016; and chapters in Schedler 2006 and Lindberg 2009.

party that expects to compete in democracy. In this context, elections provide a liberalizing push, but with less resistance from forward-thinking parties. Thus, the strategic agency of ruling parties is a critical factor in democratization through elections. Several scholars have argued that the potential to win power in democracy influences parties' choices to democratize (R. Collier 1999; Levitsky and Way 2010; Wright and Escribà-Folch 2012; Slater and Wong 2013; Riedl 2014; Miller 2015a; Ziblatt 2017; Madrid 2019). Examining Taiwan, South Korea, and Indonesia, Slater and Wong (2013) claim that parties facing a gradual decline "concede-to-thrive" and democratize while still strong enough to compete. However, there has yet to be a comprehensive global account of this route to democracy. Before further developing the theory, we must consider the fates of autocratic parties after democratization.

## AUTOCRATIC RULING PARTIES
## AFTER DEMOCRATIZATION

Former autocratic ruling parties frequently survive and prosper within democracy (Grzymala-Busse 2002; Ishiyama and Quinn 2006; Friedman and Wong 2008; Loxton 2018; Miller 2021). In competitive oligarchies, suffrage extensions usually followed from calculations they would improve parties' electoral prospects by crafting desirable electorates and earning gratitude from new voters (R. Collier 1999; Przeworski 2009a; Teele 2018). In nearly all cases, parties indeed kept power following suffrage reform. Prior to 1940, the incumbent party won 88.1% of elections held within five years of an autocratic suffrage extension, compared to 82.5% of other autocratic elections.[4]

In the modern era, democratization entails increased competition, implying a heightened chance of party turnover. Nevertheless, most ruling parties thrive well into democracy. Of the 84 democratic transitions between 1940 and 2010 from a party-led autocracy, the final party kept or regained power following 41 (defined as executive control or a legislative plurality).[5] In South Korea, Lesotho, Honduras, and elsewhere, ruling parties have even dominated democratic politics. An additional 14 parties became nationally competitive (generally defined by a threshold of 10% of legislative seats or presidential votes). This phenomenon persists: in 2015, 18 democracies had a former ruling party in power and 28 had a nationally competitive party. Figure 5.3 shows the annual fraction of post-1940 democracies meeting these two conditions.

Democratic resurgence is not limited to continuations of ruling parties. From 1940 to 2015, 37 former dictators won executive power in democracy and

---

4. This measures suffrage extensions from Przeworski 2013 and turnover from Coppedge et al. 2018. Democratic transitions are included. After 1940, the incumbent party won 89.3% of these elections (using Hyde and Marinov 2012).

5. As in Miller 2021, I end at 2010 to ensure sufficient time to observe success.

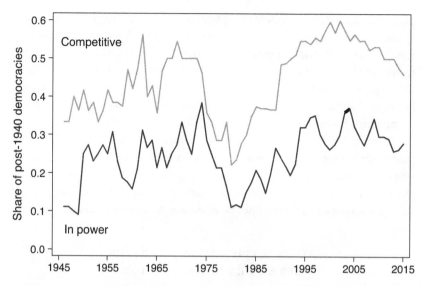

FIGURE 5.3. Former autocratic ruling parties. For each year, the figure shows the fraction of democracies (democratizing between 1940 and 2010) that have a former autocratic ruling party as a significant competitor and the fraction that have a former ruling party in power (controlling either the legislature or executive). Former ruling parties remain major players in dozens of democracies (N = 2,065).

more than a dozen founded major parties in democracy, including Hugo Banzer's Nationalist Democratic Action in Bolivia and Dési Bouterse's National Democratic Party in Suriname (Miller 2021; also Baker 1998; Riedl 2014). Still other parties were founded by autocratic elites, split from old ruling parties,[6] or present themselves as spiritual successors.[7]

Given the institutional and normative changes wrought by democratization, how can so many emblems of the autocratic past thrive in democracy? Former ruling parties enter democracy with major advantages in organization, recruitment, and brand recognition, especially if they're still in power at transition (Langston 2017; Loxton 2018; Miller 2021). In nearly all cases, they are the most professionalized and experienced party. Further, they often keep reserves of autocratic power, such as clientelist networks, state and military allies, and control of the media (Serra 2013; Langston 2017; Loxton 2018).

What predicts *which* ruling parties succeed in democracy? An initially dominant view was that ruling parties needed to engineer a "sharp break with the past" and transform themselves ideologically and institutionally to

6. In the Philippines, the Nacionalista Party and two of its offshoots made up three of the top four vote-getters in the 2016 legislative election.

7. In Peru, for instance, Popular Force has run as a continuation of Alberto Fujimori's autocratic legacy and is currently led by his daughter.

compete (Grzymala-Busse 2002; see also Orenstein 1998; Ishiyama 2008). However, this work focused heavily on post-communist states, especially Poland and Hungary. In other cases, like Mexico and Taiwan, ruling parties instead prospered with similar messaging and methods of control as in autocracy. Recent work posits that ruling party success is more about continuity than reinvention, as parties preserve their significant advantages into democracy (Serra 2013; Slater and Wong 2013; Langston 2017; Loxton 2018; Miller 2021). In turn, parties usually don't wait long in the wilderness: of autocratic parties that win democratic power, half do so in the first democratic election and more than 80% within five years.

In the most extensive cross-national test of autocratic party success in democracy, Miller (2021) compares a range of party-based and institutional characteristics for all post-1940 democracies. Several conclusions are worth highlighting. First, parties are much more successful if they accede to democratization rather than first being overthrown. Among parties still in power at democratization, nearly two-thirds win power in the ensuing democracy, compared to fewer than one in four violently ousted parties. This is due both to greater continuity in power and to their leverage over institutional choices during transition (Riedl 2014; Albertus and Menaldo 2018). Second, "pure" party regimes (those not sharing power with militaries or monarchs) are more successful, as they are institutionally stronger and better resourced. Third, parties with records of economic and military success perform better, as citizens judge them to be more competent.

Most importantly, these results, along with other complementary studies,[8] demonstrate regularities and an internal logic as to which parties succeed in democracy. In turn, this implies that parties can ground their expectations on concrete factors and not mere optimism (or its close cousin, delusion).

## Electoral Continuity Cases

With this background, we can now consider the electoral continuity cases, which are listed in Table 5.1. There are 27 primary cases and 37 total cases. To qualify, each must have an electoral ruling party in power for at least four years. This party must democratize through elections and then win either the executive or a legislative plurality within democracy.[9] With one exception (Guyana 1992), this victory occurred within two electoral cycles post-democratization.

Again, this is far from the full list of countries that democratized through elections. The four-year durability requirement ensures the parties were not created solely for democratizing elections and leaders had sufficient time to

---

8. For more on party success after democratization, see Ishiyama and Quinn 2006; Riedl 2014; and the chapters accompanying Loxton 2018.

9. An exception is made for Benin, where the former party leader won the presidency.

**Table 5.1.** Electoral Continuity Cases, 1800–2014

**Competitive Oligarchy**

| | | |
|---|---|---|
| United Kingdom 1885 | Belgium 1894 | The Netherlands 1897 |
| Denmark 1901 | Chile 1909 | Sweden 1911 |
| Argentina 1912 | Uruguay 1919 | Colombia 1937 |

**Electoral Autocracy**

| | | |
|---|---|---|
| Uruguay 1942 | South Korea 1988 | São Tomé and Príncipe 1991 |
| Benin 1991 | Cape Verde 1991 | Guyana 1992 |
| Niger 1993 | Madagascar 1993 | Guinea-Bissau 1994 |
| Malawi 1994 | Taiwan 1996 | Ghana 1997 |
| Indonesia 1999 | Mexico 2000 | Paraguay 2003 |
| Antigua and Barbuda 2004 | Zambia 2008 | The Maldives 2009 |

**Secondary Cases**

| | | |
|---|---|---|
| Indonesia 1955 | Poland 1989 | Bulgaria 1990 |
| Hungary 1990 | Mongolia 1990 | Sri Lanka 1991 |
| Albania 1992 | Lithuania 1992 | Mozambique 1994 |
| Croatia 2000 | | |

*Note:* Years shown are for democratization.

learn about their party's strength. The requirement of democratic electoral success proxies for parties' expectations at democratization. Although I don't assume these parties were absolutely certain of winning, this sets a high bar of success that essentially guarantees they knew they would be competitive. Given these restrictions, Table 5.1 is a conservative undercount of transitions with electorally confident parties. Below, I discuss several "near-misses" that still illustrate the confidence mechanism.

Among the cases, 9 were competitive oligarchies that democratized after electoral reform. In all but Denmark and Chile, democratization immediately followed reform bills that expanded suffrage.[10] The parties were highly durable, having held power for an average of 16.7 years at democratization, and with only the Netherlands and Sweden featuring parties younger than 25 years old. In turn, all but one party won the first democratic election, with Sweden's General Electoral League winning the second.

10. In Chile, suffrage was granted to male literates in 1874, a "consequence of elite strategies to maximize electoral gain" (R. Collier 1999: 59). Due to expanding literacy, the suffrage threshold was reached in 1909 (Boix, Miller, and Rosato 2013). In Denmark, 1901 marked the adoption of the secret ballot and the king's acceptance of the right of election winners to control parliament (R. Collier 1999: 81–83; Jespersen 2004).

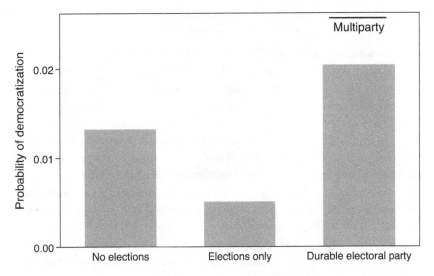

FIGURE 5.4. The annual likelihood of democratization in autocracies with no elections, with elections only, and with an electoral ruling party in power for at least four years. An additional line shows the likelihood with the added requirement of multiparty elections. Democratization is much more likely with a durable ruling party, especially compared to other electoral regimes. All autocracies are included, 1800–2014 (N = 11,489).

The 18 post-1940 primary cases also involved highly entrenched ruling parties. On average, they held power for 22.8 years at democratization, although this varied from 4 to 71 years. Seven cases (all in sub-Saharan Africa from 1991 to 1994) were single-party regimes prior to transition. The success of these 18 parties in democracy is remarkable. Up to 2015, they controlled the executive or legislature in 53.7% of country-years and were competitive in 89.8%.[11] Clearly, acceding to democratization did not amount to fully sacrificing power.

Figure 5.4 captures how the presence of a durable electoral ruling party predicts democratization. Following the electoral continuity requirement, the figure shows the annual likelihood of democratization when an autocracy has had elections and the same ruling party in power for at least four years. Only 24.7% of autocracies meet this requirement (see Figure 5.2). An additional line indicates the likelihood of democratization with the added requirement of multiparty elections. These likelihoods are compared to other autocracies with and without any elections. We can see that elections by themselves reduce the chances for democratization. In contrast, democratization is much more likely with a durable ruling party, especially combined with multiparty elections.

11. Including secondary cases, the respective totals are 57.3% and 93.1%.

## *Path to Democratization*

The electoral continuity path features established ruling parties that expect a high share of democratic power. Although the power dynamic thus differs from the violent shock cases, the pattern of events leading to democratization bears a striking resemblance. Nearly all these cases similarly experienced a trigger that disrupted the regime and heightened electoral competition. These triggers—some internal to electoral competition, but most from external causes—were generally not as cataclysmic as the shocks but were significant milestones nonetheless. As in the shock cases, the resulting disruption periods weakened the ruling party and widened opportunities for pro-democratic activity, including opposition party organization. Parties suddenly found themselves struggling to control elections and constrained in their abuses of power. When these push factors combined with high expectations of democratic competition, ruling parties calculated it was in their long-term interest to accept democratization.

### TRIGGERS

Ruling parties can survive with relative ease for decades. In Mexico, the PRI won every election from 1929 to 1985 with at least 73% of legislative seats and 74% of the presidential vote. Yet quite suddenly, everything changed: in 1988, an economic crisis and party split limited the PRI to bare majorities for the legislature and presidency. A period of rising party competition and institutional revision followed, playing out a "recurrent pattern in which crises led to reforms and opened space for the opposition," according to Ernesto Zedillo, the PRI's last autocratic president (interview, Bitar and Lowenthal 2015: 174). This culminated in the PRI's loss of the legislature in 1997 and presidency in 2000.

Nearly all electoral continuity cases experienced such a shift to heightened competition, followed by democratization within a few years to a decade or so. For 26 of 28 total post-1940 cases, events *external* to electoral politics, such as international shocks and economic crises, triggered this shift. This includes 7 cases in which the shift encompassed the adoption of multiparty competition. For 2 modern cases and all 9 older cases, the trigger was instead *internal* to electoral politics, such as party splits. To be sure, several modern cases also experienced gradually rising electoral competition and may have democratized without an external trigger. Yet a striking pattern emerges in which these triggers repeatedly pushed electoral regimes past what internal pressure had accomplished.

#### *Extra-Electoral Triggers*

The clearest trigger is the external turmoil that hit Marxist parties at the end of the Cold War, including those outside the Soviets' hegemonic control. This corresponds to 6 primary cases and 13 total. The Soviet Union's downfall

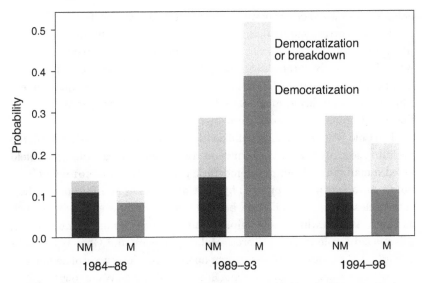

FIGURE 5.5. Non-Marxist vs. Marxist party fragility. The likelihood of democratization and party breakdown for both non-Marxist (NM) and Marxist (M) parties in three periods. Marxist parties were relatively fragile only in the five-year period surrounding the Soviet Union's fall (N = 70/66/54).

had two related effects that weakened these parties. First, starting in the late 1980s, the Soviet Union reduced the financial aid, weapons provision, and protection that had propped up allied socialist governments (McFaul 2010; Gunitsky 2017: 198–230). This led to severe economic crises in several African dictatorships, such as Cape Verde, Guinea-Bissau, and São Tomé and Príncipe. Second, Marxism's attraction as a political ideology was obliterated. The superior standards of living in Western democracies (not to mention greater freedoms) had become obvious. This naturally increased pressure to adopt successful institutions and integrate with the West (Ash 1990: 94; Miller 2016; Gunitsky 2017).[12]

The socialist leaders were well aware of the implications of communism's fall. The bloody end of Ceaușescu's government in Romania made a particular impression on African dictators, with his fate "ever-present in discussions" of the danger of delaying reforms (Reyntjens 1991: 44). Deciding to liberalize after a Tanzanian delegation witnessed Ceaușescu's fall "first hand," Julius Nyerere observed, "When you see your neighbor being shaved, you should wet your beard. Otherwise you could get a rough shave" (quoted in Levitsky and Way 2010: 16).

To see the significance of the Cold War's end, consider the 66 autocratic ruling parties in 1988 and how they fared over the following five years (1989–93). Of the 31 Marxist parties, 38.7% saw their country democratize and 51.6%

12. Even Soviet leaders embraced this logic: Foreign Minister Eduard Shevardnadze remarked to the Party Congress of 1990, "There is no sense in protecting a system that has led to economic and social ruin" (quoted in Linz and Stepan 1996: 240).

either democratized or lost power to a new autocratic regime. For non-Marxist parties, the corresponding figures are 14.3% and 28.6%. This divide was not present in other periods, as visualized in Figure 5.5. The two types of parties were about equally durable in the 1984–88 and 1994–98 periods. With Soviet decline, Marxist regimes' likelihood of losing power more than quadrupled. Their equal durability in 1994–98 likely results from the stronger Marxist parties (e.g., China, North Korea) surviving.

The Cold War's end also destabilized several non-Marxist parties. With the declining security threat, Western democracies became less willing to shield allied dictatorships from pro-democratic pressure (McFaul 2010; Gunitsky 2017). Autocrats once supported by the United States and Europe for their ruthlessness toward the Left now became expendable or even liabilities, such as South Africa's white leadership.[13] Among the electoral continuity cases, this played a role in South Korea, Malawi, Taiwan, and Ghana. The sub-Saharan African cases were also caught up in the resulting wave of democratic protests that engulfed the continent (Bratton and van de Walle 1997).

Various other triggers served a similar function, if not quite as dramatically. The most common is economic crisis, with about 40% of post-1940 cases facing a shrinking economy or inflation crisis within the five years before democratization. Besides eroding ruling parties' popularity and inspiring protest, economic declines hobble the clientelistic systems that preserve elite loyalty, encouraging ruling party defections (Greene 2007, 2010; Reuter and Gandhi 2010). Economic problems were particularly severe in Guyana, Mozambique, Indonesia, Mexico, Paraguay, and the Maldives, the last stemming from a devastating 2004 tsunami.

Civil violence destabilized several cases, with civil war in four and smaller insurgencies in another three. An assassination and coup in 1979–80 preceded an electorally competitive period in South Korea. Taiwan faced an unusual international disruption with the United States' diplomatic move to recognize China instead of Taiwan in 1979, triggering a regime crisis and an eventual liberal opening (Wu 1995; Hood 1997; Levitsky and Way 2010: 314). In Croatia, Niger, Zambia, and Guyana, the natural death of a long-tenured dictator contributed to the ruling party's fragility and electoral loss. The sudden departure of a party leader can open "the political playing field" and "increases uncertainty among the regime's rank-and-file that they have a secure future" (Howard and Roessler 2006: 372). In Croatia, for instance, the death of President Franjo Tuđman left the ruling HDZ "disoriented and divided" and "created a real opening for democracy" (Levitsky and Way 2010: 116).

---

13. A reduced fear of communism also induced many domestic elites to accept democracy. F. W. de Klerk, South Africa's last autocratic president, explained that when the Communist "threat lost the sting in its tail, it opened a window of opportunity" (interview, Bitar and Lowenthal 2015: 315).

## *Electoral Triggers*

In the competitive oligarchies and two modern cases (Uruguay 1942, Antigua and Barbuda), the shift to competitive politics was organic to electoral contestation. All were already multiparty regimes and so presented room for opposition activity and intraparty dissent. In some cases, such as the United Kingdom, party competition gradually evolved without a single signature event. This is consistent with Lindberg's (2006: 71) claim that "the electoral cycle creates a positive spiral of self-reinforcement leading to increasingly democratic elections," bolstered through institution-building, citizen acculturation, and elite accommodation.

However, citizen activism can accelerate the process. Threatening protests in the UK in 1832 encouraged limited electoral reforms (R. Collier 1999: 61–66). In Antigua and Barbuda, scandals over arms smuggling and corruption led to a 1992 general strike that convinced long-ruling dictator Vere Bird to cede power to his son, Lester.[14] Subsequent elections in 1994 and 1999 tightened given the unified opposition and new electoral commission, leading to party turnover in 2004 (Commonwealth Secretariat 2004; Schmitt 2004). As discussed below, several features of competitive elections facilitate protest.

Internal splits in ruling parties also frequently erode hegemonic party control (Brownlee 2007; Langston 2017; Madrid 2019). As Brownlee (2007: 203) puts it, "Elections alone do not capsize regimes; rather, discord among regime elites capsizes elections." Although internal regime divisions can always occur, contested elections encourage regime factions to actually defect since they have a feasible route to power (Magaloni 2006; Reuter and Gandhi 2010; Langston 2017). The disruptive effect is comparable to that of coups except that both sides typically survive and continue to divide elite and popular loyalties. This played a major role in the Netherlands, Sweden, Argentina, Uruguay 1919, Colombia, and Uruguay 1942.

Surprise electoral downturns for the ruling party can also signal the beginning of more competitive politics (Slater and Wong 2013; Pop-Eleches and Robertson 2015). In particular, they publicly demonstrate that the party is no longer impregnable, encouraging further opposition (Magaloni 2006; Domber 2013; Pop-Eleches and Robertson 2015; Knutsen, Nygård, and Wig 2017). In Denmark, for instance, the sudden rise of the peasant-allied Venstre Reform Party from 1892 to 1895 eventually deterred the recalcitrant king from propping up a series of conservative governments (Jespersen 2004).

Finally, why do external triggers play such a small role in the older cases? A potential answer is that party-specific shocks, such as economic crises, could be met with party or leader turnover rather than threatening the system itself. Like democracy, competitive oligarchy was flexible and responsive (albeit

14. The other son and former heir apparent, Vere Bird Jr., was accused of smuggling arms to the Medellín drug cartel (French 1990).

limited in who it was responding to). Even before competitive politics, monarchs could shift cabinets when individual parties failed. As a result, external crises did not erode elite control or encourage institutional reform in the same way. This was instead left to the internal evolution of electoral politics.

## PRO-DEMOCRATIC PRESSURE

Similar to the shock cases, competitive periods seriously challenge the autocratic status quo. With citizens and elites questioning regime continuity and repression constrained by the open electoral environment, democratization becomes a live goal for many actors. In particular, concerted pro-democratic activity through protests and international pressure comes to the fore. Since their democratizing effects have already been covered, I focus here on why competitive elections facilitate their emergence. I also discuss how citizen-led violence can present another source of pressure.

### Protests

By their nature, competitive electoral autocracies face bottom-up pressure from opposition parties, which have been especially effective after uniting into a single party or coalition (Howard and Roessler 2006; van de Walle 2006; Rakner and van de Walle 2009). Opposition movements have also made their mark outside the ballot box, with mass protests and strikes common features of electoral autocracies and their downfalls. From 1945 to 2015, protests or riots followed 22% of autocratic elections (using Hyde and Marinov 2012), increasing the likelihood of democratization (Bunce and Wolchik 2006, 2010; Teorell 2010). For the electoral continuity cases, 22 of 27 primary cases (30 of 37 total) featured major pro-democratic protests, with particular consequence in Belgium, South Korea, Benin, Madagascar, Indonesia 1999, and Paraguay.

How do autocratic elections contribute to mass protest? First, competitive elections necessitate a degree of openness that gives opposition groups room to organize (Meyer 2004; Chenoweth and Ulfelder 2017). Protesters can exploit various institutions—such as courts, electoral commissions, and media—that are needed to maintain the regime's electoral image and that strengthen over time (Lindberg 2006). Repression is also more costly because it damages regime legitimacy and the party's chances of competing in the future. Second, elections coordinate anti-regime organization (Bunce and Wolchik 2006; Brancati 2014; Pop-Eleches and Robertson 2015; Knutsen, Nygård, and Wig 2017). By signaling a regime's unpopularity, they can resolve uncertainties about other citizens' preferences that impede protest (Lohmann 1994; Pop-Eleches and Robertson 2015). Stolen elections are a common rallying point that drove autocratic collapse in the Philippines and the Color Revolutions of Serbia, Georgia, Ukraine, and Kyrgyzstan (Bunce and Wolchik 2006, 2010; Tucker 2007). Finally, repeated elections can raise popular demands regarding electoral conduct, increasing the likelihood of protest after violations (Lindberg 2006). As Ghana's dictator Jerry Rawlings stated, "Once you empower people and they get the taste of freedom and justice, it can be difficult to take it away from them" (interview, Bitar and Lowenthal 2015: 125).

### International Pressure

Contested elections present ideal openings for international pressure. As moments of autocratic vulnerability and potential political change, elections coordinate international attention on regime electoral behavior. Tools of international pressure include democracy assistance (Carothers 1999; Finkel, Pérez-Liñán, and Seligson 2007; Bush 2015), election monitoring (Kelley 2012; Hyde and Marinov 2014), and the conditioning of foreign aid on electoral conduct (Knack 2004; Dietrich and Wright 2014; Marinov and Goemans 2014),[15] although there are divided opinions on their effectiveness.[16] The international and protest mechanisms are also linked as international pressure is more effective when combined with electoral protest (Major 2012; Beaulieu 2014).

Although absent in the older cases, pro-democratic international pressure was a factor in 6 of 18 post-1940 primary cases (10 of 28 total). In Ghana, for instance, international relationships were "dominated by the West" and leaders believed that the continuation of aid and trade depended on further electoral reform (Handley 2013: 229). In South Korea, the regime faced U.S. pressure and sought to avoid controversy due to the upcoming Seoul Olympics in 1988 (Woo 2017).

However, external democracies often balance pro-democratic aims with concerns over stability and economic relationships (Blum 2003; Kinzer 2006; McKoy and Miller 2012; Kelley 2012). They've also too often focused on the mere presence of multiparty elections rather than deeper elements of democratic quality (Carothers 1999; Goldsmith 2008; Miller 2020b). As a result, international pressure through more diffuse channels may be more effective (Pevehouse 2005; Wejnert 2005). In Levitsky and Way's (2010) detailed account of post–Cold War electoral autocracies, the key variable explaining democratization is a country's "linkage" with the democratic West, the degree of personal interconnections through trade, travel, media, and intergovernmental organizations.[17] These linkages help spread a democratic culture, raise the cost of government abuses, and provide "critical resources to opposition and prodemocracy movements" (48).

---

15. About 12% of autocratic elections from 1945 to 2015 featured an external power influencing the election by threatening to withhold aid or another benefit (using Hyde and Marinov 2012).

16. The evidence is more positive when the regime is highly dependent on external democracies (Marinov and Goemans 2014; Gunitsky 2017).

17. A secondary role in Levitsky and Way 2010 is played by "leverage," the country's vulnerability to top-level pressure from Western countries.

*Violence*

Although protests and international pressure take precedence in these electoral openings, violent threats are also common. By definition, these ruling parties maintained uninterrupted power for four years before democratization and rarely faced threats as severe as in the shock cases. Nevertheless, many faced violent challenges from below and from fellow elites, as well as prospects of worsening challenges in the future. Of the 37 total electoral continuity cases, 4 are also civil war cases (Indonesia 1955, Sri Lanka, Mozambique, Croatia) and 3 faced lesser insurgencies (Niger, Indonesia 1999, Mexico). Of 28 post-1940 cases, 8 experienced coup attempts or plots in the 4 years preceding democratization.[18]

Other regimes faced mass political violence that threatened to spiral out of control. In Belgium, an 1893 general strike called by the Belgian Workers' Party transformed into a violent, 50,000-strong force that demanded political reforms and left leaders "genuinely harrowed by the prospect of revolution" (Luebbert 1991: 140; also Polasky 1992). Similarly, numerous states extended suffrage in the 1918–20 period out of fear their lower classes would follow Russia's example to revolution (R. Collier 1999: 84–85; Weyland 2010, 2014; Aidt and Jensen 2014; Gunitsky 2017: 60–100). In Indonesia 1999, riots in Jakarta stoked by financial crisis left more than 1,000 dead and rapidly destabilized the government (Fukuoka 2015: 427). In 1980s Madagascar, the regime faced a challenge from armed "Kung Fu societies," which claimed a membership of 10,000 concentrated around the capital (Gow 1997: 425). Ostensibly begun as Bruce Lee fan clubs, the armed groups were linked to opposition politicians and battled the regime's paramilitary forces before being violently disbanded in 1986 (Covell 1987; Levitsky and Way 2010: 277).

Mexico's pace of liberalization quickened in response to violent threats from below, which the ruling PRI sought to forestall with political concessions (Trejo 2012; Langston 2017).[19] The first major concession came in 1990 with the creation of a nominally independent electoral body, the Federal Electoral Institute (IFE), as well as several anti-fraud measures. This was a direct response to political unrest following the likely stolen 1988 election (Eisenstadt 2004; Magaloni 2006; Greene 2007). Electoral laws in 1994 and 1996 further increased electoral fairness and the IFE's independence. The armed Zapatista uprising in Chiapas in January 1994 "triggered" the electoral law adopted later that month (Diaz-Cayeros and Magaloni 2013: 263). The uprising was significant because it garnered international media attention and

18. This uses Marshall and Marshall 2018 after 1946. I also count Alfredo Baldomir's assembly dissolution in Uruguay in 1942.

19. Ernesto Zedillo, Mexico's final autocratic president, confirmed the PRI pursued liberalization from a concern that political "demands could come, at some point, in a disorderly and chaotic fashion, which [would be] . . . certainly bad for (and perhaps a mortal blow to) the party" (interview, Bitar and Lowenthal 2015: 183).

"signaled the credible possibility of violence taking root as a means to solve deadlocked political conflicts" (Diaz-Cayeros and Magaloni 2013: 251), a threat amplified by the assassination that year of the PRI's presidential candidate. The 1996 reform similarly occurred after another guerrilla movement began in Guerrero (Trejo 2012). Other major reforms in the 1994–96 period bolstered media freedom and reduced state intervention in the economy, undercutting the PRI's electoral advantages (Eisenstadt 2004; Lawson 2004; Magaloni 2006; Langston 2017).

## DEMOCRATIZATION CALCULATIONS OF AUTOCRATIC RULING PARTIES

We can now piece together the logic of electoral continuity from the party's perspective, based on the relative risks of maintaining electoral autocracy versus embracing democracy. The key mechanism is electoral confidence: The more that party leaders believe they can compete in democracy, the less threatening democratization becomes and the less resistance it should inspire. In contrast, parties with low confidence should oppose democracy, buckling only under extreme pressure or coercion.

Autocratic ruling parties would love to keep winning elections indefinitely with minimal competition, just as Mexico's PRI did for its first sixty years. However, triggering events like Soviet collapse and economic crisis disrupt hegemonic regimes, heightening competition and pro-democratic pressure. In some cases, this includes the introduction of multiparty politics. Despite the challenge, this pressure is rarely overwhelming—parties still have agency and indeed make widely varying choices in response.

Parties must then decide whether to preserve the current system or embrace greater competition, both of which carry risks. This general logic applies to multiple stages of liberalization: the acceptance of multiple parties, greater competition within autocracy, democratization, and even electoral loss. At each stage, parties trade off current threats against their long-term expected power after liberalizing. This generality is significant since we don't need to assume that liberalizing parties walk across a bright line labeled "democracy past this point." Even if they disagree on where democracy lies or they face a tougher electoral challenge than planned, confidence still explains the reforms we later recognize as democratization.

Following disruption, party leaders face major risks in struggling to maintain the status quo, both in leader security and in long-term party health. One option is increasing reliance on fraud and repression to control elections, the path taken in the Philippines 1986, Georgia 2004, and Egypt in 2011. But this erodes any remaining party legitimacy and raises the risk of a coup or protest-led overthrow, after which the party is usually uncompetitive. Regimes can also pursue a full coercive turn and end elections entirely, the path taken in

Algeria and Burma in 1990. However, this risks provoking severe international punishment and outcomes like the Algerian Civil War. In essence, parties face a dilemma in which behavior needed for control in the present compromises survival in the future.

To escape these threats, parties can instead embrace democratic competition and focus on winning through legitimate means. Although this carries some uncertainty and constrains coercive power, it becomes less risky the more confident party leaders are in their democratic electoral strength.[20] By leveling the playing field, parties accept an eventual electoral loss but get to control the transition and win without lasting damage to the party's image. As a result, democracy can maximize long-term power and security. The same logic applies to allied economic elites, who often relent to democracy only when a sufficiently competitive autocratic party can protect their interests (R. Collier 1999; Higley and Burton 2006: 101).[21] Of course, some party attributes contributing to anticipated strength in democracy could also help prolong autocracy, but the two tasks often require different tools. In fact, chapter 7's predictive modeling of a party's likelihood of turnover within autocracy and likelihood of winning power in democracy finds the two are almost uncorrelated (−0.04).

What is party confidence based on? Naturally, leaders want to believe they are revered, but there are meaningful sources of information even in self-censoring autocratic environments. Perhaps the best indicator is the party's performance in past elections, which can reveal information on party popularity despite an uneven playing field (Zeldin 1958; Magaloni 2006; Greene 2010; Miller 2015b). Parties contemplating transition have experimented with limited multiparty openings or local elections to see how they perform, as in Malawi, Ghana, Taiwan, and the Maldives. Others relied on private surveys of their popularity (Lawson 2004: 1; Handley 2013: 225; Bitar and Lowenthal 2015: 134–35). There are also objective indicators of strength and performance—such as party age, resources, and past economic growth—that predict later democratic success (Miller 2021).

Pushing forward democratization rather than waiting to be overthrown carries several political advantages and strongly predicts later democratic success (Miller 2021). Chief among the advantages is control of the transition process, including electoral timing and the adoption of favorable electoral rules. For instance, African incumbents often insisted on prohibitive party registration requirements to hamper opposition organization (Riedl 2014:

---

20. Other concerns about democracy, from radical redistribution to criminal prosecution, are similarly lessened when parties control the transition and survive into the democratic period (Baturo 2017; Albertus and Menaldo 2018; Loxton 2018).

21. See Mainwaring and Pérez-Liñán 2013: 190–92 on landed elites in El Salvador and Ziblatt 2017 on conservative party allies in the UK and Germany.

14). Elsewhere, autocrats implemented rules to fracture the opposition (Han 1988; Langston 2017: 9). By controlling the transition, a party can "create the new system according to its preferred agenda: to maintain its own power and limit the opportunities for the opposition" (Riedl 2014: 22). Further, autocratic elites can construct institutions to limit future policy change (Albertus and Menaldo 2018) and secure favors like amnesty and protections for allies in the bureaucracy and army (Mainwaring and Pérez-Liñán 2013; Friedman 2015: 298).

Another benefit of embracing democratization is that the party may be fondly remembered as a democratizer. This can help in future elections, including coalition-building (Grzymala-Busse 2002). In Indonesia, for instance, ruling party "leaders surveyed the political scene and decided that, to survive politically, they would need to burnish their own *reformasi* credentials. Only democratic elections would accomplish this" (Pepinsky 2009: 189). Avoiding the stigma of resisting democracy also helps party leaders share in international benefits and economic rewards within democracy (Baturo 2017; Albertus and Menaldo 2018).

To be clear, I do not assume that autocrats always guess right about their prospects. Many parties have made mistakes, almost always by overestimating their popular support.[22] In Poland, where the Communists failed to win a single contested seat in 1989, Przeworski (1991: 79) reports, "[Communist] Party strategists cited all kinds of reasons why Solidarity would do badly in the elections of June 1989. An eminent reformer assured me that party candidates would win a majority in the elections to the Senate." Huntington (1991: 182) notes that many "third wave democratizations moved forward on the false confidence of dictators," although his account misses how many later made comebacks. Regardless, overconfidence still induces ruling parties to embrace competition, after which parties must accept their losses (e.g., Brazil 1985) or take the extreme risk of stealing elections (e.g., the Philippines 1986).

## *Electoral Confidence and Democratization*

Let's now examine the cases in more detail. If my theory is correct, what should we see? Most importantly, we should find evidence that ruling parties' confidence in their electoral prospects facilitated their acceptance of democratization. Conversely, party leaders pessimistic about competition should fight against it. Relatedly, we should see parties gathering relevant information

22. Expectations within the party can also differ. Many soft-liner/hard-liner splits stemmed from disagreements about the party's chances in democracy (O'Donnell and Schmitter 1986; Przeworski 1991). Aleksander Kwaśniewski, a Communist reformer in Poland, described the hard-liners' opposition: "Their main argument was that if we continued with all these reforms, the Communist Party would lose power" (interview, Bitar and Lowenthal 2015: 257).

within autocracy and expending effort during transitions to maximize their chances in democracy. The alternative explanation is that democracy is forced on parties and their expectations are irrelevant, with some regaining power by happenstance. To the contrary, I show extensive evidence of party agency and the causal role of electoral confidence.

I overview four sets of cases. The first two are the electoral continuity cases in which ruling parties won their democratizing elections and those that initially lost. The former most clearly illustrate the optimistic embrace of democracy. For the latter, I show they followed the same logic and were either surprised by their initial loss or expected it but prudently anticipated later success. Third, I examine near-qualifiers for electoral continuity, namely young parties that later won democratic power and established ruling parties that failed to win power. I show many of the latter overestimated their electoral potential, encouraging them to liberalize until it was too late. Lastly, I consider the resisters, parties that fought democratization because of an anticipated inability to compete in fair elections.

## WINNERS IN THE FIRST DEMOCRATIC ELECTIONS

In most electoral continuity cases, parties expected to continue their dominance through the first democratic elections. Indeed, in 16 of 27 (59%) primary cases (56% of all 37 cases), the incumbent party won the first democratic election. These cases provide the clearest evidence of electoral confidence contributing to strategic democratization.

### Suffrage Extensions

With one exception, the pre-1940 electoral continuity cases democratized when states already enjoying robust party competition extended suffrage.[23] A recurring pattern is what Ruth Collier (1999: 55) terms the Electoral Support Mobilization path to democracy, in which reformers "calculated that a suffrage extension would play into their party's hands in the electoral arena." Thus, it was pursued with the expectation of securing power. In 8 of 9 cases (all but Sweden 1911), the party supporting reform indeed won the first post-reform election.

The prototypical case for such electoral calculations is the United Kingdom, which gradually expanded suffrage through reform bills in 1832, 1867, 1884, 1918, and 1928. In each case, reform was propelled by a competitive party seeking electoral advantage, with popular pressure a secondary factor (although most important in 1832) (R. Collier 1999: 61–66; Cunningham 2001; Machin 2001; Ziblatt 2017). The relatively modest 1832 bill was a project of the liberal Whig Party, which sought electoral reform for party advantage and to bolster the power of parliament (Machin 2001: 11–23). The result barely

23. The exception is Denmark 1901.

increased suffrage, and was not intended to seriously erode aristocratic power, but importantly redistributed parliamentary seats from overrepresented "rotten boroughs" in the countryside that advantaged the rival Conservatives.[24] In turn, the Whigs secured resounding victories in the following three elections, signaling that "the franchise they had created might well keep them in office for a very lengthy period" (Machin 2001: 23).

Following 1832, reformers failed to pass a secret ballot or a reduction in the House of Lords' power, while frustrated attempts to extend suffrage were generally "seen as methods of benefiting one or other of the parties" (Machin 2001: 37). In the late 1850s, the Conservatives' Benjamin Disraeli began pushing for suffrage reform as a way of regenerating his party: "Our party is now a corpse, but . . . [reform] might . . . put us on our legs" (quoted in Machin 2001: 53). After the Liberals (the Whigs' successor) failed to lower the wealth requirement for voting, Disraeli led a minority government starting in 1866. Appealing to working-class voters, Disraeli passed the 1867 reform bill, doubling the franchise (Rueschemeyer, Stephens, and Stephens 1992: 96).[25] Among his opponents were Conservative ministers who resigned not from principled opposition but from a belief the bill would "undermine Conservative prospects and aid the Liberals" (Machin 2001: 63). Although the Conservatives did lose again in 1868, they regained power in 1874. Meanwhile, the secret ballot was instituted in 1872 over unified Conservative opposition, as it weakened landed powers' ability to bribe and intimidate rural voters (Machin 2001: 74–83; Kasara and Mares 2017).

Reform in 1884 was more collaborative, with Liberals pushing for suffrage extension to rural working-class voters (Jones 1972; R. Collier 1999: 64) and Conservatives accepting conditional on the introduction of single-member districts (Cunningham 2001: 119–20; Machin 2001: 97–101). The resulting Arlington Street Compact was decided "with mutual advantage in mind" (Machin 2001: 98), intending to protect each party's longevity. Although two-thirds of adult men were now enfranchised, seemingly advantaging the Liberals, results were mixed (Ziblatt 2017: 111). Liberals won the first postreform election in 1885 (considered here the point of democratization) but were trounced in 1886 after a party split over Irish independence. Not until 1918 was full manhood suffrage achieved, along with the enfranchisement of women, although initially on unequal terms with men.[26]

24. Until then, tiny rural boroughs controlled by landed elites were given as much representation as entire cities (Cunningham 2001; Machin 2001). Notorious examples include Old Sarum, which had no resident voters, and Dunwich, which had largely fallen into the sea in the seventeenth century.

25. A failed amendment to the bill, offered by John Stuart Mill, was the first to propose female suffrage (Machin 2001: 64).

26. Women had to be 30 (versus 21 for men) and hold property (unlike men). Full suffrage equality was achieved in 1928.

Other cases worked similarly, with variation in the ideology and electoral support strategy of the democratizer. In 1930s Colombia, the Liberals under Alfonso López Pumarejo "pushed through a major democratization of the suffrage, and . . . made an explicit bid to capture the political support of the newly enfranchised masses" (Peeler 1977: 29), whereas the rival Conservatives regarded this as a maneuver to entrench Liberal rule (Rueschemeyer, Stephens, and Stephens 1992: 189; Kline 1995; Peeler 1977).[27] Indeed, the Liberals controlled the legislature until 1951. In Belgium 1894, the conservative Catholic Party pushed universal manhood suffrage because "the right wing could count on the mass of peasant voters who were Catholics" (Carstairs 2010: 51; also Vander Linden 1920; Witte, Craeybeckx, and Meynen 2009: 115). In turn, the Catholics retained a legislative majority until 1919. In the Netherlands, the moderate Liberal Union expanded suffrage to a quarter of men in 1887, "seeking new voters to outvote the more conservative clerical parties" (van der Laarse 2000: 65–66). A further suffrage extension followed in 1896, after which the Liberals maintained a plurality until 1909.

Lastly, in Argentina, President Roque Sáenz Peña of the conservative PAN passed a major electoral reform in 1912 with universal male suffrage, a secret ballot, and various fraud protections. Although partly in response to the Radical Civic Union (UCR), a middle-class party that had led two unsuccessful revolutions, the law's passage hinged on Peña's belief that "the political status quo would be maintained" (R. Collier 1999: 46) and conservatives "would continue to win elections" (Mainwaring and Pérez-Liñán 2013: 131; also Rock 1987: 190; Madrid 2019). In particular, Peña believed the PAN was "a tradition and an historic force [that] rules without opposition in the whole society" (Rock 1975: 35). This was overconfident: the PAN retained a plurality in 1912 but narrowly lost the legislature in 1914 and the presidency in 1916 to the UCR, which dominated elections until a 1930 coup.

### Modern Cases

The contemporary cases democratized by allowing freer competition. In 8 of the 18 post-1940 primary cases (13 of 28 total), the party then won the first democratic election.[28] Further, the parties in Uruguay, South Korea, Taiwan, Guinea-Bissau, Ghana, and Paraguay have arguably been the most successful parties in democracy. Across the 8 cases, the parties held power in 68.1% of democratic country-years up to 2018 and were competitive in 100%.

27. Ironically, one of the Conservatives' complaints was that a new system of voter ID cards would be used by Liberals to inhibit voting (Henderson 1985: 84).

28. The primary cases are Uruguay 1942, South Korea, Guinea-Bissau, Taiwan, Ghana, Paraguay, Zambia, and the Maldives. The secondary cases are Indonesia 1955, Mongolia, Bulgaria, Lithuania, and Mozambique.

Anticipating this strength, these parties approached democracy with high confidence. This made democratization the more appealing option, especially when facing protests and international pressure. The parties were also adept at controlling transitions to craft favorable institutional rules and maintain autocratic resources, maximizing "the chance of creating a one-party dominant system under democracy" (Cheng 2008: 130). Particularly in Taiwan, Ghana, Guinea-Bissau, and Zambia, regimes pursued a carefully controlled, multiyear transition to democracy.

In Taiwan, the Kuomintang (KMT) maintained single-party rule from 1949, tolerating an independent (Tangwai) movement but freezing legislative membership so that elections only occurred after a death or retirement (Hood 1997; Langston 2017: 208). The U.S. derecognition of Taiwan in 1979, plus rising discontent from native Taiwanese and the growing middle class, presented a looming crisis for single-party rule (Chao and Myers 1998; Wong 2008; Levitsky and Way 2010: 309, 314). However, party leaders were split, with hardliners "against opening the political sphere while moderates believed the KMT could continue to win in multiparty elections" (Langston 2017: 208). President Chiang Ching-kuo finally opted for a political opening in 1986–87, ending martial law and accepting the opposition DPP (Rigger 2001; Levitsky and Way 2010: 314). The opening was continued by Lee Teng-hui, the first native Taiwanese president, after Chiang's 1988 death.

At its heart, this choice stemmed from confidence in the KMT's "ability to win elections" (Levitsky and Way 2010: 357) and a strategy of "setting and enforcing the terms and pace of political change" for maximal advantage (Dickson 1997: 213). The slow reform process that followed over 1986–96 "gave the party assurances of its ability to stay in power beyond political liberalization, thus greatly facilitating the regime's willingness to undertake and oversee liberalization" (Mattlin 2011: 12–13; also Hood 1997; Cheng 2008: 130; Slater and Wong 2013). Besides securing favorable electoral rules, the KMT ensured it could retain its considerable resources, including up to $500 million a year in business revenue (Levitsky and Way 2010: 312, 315; also Greene 2007; Wong 2008).[29] In turn, the KMT won the first direct presidential election in 1996, lost the presidency and legislature in 2000–2001 after a party split and corruption scandal, and then regained both in 2008.

Ghana 1997 was a quicker process but similarly grounded in electoral confidence. It also began by testing the waters with a controlled shift to multiparty autocracy, a process that "seemed eminently reasonable, yet was carefully designed to maximize every advantage for the incumbent" (Bratton and van de Walle 1997: 172). Facing international and domestic pressure,

29. The KMT also became increasingly adept at policy competition to nullify the DPP's social welfare appeals, including a major health care extension in 1995 (Haggard and Kaufman 2008; Kosack 2014).

military dictator Jerry Rawlings announced a liberalizing plan in 1991, with a 1992 constitutional assembly (packed with regime supporters) and referendum legalizing parties (Reyntjens 1991; Bratton and van de Walle 1997: 113). Rawlings also transformed an existing mass organization into the National Democratic Congress (NDC), which dominated the (partly boycotted) 1992 elections, the first since 1979 (Levitsky and Way 2010: 300–301; Riedl 2014). Rawlings accepted elections based on a belief "he would likely win them" given his popularity, opposition weakness, and access to state resources (Handley 2013: 222; also Riedl 2014: 138), reinforced by multiple regime-commissioned surveys showing popular support (Sandbrook and Oelbaum 1999; Handley 2013: 225; Bitar and Lowenthal 2015: 134–35). As a result, democracy "offered the NDC the best of both worlds: It would retain power and enhance its international legitimacy" (Levitsky and Way 2010: 303). The NDC maintained its advantages and convincingly kept power in heavily monitored 1996 elections. Although the opposition won in 2000 with Rawlings term-limited out, the NDC rebounded in 2008 and 2012 (Handley 2013; Riedl 2014).

In South Korea 1988, the transition was propelled to a greater degree by protest, but the regime still maintained sufficient control to set the terms of democratization to the ruling party's advantage. After an assassination and coup, Chun Doo-hwan consolidated power in 1980 and formed the Democratic Justice Party (DJP), which won flawed legislative elections in 1981 and 1985.[30] A large protest movement led by the "two Kims" (rivals Kim Dae-jung and Kim Young-sam) subsequently demanded direct presidential elections. It peaked in 1987 after negotiations stalled and Roh Tae-woo, Chun's coup partner, was announced as the next president (Casper 2000a; Kim 2000; Slater and Wong 2013). Bucking international pressure, Chun arrested the protest leaders, but Roh broke with Chun and accepted their demands (Casper and Taylor 1996; Woo 2017). A central motive was Roh's recognition "that he could prevail in a free and fair election" (Adesnik and Kim 2013: 267). To assist this, the regime released Kim Dae-jung from jail to divide the opposition and adopted a single-round presidential election to allow Roh to win with only 36.6% of the vote (Han 1988; Adesnik and Kim 2013). The DJP retained the legislature in 1988, then merged with Kim Young-sam's party in 1990 to secure his presidential win (Lee 1993; Kim 2000). Kim Dae-jung followed as president in 1997. After retiring to a Buddhist monastery for two years, Chun was tried for treason and bribery (along with Roh) and initially sentenced to death, although this was later commuted (Casper and Taylor 1996; Kim 2000; Saxer 2013).

The critical role of democratic anticipation in South Korea is perhaps best illustrated by comparison with the *lack* of opening in 1979, when another

---

30. Some accounts point to 1985 as a major setback for the regime, but the DJP's vote and seat totals were virtually unchanged from 1981. However, with 35.2% of the vote, the DJP's victory clearly remained dependent on opposition fragmentation.

large protest movement pressured the Park Chung-hee regime to liberalize. In this case, the regime cracked down, triggering Park's assassination by the Korean CIA. When the succeeding regime signaled a liberalizing turn, this was stopped by the Chun-led coup and further repression in 1980, including a massacre of several hundred protesters in Kwangju (Savada and Shaw 1990). Two features of the expected aftermath of liberalization help to explain the divergence. First, the 1979–80 protest movement was led by students and left-ists, which prompted domestic and U.S. fears of policy radicalism if democracy took root (McKoy and Miller 2012; Adesnik and Kim 2013). Second, Park's ruling party was not well-positioned to retain power (Adesnik and Kim 2013: 267–68). Facing a unified opposition, it failed to gain even a plurality of votes in the 1978 legislative election, with a seat majority secured only with presidential appointees. Further, Park's narrow presidential win in 1971 (over Kim Dae-jung) had led the regime to abandon direct presidential elections. In 1987–88, in comparison, a more moderate democratic movement and Roh's prospects against a split opposition left the regime "confident that neither the economic nor the diplomatic pillar of [Chun's] agenda would crumble as a result of a democratic transition" (Adesnik and Kim 2013: 285).

## LATER WINNERS

A tougher test of the theory concerns parties that initially lost. I examined each electoral continuity case in which parties lost the first democratic election to see whether they approached the election with high confidence. In particular, I looked for private statements of rulers' expectations,[31] expressions of shock after losing, and contextual evidence like recent victories or strong polling. Of the 11 primary cases (16 total), in 5 (8 total) I found clear evidence of the party entering with confidence and miscalculating (Sweden, Cape Verde, Niger, Indonesia 1999, Mexico).[32]

For instance, Cape Verde's PAICV was "completely confident of victory" (Lobban 1995: 116) and "could scarcely conceal their shock" after losing in 1991 (Meyns 2002). Outgoing prime minister Pedro Pires reported, "We never imagined we could lose," while PAICV official Georgina de Mello noted "even our most pessimistic forecasts predicted victory" (quoted in Traore 1991: 11). It was precisely this overconfidence that led the PAICV to initiate the opening, attempting to weaken the opposition by grabbing the pro-democratic mantle (Traore 1991; Lobban 1995: 116–17; Meyns 2002). The party won back the legislature in 2001, with Pires winning the 2001 presidential election by 12 votes (a margin of 0.008%)!

---

31. By "private statements," I'm distinguishing rulers' opinions given behind the scenes (such as at party meetings or to confidantes) from campaign boasts or empty reassurances to allies, i.e., not all claims are taken at face value.

32. The secondary cases are Poland, Sri Lanka (1994 election), and Albania.

In most cases, this confidence was far from delusional. In Niger, despite failing to control the national conference that designed electoral reforms and having its leader barred from the presidential election, the ruling MNSD remained the advantaged party entering the 1993 elections given its continued support from business and the opposition's lack of experience (Gervais 1997; Villalón and Idrissa 2005). As Ibrahim and Souley (1998: 151) explain, "The MNSD was a party that assumed that it was destined to win the scheduled elections that were to mark the Nigerien transition. This is because it had within it almost all the people of wealth and influence in the country. Its self-assured campaign slogan was *nassara*, meaning victory." Indeed, the party narrowly lost the presidential contest (after leading in the first round) and won a legislative plurality but was blocked from forming a government by an opposition coalition. The MNSD regained legislative power in 1995, then won both the presidency and legislature in the next democratic elections in 1999.[33]

This leaves 6 primary cases (8 total) in which parties expected to lose the first democratic election and did so.[34] Nevertheless, their acceptance of defeat was logically sound given a long-term perspective, assuming party leaders didn't expect rivals to consolidate hegemonic control. Maintaining their democratic commitments retained their political influence within democracy and secured future opportunities to contest for power, when persistent advantages could win out over inexperienced newcomers. In fact, a period of loss and reinvigoration may be quite attractive to party reformers (Grzymala-Busse 2002). This is doubly true when leaders expect the immediate post-democratization period to be economically or politically unstable, such as during post-communist economic liberalization. An early crisis under the opposition provides the autocratic old guard an ideal chance to rebound as representatives of stability and expertise, as occurred in Poland, Albania, Mexico, and Madagascar. Indeed, the wait to victory was generally brief for these parties. In 7 of 11 primary cases (9 of 16 total), the party (or party leader in Benin) regained power in the second cycle of elections, with all but one back in power by the third cycle.

São Tomé and Príncipe 1991 illustrates how patience can pay off in later democratic power, for both parties and individuals. From 1975, the country was led by Pinto da Costa's single-party MLSTP, which won independence from Portugal. In 1978, the government defeated the attempted invasion of a mercenary army led by exile Carlos da Graça (an MLSTP cofounder who

---

33. The 1999 elections followed a 1996 coup, an electoral authoritarian interregnum under coup leader Ibrahim Baré Maïnassara, his 1999 assassination during a coup, and a quick restoration of democracy.

34. The primary cases are Benin, São Tomé and Príncipe, Guyana, Madagascar, Malawi, and Antigua and Barbuda. The secondary cases are Hungary and Croatia.

opposed the party's socialist turn), followed by the ouster and exile of Prime Minister Miguel Trovoada for perceived opposition (Seibert 2002; Francisco and Agostinho 2011). Incredibly, both were allowed back prior to democratization (with Graça becoming a government minister) and both then won power within democracy. After an economic crisis and ruling party split in 1990, the regime was in disarray (Brooke 1988; Francisco and Agostinho 2011). A breakaway faction of MLSTP dissidents won free elections in 1991, with Trovoada winning the presidency unopposed after Pinto da Costa chose not to run (Reyntjens 1991: 53). Despite this disastrous 1989–91 period, the MLSTP's eclipse was brief, as it won local elections in 1992, regained the legislature in 1994 (with Graça as prime minister), and won again in 1998 and 2002. Pinto da Costa also engineered a remarkable comeback, winning the presidency in 2011. Persistent parties and leaders can achieve surprising turns of fortune in democracy.

Guyana 1992 is the lone electoral continuity case with the party or leader failing to win in the first three electoral cycles, but it is no exception to the power logic. The long-ruling PNC lost in 1992 but by less than 10% of legislative seats. It would also lose the following four elections, finally regaining power by a single seat in 2015. The losses were unsurprising given that the PNC primarily represents the Afro-Guyanese minority, whereas its longtime rival, the PPP, represents the Indo-Guyanese majority (Premdas 1995; Singh 2008; Hinds 2011). As a result, the democratic opening was opposed by "hardliners in the PNC who viewed free and fair elections as a sure recipe for the party's removal from office . . . [and] were 'traumatized' and 'puzzled by its underlying political calculations'" (Hinds 2011: 19). Unlike these "antediluvian political dinosaurs" (to quote a newspaper editorial; "Thank you Jimmy" 1990), the incumbent president Desmond Hoyte believed he could leverage his economic reforms and record of growth to win in 1992. Combined with domestic pressure and a shutoff of American aid, Hoyte's self-assurance encouraged him to accept free elections over several of his party leaders' objections. Arguing past elections were reasonably fair, he claimed he "had no doubt of the PNC being returned to power" (Premdas 1999: 150) and "predicted a 'crushing defeat' of his rivals at the polls" (Khan 1992). Alas, it was not to be, but the sentiment influenced his acceptance of democracy. This includes his opposition to an aborted attempt by PNC leaders to challenge the 1992 election results, which allowed Hoyte to maintain his pro-democratic mantle for future elections (Hinds 2005: 80). Guyana thus represents a partial case of near-term confidence, with the PNC's consistent performance[35] and 2015 win supporting the role of expected power in democratizing calculations.

---

35. Its coalition only once dropped below a 40% vote share in the last seven elections (1992–2020).

## NEAR-QUALIFIERS AND FALSE EXPECTATIONS

Looking solely at established ruling parties that successfully regained power within democracy undercounts the number that *expected* to seriously compete and democratized with this in mind. I count 20 other cases (including 5 of the 12 path outliers) as resembling the electoral continuity path. All 20 feature autocratic parties that acceded to democratization (i.e., without being violently overthrown) but fail some other requirement. Exactly half gained power within democracy and half did not. In nearly every case, the expectation of holding some power within democracy shaped their responses to democratization.

Ten cases feature an autocratic party or coalition that later won democratic power but was not sufficiently long-lived within autocracy to qualify.[36] For instance, in El Salvador, death-squad leader Robert D'Aubuisson founded ARENA in 1981 with military and business leaders (Ladutke 2004). Although it lost the initial democratic election in 1984 (to the civilian junta leader from 1980 to 1982), ARENA won the legislature in 1988 and controlled the presidency from 1989 to 2009 (Wood 2003). Similarly, Guatemala's MLN, founded by coup leader Castillo Armas, relented to democratization in 1958 after Castillo Armas's assassination and a disputed election (Schlesinger and Kinzer 1982; Gleijeses 1991; Yashar 1997). It reclaimed power in 1961.[37]

Cuba 1940 presents another interesting case. After a highly unstable 1933–34 period featuring multiple coups, military dictator Fulgencio Batista (a sergeant stenographer when he led his first coup) ruled through a "succession of puppet presidents from the ranks of the old politicos, each of whom was removed as soon as he tried to assert any degree of independence" (Halperin 1970: 17; also Alexander 1973; Duff 1985). Lacking a civilian base or his own party, Batista crafted several shifting party coalitions that won highly flawed elections in 1936 and 1938. His choice to allow constitutional assembly elections in 1939 and a democratic constitution in 1940 stemmed from both electoral confidence and other strategic considerations. Batista "believed he could risk playing the democratic statesman and restore legitimate government" (Ameringer 2000: 13), as he was "feeling politically secure and [wished] to improve his image in the United States and to align with reformist tendencies emerging in Latin America" (Del Aguila 1984: 26). The calculation paid off as Batista (then allying with the Communists) won the presidency in 1940,

---

36. All are primary coup, civil war, or foreign war cases. These are Cuba 1940, Panama 1952, Guatemala 1958, Guatemala 1966, Honduras 1971, El Salvador 1984, Nicaragua 1984, Suriname 1991, Lesotho 2002, and Sierra Leone 2002.

37. The same pattern recurred a few years later, when a 1963 coup ousted the 1958 presidential winner, followed by a military party creation (PID), a 1966 transition, and the PID's return to power in 1970.

although the opposition (led by Ramón Grau, whom Batista overthrew in 1934) won the legislature.

Clearly, such cases can follow the same logic as the main electoral continuity cases if leaders correctly anticipate the success of their young parties. As with Batista, the same applies to individual *dictators* who later gain power, often with entirely new parties founded in democracy, as occurred in Bolivia, Guatemala, the Maldives, and Fiji. In still other cases, military governments acceded to democracy believing a new party, created or revived for democratic elections, would win and protect its interests.[38]

Ten other cases feature a sufficiently long-ruling party that acceded to democratization and continued to compete but failed to regain power.[39] Many of these parties expected to win, at least when liberalization began, encouraging them to accept an electoral opening over which they subsequently lost control. This logic held even in cases with a less consensual endgame: in the Philippines 1986, Ferdinand Marcos's New Society Movement (KBL), formed in 1978, was a weak party mainly held together by graft. Facing international pressure, Marcos opted for snap elections in February 1986, "confident that he would win handily and so prove his democratic bona fides to skeptical Americans" (Ackerman and Duvall 2000: 379). Believing the opposition was too divided, Marcos "fully expected to remain in power" (Schock 2005: 76) and "presumably never contemplated electoral defeat," according to the American ambassador (Armacost 1987: 302). This was mere delusion, as Marcos was extremely unpopular and thus was forced to steal the election (Ackerman and Duvall 2000; Franco 2001; Thompson 2002). KBL limped on, most recently getting 0.61% of legislative votes in 2016.

Brazil's military government stands out for its hubris, despite repeated signals of electoral vulnerability. After a 1964 coup, the military created a controlled two-party system with the ruling party ARENA and the opposition Brazilian Democratic Movement (MDB) (Stepan 1988, 1989; Hunter 1997; Fausto and Fausto 2014). Following a repressive period targeting labor, President Ernesto Geisel moved toward softer rule in 1974 out of "confidence that the regime could win competitive elections" (Bitar and Lowenthal 2015: 6). Given ARENA's overwhelming victory in 1970, "no one expected the opposition to win" in 1974 and the MDB even "seriously contemplated its own dissolution" (Binnendijk 1987: 260). The election results "stunned everyone" (Huntington 1991: 175), with the MDB gaining 48% of the lower house vote

38. This strategy is risky: in Honduras 1982 and Turkey 1983, militaries struck deals with parties to retain significant political control, but those parties unexpectedly ended up losing (Casper and Taylor 1996: 97, 101).

39. These are Brazil 1985, Czechoslovakia 1990, Bangladesh 1991, Central African Republic 1993, South Africa 1994, Senegal 2000, Serbia 2000, Peru 2001, Kenya 2002, and Pakistan 2008. Significantly, five of these are non-path cases, representing nearly half of these outliers.

and winning the Senate. Despite the evident danger, opposition leader (and later president) Fernando Cardoso argues the military was unwilling to "let go of the appearance of liberal institutions" and the use of elections as a release valve for social pressure (Bitar and Lowenthal 2015: 12).

After another narrow escape in 1978, the military turned to institutional reforms designed to preserve its power but which merely accelerated the path to democracy (Huntington 1991: 183; Hunter 1997). The first tack, under President João Figueiredo, was to allow multiparty elections to split the opposition (Hoge 1981; Hunter 1997). Although most MDB members shifted to the new PMDB, several other opposition parties did form, including the labor-centric Workers' Party that dominated Brazilian politics in the 2000s. ARENA also transformed into the Democratic Social Party (PDS). Ahead of 1982 elections, PDS "used every possible legal instrument to secure a priori advantage" (Przeworski 1988: 69), even making sure that beans (a staple of the Brazilian diet) were selling at 40% of their normal price (Fraser 1982). Despite narrowly losing its legislative majority, the military "appeared satisfied with the overall outcome," as it expected to retain an electoral college majority for the indirect presidential election in 1985 (Hoge 1982). Thus, the presidency was "still firmly in the grip of the military" (Fraser 1982).

In two different spheres, democratic actors then took advantage of the liberal opening to derail the regime's plans. First, the opposition built a mass movement pushing for direct presidential elections ("Diretas Já"), organizing strikes and rallying nearly one million protesters in 1984 (Hunter 1997; R. Collier 1999: 134–38; Fausto and Fausto 2014). Already facing economic problems, the military compromised by promising that electoral college members would have a free choice, believing it could easily control the vote (Hoge 1982; Casper and Taylor 1996: 111). Second, after years of tension, the ruling party split, with the liberal wing forming the PFL. In turn, controversy over the military's presidential nominee led to numerous electoral college defections to the PMDB's candidate, Tancredo Neves, including his running mate, José Sarney (Sun-Sentinel Wires 1985; Hunter 1997). This was the fatal stroke, as Neves easily won. Tragically, he was unable to serve due to ill health and Sarney was inaugurated as president in March 1985. The military relented with assurances of no human rights prosecutions and "unfettered influence in key policy areas" (Casper and Taylor 1996: 109–12; also Stepan 1988; Hagopian 1996). Subsequently, the PMDB dominated the 1986 legislative election and remains a major party, controlling the presidency from 2016 to 2018. The PDS rapidly declined, dissolving through merger in 1993, while the PFL remained competitive through the 2000s.

Even when parties did not realistically expect to win power, their survival as political parties helped to smooth their acceptance of democracy, especially where they bargained out favorable electoral and institutional arrangements. In South Africa, the white-supremacist National Party (NP) famously agreed in 1993 to free elections and an end to apartheid after years of grueling, stop-and-start negotiations with the African National Congress (ANC). The NP's return to power was unlikely, and indeed their high point was 20% of the vote in 1994, after which the party abruptly declined. As Friedman (2015: 293–94) writes, "Both sides assumed that the ANC would win a free election. . . . This made for a difficult transition." However, several elements of the agreement allowed the NP to keep a fleeting share of power. Perhaps most critical to their acceptance was the "sunset clause" mandating a five-year power-sharing government (although it would collapse after two years).[40] Other favorable provisions included proportional representation, constitutional guarantees for minority rights and property, and employment protections for the predominantly white bureaucracy. Forced to accept majority rule, "NP strategists concluded that their control over the military, police, and bureaucracy—as well as skills and capital—would ensure continued white influence" (Friedman 2015: 298). Further, the NP's continuation as a party led them to expect residual power in coalition governments and at the provincial level. Ultimately, the party was outbid as a government critic by the Democratic Alliance and (after an uninspired name change to the New National Party) formally merged in 2005 with its old enemy, the ANC.

## RESISTERS

Finally, we consider the autocrats who recognized that democracy meant their oblivion. In total, 64 transitions featured an autocratic ruling party or coalition that acceded to democracy without being violently overthrown. In 47 (73%), the party won power in democracy, a remarkable record of success.[41] This leaves 17 unsuccessful parties, including the 10 long-ruling parties mentioned above.

Although some of these party leaders incorrectly believed they would be competitive, especially at the start of liberalization, most had no such illusions. As expected, they fiercely resisted democratization until their hands were forced by internal weakness and international and domestic pressure. Across the 17 failed cases, 14 featured major pro-democracy protests—particularly robust in South Korea 1960 and Serbia 2000—and 6 featured strong pro-democratic international pressure.[42] Eleven fit a violent shock path, including civil war in 6. Several cases also featured the military abandoning the

---

40. In a grand irony given the NP's use of Communist fears to prop up their rule, the sunset clause was first proposed by Joe Slovo, the head of the South African Communist Party (Sparks 1996: 181).

41. In all but one (Spain 1977), the party competed electorally within democracy. Of the parties in power for at least four years, 37 of 51 (73%) won power in democracy.

42. The lone case with neither is Senegal 2000, an exceptional transition in many respects.

dictator, as in South Korea, the Philippines, Bangladesh 1991, Serbia, and Ecuador 2003.

The Central African Republic's path to democracy is a model of autocratic intransigence. After a 1981 coup, military dictator André Kolingba formed the Central African Democratic Rally (RDC) in 1986. A sham referendum that year made it the sole legal party and affirmed Kolingba's presidency, followed by assembly elections in 1987 (Kalck 2005). Young and little more than Kolingba's personal vehicle, the RDC was ill-suited to real competition. As a result, RDC leaders met the democratic storm sweeping Africa in 1990 by "explicitly rul[ing] out multi-partyism as 'unsuitable'" (Reyntjens 1991: 46), with Kolingba proclaiming his country "not ready for multiparty democracy" (Bratton and van de Walle 1997: 108). Domestic and international audiences disagreed: mass protests and a reported French search "for a successor to General Kolingba" forced the RDC to allow multiple parties in 1991 (Reyntjens 1991: 46). In the 1992 presidential election, Kolingba's dismal performance (possibly as low as 2%) prompted him to nullify the election and extend his rule by fiat (Bratton and van de Walle 1997: 203). Intense international pressure and rising coup threats forced Kolingba to allow new elections in August 1993, in which he placed fourth and the RDC gained 15% of the legislature (Kalck 2005; O'Toole 2018). His move to again nullify the result through the courts was dissuaded with an immediate shutoff of French aid (O'Toole 2018: 118). Kolingba wasn't done, as he supported mutinies in 1996–97 and a coup attempt in 2001 (O'Toole 2018).

*Madagascar: Resistance without Future Competition*

Madagascar further illustrates the resistance that dictators will mount to democratization if denied the prospect of competition, although it ultimately qualified for electoral continuity. Didier Ratsiraka, nicknamed the "Red Admiral" for his ardent socialism and naval background, ruled Madagascar following a 1975 coup. In 1976, he founded a socialist party, later called the Association for the Rebirth of Madagascar (AREMA), that ruled uncontested until opposition parties were legalized in 1990. The fledgling opposition, initially organized as a religious coalition, formed the Active Forces movement and led a series of crippling general strikes and mass protests that grew to as large as 400,000 (Allen 1995; Gow 1997; Levitsky and Way 2010: 276–82). Ratsiraka responded with violence, but under French pressure conceded to a political reform package in May 1991 and a dismissal of his cabinet and prime minister (Gow 1997). The final break was an August march on Ratsiraka's private bunker that was dispersed by artillery and a helicopter gunship, leaving 50 dead and prompting military defections (Allen 1995; Gow 1997: 435). With opposition groups controlling large swathes of territory and Active Forces leader and surgical professor Albert Zafy declaring himself head of a parallel government,

Ratsiraka was forced into a transitional power-sharing deal in October 1991 (Covell 1987; Gow 1997).

After this initial capitulation, President Ratsiraka and his allies returned to violence to influence constitutional negotiations in the National Forum. In March 1992, an attempted assassination of Zafy failed when a truck loaded with containers of cooking gas and gasoline rammed into his home and exploded, but the fire failed to spread (Gow 1997: 437). A month later, a pro-Ratsiraka crowd broke into a constitution-drafting meeting, provoking a firefight (Gow 1997: 436).

The next crisis for Ratsiraka occurred when the National Forum moved to ban him from running for president. Faced with permanently losing power, Ratsiraka shifted to outright rebellion as "he worked secretly against the interim Government by financing instability" and encouraging ethnic separatism (Gow 1997: 437). Ratsiraka "opened a private, powerful radio station which jammed the national transmitter in Antananarivo, and set up his own television station to carry personal messages to the people," successfully leading three coastal provinces to declare autonomy (Gow 1997: 437). Like Milton's Satan, Ratsiraka preferred to rule in Hell than to serve in Heaven. Burdened with an already weak state, the opposition agreed to let Ratsiraka run for president.

Zafy and the opposition emerged victorious in the inaugural multiparty elections in 1993, with Zafy defeating Ratsiraka 2-to-1 in the second round of the presidential election. Zafy's party also won a legislative plurality but in a highly fragmented parliament. Political deadlock combined with severe economic problems, leading to Zafy's impeachment in 1996. Ratsiraka then got his revenge, narrowly defeating Zafy for the presidency in 1996 (although Zafy claimed fraud, courts upheld the win) and expanding his power in a 1998 referendum (Marcus 2004; Levitsky and Way 2010: 276–82). The triumph was short-lived, as Ratsiraka was overthrown in a 2002 revolt by Antananarivo's mayor, Marc Ravalomanana, after a disputed presidential election (Marcus and Razafindrakoto 2003; Marcus 2004). In turn, another Antananarivo mayor, Andry Rajoelina, rebelled in 2009. With civil war looming, there followed an extraordinary crisis mediation featuring all four leaders—Ratsiraka, Zafy, Ravalomanana, and Rajoelina—that established a nominal power-sharing deal but essentially affirmed Rajoelina's rise to power (Bearak 2009). Ratsiraka received amnesty from prior corruption charges and returned from exile in France.

Madagascar fits both sides of this book's theory: extreme insecurity within autocracy (combining mass protest, international pressure, and elite defections, including a 1990 coup attempt) that pushed Ratsiraka and the prospect of democratic power that pulled him. When the latter was threatened, Ratsiraka was willing to undermine the state and risk civil war rather than fully give up power. In contrast, with the accurate expectation of later competing in elections, Ratsiraka stepped down in 1993. In every other moment of serious challenge—the 1991 protests and the 2002 revolt—it took overwhelming coercive force, including his abandonment by the military, to convince Ratsiraka to sacrifice power. The Red Admiral's machinations display well how power calculations influence democratization.

## Summary

This chapter detailed the electoral continuity path to democratization, characterized foremost by ruling parties' confidence in their retention of power within democracy. When parties believed they would successfully compete in fair elections—in competitive oligarchies like the UK and the Netherlands, and modern electoral autocracies like Taiwan, Ghana, and South Korea—they willingly acceded to democracy and remained significant political actors. In other transitions, such as the Philippines and Brazil, parties overestimated their chances and liberalized until it was too late. In contrast, parties in Central African Republic, Serbia, and Bangladesh recognized their deficiencies and resisted democratization until their hands were forced.

In addition, nearly all electoral continuity cases featured distinctive periods of heightened competition before democratization, mainly brought on by external causes like economic and geopolitical crises. These periods provided openings for pro-democratic protest, international sanctions, and threats of violence. Collectively, this pressure supplied a push factor that undermined autocratic stability and induced parties to accept their share of democratic power. Like the shock cases, we find a distinctive combination of triggering events, pro-democratic activity, and power calculations leading to democratization.

# CHAPTER SIX

# Other Autocracies

THIS CHAPTER TACKLES all remaining autocracies. I first discuss the twelve democratic transitions that do not satisfy the strict criteria for the paths. Several are near-misses that fit the underlying logic of minimal power loss from democratization, while others are true outliers. After discussing commonalities across the outliers, I examine whether other crises should be added to the paths but argue none add much explanatory power.

Next, I overview all cases of non-democratization, emphasizing how this book's framework can explain many cases of stability. Specifically, most non-democratizing countries lack both a recent shock and a durable ruling party, making their stability expected. However, many had shocks or competitive parties and yet failed to democratize, prompting the question of what other conditions are needed (further explored in chapter 8).

## Outlier Transitions

Democratization is a complex, multidimensional process, with every case marked by idiosyncrasies. It's therefore unsurprising if we can't fit every case into a parsimonious set of categories. This is certainly true here, as 12 of 139 transitions (listed in Table 6.1) fail to satisfy any of the six criteria that define this book's paths. However, I argue that four cases closely fit the paths logic. The remaining outliers are a mix of pacted and protest-driven cases, which still illustrate the importance of crises and weakness. I further discuss the commonality of protests and uncontrolled elections among the outliers, adding clarity to these alternative routes to democratization. Lastly, I overview additional shock candidates but show they played little role among the outliers.

**Table 6.1.** Outliers, 1800–2014

**Protest/Opposition-Led**

| | | |
|---|---|---|
| France 1848 | South Korea 1960 | Nepal 1991 |
| Central African Rep. 1993 | Peru 2001 | Kenya 2002 |
| Georgia 2004 | | |

**Pacted/Regime-Led**

| | | |
|---|---|---|
| Peru 1956 | Brazil 1985 | Uruguay 1985 |
| Chile 1990 | South Africa 1994 | |

## NEAR-MISS TRANSITIONS

Although this is somewhat impressionistic, I count four outliers as "near-misses" that illustrate the paths' essential logic: Peru 1956, South Korea 1960, Brazil 1985, and Georgia 2004. The most straightforward is South Korea, which was seven years removed from a devastating civil war that caused nearly one million civilian casualties (Han 1974; Savada and Shaw 1990). Although the war was slightly too distant and not a true defeat, its lingering effects contributed to regime weakness and vulnerability to U.S. pressure (Trumbull 1960; Kim 1996).[1]

Five outliers had a durable ruling party that failed to regain power: Brazil, Central African Republic, South Africa, Peru 2001, and Kenya. Of these, Brazil 1985 is the only case that fits the electoral continuity logic, with its military rulers' consistent overconfidence motivating them to liberalize from the 1970s (see last chapter). In South Africa and Kenya, party leaders believed they could retain vestiges of power, but opposition and international pressure were more decisive (Casper and Taylor 1996: 86).[2] In Central African Republic and Peru, the parties were extremely weak, although a spiritual successor in Peru won a legislative majority in 2016.

Like many shock cases, Georgia 2004 was driven by state weakness and elite divisions, with the country in a state of virtual civil war for over a decade (Hale 2005; Levitsky and Way 2010: 220–28; Welt 2010; Way 2015: 153–55). Immediately after independence, a bloody 1991 coup ousted the elected president Zviad Gamsakhurdia, who fled to Chechnya to form a government-in-exile. Simultaneously, Russian forces aided separatist movements in South Ossetia and Abkhazia, leading to a costly Georgian defeat in 1993 and de facto independence for both. Taking advantage of state weakness, a warlord took control of the Adjara region and Gamsakhurdia returned to conquer much of

---

1. For more on South Korea 1960, see chapter 2.

2. South Africa and Kenya also followed extensive civil violence, but connected to fights for political equality, violating the civil war criteria.

western Georgia, although he was defeated with Russian assistance (Curtis 1994). Meanwhile, former Soviet foreign minister Eduard Shevardnadze consolidated power, founding the Union of Citizens of Georgia (UCG) and officially becoming president in a flawed 1995 election. Yet the "state remained strikingly weak" and violence crackled on, with attempted assassinations of Shevardnadze in 1995 and 1998, extended paramilitary activity, and a failed invasion to retake Abkhazia in 1998 (Levitsky and Way 2010: 222; also King 2001).

Corruption and rising repression led to several elite defections from UCG in 2001, including Minister of Justice Mikheil Saakashvili and the chairman of the parliament Zurab Zhvania, both of whom founded new parties. This led to the UCG's implosion, culminating in its winning 70 of 4,850 seats in 2001 local elections (Welt 2010: 159). Starved of elite supporters, Shevardnadze allied with the "widely reviled" strongman ruler of Adjara, who promised to help organize electoral fraud (Welt 2010: 156, 167). The 2003 legislative election was flagrantly stolen, with thousands of opposition voters mysteriously purged from the voter rolls, prompting international rebukes and rising opposition (Bunce and Wolchik 2011: 148–76). Yet protests remained fairly small (Levitsky and Way 2010: 225; Welt 2010: 156). What decided the regime's collapse was not opposition numbers but "party and state weakness" (Levitsky and Way 2010: 224) and the defection of security forces, who stepped aside as protesters stormed parliament while Shevardnadze was speaking (Mydans 2003; Welt 2010: 176–78). He was forced to resign and 2004 elections were won by Saakashvili, Shevardnadze's former protégé forty years his junior (Fairbanks 2004; Welt 2010).

Throughout the 1991–2003 period, Georgia was a "weak state scrambling to maintain order" (Welt 2010: 155), which meant "the political arena was wide open to competition and protest" (Welt 2010: 163). The 2003 Rose Revolution was the culmination of this opening, organized by a small but determined protest movement under Saakashvili. As the post-Gamsakhurdia outcome shows, this opening could as easily have ended in anarchy or renewed authoritarianism but was pushed toward democracy by international pressure and an influential protest model from Serbia 2000 (Fairbanks 2004; Bunce and Wolchik 2006, 2011: 148–76; Levitsky and Way 2010: 220–28). Although too distant from the 1991–93 civil war to qualify as a shock case, Georgia illustrates the core logic of state weakness, disruption, and opportunities grasped by pro-democratic actors.

Peru 1956 is a near-qualifier for both the post-coup and electoral continuity paths. In 1948, a military coup under Manuel Odría aimed to repress the leftist APRA party (Masterson 1991: 114–15; Hunefeldt 2004). Odría subsequently won a 1950 election by disqualifying the main opposition candidate (Werlich 1978: 249). A repressive period yielded to a populist turn, weakening Odría's support from landed oligarchs. This combined with opposition from military factions concerned that Odría aimed to permanently keep power, prompting an attempted coup by the minister of war (Astiz 1969: 140; Masterson 1991: 144–46). Rising popular pressure, including land seizures and labor organization, added to Odría's vulnerability (Cleaves and García 1983: 215). Desperate and isolated, Odría "resorted to gangsterish tactics" but "with scant elite or military support" was forced to hold 1956 elections (McClintock 1999: 320). Despite clear weaknesses and signs that "General Odría never succeeded in stabilizing his regime" (Kantor 1969b: 476), the 1948 coup is judged too causally distant to count this as post-coup.

In the 1956 presidential election, Odría attempted to disqualify a major opposition figure, Fernando Belaúnde, but relented after protest threats (Masterson 1991: 148). Surprisingly, the military's favored candidate, former president Manuel Prado, won after making a deal to legalize APRA in exchange for its support (Kantor 1969b: 476; Masterson 1991: 147). Odría remained active in electoral politics, founding a new party in 1961. In 1962, after an inconclusive presidential election, Odría nearly became president in a deal with APRA, but this was blocked by a military coup. Since Odría didn't have a real party from 1948 to 1956, this cannot qualify for electoral continuity but bears some resemblance given Prado's victory and Odría's electoral prospects.

## TRUE OUTLIERS

This leaves eight "true outliers" without a major preceding shock or a ruling party capable of regaining power. This is a small collection indeed, representing less than 6% of all transitions. Nevertheless, it's worth examining whether these cases fall into any illuminating patterns. For starters, none were primarily pushed by regime elites; among all outliers, I credit only Peru 1956 and Brazil as transitions "from above." Instead, the eight resulted from either pacts or bottom-up pressure.

Three cases (Uruguay, Chile, South Africa) nicely conform to the "transitional theory" of O'Donnell and Schmitter (1986), Przeworski (1991), Colomer (1991), and others. In each, regime hard-liners and soft-liners split over liberalization, domestic opposition rose, and soft-liners and moderates bargained out democratic pacts. In South Africa and Uruguay, regime elites oversaw a lengthy, determined reform process, whereas the capitulation in Chile was more sudden. In each, regime choices were shaped by popular pressure. In Uruguay and Chile, military rulers lost major plebiscites that signaled mass opposition.[3] Mass violence also engulfed South Africa and threatened Chile, where Communists attempted to assassinate President Pinochet and compiled a large

3. A South African plebiscite signaled white opposition to apartheid, but in 1992, well into the negotiation period.

arms stockpile confiscated in 1986 (Arriagada 1988; Huneeus 2007). As opposed to purely top-down or bottom-up transitions, these involved joint activity. In turn, the pacts had highly favorable terms for outgoing rulers, with Pinochet remaining head of the army until 1998 and a power-sharing deal in South Africa.

The remaining five cases (France, Nepal, Central African Republic, Peru, Kenya) were propelled from below by mass protest movements. International pressure also played a major role in Central African Republic and Kenya. As expected, rulers relented from a position of weakness, stemming from elite splits in Peru and Kenya and economic crises in France and Central African Republic. In Nepal, a 1988–90 diplomatic crisis with India "weakened the government and strengthened the leverage of the opposition movement" (Schock 2005: 136). Despite this weakness, the regimes hardly went willingly. In 1990, Nepal's regime repeatedly fired on demonstrators, "ushering in a period of terror unprecedented in recent Nepalese history" (Schock 2005: 124). In Kenya, Moi used extensive ethnic violence to divide and intimidate the opposition (Baker 1998: 122–24; Klopp and Zuern 2007: 137–38; Levitsky and Way 2010: 271). Lastly, in Peru, the regime repressed protests over a fraudulent 2000 election until the release of a video showing the intelligence chief bribing an opposition legislator, which rapidly disintegrated elite cohesion (Carrión 2006; Burt 2007). President Fujimori was forced to resign by fax while hiding in Japan, although the congress ignored this and impeached him for "moral incapacity" (Conaghan 2005: 241).

The cases that most clash with this book's power logic are probably France, Uruguay, Chile, Nepal, and Central African Republic. In each, rulers lost significant power and didn't face major elite divisions or large-scale violence leading up to democratization.[4] Rather, events like economic crisis (in Uruguay, Central African Republic, and France, which faced a financial crisis and spike in food prices) and the Soviet collapse (affecting Chile, Nepal, and Central African Republic) combined with domestic and international pressure to force regime change. Thus, the path categories and the minimization of power loss are not *absolutely* necessary, but democratization outside them is very rare and still requires a significant crisis.

Lastly, it's worth noting that many of the outliers have had a disproportionate influence on democratization theory. Brazil and Uruguay were central cases in O'Donnell and Schmitter 1986, Huntington 1991, Linz and Stepan 1996 and R. Collier 1999. Chile, South Africa, and Kenya have also received outsize attention. Although all cases are worthy of focus, researchers should be wary of drawing conclusions from a small number of familiar

---

4. To lean against my own theory, I'm not counting the internal hard-liner/soft-liner splits in Chile and Uruguay.

cases, especially when these cases become familiar due to their conformation with existing theory.

## COMMON ELEMENTS

What common elements are shared among the 12 outliers? The clearest commonality is major pro-democratic protest, which was present in all 12 cases, as compared with 68% of path cases.[5] Protest directly ousted dictators in France, South Korea, Peru 2001, and Georgia. In the latter three, this was in reaction to stolen elections. In France, King Louis-Philippe's 1848 ouster followed long-simmering discontent over economic problems and political stagnation (Zeldin 1958; R. Collier 1999: 40–44; Rapport 2009). "I believe that right now we are sleeping on a volcano," Alexis de Tocqueville commented in a January 1848 legislative speech. "Can you not feel . . . the wind of revolution in the air?" (quoted in Rapport 2009: 42). The following month, the king outlawed the politically charged food banquets that had been used to skirt anti-association laws, triggering mass protest. One night, after a mystery gunshot rang out, soldiers fired on a Parisian crowd and revolution followed (Ellis 2000; Rapport 2009: 52). Within days, the king fled and rioters broke into the presidential palace, each taking "turns to sit on the throne," which they dragged outside and burned (Rapport 2009: 56).

Elections within autocracy (i.e., not counting founding democratic elections) played a major role in 9 of 12 cases, although in very different ways. In Uruguay and Chile, plebiscites came as surprise defeats for the government and may have been pivotal in pushing democratization forward. In South Korea, Peru 2001, and Georgia, protests ousted dictators after they stole elections. In Central African Republic, Kenya, and Brazil, autocrats lost control of a guided electoral process. In each case, domestic and international pressure targeted electoral abuses, which combined with internal regime splits in South Africa, Kenya, and Brazil to fatally weaken regimes and enable electoral turnover.

In general, bottom-up pressure was key for the outliers, as manifested in protest movements and electoral opposition. Thus, without a shock or competitive ruling party, the slim potential for transition requires major protests *and* regimes sufficiently weakened through an event like economic crisis, elite split, or Soviet collapse.

## OTHER CRISES?

To complete the outlier discussion, I consider other destabilizing events omitted from this book's shock path. Besides potentially adding clarity to the outliers, this can suggest whether some events ought to be added to the list of

---

5. International pressure influenced half the outliers, a slightly higher fraction compared to the rest.

shocks. As it happens, these events impact very few outliers. Although some are more common in the path cases, they are better understood as mechanisms rather than independent shocks.

*Natural deaths*: Although natural deaths of dictators can have similar effects as assassinations, they've rarely impacted democratization and played no role among the outliers. An autocratic executive's natural death preceded only three cases of democratization within five years (Greece 1944, Spain 1977, Croatia 2000), with another five involving a resignation due to poor health (using Goemans, Gleditsch, and Chiozza 2016). Even including larger windows than five years, natural death or illness played a meaningful role in perhaps seven transitions (Panama 1950, Honduras 1957, Spain 1977, Guyana 1992, Niger 1993, Croatia 2000, Zambia 2008), all of which already fit one of the paths.[6] In Spain, Guyana, Croatia, and Zambia, the outgoing executive was an entrenched dictator, but only in Spain and Guyana did this exit produce a liberalizing successor. In Honduras, precisely the opposite occurred: when President Juan Manuel Gálvez resigned due to poor health in 1954, his successor instituted a political crackdown, prompting a 1956 coup partly led by Gálvez's son. In Croatia and Zambia, the exit immediately preceded elections and contributed to the ruling party's loss. Thus, we again find leader exits generating a mix of paths to democracy, with some shifting power to reformist leaders, some contributing to instability, and some weakening the regime against electoral opposition.

*Elite splits*: Elite division is a central mechanism for the shock path, especially after coups and civil wars. Of course, there are other markers of elite splits, such as executive-led purges and failed coups. Both capture intraregime division but also imply the executive retained power, making them uncertain markers of weakness. Indeed, among the outliers, only Peru 1956 experienced a failed coup attempt in the five years before democratization (using Powell and Thyne 2011) and only Peru 1956 and 2001 had meaningful purges in this window (using Banks and Wilson 2017).[7] Elite divisions played a significant role in Brazil, South Africa, Kenya, and Georgia but did not manifest quite so dramatically.[8]

*Economic crises and natural disasters*: Economic crises are another mechanism connected to shocks that could have an independent effect. Of the 12 outliers, half experienced a negative two-year growth rate within five years of democratization, but only one-third (South Korea, Brazil, Uruguay, Central

6. For a similar view that autocrats' natural deaths rarely produce regime change, see Kendall-Taylor and Frantz 2016. However, Treisman (2015) argues they predict democratization when combined with economic development and Besley, Persson, and Reynal-Querol (2013) find they increase executive constraints.

7. Both are more common among the shock cases (roughly one-fifth with failed coup attempts and one-half with purges), but they're usually closely connected to the shocks.

8. In all but South Africa, ruling party factions broke off to form major opposition parties.

African Republic) experienced a more serious crisis (5% income decline or 50% inflation rate over 2 years). For the path cases, the corresponding figures are 71% and 40%, confirming that economic crises are related to political instability (especially civil and international war). Even further removed from regime politics, natural disasters affected a small number of transitions and no outliers. For instance, an earthquake destabilized the Somoza dictatorship in Nicaragua, a hurricane contributed to a 1975 coup in Honduras, and a 2004 tsunami weakened the ruling party in the Maldives.

*Protest waves*: Given the significance of protest among the outliers, how many were a product of contagious protest waves? Various regional waves saw the rapid diffusion of protest among neighbors, including 1848 in Europe, the post-Soviet wave in Eastern Europe and sub-Saharan Africa, the Color Revolutions, and the Arab Spring (e.g., Ash 1990; Bratton and van de Walle 1997; Rapport 2009; Weyland 2010; Bunce and Wolchik 2011). However, scholars have questioned whether they resulted from contagion as opposed to common political and economic shocks (Hale 2013; Brancati 2014; Houle, Kayser, and Xiang 2016; Gunitsky 2017). As discussed in chapter 4, the post-communist cases in Eastern Europe are best understood as stemming from Soviet withdrawal, with contagion and learning secondary factors. Among the outliers, only two cases (Central African Republic, Georgia) fit the contagion dynamic, although a few others (Chile, Nepal, South Africa) were influenced by the underlying geopolitical shifts. In contrast, France was the initial trigger in 1848, not a result of contagion.

## Negative Cases: Patterns of Non-Democratization

What can this book's framework tell us about stable autocracies? The paths describe common antecedents of democratization, which together form a virtually necessary condition for transition. Therefore, autocracies without recent shocks or a competitive ruling party are very unlikely to democratize. As this section shows, this accounts for most cases of autocratic stability.

Yet there are also numerous cases of reconsolidated authoritarianism after shocks, long periods of state collapse, and ruling parties that successfully resist democracy. Indeed, a central part of my theory is that the path conditions are *not* sufficient to produce democratization. Although they create openings for change, success depends on pro-democratic pressure, country structure, and actors' choices. I consider below how conditions discussed in the last three chapters can account for many cases of non-democratization. However, the primary analysis of the extra ingredients needed to secure democracy is in chapter 8, where I test how protest and economic factors combine with the path conditions. I show not only that these factors take on greater importance in the path contexts but that favorable conditions can make it much more likely than not that countries democratize within five years.

To explore further, I assign all cases of autocratic stability to four groups, discussing each in turn and noting some representative examples. First, there are cases without a recent shock or a durable electoral ruling party. These comprise the majority of stable autocracies and are well explained by my framework. Second, there are autocracies with a ruling party but no shock. Since there are additional mechanisms in electoral continuity, including triggers and sufficient confidence, many of these cases are predicted by chapter 5. Third, there are autocracies that suffer repeated shocks and persistent weakness, often with state collapse. Since democratization requires a usable state, many of these cases are also expected. Lastly, there are autocracies where shocks were followed by reconsolidated authoritarianism.

To define the groups, I continue to use the measures of recent shocks (within five years) and durable electoral ruling parties (with control for 4+years). I want to avoid including countries that democratize in the near future, which are hardly representatives of stability. Thus, the sample is all autocracies that remain autocratic for the following five years, corresponding to 10,518 country-years. The percentages that fall into each group are shown in parentheses.

### *No Shock and No Qualifying Party (52.2%)*

The group best explained by this book includes the autocracies without shocks or qualifying ruling parties, which comprise a narrow majority of all stable autocracies. These are among the strongest and most politically closed dictatorships, successfully preventing both violent challenges from below and major internal splits. Without shocks, their coercive dominance avoided suitable openings for pro-democratic activity. Further, the absence of an electoral ruling party implies a lack of electoral pressure and poor prospects within democracy, making strategic democratization much less likely.

Stability in these regimes goes well beyond escaping democratization. In general, they've rarely succumbed to pressure from below: in only 0.27% of country-years was there executive turnover from popular protest or revolution, less than one-seventh the rate for other autocracies. Organized opposition was not entirely absent—from 1919 onward, they faced protests in just under 12% of country-years, compared with over 20% in other autocracies (using Banks and Wilson 2017)—but it has rarely seriously challenged them. Overall, these regimes had a 3% risk of autocratic regime change, about one-third the rate for other autocracies.

The majority of these regimes are monarchies (55.7%), with party-based, military, and personalist regimes each comprising between 13 and 15.5% of country-years. The monarchies include modern Swaziland, Morocco, Jordan, Saudi Arabia, Kuwait, Bahrain, United Arab Emirates, Oman, and Bhutan, with only a few country-years omitted after assassinations or coups. These monarchies have retained high elite loyalty, while stifling popular organization.

In fact, only two cases ever experienced a turnover from below (Spain in 1919, Nepal in 1951), a rate 1/25 that of other autocracies, and fewer than 7% of country-years featured a protest. Simply put, they've virtually eliminated any meaningful internal pressure for democratization.

Several party-based regimes, including modern China and Eritrea, end up here because the parties either were not sufficiently durable or didn't hold elections. Although China's party is very strong and might win in democracy, it has not established national elections and, with the possible exception of the 1989 protests, has not recently faced a trigger sufficient to incentivize liberalization (Dickson 1997; Dobson 2012; Slater and Wong 2013). In fact, China has not faced a qualifying shock since 1968.

Burma from 1993 onward qualifies among the military regimes. Although it is currently attempting a gradual liberalization, this has been hampered by its lack of competitiveness. In 2010, the regime founded the Union Solidarity and Development Party, which won boycotted 2010 elections, but was badly defeated in 2015. Despite allowing the opposition to take the presidency, the military remains politically dominant and full democratization may remain elusive as long as the military believes it is unlikely to win power (Morgenbesser 2016; Zin 2016).

### Party and No Shock (19.2%)

The next group features durable electoral ruling parties without recent shocks. In the previous chapter, I argued that many such regimes support democratization because of confidence in their electoral prospects, minimizing the expected loss of power. The argument was *not* that every regime with a durable ruling party will democratize—several further conditions are needed to make this likely. As a result, the stability of many of these parties is expected.

First, weak parties unable to compete for power within democracy should resist democratization. For instance, party leaders in Central African Republic and South Africa (until the late 1980s) did not expect to fare well in democracy and relented only with intense international pressure and internal threats of violence. In contrast, many other parties with poor prospects successfully resisted democratization. To proxy for low expectations, we can use the predictive model from chapter 7 that estimates each party's likelihood of gaining power within democracy. Among the parties with less than half the average annual chance of holding power (about 19%) are Haiti's Fanmi Lavalas, the Socialist Party of Serbia, United Russia since 2008, and the Ba'ath Party in Syria and Iraq. Despite successfully avoiding democratization, many of these weak parties instead succumbed to competing elites through coups or civil wars.

Second, ruling parties need a triggering event to push them into a period of heightened vulnerability. It follows that especially strong parties can forestall democratization by avoiding moments of weakness and firmly controlling elections. Fitting examples include modern-day Singapore, Namibia, Cameroon, Azerbaijan, Uzbekistan, and Algeria, all of which exert hegemonic control and prevent major disruptions that could spark rising competition. Although many of these parties would likely succeed in democracy, they have no need to take that risk. As a result, it is often parties at *middle* values of strength that accept democratization, as they are sufficiently strong to compete in democracy but eventually face vulnerable moments like economic crises, succession battles, and international disruptions. To proxy for these strong parties, we can use a different predictive model from chapter 7 that estimates each party's annual likelihood of turnover within autocracy. In about one-fifth of the group, this risk is less than 1%.

Third, single-party regimes, which make up 52.5% of the group, rarely accede to democratization and have only done so under very specific conditions. More than three-fourths of the electoral continuity cases were multiparty regimes prior to democratization, with the nine exceptions all sub-Saharan African countries between 1991 and 1994 (during a regional wave of protests and transitions). Single parties are unlikely to democratize since they lack a legal opposition and an electoral source of rising competition, while the absence of a competitive history makes their democratic prospects highly uncertain. Thus, it took the disruption from the Soviet Union's fall, combined with increasingly pro-democratic foreign aid conditionality, to overwhelm the African regimes and convince them to democratize.

Conservatively, this book's theory accounts for parties with a low likelihood of gaining democratic power or that are highly secure within autocracy. It also makes sense to include the country-years that are early in ruling party spells that later democratize through electoral continuity. In total, this corresponds to 41.5% of the group. Adding single-party regimes would raise this further, but this is more tenuous since there are exceptions. For the remaining unexplained cases, stability could still be tied to a lack of appropriate triggers, insufficient pro-democratic pressure, or personal caution among party elites.

### Shock and Persistent Weakness (16.3%)

For the cases following shocks, I distinguish between countries with lengthy periods of repeated shocks, violence, and instability versus those regimes able to quickly reconsolidate power. As a reasonable proxy, I count a case as reconsolidating following a shock if it survives five years without another shock, authoritarian regime change, or state collapse. The remainder (comprising this group) are considered unstable until they reach the *beginning* of a five-year stable period.

Illustrative examples of persistent weakness include modern-day Sudan, South Sudan, Afghanistan, Guinea-Bissau, and Somalia, plus Haiti 1986–94, Burkina Faso 1974–87, Liberia 1989–2000, Chad 1966–2006, and Cambodia in the 1970s and 1990s. In Haiti, for instance, 1986–94 featured five irregular turnovers, including three coups and a foreign-imposed regime change. The 1966–2006 period in Chad included five separate civil war spells and four irregular turnovers. Following a brief democratic period, Guinea-Bissau from 1998 to 2009 saw a civil war, two coups, and a military-led assassination of the president.

Instability of this kind does not preclude democratization. Many transitions (e.g., Dominican Republic 1966, Bolivia 1982, Sierra Leone 2002) followed repeated shocks or civil war. However, persistent state weakness presents a significant obstacle to democratization just as it does to stable autocracy. Highly insecure autocratic leaders may even favor democratization yet lack sufficient control to implement the process. Indeed, 14.6% of the country-years in this group are counted as in state collapse, a condition that makes democratization virtually impossible.[9]

### *Shock and Reconsolidated Autocracy (12.2%)*

The final group consists of autocracies that face a shock followed by the (possibly new) regime reasserting control and maintaining stability for at least five years. They appear in this group from the shock year until they "graduate" to the first group after five years. Although the smallest group, these cases are significant because they ultimately break from the high-propensity period for democratization, unlike the previous two groups. Thus, they are especially illuminating regarding how autocratic stability is constructed.

Although coups often trigger repeated countercoups and other shocks, about one-third led to 5+ years of autocratic stability, including Indonesia in 1966, Libya in 1969, Tunisia in 1987, and Qatar in 1995. In Tunisia and Qatar, coups ousted the executive but maintained overall regime continuity. In Indonesia and Libya, the new leadership radically changed the regime alongside bloody purges. Similarly, autocracy successfully reconsolidated after assassinations in Saudi Arabia in 1975, Egypt in 1981, and Armenia in 1999; after civil wars in Russia, Algeria, and Iran; and following Spain's defeat in the Spanish-American War, Libya's defeat to Chad in 1987, and Iraq's loss in the first Persian Gulf War.

In some cases, shocks produced a liberal opening or restoration of elected government short of democracy. Historical cases include Serbia's 1903 May Overthrow (an anti-royalist coup that ushered in parliamentary rule), Sweden's 1809 anti-royalist coup after the loss of Finland to Russia, and Russia's 1905 revolution after its defeat in the Russo-Japanese War (Ackerman and Duvall 2000: 13–59). In Paraguay, the 1989 military ouster of Alfredo Stroessner, forty-five years into his tenure, led to a relatively open competitive

---

9. The sole case of democratization with continuing state collapse is Dominican Republic 1966. In seven other cases, state collapse ended the previous year due to the end of war or occupation.

authoritarian period (Abente-Brun 2009). In other cases, a brief liberal opening was quashed by hard-liners, who then reconsolidated autocratic rule. Examples include Hungary's 1956 opening (crushed by the Soviets), South Korea in 1979, Burma in 1988–90, and Egypt in 2011–13.

These varied paths to reconsolidated autocracy again illustrate how shocks present openings for change. Although the old leadership quickly reasserted power in some cases, in others the shock produced radical autocratic transformation, a sustained liberal opening, or a quick hard-liner reaction. Yet the puzzle most relevant for this book is how these regimes escaped democratization. In part, this reflects the difficulty and rarity of democratization, but we can also explore what sets these regimes apart.

There are two key requirements for post-shock democratization. The first is leader insecurity, implying little to lose from democratizing. Whether this is satisfied can depend on the shock itself and leader agency. If autocrats can command sufficient coercive power and quickly build cohesive elite coalitions, they can escape insecurity and will spurn democratization. This should be especially likely following revolutionary takeovers or coups with unified military backing. The second requirement is sufficient pro-democratic pressure, a product of opposition mobilization, country structure, and international dynamics. Democratic actors must grasp the opening and win out against the alternatives.

Although more rigorous tests are in chapter 8, a few simple comparisons reveal how these cases of reconsolidated autocracy sharply differ from the successful post-shock transitions. Regarding the first requirement, the democratizers faced a risk of irregular turnover that was about one-third higher, using the predictive model from chapter 7. Regarding the second, the stable autocracies faced protests in only 13% of country-years, less than one-third the rate for the democratizers (using Banks and Wilson 2017). Further, a quarter more of the population was literate in the democratizers and the surrounding region had 2.5 times the fraction of democracies. Lastly, 37% of the reconsolidated autocracies are from before 1900, an era when democratization was extremely rare (0.15% per year) and which includes only 2 of 100 shock cases. Thus, reconsolidated autocracy is less puzzling when we consider the general absence of pro-democratic mobilization and supporting structure.

## Summary

How many cases of stable autocracy can be explained by this book's framework? Conservatively, we can include the cases without shocks or durable parties, the set of durable parties noted above, and regimes in state collapse. In total, this accounts for 63% of country-years. For the remainder, we need to look more deeply at the interactive role of favorable socioeconomic conditions and pro-democratic activity, a subject explored in chapter 8.

# CHAPTER SEVEN

# Direct Effects of the Paths

THE PREVIOUS CHAPTERS showed that democratization almost always follows one of five shocks or occurs with a durable ruling party that regains power in democracy. Either path helps to disrupt the autocratic status quo and shift to a political context in which autocratic leaders are less threatened by democratization. How well do these conditions predict democratization? Is there comprehensive evidence that the key mechanisms of leader insecurity and party confidence matter as expected?

This chapter begins the quantitative testing, focusing on the direct relationship between the path conditions and democratization. I start by translating the preceding discussion into testable hypotheses. I then clarify my empirical approach, followed by the empirical setup and results. To improve causal inference, I contrast the key predictors with other events that should be similarly predicted by potential confounders, examine a difference-in-differences model, and stress the robustness of the findings to additional controls and model variations. Finally, to test the mechanisms, I use an imputation technique that estimates the likelihood of a dictator's irregular ouster and a party's chance of winning power in democracy. Results provide strong support for the book's theory on shocks and ruling parties, as well as the predictive power of leader insecurity and democratic prospects.

In the next chapter, I focus on conditional and mediated relationships in which shocks and ruling parties interact with pro-democratic activity and country-level characteristics in predicting democratization. The final empirical chapter examines how the paths impact later democratic survival.

## *Predictions*

Up to now, this book has defended the main claims summarized in chapter 1 through qualitative case studies and descriptive statistics. Building on the theory and further nuances developed in the preceding chapters, I now clarify the specific hypotheses that I empirically test. Although I chose not to repeat the phrase, each hypothesis can be prefaced with an *"All things equal . . ."* stipulation.

As explained in chapters 1 and 2, a primary motivator for autocrats to democratize, particularly following shocks, is the threat of a coercive ouster. Given the dire consequences of this outcome, including potential imprisonment and death, dictators are more favorable toward democratization when this risk is higher. The same logic applies to ruling parties if they are uncertain about their chances of retaining power in autocracy. In addition, parties have a tempting option of competing within democracy, although their chances of success vary depending on party history and country factors. We can specify these mechanisms as follows:

> *Hypothesis 1*: Democratization is more likely when autocratic leaders face a higher likelihood of coercive overthrow.

> *Hypothesis 2*: Ruling parties are more likely to allow democratization when their likelihood of winning power in democracy is higher and when their likelihood of retaining power in autocracy is lower.

To test these claims at the end of the chapter, I estimate the risk of each outcome and show this risk predicts democratization as the theory suggests.

As discussed at length, violent shocks are central to exacerbating regime weakness and leader insecurity. These shocks have further effects that feed into democratization, including heightened supporter uncertainty and openings for pro-democratic actors. Therefore, democratization should be more likely following these shocks.

> *Hypothesis 3*: Democratization is more likely in the aftermath of coups, civil wars, assassinations, defeat in foreign war, or the withdrawal of an autocratic hegemon.

For empirical testing, I focus on whether any shock has occurred in the previous five years, with robustness checks varying this window. I also test the shocks individually, disaggregate them, and contrast them with comparable events, particularly those that should be similarly predicted by regime weakness. This is not the first study to relate these shocks to democratization, but it does apply the widest scope and is the first to integrate the shocks together and with the electoral path.

Although this is expanded upon below, it's useful to specify here three further hypotheses derived from the preceding chapters. The first disaggregates by the civil war outcome. The second clarifies the contrast between defeat in war and other occurrences of war. The last makes clear that autocratic turnovers driven purely from below are not predictive of democratization.

> *Hypothesis 4*: Democratization is more likely during ongoing civil wars and after civil wars ending in stalemate, but not after civil wars ending in rebel or government victory.

*Hypothesis 5*: Democratization is more likely following defeat in foreign war, but not during an ongoing war or after victory in war.

*Hypothesis 6*: Absent recent shocks, democratization is not more likely following revolutions or other autocratic ousters from below.

The final hypothesis on direct effects concerns durable ruling parties. As discussed in chapter 2, although the electoral continuity path requires an established ruling party that regains power in democracy, this obviously cannot be used to predict democratization. Therefore, I focus on the simpler question of whether an electoral ruling party exists and has continuously ruled for at least four years. This helps to ensure the party was not created for democratization and provides sufficient time for leaders to develop the capacity to continue competing electorally. Indeed, about three-fourths of these parties that acceded to democracy ultimately won democratic power.

This party measure combines the requirements of an established ruling party *and* holding elections, but these can be further distinguished. At first glance, this may seem like splitting hairs: Don't nearly all electoral autocracies have powerful ruling parties that routinely win elections? In fact, of all electoral autocracies, only a slight minority (49.3%) have an identifiable ruling party and only 37.5% have a ruling party in power for at least four years (without turnover or overthrow). If we restrict our attention to post–World War II, ruling parties are more common but far from universal: 72.7% of electoral autocracies have a ruling party and 57.7% have a party lasting at least four years. The final hypothesis makes clear that it's the *combination* of an established ruling party and elections that predicts democratization, not elections alone.

*Hypothesis 7*: Democratization is more likely with an established ruling party that holds elections, but not more likely with elections absent such a ruling party.

## *Empirical Setup*

### MODELS AND CONTROLS

Unless noted otherwise, I predict democratization using a dynamic logit model (sometimes called a "Markov transition model") in a sample of autocracies covering 1800–2014. The dependent variable is 1 if the country democratizes and 0 otherwise, with all independent variables lagged by at least one year. Because I account for the country's consecutive years as an autocracy, this is a form of duration model. Except as noted below, I use heteroskedasticity-robust standard errors. As throughout the book, I use Boix, Miller, and Rosato 2013 to define democracy. Given missing data for other variables, the tested sample leaves out microstates but still encompasses 132 democratic transitions.

For the shocks, I combined existing data sets and my own coding to derive annual measures of each back to 1800 (see the appendix). Again, coups require a successful coercive executive ouster or change to the regime. Civil wars are the only shock not dated to a specific year and continue as long as the war is active. Assassinations count killings of either the head of state or head of government. A defeat in foreign war is dated to either the capitulation or the end of foreign occupation if applicable. Hegemonic withdrawal is dated to 1944 for Nazi-dominated countries and 1989 for Soviet-dominated countries. The main variable I test is *Shock (5 years)*, coded 1 if any shock occurs in the five-year window ending the current year. This is 1 in 29.4% of autocratic country-years. The other main variable, *Durable Ruling Party*, requires an electoral ruling party in uninterrupted power for 4+ years. This is 1 in 24.5% of autocratic country-years.

For controls, I begin with a fairly stripped-down set of models, which has the advantage of maximizing the sample size and avoiding post-treatment bias. The most minimal model controls for the year, a cubic function of the autocracy age (a flexible approach to account for duration dependence), the country's previous number of democratic spells (to proxy for democratic experience and country-specific predispositions for regime type), and the surrounding region's fraction of democracies (to proxy for regional diffusion).[1] Since this leaves out any socioeconomic controls, the "base model" I focus on adds controls for average income (*GDP/capita*, natural-logged, in real 2000 dollars), *Economic Growth* (the two-year average change in *GDP/capita*, as a %), and *Population* (natural-logged). See the appendix for how these are constructed. The base model keeps the complete date range and preserves about 93% of the full autocracy sample. Many further controls are considered below.

## CAUSATION AND ANALYSIS

Although all quantitative tests must be interpreted with caution, several features of the analysis further bolster the causal evidence for the effects of shocks and ruling parties. In particular, I argue it is unlikely that omitted confounders are driving the findings. This is reinforced by the strong robustness of the results to alternative controls and models, the use of difference-in-differences and placebo tests, checks for post-treatment bias, and the sheer magnitude of the findings.

It should be stressed that major predictors of democratization are generally not thought to also positively predict violent shocks. For instance, of the 14 structural predictors of democratization I examine in the next chapter, only 2 have significant relationships with both democratization and shocks in the same direction, compared with 10 that have significant relationships

---

1. This uses the same region definitions in Miller 2015a, 2021. If a country is the only one in its region, this is measured as 0.

in opposite directions.[2] Thus, it's just as plausible that omitting some confounders *underestimates* the true causal relationship between shocks and democratization. The same applies to *Durable Ruling Party*, which combines autocratic *stability* and the holding of elections. As I've shown previously, autocratic election adoption and democratization are predicted by entirely different factors (Miller 2020b).

Nevertheless, potential confounding must be taken seriously. I explore a large range of controls, including measures of regime strength, autocratic regime type, civil liberties, economic crises, and other socioeconomic conditions. I also apply a technique called *extreme bounds analysis* that tests the robustness of findings to thousands of control combinations. In the first set of tests, I include a *difference-in-differences* model with country and year fixed effects (Athey and Imbens 2006; Lechner 2011). Besides this, related methods like synthetic control, and placebo tests, I don't regard other causal inference techniques as feasible for testing shocks or ruling parties.[3] Further robustness checks vary the window for shocks, the minimum durability of ruling parties, the year range, control lags, and so on. The main results are highly robust to these variations.

Special emphasis is also placed on contrasting shocks and parties to parallel events and institutions that should be similarly predicted by confounders like regime weakness. For instance, it's shown that revolutions, failed coups, and elections by themselves do not positively predict democratization. Like the dog that didn't bark, these act as *placebo tests*, an underutilized causal inference technique that shows a non-result where an alternative theory predicts a positive result.

Because *Shock (5 years)* and *Durable Ruling Party* are 1 for multiple years, a concern is this could induce post-treatment bias as the controls are often measured after the shock or party rises to power. I explore two model variations to address this. First, I shift the window for shocks down to 1 year, in which case the controls are no longer post-treatment. As shown below, results hold. Second, I lagged all controls by up to 10 years. Results are virtually identical, with the effect of shocks slightly stronger for longer lags.

To improve clarity, I stress throughout the effects on actual probabilities, although I also show logit results for the main findings. Unless mentioned otherwise, everything shown visually is an estimated annual probability of democratization or change in this probability, derived from a logit using the base model. For instance, I show how the probability changes moving from no

---

2. Results are unchanged controlling for the two same-direction variables (economic crisis and military regimes).

3. The only instance of credible quasi-random variation in a shock (or durable ruling parties) that I'm aware of is Jones and Olken's (2009) comparison of successful and unsuccessful assassinations (see chapter 3).

recent shock to at least one. Whenever deriving estimated probabilities from a logit, the result depends on assumptions about the values of the model's other variables. I use the "margins" command in Stata, which derives probabilities and shifts based on the actual observed values in the sample.[4] In other words, it gives the predicted effects as applied to real-world cases.

An important note is needed on the *magnitude* of effects. The effects of variables like shocks and ruling parties can misleadingly appear quite small, usually on the scale of a 1–2% increase in democratization's chances. Two pieces of context are needed to appreciate the findings. First, although I show *annual* likelihoods, the variables operate on longer timescales. For instance, an individual shock will cause *Shock (5 years)* to be 1 for five years. Therefore, the implied effect of a shock on democratization in the near term is approximately five times the estimated annual effect. This is even more significant for *Durable Ruling Party*, as this is 1 for as long as the party survives in power. On average, parties that meet the four-year durability requirement satisfy this for about 12 years, so the long-term effect of such a party existing is around 12 times the annual effect. Second, it should be appreciated anew how low the likelihoods of democratization are in general: only 1.15% from 1800 to 2014. Therefore, a 1% increase in this likelihood is roughly a *doubling* of democracy's chances. Needless to say, understanding what doubles or triples the incidence of an important political outcome is substantively significant.

## Empirical Results

### MAIN RESULTS

Table 7.1 presents the main results, predicting democratization from *Shock (5 years)*, *Durable Ruling Party*, and varying controls. Model 1 uses the most basic set of controls (preserving the entire autocracy sample). Model 2 uses the base model that, unless mentioned otherwise, is used for all further results. Model 3 adds three institutional variables that go back to 1800: dummies for *Military Regime* and *Personalist Regime* (an extension of Geddes, Wright, and Frantz 2014; see the appendix) and a 0–1 measure of civil liberties (from Coppedge et al. 2018). Model 4 adds country fixed effects and Model 5 further adds year fixed effects, making it a difference-in-differences model. Following recommended practice with fixed effects, Models 4 and 5 use a linear probability model (OLS applied to a binary outcome; see Caudill 1988).

---

4. To be more specific, "margins" calculates the estimated probability of democratization for each unit from assumptions about a key variable (e.g., a recent shock) and the actual values of all other variables. It then averages these unit probabilities across the sample. The same approach applies to probability shifts. When calculating how the probability shifts when continuous variables change, it technically gives the probability derivative (on the scale of a one-unit shift in the variable).

**Table 7.1.** Models Predicting Democratization

| | Dynamic Logit | | | OLS | |
|---|---|---|---|---|---|
| | (1) | (2) | (3) | (4) | (5) |
| **Shock (5 years)** | 1.381*** | 1.362*** | 1.405*** | 0.018*** | 0.016*** |
| | (7.03) | (6.72) | (6.05) | (5.10) | (4.77) |
| **Durable Ruling Party** | 0.643** | 0.658** | 0.861*** | 0.016** | 0.014** |
| | (3.11) | (3.09) | (3.72) | (2.92) | (2.66) |
| Regional Democracy | 2.401*** | 2.161*** | 1.609*** | 0.032** | 0.038** |
| | (6.64) | (6.01) | (3.48) | (2.88) | (3.25) |
| Previous Dem. Spells | 0.451*** | 0.431*** | 0.571*** | 0.008 | 0.011 |
| | (4.22) | (4.06) | (4.25) | (0.57) | (0.77) |
| GDP/capita (ln) | | 0.226* | 0.123 | 0.008 | 0.006 |
| | | (2.35) | (1.15) | (1.73) | (1.23) |
| Economic Growth | | −0.050*** | −0.054*** | −0.001** | −0.001* |
| | | (−3.48) | (−3.34) | (−3.07) | (−2.42) |
| Population (ln) | | 0.059 | 0.119 | 0.008 | −0.002 |
| | | (0.93) | (1.86) | (1.40) | (−0.19) |
| Military Regime | | | 0.845** | 0.008 | 0.009 |
| | | | (3.19) | (1.50) | (1.78) |
| Personalist Regime | | | −0.025 | −0.004 | −0.003 |
| | | | (−0.10) | (−0.73) | (−0.63) |
| Civil Liberties | | | 4.619*** | 0.087*** | 0.110*** |
| | | | (8.31) | (5.28) | (5.89) |
| Year | 0.010*** | 0.007* | 0.008** | 0.000 | |
| | (3.69) | (2.58) | (3.00) | (0.55) | |
| Autocracy Age Cubic? | Y | Y | Y | Y | Y |
| Country FE? | | | | Y | Y |
| Year FE? | | | | | Y |
| N | 11,459 | 10,618 | 9,805 | 9,805 | 9,805 |
| Countries | 165 | 151 | 150 | 150 | 150 |
| Pseudo/Adjusted R² | 0.160 | 0.159 | 0.222 | 0.049 | 0.051 |

*Notes:* The table displays dynamic logits and regressions (OLS) predicting democratization in a sample of autocracies. All independent variables are lagged by one year. Years are 1800–2014. $t$- and $z$-values (based on robust standard errors) are in parentheses. *$p<0.05$, **$p<0.01$, *** $p<0.001$

Both *Shock (5 years)* and *Durable Ruling Party* strongly and significantly predict democratization across all models. In fact, the addition of the institutional variables makes the relationship stronger. Figure 7.1 shows the relevant probabilities derived from Models 2 and 3. Without either main variable, there is only about a 0.5% chance of democratization. With a durable party or recent shock, this jumps to 1.8% and 2.5%, respectively, a proportional increase of

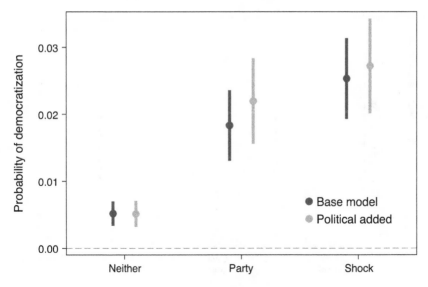

FIGURE 7.1. Two paths and democratization. Estimated likelihood of democratization based on a recent shock, a durable ruling party, or neither, from Models 2 and 3 of Table 7.1. Bars = 95% CI.

3.5–5 times. According to Model 5, a recent shock raises the likelihood of democratization by 1.6% per year, while a durable ruling party raises the likelihood by 1.4%.

Again, speaking in terms of 1–2% increases in annual probability may misleadingly seem small. To see the substantive impact, consider a thought experiment. Suppose we begin in our current world and assume the democratization rate is the estimated likelihood absent any shocks or a durable party. For simplicity, let's fix the democratic breakdown rate at its observed value since 1980: 1.17% per year. What would the world's long-run equilibrium fraction of democracies be? Only 30.8%. In comparison, if we take the average democratization rate given shocks or durable parties, the long-run fraction would be 64.8%, or a difference of around 65 democracies. The percentages add up.

## DISAGGREGATED TRIGGERS AND COMPARISONS

We begin a deeper look into these effects by disaggregating the individual shocks. Figure 7.2 visually summarizes the *increase* in democratization's likelihood from two tests, both using the base model and controlling for *Durable Ruling Party* (not shown). The first result is for the *number* of recent shocks. On average, each additional shock raises the annual likelihood of democratization by 0.9%. The next model includes each shock type separately, all dummies for an occurrence within five years. Recent coups, defeats in war, and

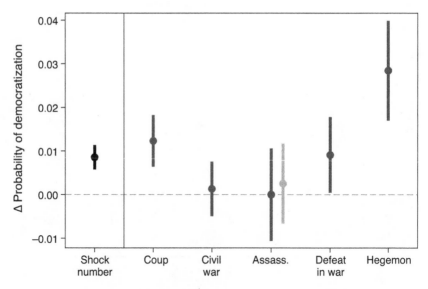

FIGURE 7.2. Shocks and democratization. Estimated increase in democratization likelihood from the number of recent shocks (left side) and each recent shock tested simultaneously. Recent assassinations are tested with (dark bar) and without (light bar) counting the current year. Recent coups, defeat in war, and hegemonic withdrawals significantly predict democratization even in this disaggregated test. Bars = 95% CI.

hegemonic withdrawals are all significant, with the latter having the strongest effect, followed by coups. A recent civil war is not significant, but this is consistent with the hypothesis on different civil war resolutions. The estimated effect of assassinations is essentially 0. As noted in chapter 3, this test suffers from a lack of variation and overlooks two assassinations that occurred early in the democratization year. The lighter line shows the effect if the following year is included in the assassination window; this is now positive but remains insignificant. Thus, we find supportive evidence for three of the shocks and mixed evidence for civil wars and assassinations. Combined with the main results, we find strong overall support for Hypothesis 3.

Figure 7.3 captures several further tests contrasting or disaggregating the shocks. Except for the bottom right, these expand the disaggregated shocks model just discussed. First, in the upper left, I added a measure of any recent *failed* coup (from Powell and Thyne 2011). This has a positive but insignificant effect, while successful coups are significantly stronger. In fact, the coup effect is heightened because it's now being compared to autocracies with no coup attempts. This indicates there is something distinct about the instability stemming from actual regime change.

The upper-right test disaggregates civil wars into ongoing wars (those continuing into the next year) and three types of resolution: rebel wins,

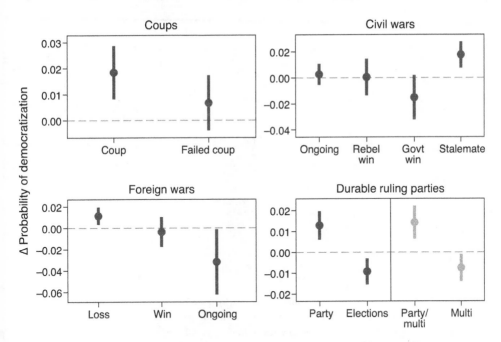

FIGURE 7.3. Contrasting effects on democratization. Estimated increases in democratization likelihood from several tests, disaggregating or contrasting shocks and durable parties. Bars = 95% CI.

government wins, and stalemates. Each is counted if occurring in the five-year window. Consistent with Hypothesis 4, recent stalemates are strongly related to democratization, equivalent to an 8.5% higher chance of democratization over five years. In contrast, government victories are negative for democratization and rebel wins have no effect. Inconsistent with Hypothesis 4, ongoing civil wars are positive but not significant for democratization. However, this becomes significant when the political controls (from Table 7.1, Model 3) are included.

The bottom-left test adds ongoing foreign wars and recent victories in war as a comparison to defeat in war. Confirming Hypothesis 5, defeat in war predicts democratization, but victories do not and ongoing war is strongly negative. This presents an instructive contrast with the pattern for civil wars. Although they divert coercive resources, foreign wars do not imply state weakness as civil wars do and generate rally-round-the-flag effects that solidify regime control (unless they lose).

Finally, the bottom-right panel summarizes two tests, both of which include the aggregate *Shock (5 years)* since the focus is on durable parties. The first adds a separate measure of elections alongside *Durable Ruling Party*. The second alters the *Durable Ruling Party* measure by additionally requiring multiparty electoral competition for 4+years, tested alongside a measure of multiparty elections. The surprising finding is that absent a ruling party,

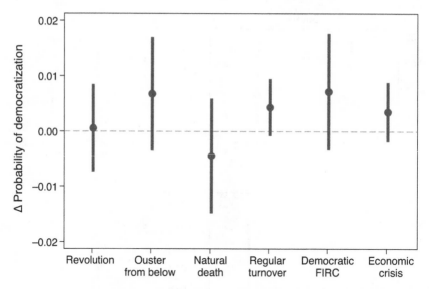

FIGURE 7.4. Other events and democratization. Estimated increases in democratization likelihood from various non-shock events, including ousters from below and economic crisis. Bars = 95% CI.

both elections and multiparty elections are significantly *negative* for democratization. This confirms Hypothesis 7 and reflects the fact that autocracies will resist electoral pressure to liberalize if they lack a vehicle for preserving their power. The finding informs the ongoing debate as to whether autocratic elections and parties contribute to democratization (e.g., Lindberg 2006; Wright and Escribà-Folch 2012; Knutsen, Nygård, and Wig 2017). As a corrective, the results imply that the *interaction* between elections and ruling parties is critical to understanding their democratizing effects.

As a final set of contrasts with the shocks, Figure 7.4 summarizes tests of six additional events, each tested alongside *Shock (5 years)*, *Durable Ruling Party*, and the base model. With the exception of economic crisis, each is tested in a five-year window. First, I test revolutions and then any autocratic ouster from below, including protest-based ousters like Tunisia in 2011 (see the appendix). Since popular activism is one of the paths' mechanisms and I want to contrast the paths with independent from-below activity, the latter measure only counts ousters outside the paths (i.e., those that don't follow shocks or coincide with ruling parties). Confirming Hypothesis 6, both are insignificant, demonstrating that not all forms of regime instability promote democratization.

Second, I test recent natural leader deaths (Goemans, Gleditsch, and Chiozza 2016) and any regular executive turnover, both required to occur within autocracy. The former is negative for democratization and the latter just misses positive significance, although it's small in magnitude. This demonstrates that leader change in general is not predictive; rather, a necessary part of the shocks path is disruption and uncertainty. Third, the next model tests foreign-imposed regime change (FIRC) by a democracy (from Downes and Monten 2013, extended by Downes to 2015). This is slightly positive but misses significance. Lastly, the sixth model tests a major economic crisis within the previous two years (defined as a 5% economic decline or 50% inflation rate averaged over two years), which surprisingly misses significance. If *Economic Growth* is removed from the controls, economic crisis edges into significance, but the effect is relatively small (0.57%).

## ROBUSTNESS

### Controls

An enormous range of variables have been related to democratization, from levels of rainfall to the fertility rate to whether the country is an island. I've similarly checked the robustness of the main findings to a wide variety of further controls. However, my primary concern here is not to canvass the universe of controls but to account for plausible confounders and confirm the findings' robustness to the most relevant institutional and socioeconomic variables. For the initial discussion, each variable is tested individually (or as related pairs) after being added to the base model. I then discuss a technique that looks at several in combination. Many of these variables' effects on democratization are explored further in the following chapter.

Most importantly, I investigate robustness to controls for state and regime weakness. Although weakness is a mechanism for the shocks' influence on democratization, it is also a plausible confounder since it encourages violent regime challenges. Controlling for weakness risks post-treatment bias, but my theory posits other effects of shocks (such as uncertainty and pro-democratic openings), so I still expect a positive effect. I control separately for the following: measures of fiscal capacity, state control of the economy, party system strength, and autonomy from foreign actors (all from Coppedge et al. 2018); measures of military size (as % of population) and military spending (as % of GDP) (see the appendix); and a measure of state capacity (a 0–1 aggregate of 24 variables capturing administrative and coercive capacity, from Hanson and Sigman 2013). The effect of *Shock (5 years)* remains significant after controlling for each, with the effect magnitude virtually unchanged or stronger.[5] The same applies to *Durable Ruling Party*, with the sole exception of controlling

5. The lowest effect magnitude is 1.2%, compared to the base model estimate of 1.6%.

for state capacity. However, this partly stems from the smaller sample size (40% that of the base model) and it only narrowly misses significance. Thus, regime weakness does not appear to be a strong confounder for either main variable.

Among other institutional/political variables, I explored controlling for freedom from repression, horizontal and vertical accountability, civil liberties, political liberalism, gender equity in power, the level of participatory democracy, free and fair elections, clientelism, and dummies for presidential and semi-presidential systems (all from Coppedge et al. 2018), as well as a dummy for communism (Gunitsky 2017) and a measure of autocratic personalism (Geddes, Wright, and Frantz 2018). Both main variables remain significant with all these controls. Among socioeconomic variables, I controlled for oil dependence (as % of GDP), natural resource dependence, inequality (as a Gini coefficient), education (average school years in adult population), literacy, urbanization, religion, ethnolinguistic fractionalization, colonial history, and the country's external dependence on democracies through trade, military alliances, and foreign aid (see the appendix on each). Both main variables remain significant across all checks, with the sole exception of *Durable Ruling Party* when inequality is included (which again relates to a small sample size, about one-third that of the base model).

To fully capture the robustness of the main findings, I apply a technique called *extreme bounds analysis* (EBA). Most models have numerous defensible options, particularly over which controls to include. Rather than basing one's conclusions on a single decision, EBA cycles through all possible combinations of options to provide a range of estimates (Leamer 1985; Sala-i-Martin 1997). Beginning with the base model, I tested every combination of 12 sets of additional controls in separate dynamic logit models, producing 4,096 estimates for each main variable. The 12 were chosen for having little missing data, displaying predictive power for democratization when added alone, and encompassing state strength, political attributes, and socioeconomic factors. Most are single variables: measures of civil liberties, civil society strength, state control of the economy, military spending, communism, gender equity in power, natural resource dependence, and literacy. Those included as sets are the military and personalist regime dummies, measures of horizontal and vertical accountability, dummies for semi-presidentialism and presidentialism, and region dummies.

Each of the 4,096 models produced distinct estimates for shocks and durable ruling parties. Since the samples change across models, I consider *t*-values to be the best metric of comparison as opposed to coefficients (see Miller, Joseph, and Ohl 2018). Figure 7.5 shows ranges of *t*-values for the shock and ruling party estimates. Shocks are highly robust, with every estimate remaining significant at the .001 level. The ruling party estimates are not quite as

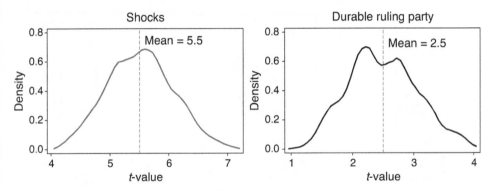

FIGURE 7.5. Distributions of *t*-values for *Shock (5 years)* and *Durable Ruling Party* from extreme bounds analysis, summarizing 4,096 separate tests with varying controls.

robust, but 82.7% remain significant at the .05 level and no *t*-value is below 1. In sum, the main variables display a very low dependence on controls, especially for the shocks.

### Other Robustness Checks

I consider a number of other modeling variations. Since the five-year window that defines recent shocks is somewhat arbitrary, Figure 7.6 shows the estimated effect for each window from 1 to 10 years. The estimates are remarkably consistent across this range, although highest in the three- to five-year range. Figure 7.7 repeats this for the minimum party durability to qualify for *Durable Ruling Party*, with the effects on democratization remaining significant between 3 and 7 years. The insignificance at the low end is expected, as these are not parties with sufficient experience to be confident in their democratic prospects. At the high end, estimates are similar in magnitude up to 9 years. Entrenchment beyond that is likely proxying for parties that are the most resistant to democratization.

Figure 7.8 shows the main variables' effects when the sample is limited to specific time periods: 1800–1945 (roughly corresponding to the First and First Reverse Waves of democratization), 1946–73 (Second and Second Reverse Waves), 1974–2014 (Third Wave), and 1989–2014 (post–Cold War). The effect of shocks is significantly positive in every period but much smaller in the earliest, in part reflecting the relative rarity of democratization. Thus, the long temporal scope of this study is somewhat underplaying the effect of shocks as it applies to the modern period. Variation for *Durable Ruling Party* is more complex: it's significant only in the earliest period and post–Cold War, exactly matching the temporal pattern for the electoral continuity path (with cases

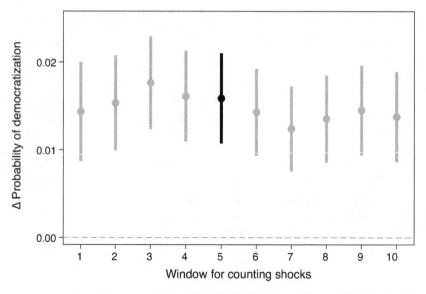

FIGURE 7.6. Shock effects for different windows. Estimates of increased likelihood of democratization when varying the window for recent shocks. The main window used in the book is five years. Bars = 95% CI.

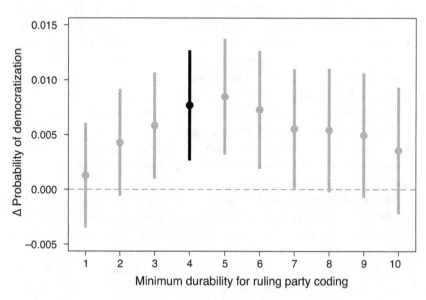

FIGURE 7.7. Variation in ruling party effects. Estimates of increased likelihood of democratization when varying the minimum durability for *Durable Ruling Party*. The main time span used in the book is four years. Bars = 95% CI.

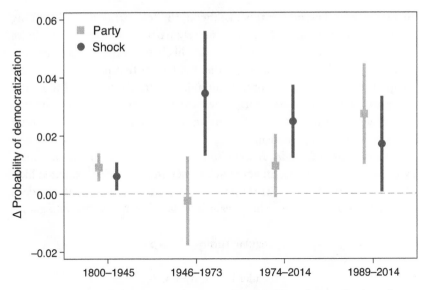

FIGURE 7.8. Path effects by time period. Estimated effects of recent shocks and durable ruling parties on democratization, stratifying by four different time periods. Bars = 95% CI.

from 1885–1942 and 1988–2009).[6] Significantly, durable parties are slightly more positive for democratization than shocks post–Cold War.

I further tested the main models using alternative democracy measures, specifically by requiring democracy to additionally score 6 or above on Polity (Marshall and Jaggers 2017) or above 0.5 on V-Dem's polyarchy measure (Coppedge et al. 2018). Shocks remain significantly predictive, but ruling parties narrowly miss significance for the Polity measure. Lastly, I confirmed all of the main results using OLS, a multinomial logit that simultaneously predicts democratization and autocratic breakdown, lagging controls by 5 or 10 years, and only counting shocks that occur within autocracy.

## TESTING THE MECHANISMS

Finally, I directly test the mechanisms of leader insecurity and party power calculations through an imputation technique. The idea is to estimate a leader's annual likelihood of being violently overthrown, given leader and country

6. This pattern is likely connected to the changing techniques of autocratic electoral control. In the earlier period, autocracies limited suffrage and democratized by gradually extending it. When this technique became unviable, the model for an autocratic party that could control contested full-suffrage elections, let alone survive into democracy, remained underdeveloped. With the spread of dominant electoral parties as in Mexico, Taiwan, and Senegal, the electoral continuity path was reopened.

characteristics. The higher this likelihood, the less attractive maintaining autocracy will be for most dictators. Similarly, parties with greater confidence in their democratic prospects will be more likely to accept democratization. An added complication, however, is that the factors that predict democratic competitiveness might also predict durability within autocracy. I therefore generate two predicted risks for parties: their chances of winning power in democracy and their likelihood of losing power in autocracy. Both should make democratization more likely.

The measure of *Leader Insecurity* is generated by predicting irregular executive turnover across all autocracies, then imputing the estimated likelihood for each autocracy. This provides a reasonable proxy for the leader's expected risk of overthrow. Thus, I calculate the following within autocracy:

$$P(\text{Irregular Turnover}) \sim \boldsymbol{X\beta} + \varepsilon$$

$$\text{Leader Insecurity} = \boldsymbol{X\hat{\beta}}$$

where $\boldsymbol{X}$ are leader- and country-specific variables and irregular turnover is predicted with a logit. I use the following predictors, all lagged by one year: indicators for any irregular turnover, coup, or regular turnover in the last five years, *GDP/capita*, *Economic Growth*, *Regional Democracy*, dummies for military and personalist regimes, a dummy for a legislature (from Coppedge et al. 2018), ethnic fractionalization, the military size (as % of population), the leader's tenure in office, the leader's age (Goemans, Gleditsch, and Chiozza 2016), and region dummies. Among the strongest predictors are average income, recent irregular turnover, and regime type. The resulting estimated risk varies from 0.5% to 33.4% (in Cambodia 1975).

To capture a party's *Democratic Prospects*, I use the main model from Miller 2021, which examines former autocratic ruling parties' likelihoods of winning power in democracy. I translate the model to autocracy by imputing each party's chances of winning power assuming it democratizes the following year. For instance, a key predictor in the model is the average economic growth under party rule; I therefore input a party's average growth rate to the current year. Other predictors include party age, years in power, average opposition party freedom, and whether the party ever experienced a territorial loss, in addition to *GDP/capita* (ln), regional democracy, previous democratic breakdowns, year, and a post–Cold War dummy.

*Party Insecurity*, the risk of party turnover in autocracy, is estimated from the same variables as *Leader Insecurity*, with the addition of party system strength (from Coppedge et al. 2018) and the same party variables as for *Democratic Prospects*. I count turnover either to a new party or to a non-party regime, but not voluntary democratization. Since the most accurate ruling-party data and the model from Miller 2021 are for a post-1940

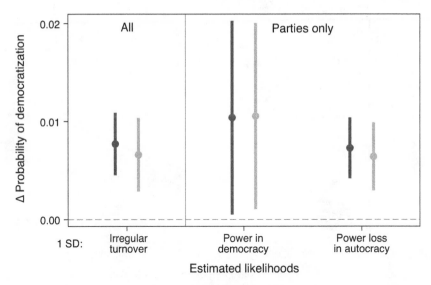

FIGURE 7.9. Autocratic security and democratization. Estimated effects on democratization from one-standard-deviation increases in the estimated likelihoods of irregular
turnover, democratic power (assuming democratization occurred that year), and party
turnover (latter two for post-1940 party regimes). For each risk factor, the two displayed
estimates respectively omit and include controls for shocks and durable ruling parties.
The estimates show that regime insecurity and party prospects in democracy are
important motives for democratization. Bars = 95% CI.

sample, both *Democratic Prospects* and *Party Insecurity* are only imputed for
this period.

Figure 7.9 shows how each risk factor predicts democratization, tested with
the base model.[7] On the left, *Leader Insecurity* is tested in a full sample of
autocracies, with the estimates showing the heightened probability of democratization from a one-standard-deviation (1 SD = 5.2%) increase. Since *Leader
Insecurity* is intended to capture overall risk, it's not clear whether shocks and
ruling parties should still be included in the model. The dark and light bars
indicate their respective omission or inclusion, with little effect. The results
show a significant effect of leader insecurity, with every 5% increase in irregular turnover risk translating to roughly a 0.8% increase in democratization.
Figure 7.10 displays the estimated probability of democratization (with shocks

7. Given that these risk factors are estimated, statisticians argue that their standard
errors in testing may be too conservative (Pagan 1984). As a standard response, I investi-
gated a bootstrap technique. This samples data points with replacement to generate a new
autocratic sample, calculates the risk factors, and finally tests them on the corresponding sample. This is repeated 1,000 times, with the standard errors calculated from the
observed distribution of each coefficient. However, this resulted in smaller standard errors
for *Leader Insecurity* and *Democratic Prospects* (with results for *Party Insecurity* remaining highly significant), so I decided to preserve the simpler and more conservative method.

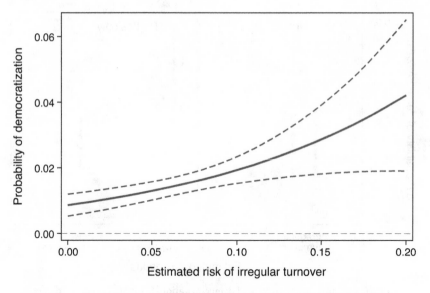

FIGURE 7.10. Leader insecurity and democratization. Estimated likelihood of democratization from estimated risk of irregular turnover. Area = 95% CI.

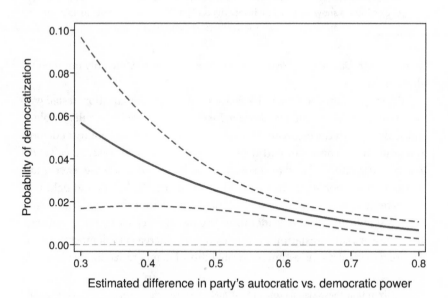

FIGURE 7.11. Party prospects and democratization. Estimated likelihood of democratization from estimated difference in a ruling party's chances of retaining power in autocracy versus winning power in democracy. Area = 95% CI.

and ruling parties included) across a wide range of *Leader Insecurity*, demonstrating a roughly sevenfold increase in democratization's chances.

The right side of Figure 7.9 summarizes the results from testing *Democratic Prospects* and *Party Insecurity* in a sample of ruling-party regimes. Both are significantly predictive. A 1 SD increase in *Democratic Prospects* (22.5%) has the largest effect of any risk factor, although the standard error is larger. Figure 7.11 displays the estimated probability of democratization (with shocks and ruling parties included) from the *difference* in these two risks, that is, a party's increased chance of retaining power in autocracy versus democracy. Variation in this relative risk predicts a roughly tenfold shift in the likelihood of democratization.

The findings provide strong support for Hypotheses 1 and 2: Autocrats and ruling parties make democratization decisions in part based on power calculations. The more insecure their hold within autocracy, the more that democracy can be regarded as a salvation. And the less risky democracy is for party power, the more willing they are to make the leap. In addition, recent shocks significantly predict *Leader Insecurity* and *Party Insecurity*, while durable parties significantly predict *Democratic Prospects*, further confirming that the paths operate through these mechanisms.

## Conclusion

The findings are very clear: both shocks and durable ruling parties strongly predict democratization. Moreover, the effect sizes are large enough to fundamentally shape the global prevalence of democracy. Indeed, the main result confirmed that countries have about a 1-in-200 annual chance of democratization absent shocks or ruling parties. The results are highly robust to varying controls and model alternatives, especially for shocks. A partial exception is the period-dependence for durable parties. However, they are strongest in the modern period, so this only amplifies their relevance to current and future democratization.

Results also offer strong support for other elements of the book's theory. Leader and party insecurity and ruling party prospects in democracy—key mechanisms for the theory—predict democratization. Among individual shocks, coups, hegemonic withdrawals, civil war stalemates, and defeats in foreign war each individually predict democratization, with more mixed evidence for ongoing civil wars and assassinations. No effect was found for failed coup attempts, other civil war resolutions, or victories in war, nor for ousters from below independent of the paths. Thus, a consistent pattern is that the violent events most predictive of weak regimes are the most conducive to democratization. The next chapter investigates the implications of the paths for structural variables and protest.

# CHAPTER EIGHT

# Mediated Effects of the Paths

WHEN ARE PRO-DEMOCRATIC protests most likely to succeed? How do country characteristics like economic development, oil dependence, and gender inequality influence democratization? With the last chapter demonstrating the average effects of recent shocks and durable ruling parties, the current chapter turns to how they interact with pro-democratic activity and socioeconomic structure. This can give protest movements and democracy promoters valuable insight as to when autocracies are most vulnerable to pressure.

The results provide strong empirical support for the book's theory that pro-democratic activity and structure have heightened importance when shocks or confident ruling parties disrupt the autocratic status quo. When the dam breaks, the land steers the water. In fact, the interaction with structure is powerful enough that it can largely fill the theoretical gap between opening and successful democratization. Given shocks or durable ruling parties, autocracies with sufficiently favorable structural conditions are much more likely than not to democratize within five years.

On the methodological side, this chapter proposes a shift in how scholars test country-level factors and democratization. Rather than focusing on direct effects, given that shocks and ruling parties precede nearly all cases of democratization, a better approach is to capture how structure flows through these conditions. I introduce a framework that tests how structure first predicts and is then conditioned by shocks and ruling parties, which helps to illuminate *how* and *why* specific factors predict democratization and why many do not. In particular, I show this framework can break down the fraction of a variable's effect on democratization that runs through each path (or neither path), revealing what pushes countries down their specific paths. As an exploratory exercise, I apply the framework to 14 structural factors, with the deepest analysis on average income and why it has such a weak relationship with democratization.

## *Predictions*

It's again helpful to summarize the theoretical claims into a few testable hypotheses. Each can be prefaced with an *"All things equal . . ."* stipulation. As predicted by the theory, I found extensive qualitative evidence that shocks and durable ruling parties produce destabilized periods that both facilitate pro-democratic activity and make it more likely to succeed. Following shocks, this is due to coercive and institutional weakness, elite uncertainty about regime survival, and the increased danger of resorting to repression. With ruling parties, this is due to wider opportunities for opposition organization and drawbacks of repression for forward-thinking parties.

> *Hypothesis 8*: Pro-democratic activity is more likely following recent shocks or with durable ruling parties.

> *Hypothesis 9*: Pro-democratic activity is more predictive of democratization following recent shocks or with durable ruling parties.

To anticipate the terms defined in the next section, pro-democratic activity acts as both a mediator and a moderator for the effects of shocks and parties.

What does this imply for structural factors like economic development? All such factors ultimately influence democratization by affecting the preferences and power of elites, opposition actors, and regime leaders. A range of socio-economic conditions have been found to predict wider pro-democratic preferences and greater economic and political power for pro-democratic actors (e.g., Lipset 1959, 1960; Dahl 1971; R. Collier 1999; Inglehart and Welzel 2005; Mainwaring and Pérez-Liñán 2013; Sanborn and Thyne 2014). It follows from Hypothesis 9 that structure should therefore be more predictive following shocks or with ruling parties, when popular preferences will be most pivotal. This does not necessarily hold universally and uniformly across all factors, but those that facilitate pro-democratic activity (either through democratic preferences or organizational capacity) are the most likely to fit this pattern.

> *Hypothesis 10*: On average, structural factors are more predictive of democratization following recent shocks or with durable ruling parties, especially when these factors predict pro-democratic sentiment.

Below, I test various structural factors, allowing their effects to be conditional on recent shocks and durable parties. The framework I develop also incorporates these factors' initial predictions of shocks and durable parties, which is critical to understanding how they ultimately lead to democratization. Indeed, an extensive literature on the predictors of coups, civil wars, and other shocks (e.g., Londregan and Poole 1990; Belkin and Schofer 2003; Iqbal and Zorn 2006; Powell 2012; Gates et al. 2016; Bodea, Elbadawi, and Houle 2017)

has found starring roles for many of the same factors that predict democratization, although often in different directions. Thus, shocks and parties act
as both mediators and moderators for structural effects on democratization.

This discussion has left somewhat open *which* specific structural factors
are expected to have which patterns. This is intentional, as the empirical
framework and hypotheses are general in scope. I predict that most structural
factors with a total effect on democratization will have significant interactions with the paths, as well as a number of variables with *null* total effects.
However, as a straightforward expectation, the factors most likely to predict
pro-democratic sentiment (and therefore lead to strong conditional effects)
should be "modernization" variables like average income, education, and literacy (Lipset 1959, 1960; Inglehart and Welzel 2005; Sanborn and Thyne 2014).
For the empirical analysis below, I focus on the most theoretically significant
and well-studied factors, beginning with average income.

## *Mediation, Moderation, and Democratization*

Mediation analysis is a way of unpacking *how* causal relationships work by
testing for intermediate variables on the causal path. Figure 8.1 shows the simplest version of a mediation model. A variable $X$ can have a *direct effect* on $Y$
and an *indirect effect* mediated through $M$. The *total effect* is the sum of the
direct and indirect effects. A similar setup can incorporate multiple mediators, each with their own indirect effect. For interpretation, researchers tend
to focus on the size of mediation effects and the fraction of the total effect
explained by mediators.

Estimation is straightforward: each mediator is predicted by $X$ in a separate model (the first stage) and then the outcome $Y$ is predicted by $X$ and each
mediator together (the second stage). Indirect effects are calculated by combining estimates from the two stages.[1] Estimating mediation through $M$ without bias requires two main assumptions beyond the lack of omitted variables
mutually affecting $X$ and $Y$ (Imai et al. 2011; Glynn 2012; VanderWeele 2015).
First, there must also be no omitted variables mutually affecting $M$ and either
$X$ or $Y$. Otherwise, either the estimated effect from $X$ to $M$ or from $M$ to $Y$ will
be biased. Second, a more often overlooked assumption is there cannot be unit
heterogeneity in the effect of $X$ on $M$ that is correlated with unit heterogeneity
in the effect of $M$ on $Y$ (see Glynn 2012).

We can also test for *moderation* or *conditional effects*. Instead of $M$ acting
as an intermediate step from $X$ to $Y$, $M$ can affect the strength of association
between $X$ and $Y$. For instance, a sudden fright might better predict a heart

---

1. If both stages are linear models, this combination is a simple product of coefficients
(Baron and Kenny 1986; Glynn 2012). With binary models, a slightly more complicated
calculation is needed (Imai et al. 2011; VanderWeele 2015).

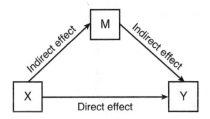

FIGURE 8.1. General setup for causal
mediation, with mediator $M$.

attack if a person is already overweight. In this case, weight acts as a moderator. A mediator can simultaneously act as a moderator if $X$ predicts $M$ and
$M$ affects the strength of relationship between $X$ and $Y$. Testing this requires
including the appropriate interactions with $M$ in the second stage or stratifying by $M$ (Edwards and Lambert 2007; VanderWeele 2015).

This chapter examines two frameworks combining mediation and moderation. First, I validate Hypotheses 8 and 9 by showing that shocks and ruling
parties predict pro-democratic activity and interact with it in predicting
democratization. Second, I examine how shocks and ruling parties both
mediate and moderate the democratizing influence of structural variables, including economic development, institutions, and regional democracy. Rather than picturing these variables as directly predicting democratization, as in most research, we can think of them as flowing through
the preceding context. The two frameworks are closely connected, as the
moderating effect of pro-democratic activity helps to explain the parallel
patterns for structural factors, especially those that predict pro-democratic
sentiment.

## The Paths, Pro-Democratic Activity, and Democratization

### FROM THE PATHS TO PRO-DEMOCRATIC ACTIVITY

We begin by examining how the paths provide openings for pro-democratic
pressure. I predict four measures of pro-democratic activity: *Protest* (a dummy
for any protest or strike, from Banks and Wilson 2017), *Nonviolent Movement*
(using NAVCO, from Chenoweth and Lewis 2013), *Civil Society* strength (0–1
measure, from Coppedge et al. 2018), and a count of international *Political
Sanctions* aimed at regime change or human rights (from Morgan, Bapat,
and Kobayashi 2014). These were previously used for descriptive statistics in
chapter 2. Note that *Nonviolent Movement* primarily picks up large and well-
organized campaigns and, as a result, is about five times rarer in autocracies
than *Protest*. The first two are predicted with logits and the latter two with

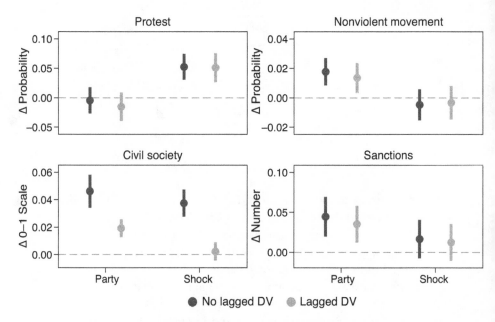

FIGURE 8.2. Predictions of pro-democratic activity. Estimated increases on four measures of pro-democratic activity from recent shocks and durable ruling parties. The tests vary by whether they include a lagged dependent variable (light bars) or not (dark bars). Bars = 95% CI.

OLS,[2] each with a sample of autocracies and the base model from chapter 7. The independent variables of interest are *Shock (5 years)* and *Durable Ruling Party*. All independent variables are lagged by one year. To account for potential reverse causation from pro-democratic activity to shocks or ruling parties, I run the models with and without a five-year lagged dependent variable (DV).

Figure 8.2 summarizes the results, showing the increased probability of *Protest* and *Nonviolent Movement* and increases in *Civil Society* and *Political Sanctions* for each path condition and the two models. With the exception of *Civil Society* (which is much stickier over time), results are similar with and without the lagged DV. Consistent with Hypothesis 8, shocks and parties predict more pro-democratic activity but differ on the types. *Protest* is 5% more likely following recent shocks, roughly a 30% proportional increase. Besides protest, shocks are significantly related to *Civil Society* but only without a lagged DV. In contrast, durable parties do not predict *Protest* but do robustly predict each of the other three DVs, proportionally increasing the likelihood of *Nonviolent Movement* by over 60%. A likely reason for this pattern is that durable parties often introduce broad liberal reforms that enable civil society development and give sufficient room for large nonviolent

2. Results are virtually identical if *Political Sanctions* is predicted with a count model.

movements. In contrast, individual protests can occur in disordered and violent environments.

Results are similar for other outcomes. The overall strength of anti-regime organization (from Coppedge et al. 2018) is predicted by durable parties, whereas violent activity like riots and guerrilla movements (from Banks and Wilson 2017) is predicted by shocks. However, these are less likely to be pro-democratic, so I favor the DVs shown in Figure 8.2. In sum, both shocks and durable parties predict a range of anti-regime and pro-democratic activity, although interestingly differ on the exact types.

## FROM PRO-DEMOCRATIC ACTIVITY
## TO DEMOCRATIZATION

We now examine how pro-democratic activity predicts democratization, allowing for differences across contexts. Specifically, I stratify by separately examining samples of autocracies following shocks, with durable ruling parties, and with neither. Each pro-democratic measure is tested with a separate dynamic logit in each sample, with the base model of controls. Stratifying like this is important because controls also have distinct effects in each context, as the next section will show. Stratifying is equivalent to including a full set of interactions between the context and each independent variable. I use the four pro-democratic measures tested above, along with *Regional Democracy* (the surrounding region's fraction of democracies). The latter has been shown to encourage democratic change through emulation and direct pro-democratic pressure (Starr 1991; Wejnert 2005; Gleditsch and Ward 2006) but was not appropriate to test as an outcome of domestic events.

Figure 8.3 shows the increased likelihood of democratization in the three contexts from 0–1 shifts in *Protest* and *Nonviolent Movement* and one-standard-deviation shifts in the remaining measures. In every case except *Political Sanctions*, pro-democratic activity has a minuscule effect without shocks or ruling parties and a significantly positive effect on democratization given either path condition.[3] The effect sizes are also enormous: a nonviolent movement raises the annual likelihood of democratization by more than 5% with either path condition, in addition to the latter's direct effect. Effect sizes are similar for shocks and ruling parties, with the exception of *Regional Democracy*, which has about twice the impact after shocks. *Political Sanctions* has no effect in any context, which is not too surprising given past results on the inconsistent application and weak leverage of international democracy promotion (Goldsmith 2008; Dietrich and Wright 2014; Bush 2015; von Borzyskowski and Vabulas 2019).

One concern when comparing probability effects from a binary model like logit is that effects can appear larger or smaller depending on your location on

---

3. The differences are all significant if tested in the same sample with interactions.

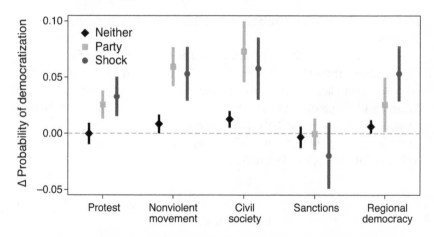

FIGURE 8.3. Conditional effects of pro-democratic activity. Estimated effects of five measures of pro-democratic activity or pressure on likelihood of democratization, dividing between countries with recent shocks, durable ruling parties, and neither. Each effect is the increased probability given a one-standard-deviation increase in the predictor, or a shift from 0 to 1 for protests and nonviolent movements. Except for political sanctions, there is a consistently stronger effect with recent shocks or ruling parties. Bars = 95% CI.

the logit curve (Frant, Berry, and Berry 1991). The logit function resembles a stretched-out S shape, which is shallower at very low and very high probabilities. Thus, a factor like protest can appear to have a larger effect if you begin at a moderate probability, such as after shocks. To ensure this is not generating the comparisons in Figure 8.3, I reran each test with a linear probability model (using OLS), which is not affected by this issue. In every case, the same patterns appear. Excluding political sanctions, the pro-democratic variables average 7.3 times the probability effect after shocks and 6.3 times the effect with durable ruling parties compared to neither. There is therefore overwhelming support for Hypothesis 9: pro-democratic activity is more effective following shocks or with ruling parties.

Combined with the results in Figure 8.2, we see that pro-democratic activity both mediates and moderates the effects of shocks and parties on democratization. It's straightforward to calculate the fraction of the total effects mediated in this way.[4] Looking only at path conditions and mediators that are significantly related in Figure 8.2, I find that *Protest* explains 8.4% (SE = 3.9%)

---

4. To calculate this fraction for shocks, for example, I first determine the expected value of the mediator with and without a recent shock, using the model with the lagged DV. The mediated effect is the estimated difference in democratization likelihood between these two values of the mediator, holding the shock measure fixed at 1 (VanderWeele 2015). This mediated effect is then divided by the total effect of shocks. Standard errors were calculated by bootstrapping the sample and repeating this procedure 1,000 times (Imai et al. 2011).

of the shock effect, while *Nonviolent Movement* and *Civil Society* respectively explain 8.8% (SE = 5.5%) and 25.3% (SE = 7.8%) of the ruling party effect. This supports the theory that pro-democratic openings are significant facets of how the paths produce democratization.

Another important implication of these results is the diminished effectiveness of pro-democratic activity without the right contexts. Again, this helps to explain the varying success of protests, including prominent failures in the 1848 revolutions, the Arab Spring, Iran, Burma, China, and Venezuela. On the flip side, the results provide guidance to the most propitious moments for opposition movements to apply pressure.

## Structural Factors and Democratization: A New Empirical Framework

I now turn to examining how socioeconomic and political factors predict democratization. Rather than simply testing total effects, as is common in empirical research, I try to answer *why* they predict democratization by examining their effects through the paths. This incorporates the variables' initial predictions of shocks and ruling parties, as well as their varying effects on democratization by context. Combining these effects can uncover illuminating and often unexpected patterns. After motivating and outlining the empirical framework, I examine the results in detail for average income, then overview thirteen other structural variables. Finally, I show how the framework can calculate how much of a variable's total effect on democratization runs through each path.

### A NEW FRAMEWORK FOR PREDICTING DEMOCRATIZATION

Since virtually all democratic transitions follow shocks or ruling parties, it makes sense to analyze how predictors of democratization flow through these preceding conditions. Figure 8.4 shows the proposed structure. A given predictor can have five relevant effects. First, it can predict the initial occurrence of shocks and durable ruling parties (effects 1, 2). Second, its prediction of democratization can interact with shocks and ruling parties in a moderating relationship (effects 3, 4). Third, it can directly predict democratization outside of the paths (effect 5). Of course, a predictor can satisfy one or more of these effects without satisfying others. To simplify slightly, if each of the five effects can be positive, negative, or zero, there are 243 possible combinations, each with a different implication. The only case in which the paths do not help to explain a connection to democratization is if the predictor is positive for effect 5 alone.

A virtue of this framework is that it can uncover a range of complex and theoretically interesting patterns. First, combinations of effects can shift the most likely path taken to democratization, a more specific outcome with

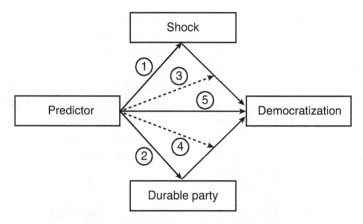

FIGURE 8.4. A new empirical framework for predicting democratization.
Rather than conceptualizing variables as directly predicting democratization,
we can see them as flowing through preceding events and institutions,
chiefly shocks and ruling parties. A variable can predict these antecedents
(effects 1, 2), moderate the democratizating effect of shocks and ruling
parties (effects 3, 4), or directly predict democratization (effect 5).

implications for democratic survival. Second, understanding moderation
effects may be especially important to pro-democratic actors who want to
identify the most favorable times to push for liberalization. For instance, a
variable positive for effect 4 alone implies that it can contribute to democratization, but only with a durable ruling party, potentially shaping opposition
strategy. Third, whether variables predict shocks or ruling parties is itself significant and should be considered alongside any democratizing effects.

Further, the framework can also help to explain predictors' *null* relationships with democratization, which are typically ignored. For instance, a predictor might encourage one type of democratization and discourage another,
still a substantively meaningful effect. Another possibility is a variable boost-
ing effect 1 and reducing effect 3, meaning it predicts shocks but lessens the
likelihood these shocks result in regime change. This can balance out for
democratization but implies a noteworthy destabilizing effect.

To be clear, this framework is still sensitive to many of the same concerns
as traditional tests, including omitted variables. However, accounting for the
paths can eliminate one source of omitted variables and clue researchers into
others. Further, the framework is not designed to select between structural
causes of democratization as more or less important, although it does reveal
which causes predict desired routes to democratization.

The goal is to improve on traditional tests by unpacking and deepening the
prediction of democratization in a theoretically meaningful way. The payoff is
improved insight into the how and why of democratizing effects, with potential
for more effective democracy promotion and strategic opposition to autocracy.

## EMPIRICAL SETUP

Let's consider testing a structural factor $X$, such as economic development. As shown in Figure 8.4, we want to include both mediating and moderating effects of each path. Therefore, the analysis must predict shocks and ruling parties from $X$, as well as predict democratization with interactions between $X$ and each context. A major complication concerns timing and causal ordering. The shocks and ruling parties must precede democratization. Further, the shock can have up to five years to result in democratization, while ruling parties are counted as long as the party endures. In addition, $X$ must precede the tested shock and predict the future presence of ruling parties, otherwise it could reflect reverse causation (VanderWeele 2015: 53–54).

I propose the following setup to account for this timing.[5] Let's say that $X$ and all controls are measured in Year 0, with this year required to be within autocracy. First, I predict whether a *Shock* occurs within autocracy in Years 1–5. Second, I predict whether *Durable Ruling Party* is satisfied at any point in the same window. These two models correspond to effects 1 and 2 in Figure 8.4.[6] Third, I predict whether the country democratizes within Years 2–6 from $X$, shocks and durable parties (in their five-year windows and only counted if they precede democratization), and their interactions with $X$. This allows for the calculation of effects 3–5.

Note the timing is very flexible. A shock might occur in Year 1 and produce democratization in Year 6 or might occur in Year 3 and produce democratization in Year 4. Also note that $X$ is predicting democratization up to six years later, so this arguably works best for either slow-moving structural variables (such as economic development and oil dependence) or factors that can plausibly exert long-term effects (such as institutions and economic crises).

### MEDIATED AND CONDITIONAL
### EFFECTS OF AVERAGE INCOME

I begin by applying the framework to average income (*GDP/capita*, natural-logged, in real 2000 dollars), probably the single most-studied characteristic in relation to democratization (e.g., Lipset 1959; Burkhart and Lewis-Beck

---

5. To my knowledge, no existing mediation/moderation setup can incorporate such a complex timing structure. VanderWeele (2015: 155–59) recommends using marginal structural models for longitudinal data, but these work best with a fixed number of periods and can't recover mediated effects.

6. An option is to include lags for past shocks and parties in these first-stage predictions, which will then measure shifts in these outcomes. This is a particular concern for civil wars and durable parties, which can persist for several years. Yet this has a minimal effect on results for the 14 variables I examine—all significant first-stage results retain the same sign and only in 2 cases do they become insignificant.

1994; Barro 1999). For years, scholars saw high average income as intimately connected to democracy as a consequence of modernization theory (Lerner 1958; Lipset 1959, 1960; de Schweinitz 1964). Wealthier countries tend to have better-educated and politically moderate citizens (Lipset 1959, 1960; Dahl 1971; Sanborn and Thyne 2014), translating to greater mass and elite support for democracy (Huntington 1991; Boix 2003; Lizzeri and Persico 2004; Inglehart and Welzel 2005; Mainwaring and Pérez-Liñán 2013; Treisman 2015). Development also predicts the growth of strong working and middle classes, who favor greater freedom and have the organizational resources to push for democracy (Huntington 1991; Rueschemeyer, Stephens, and Stephens 1992; R. Collier 1999; Inglehart and Welzel 2005; Haggard and Kaufman 2016; Dahlum, Knutsen, and Wig 2019). Overwhelmingly, these theories presume that economic development fosters democracy by tilting popular and elite preferences toward the regime type.

Yet things are not so simple. Przeworski and Limongi (1997) and Przeworski et al. (2000) shocked comparative scholars by showing that income predicts democratic survival but not democratization, at least not after 1950. Acemoglu et al. (2009) went further by arguing that income's correlation with democracy is a spurious consequence of historical institutions. The income-democracy relationship remains much debated, with Boix and Stokes (2003) and Boix (2011) responding that a positive effect on democratization is restored if one considers a sufficiently long time period. More recent work has shifted to identifying conditional relationships in which income's effect depends on the time period (Boix 2011; Boix, Miller, and Rosato 2013), leader change (Miller 2012; Treisman 2015), or structural characteristics like the state's control of the economy (Tang and Woods 2014).

Even if average income positively predicts democratization, there remains the puzzle of why this relationship is so weak, especially relative to its effect on democratic survival (Miller 2012). I argue that political context—as captured by recent shocks and durable parties—is a critical missing piece of this puzzle, which past work has neglected by focusing on actor preferences. Income relates to this context in two ways. First, it's well understood that income is a general stabilizing force, with an especially strong negative effect on political violence (Londregan and Poole 1990; Feng 1997; Miller 2012; Singh 2014). Other research shows average income negatively predicts the adoption of multiparty elections because wealthier citizens are harder to control (Miller 2020b). Second, if average income predicts pro-democratic sentiment, we should expect it to have a stronger effect when political openings provide room for opposition organization. Specifically, it should be more predictive of democratization following violent shocks or with destabilized electoral politics. Thus, average income should strongly predict democratization during political openings but makes these political openings less likely in the first place. The balance of income's stabilizing and pro-democratizing forces explains why its total effect on democratization is so weak.

**Table 8.1.** Average Income: Predictions of Paths and Democratization

| DVs (5-year periods) | Shock | Durable Ruling Party | Democratization 1800–2014 | | Democratization 1950–2014 | |
|---|---|---|---|---|---|---|
| | (1) | (2) | (3) | (4) | (5) | (6) |
| GDP/capita (ln) | −0.317*** | −0.123*** | 0.215*** | 0.205*** | 0.048 | −0.066 |
| | (−12.09) | (−4.48) | (4.97) | (3.39) | (1.07) | (−1.01) |
| GDP/capita (ln)× Shock (5 years) | | | | 0.485*** | | 0.558*** |
| | | | | (4.39) | | (5.81) |
| GDP/capita (ln)× Durable Ruling Party | | | | −0.203* | | −0.058 |
| | | | | (−2.35) | | (−0.58) |
| Shock (5 years) | | | | −2.852*** | | −3.484*** |
| | | | | (−4.34) | | (−4.56) |
| Durable Ruling Party | | | | 1.912** | | 0.468 |
| | | | | (2.77) | | (0.59) |
| Regional Democracy | −1.204*** | 1.785*** | 1.490*** | 1.701*** | 0.826*** | 1.067*** |
| | (−9.91) | (14.44) | (8.11) | (8.78) | (3.44) | (4.17) |
| Previous Dem. Spells | 0.447*** | −0.699*** | 0.686*** | 0.618*** | 0.687*** | 0.594*** |
| | (9.13) | (−12.98) | (10.51) | (8.83) | (10.24) | (8.23) |
| Economic Growth | −0.033*** | 0.014** | −0.033*** | −0.029** | −0.023* | −0.019* |
| | (−5.27) | (2.99) | (−3.66) | (−3.23) | (−2.40) | (−2.08) |
| Population (ln) | 0.077*** | 0.080*** | 0.090** | 0.092** | 0.083* | 0.090* |
| | (5.51) | (4.98) | (3.13) | (3.02) | (2.27) | (2.32) |
| Year | 0.000 | 0.024*** | 0.009*** | 0.007*** | 0.007* | 0.010** |
| | (1.06) | (35.03) | (7.18) | (4.95) | (2.10) | (3.05) |
| Autocracy Age Cubic? | Y | Y | Y | Y | Y | Y |
| N | 10,487 | 10,487 | 10,470 | 10,470 | 5,035 | 5,035 |
| Countries | 151 | 151 | 151 | 151 | 137 | 137 |
| Pseudo R² | 0.047 | 0.230 | 0.143 | 0.170 | 0.073 | 0.101 |

*Notes:* The table displays logits predicting shocks, durable ruling parties, and democratization in a sample of autocracies. Models 1 and 2 predict any autocratic shock or durable ruling party within the following five years, respectively. Models 3–6 predict democratization over a five-year period, with shocks and ruling parties lagged by one year and remaining controls lagged by two years. Years are 1800–2014, except for Models 5 and 6. $z$-values (based on robust standard errors) are in parentheses. $*p < 0.05$, $**p < 0.01$, $***p < 0.001$

Table 8.1 shows the results from applying the empirical framework to average income. The first two models are logits predicting *Shock* and *Durable Ruling Party* within five-year windows. The third model shows the prediction of democratization (also within a five-year window) if we ignore the path context. The fourth model then adds the measures of shocks and durable parties (the DVs from Models 1 and 2) and their interactions with average income. To aid comparison with Przeworski et al. 2000, Models 5 and 6 repeat this pattern for 1950–2014 only. Each model includes the base set of controls, with all independent variables lagged.

As expected, average income is strongly negative for both shocks and durable parties, with a one-standard-deviation (1 SD) increase lowering the five-year likelihood of shocks by 6.2% and durable parties by 2%. This reflects higher income's general stabilizing effect and its negative relationship with election adoption.

Consistent with Boix and Stokes 2003, Model 3 shows that average income has a positive total effect for democratization, although the effect size is modest—a 1 SD increase raises democratization's five-year likelihood by only 1.1%. The most significant finding is in Model 4: *income interacts with the political context*, showing a much stronger effect following shocks and a modestly weaker effect with ruling parties. Figure 8.5 shows the predicted probability of democratization for a range of *GDP/capita* (ln) with and without a shock. With a shock, moving from the 5th to 95th percentile on average income within autocracies roughly *quadruples* the likelihood of democratization. Without a shock, the probability is unchanged. This general pattern holds for the 1950–2014 sample, but consistent with Przeworski et al. 2000, the total effect of average income is now insignificant. Once again, average income has a strong positive effect on democratization only after a shock occurs.

We now get a fuller picture of average income's connection to democratization and why its net relationship is so weak. When wealthier, pro-democratic citizens combine with the regime instability surrounding shocks, pro-democratic change becomes especially likely. However, average income's stabilizing effect makes these openings rarer. These pro-democratic and stabilizing effects balance out in the 1950–2014 sample and have a small net effect in the full sample. An implication of this is many wealthy autocracies should experience long periods of quiescence followed by a sudden shock and a broadly popular shift to democratization, a fitting description of cases like Spain 1977, Argentina 1983, Hungary 1990, and Croatia 2000. These patterns are explored more fully in Miller 2012, which examines the similar interaction of average income and recent irregular turnover for democratization and explains why income's effect is stronger for democratic survival.[7]

## MEDIATED AND CONDITIONAL
## EFFECTS OF OTHER VARIABLES

Having seen how this works for average income, we can now extend this framework to other variables. I consider 13 further variables spread across four categories (see the appendix if source is not cited). I begin with three

---

7. In brief, the pro-democratic and stabilizing effects of average income work together within democracy, producing a strong positive effect on democratic survival.

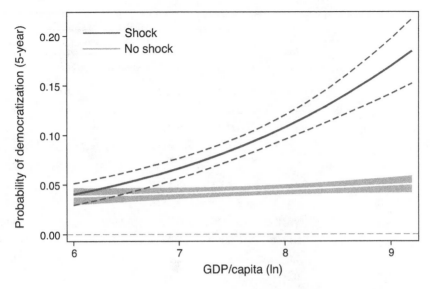

FIGURE 8.5. Conditional effect of income. Estimated five-year likelihood of democratization from *GDP/capita* (ln) with and without a preceding shock. Area = 95% CI.

variables likely to track pro-democratic sentiment: *Literacy* (as % of adult population), *Education* (average schooling years in adult population), and *Regional Democracy*. For further socioeconomic factors, I include *Oil Dependence* (oil revenue as % of GDP), *Equal Resources* (a measure of equal distribution of public goods and power across social groups, from Coppedge et al. 2018), and *Gender Equality* (the same distribution measure applied to gender, from Coppedge et al. 2018). The first is much-studied in connection to democratization, while the latter two capture substantive equality. I also include *Economic Crisis* (a 5% economic decline or 50% inflation rate averaged over two years), tested after omitting *Economic Growth*. To track regime strength, I use *State Capacity* (an aggregate measure of administrative and coercive capacity, from Hanson and Sigman 2013), *Party Strength* (Coppedge et al. 2018), and *Military Spending* (as % of GDP). Finally, for further institutions, I test a *Military Regime* dummy, *Freedom from Repression*, and *Horizontal Constraints* on the executive (latter two from Coppedge et al. 2018).

Table 8.2 summarizes the results for these variables (tested separately), as well as *GDP/capita* for comparison. The equivalent of Models 1–4 from Table 8.1 were run for each. In order, the columns show the variable's total effect on democratization (in gray), the effect on shocks, the effect on durable parties, and the effects on democratization conditional on shocks, parties, and neither. These conditional effects are calculated from the equivalent of Table 8.1's Model 4. Thus, the gray column shows the net effect explained by

**Table 8.2.** Mediated Effects of Paths and Democratization (in %)

| Predictors | Total Δ Demz. | Δ Shock | Δ Party | Δ Democratization Given Shock | Party | Neither |
|---|---|---|---|---|---|---|
| *GDP/capita* (ln) | 1.05*** | −6.18*** | −2.04*** | 4.74*** | 0.01 | 0.70*** |
| *Literacy* | 3.11*** | −6.81*** | 5.07*** | 7.23*** | 1.74** | 1.90*** |
| *Education* | 1.58*** | −5.95*** | 0.91 | 5.49*** | 0.56 | 0.98** |
| *Regional Democracy* | 1.57*** | −5.13*** | 6.35*** | 4.43*** | 0.08 | 1.79*** |
| *Oil Dependence* | −3.76*** | 1.28** | −1.87*** | −3.10* | −4.91*** | −2.22** |
| *Equal Resources* | −0.08 | −7.23*** | −6.11*** | 1.77 | 0.21 | −1.89*** |
| *Gender Equality* | 1.39*** | −6.07*** | 0.04 | 3.99*** | 0.87* | 0.88*** |
| *Economic Crisis* | 1.99*** | 10.31*** | 0.74 | 2.99* | 0.95 | 3.09*** |
| *State Capacity* | 2.31*** | −10.00*** | 1.72 | 5.44*** | 2.03** | −1.29 |
| *Party Strength* | 1.77*** | −3.87*** | 11.63*** | 1.09 | 2.45*** | 1.29*** |
| *Military Spending* | −2.03** | 1.12* | −2.48*** | −6.73*** | −1.18 | −4.10*** |
| *Military Regime* | 3.77*** | 10.45*** | −11.11*** | 4.28*** | 3.10*** | 4.79*** |
| *Freedom from Repression* | 1.34*** | −2.52*** | 1.01* | 1.21 | 2.11*** | 0.01 |
| *Horizontal Constraints* | 2.69*** | 0.58 | 0.32 | 0.22 | 3.86*** | 2.24*** |

*Notes:* The table summarizes how each of 14 variables predicts democratization, shocks, and durable ruling parties over five-year periods. The final three columns show how the variables predict democratization conditional on a shock, party, and neither. Each number is the increased probability (in %) given a one-standard-deviation increase in the predictor, or a shift from 0 to 1 for *Economic Crisis* and *Military Regime*. The numbers were calculated from logits with the base model. *$p < 0.05$, **$p < 0.01$, ***$p < 0.001$

the subsequent columns, which respectively correspond to effects 1–5 from Figure 8.4. All estimates are taken from logits with the base controls (including *GDP/capita*). The effects are shown as predicted percentage changes in the outcome's five-year probability from a 1 SD increase in the variable, or 0–1 shifts for *Economic Crisis* and *Military Regime*.

There is a lot to unpack here. For starters, every variable but *Equal Resources* has a significant total effect on democratization. All but one significantly predict shocks, with nine showing an effect magnitude above 5%. In comparison, nine variables significantly predict durable parties and five have an effect magnitude above 5%. The conditional effects on democratization display several patterns. Most significantly, shocks yield the strongest-magnitude effect for 7 of 14 variables and parties 4 of 14. For the remaining three variables, the effect absent shocks or parties is just barely stronger than with shocks. On average, the effect magnitude with shocks is about double that absent shocks or parties. This provides strong support for Hypothesis 10.

Results for the pro-democratic variables are consistent and fit expectations. As with average income, each of *Literacy, Education*, and *Regional Democracy* are negative for shocks and have by far the strongest positive effects on democratization with shocks. In contrast with average income, *Literacy* and *Regional Democracy* positively predict durable ruling parties and have small positive effects on democratization given parties. Especially for *Literacy*, this additional path effect boosts the net effect above that of average income.

Turning to other socioeconomic variables, *Oil Dependence* has a strong negative total effect on democratization. In fact, the effect is negative under all three conditions. Yet the strongest contribution is through parties, as *Oil Dependence* is negative for parties and has the strongest negative effect on democratization given parties, likely because ruling parties use oil wealth to maintain control (Greene 2007, 2010). In contrast, oil predicts violent shocks, but this is balanced by the negative conditional effect with shocks.

*Equal Resources* is an instructive case. Despite having no net relationship with democratization, there is a lot going on under the placid surface. The variable is strongly negative for both shocks and parties, but this is balanced by marginally positive effects on democratization after each. Only with neither does it have a significantly negative effect on democratization. A potential explanation for this is that *Equal Resources* predicts wider satisfaction among social groups, as reflected in the reduced chance for violent disruption. In turn, it becomes especially unlikely for actors to suddenly force a democratic opening without any preceding shock or electoral trigger. *Gender Equality* works differently, as it's similarly negative for shocks but now has a strong positive effect after shocks. Combined with a non-relationship with ruling parties, this results in a modest net positive effect on democratization.

*Economic Crisis* presents a highly intuitive pattern. As a destabilizing factor, it's strongly positive for shocks and has a positive effect on democratization in each context except with ruling parties. A likely reason for the latter pattern is that weak growth negatively predicts ruling parties regaining power post-democratization (Miller 2021). Therefore, economic crisis undermines the fundamental logic of the electoral continuity path: party leaders' confidence in their democratic chances. Although it may contribute to the initial competitive opening, forward-thinking parties will want to delay democratization until the crisis has faded from memory.

Turning to markers of regime strength, *State Capacity* and *Party Strength* are actually positive for democratization despite both being negative for shocks. We can pinpoint the primary reason for each. For *State Capacity*, it's the strong positive relationship to democratization following shocks. For *Party Strength*, it's the positive prediction of ruling parties and the positive effect on democratization with parties. The latter effect again reflects the heightened chances for strong parties to gain democratic power. More intuitively, *Military*

*Spending* is negative for democratization due to strong negative effects in each context except with parties. This is sensible, as military strength helps regimes reconsolidate control following violent ruptures, whereas ruling parties are less likely to rely on mass coercion and past military spending is minimally helpful for gaining democratic power.

Turning to institutions, several scholars have puzzled over the positive democratizing effect of *Military Regimes* (Geddes 1999; Pepinsky 2014; Geddes, Wright, and Frantz 2018). Consistent with the coups section of chapter 3, military regimes are strongly positive for shocks and negative for durable ruling parties. In turn, military regimes are positive for democratization in each context, especially without parties. This coheres with the idea of military governments as both destabilizing and fragile. Both *Freedom from Repression* and *Horizontal Constraints* are positive for democratization. Interestingly, in both cases, the primary reason is the strongly positive effect with parties. As with *Economic Crisis* and *Party Strength*, this is likely explained by the effects on parties' expectations of democratic power. As Miller 2021 shows, the party's average record of *Freedom from Repression* is positive for later success.

## HOW STRUCTURAL FACTORS PREDICT THE PATHS

Having laid out these varying patterns through the paths, we can go one step further and use the results to estimate *how much of a variable's total effect on democratization is explained by each path*. This is subtly different from the traditional mediated effect, or what VanderWeele (2015) calls the "natural indirect effect." To see this, suppose a variable's sole effect is to increase the likelihood of democratization following shocks. It has no effect on shocks or democratization otherwise. Logically, this means all of the variable's effect on democratization runs through the shock path. However, the variable's mediated effect would be 0 because it doesn't predict shocks (VanderWeele 2015: 22).

I consider the following procedure to capture each path's contribution to democratization. To introduce the idea, let's simplify slightly and suppose that democratization (D) can either follow an event A or not ($\neg A$). We can thus divide the probability of democratization into the probability with and without A:

$$P(D) = P(A, D) + P(\neg A, D)$$
$$= P(A) * P(D \mid A) + (1 - P(A)) * P(D \mid \neg A)$$

Suppose we're interested in how a variable $X$ contributes to D. In particular, we want to know to what degree $X$ predicts the combination of A followed by D. This is given by:

$$\frac{\partial P(A,D)}{\partial X} = P(A) * \frac{\partial P(D \mid A)}{\partial X} + \frac{\partial P(A)}{\partial X} * P(D \mid A)$$

and the same in parallel for D without A. Moreover, the two in combination will sum to $\dfrac{\partial P(D)}{\partial X}$ and therefore can be used to calculate the fraction of $X$'s total effect on D attributable to each path.

We can straightforwardly apply this framework to democratization occurring after a shock, with a durable ruling party, and neither.[8] For shocks, for example, we only need four quantities: the average likelihood of a shock, the increased likelihood of post-shock democratization from $X$, the increased likelihood of a shock from $X$, and the average likelihood of democratization given a recent shock. These quantities are defined and calculated as in the previous subsection. Therefore, the second and third quantities are already shown in Table 8.2, with the others easily computed. The same calculations are repeated for ruling parties and for neither, predicting "no shocks or ruling parties" as a discrete category.

This produces $X$'s effect specific to three types of democratization, corresponding to the two paths and outside the paths. We can then divide each contribution by the total effect of $X$ to get the fraction running through each path. To calculate standard errors, I use a bootstrap that randomly generates a new autocracy sample with replacement and repeats the above calculations. This is repeated 500 times for each predictor, with the standard errors taken as the observed standard deviation across the estimates.

Figure 8.6 summarizes the results for each structural variable discussed above except *Equal Resources* (which has no total effect to explain). The horizontal axis captures the fraction of each variable's total effect explained by the shock path. The vertical axis shows this for the ruling-party path. For each fraction, the bars show a one-standard-error deviation on either side of the estimate. The remaining fraction corresponds to democratization outside the paths. To better picture this, I include a diagonal line for where the shock and party fractions would sum to 1. The distance to this line is the fraction due to neither. Note that a fraction can be negative if the path-specific effect is opposite in sign to the total effect.

Examining Figure 8.6, we see a broad distribution in how variables relate to the paths. First, most measures of regime strength and institutions cluster in the upper left and thus primarily affect democratization through parties. Again, this can be explained by their contributions to ruling parties' confidence in their democratic prospects. The exceptions are for military spending and military regimes, coercive factors that are less useful for ruling parties but directly relate to shocks.

---

8. That shocks and parties can overlap presents only a slight complication. Assuming the two effects are additive for democratization, we simply take P(Shock) across the whole sample (including overlaps) and take P(D|Shock) as the effect of shocks alone. This avoids double-counting effects.

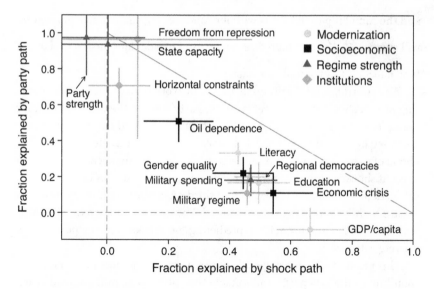

FIGURE 8.6. Mediated effects on democratization. Plot of how each of 13 variables predicts shifts in the likelihood of democratization. The horizontal axis captures the fraction of the variable's democratization effect that runs through shocks, while the vertical axis captures the fraction through durable ruling parties. For instance, virtually all of the effect from party system strength to democratization runs through the party path. The bars show one standard deviation of uncertainty for each dimension, calculated from a bootstrap.

Second, all of the pro-democratic "modernization" variables and all the socioeconomic variables except *Oil Dependence* cluster in the bottom right, meaning they primarily affect democratization through shocks. On average, just over half of their effects (50.2%) run through shocks and 15.7% through parties. This is despite all but one of these variables *negatively* predicting shocks, which is overwhelmed by the positive conditional effect on democratization after shocks. Thus, understanding this post-shock effect is critical to further work on socioeconomic predictors of democratization. Third, *Oil Dependence* is an outlier, with a slightly larger fraction explained by parties. Although *Oil Dependence* has a negative democratizing effect in all contexts, it's positive for shocks, balancing out some of this negative effect.

On average, the two paths account for about three-quarters of the total effects on democratization, again indicating their significance in understanding democracy's origins. Needless to say, this is far from a full catalog of democracy's predictors, a likely impossible task. Rather, my goal has been to show how the empirical framework spreads some light within the "black box" of causation from structure to democratization. Rather than limiting tests to total effects of structural variables, it is fruitful to think of structure flowing through preceding conditions and interacting with them. This framework provides valuable insight to *why* specific variables predict democratization and how the effects may vary with political context, time period, and other conditions.

## The Paths' Predictive Power

We can now bring this chapter's results together to address a lingering puzzle for this book's theory. As repeatedly emphasized, shocks and durable parties by themselves cannot guarantee democratization. Rather, they provide openings that pro-democratic actors must grasp more effectively than their competitors. Indeed, the majority of autocracies satisfying the path conditions fail to democratize. Given the interactive results with pro-democratic activity and structure, how well can we now fill the gap from the paths to successful transition? In particular, how strongly do shocks and parties predict democratization when structural conditions are favorable?

Let's consider two theoretical countries, one with good conditions for democratization and one with poor conditions. Specifically, I set values for four moderating variables: *Civil Society, Literacy, GDP/capita* (ln), and *Oil Dependence*. These cover both pro-democratic potential and economic structure and are all fairly stable over time. For good conditions, I assume full literacy, no oil revenue, and values for civil society and average income 1 SD above the average in post-2000 autocracies. For poor conditions, I assume oil revenue at 5% of GDP and the remaining variables at 1 SD below average. To predict democratization, I stratify the sample by autocracies after shocks, with durable ruling parties, and with neither, then test these structural variables along with the base model of controls. Finally, I impute predicted democratization (for a five-year period) from the given values of these four variables.

Table 8.3 shows the results at the top. A country with poor structural conditions and neither path condition has about a 0.1% chance of democratizing within five years. In stark contrast, an autocracy with a recent shock and good structural conditions has a 65.5% chance of democratizing. This is more than a *500-fold increase*. Structure alone increases democracy's chances 13-fold following shocks and 27-fold with durable parties. Thus, once we consider the interaction of the paths with structure, the gap from opening to success is nearly closed. Of course, we could consider other variable combinations and values, but the point remains that favorable structural conditions can shift countries following shocks from virtually zero chance of democratization to overwhelmingly likely.

Table 8.3 also shows the results for five autocracies (the three with the largest current populations and two with favorable structural conditions), using their 2014 values for the moderating variables (except *Civil Society*, which is averaged from post-2010). Again, their five-year likelihoods of democratization are shown assuming they faced a shock, had a durable ruling party,

**Table 8.3.** Five-Year Likelihood of Democratization (in %)

| Civil Society, Literacy, GDP/capita, Oil Dependence | Democratization Given | | |
|---|---|---|---|
| | Shock | Party | Neither |
| Good Conditions | 65.5 | 52.0 | 26.0 |
| Poor Conditions | 5.1 | 1.9 | 0.1 |
| China | 28.2 | 11.3 | **4.8** |
| Bangladesh | 42.7 | 37.3 | **22.5** |
| Russia | 13.1 | **2.2** | 0.1 |
| Singapore | 54.6 | **29.9** | 35.2 |
| Armenia | 65.6 | **53.5** | 24.3 |

*Notes:* The table displays estimated five-year likelihoods of democratization given a shock, durable ruling party, or neither, assuming specific values for *Civil Society, Literacy, GDP/capita* (ln), and *Oil Dependence*. Values for the good and poor conditions are approximately one-standard-deviation above and below the means for post-2000 autocracies. The five countries take their values as of 2014. The bolded estimates are the correct columns for that country as of 2014 (and up to 2017).

and neither. Their actual contexts as of 2014 (which held up to 2017) are in bold.[9] Since the structural variables are fairly sticky, these likelihoods should approximately hold to the current year. Not too shockingly, there is a low likelihood of either China or Russia democratizing, although it may be surprising that China is the more likely. Bangladesh has a moderate chance of democratizing, especially now that the Awami League satisfies the durable-party threshold. Singapore, a long-noted autocratic outlier given its economic development, has a lower chance of democratizing than one might guess because of its low score on *Civil Society*. The highest estimated likelihood by far is Armenia, a well-grounded prediction given the country's protest-driven ouster of its ruling party and dictator in 2018 that may have ushered in democracy.

## Conclusion

To secure democratization, shocks and durable parties require pro-democratic actors to grab the openings they provide and regime leaders to relent to change. It is therefore crucial to understand not just the average effects of shocks and durable parties but how they vary by structure and pro-democratic activity.

As predicted, shocks and durable parties generate varying forms of pro-democratic activity and in turn make this activity more effective. Protests and

9. As of 2018, Bangladesh would satisfy *Durable Ruling Party* and Armenia would not. Because China lacks national elections, it does not satisfy *Durable Ruling Party*.

other civil society movements are much more likely to succeed following violent shocks or when facing durable ruling parties. Without either, they are generally ineffectual, a useful guide for protest movements plotting the best time to strike.

Structural factors, especially those that predict pro-democratic sentiment, also interact with these contexts in predicting democratization. This goes far in explaining why only some countries democratize after satisfying the path conditions and why many fail. It also suggests a fundamental shift in how we think about structure leading to democratization. Rather than focusing on total effects, it's more instructive to test how structure is mediated through and conditioned by shocks and ruling parties. This framework can also apply to variables *without* a net effect on democratization and establish why.

Exploring several structural variables, this chapter only skimmed the surface of a deep pool of contextual effects. For instance, average income strongly predicts democratization following a violent shock but not otherwise. Combined with income's negative effect on shocks, this explains its weak total relationship with democratization. The framework can also break down how much of each structural variable's effect on democratization is attributable to each path. As we saw, institutions and regime strength primarily affect democratization through the party path, whereas socioeconomic conditions mainly run through the shock path. In the next chapter, I establish why this matters by showing how the path taken to democratization predicts the quality and durability of democracy.

# CHAPTER NINE

# The Paths and Democratic Survival

HOW DO THE PATHS predict political trajectories *after* democratization? Democracy never begins as a clean slate, free from the past and its lessons. The paths correspond to significant events that can influence politics for decades, well past the transition itself. In some cases, the same conflict persists into democracy and inspires further coups or a revival of civil war. In others, shocks and surviving ruling parties subtly shape the party system, economic health, and popular opinions about democracy.

This chapter explores how the paths affect democratic survival and quality. Although I don't attempt a full theory of either, I build on past work connecting transitions to the ensuing democracy to develop expectations for the paths. I then test the distinct transition types on a full sample of democracies from 1800 to 2014, predicting survival and four measures of quality. The findings are clear: democracies are significantly more durable and of higher quality when transitions follow regimes with established ruling parties compared with domestic shocks. International shocks and other transitions are more mixed. Thus, the paths carry legacies for democracy, with implications for how democracy can best continue to spread. In particular, electoral continuity stands out as the most favorable route to democracy, although it comes at a cost of greater institutional persistence from autocracy.

## Legacies of Transition: Democratic Survival and Quality

We first need to specify the outcomes to be explained. Democratic survival simply indicates the continuation of democracy. This faces two primary threats: military coups (sometimes in league with other autocratic elites) and self-coups by democratic leaders (Maeda 2010; Svolik 2015). Since the Cold War, the latter has become the dominant threat. Given that elites initiate nearly all breakdowns, much of the literature on democratic survival has focused on elite norms, intragovernmental constraints, and military dynamics (Dahl 1971; Higley and Burton 2006; Houle 2009; Mainwaring and Pérez-Liñán 2013). However, opposition parties and citizens are also crucial actors that can mobilize to defend democracy. As a result, democracy is stabilized by both popular and elite support for democracy (Diamond 1999; Brancati 2014; Graham, Miller, and Strøm 2017).

Democratic quality is a multivaried concept encompassing electoral fairness, civil liberties, citizen participation, leader responsiveness, and other factors. As such, there is a greater range of potential influences, including institutions, political norms, and economic structure. The role of political agency also cannot be ignored. Democratic erosion, a decline in democratic quality typically engineered by elected leaders, is an increasingly common tool for consolidating power while maintaining the outward veneer of democracy (Bermeo 2016; Waldner and Lust 2018).

## MECHANISMS

A range of work argues that the style of democratization affects democratic survival and quality, but there are divided opinions on what's best for democracy. Before discussing the paths, we first need to identify *how* the transition influences democracy. I focus on two mechanisms: institutions and attitudes.

First, democratic institutions are frequently established during transitions in pacts with autocratic elites. This includes constitutions (which can alternatively be carried over from autocracy), electoral rules, and residual power for autocrats (Karl 1990; Riedl 2014; Albertus and Menaldo 2018). In Portugal 1976 and Turkey 1983, for instance, militaries retained the power to veto legislation for several years. These compromises present mixed benefits. Several authors claim that transitions involving pacts encourage democratic stability by building elite cooperation and acceptance of the new regime (Dahl 1971; O'Donnell and Schmitter 1986; Munck and Leff 1997; Casper 2000a; Guo and Stradiotto 2014). Yet autocratic control over democratic design can also lead to unresponsive institutions, less participation, and widespread popular dissatisfaction (Przeworski 1991; Munck and Leff 1997; Bermeo 2003a), an outcome that Karl (1990) refers to as "frozen democracy."

Second, both elite and popular attitudes about democracy affect democratic health. Several authors stress the need for cooperative norms among elites, who must prefer competing within democracy to violently challenging the system after electoral losses or abusing their power after victories (Dahl 1971; Przeworski 1991; Diamond 1999; Higley and Burton 2006; Graham,

Miller, and Strøm 2017). Democratic consolidation ultimately requires elites to accept democracy as the "only game in town" (Linz and Stepan 1996). Thus, a recent history of elite violence can harm democratic stability and quality by leaving aggrieved opponents and establishing a norm of competitive coercion for settling disputes (Huntington 1991; Cervellati, Fortunato, and Sunde 2014). Popular support for democracy also matters for survival, with greater mobilization during the transition potentially leaving a legacy of participation and popular ownership of democracy (Ekiert and Kubik 1998; Chenoweth and Stephan 2011; Bayer, Bethke, and Lambach 2016).

Finally, characteristics of the previous autocracy can affect democratic performance independent of the transition. As many authors emphasize, norms of elite contestation and political networks build up gradually within autocracy (Dahl 1971; Higley and Burton 2006). Institutions like parties, legislatures, and militaries are rarely entirely remade by the transition, imparting their character from autocracy (Bratton and van de Walle 1997; Riedl 2014; Albertus and Menaldo 2018). This is clearest in the case of persistent ruling parties but also holds more broadly. For instance, Miller (2015a) finds that greater electoral experience within autocracy promotes democratic survival as it establishes key supporting institutions and acculturates elites and masses to competition.

## FROM THE PATHS TO DEMOCRATIC
## SURVIVAL AND QUALITY

What does this imply for the specific paths? Both shocks and electoral continuity leave complicated legacies. For shocks, cycles of violence and elite insecurity threaten to carry over to democracy like rotten wood in a home's foundation. For electoral continuity, the most complex issue is the continuing influence and even dominance of autocratic ruling parties, who often control transitions to their benefit. Although each path presents trade-offs, there are strong reasons to expect electoral continuity to produce more durable and higher-quality democracies. Post-shock democracies should be weakest, although there may be a divide between domestic and foreign shocks.[1]

Electoral continuity has the advantage of a smooth transition with minimal elite dissatisfaction. Successful former ruling parties give autocratic elites a stake in the young democracy (Riedl 2014; Langston 2017; Ziblatt 2017). Moreover, the parties' prior dominance under autocracy lowers the risk of

---

1. Only scattered prior research examines how specific shocks affect democratic survival. Andrew Miller (2011) and Tansey (2016) give a negative verdict for democracy following coups. Although a large literature predicts peace and democracy after civil war, it rarely contrasts this with other transitions. However, Bermeo (2010a) argues that post-conflict democracies tend to be more durable, crediting this to peace accords and strong ex-rebel political parties.

military or other elite-led coups. Another benefit of electoral continuity is that experience with elections aids both institutions and attitudes. Unlike many other transitions, these cases avoid the rapid and chaotic development of parties and electoral processes around democratization. The continued strength of the ruling party adds structure and legibility to the country's electoral politics and provides a valuable organizational model for opposition parties (Grzymala-Busse 2002; Riedl 2014; Loxton 2018). Further, electoral continuity facilitates well-organized opposition movements with experience in electoral competition and protest mobilization under autocracy. In turn, stronger parties and civil society movements are positive for democratic survival and quality (Kuenzi and Lambright 2005; Brancati 2014; Bernhard et al. 2020).

The negative side of electoral continuity turns on the agency of these former autocratic parties. Seeking to perpetuate their dominance, these parties frequently use their leverage over the transition and similar tools as within autocracy to control elections (Serra 2013; Riedl 2014; Loxton 2018; Miller 2021). Citizens may also react to the resilience of these parties with cynicism about democracy or as a sign their fellow voters are nostalgic for autocracy, weakening the popular coalitions defending democracy (Seligson and Tucker 2005; Loxton 2018; Miller 2021). Recent erosions of democracy were overseen by former ruling parties in Nicaragua, Mozambique, and Zambia. Indeed, I show (Miller 2021) that having a former ruling party in power is negative for democratic survival and quality, but only compared to other democracies that follow ruling-party autocracies. The implication is that electoral continuity presents trade-offs while the ruling party remains dominant but will be especially favorable for democracy once the party fades or acculturates to democratic norms.

The shock path, with low elite cooperation and a high propensity for violence and disorder, holds clear problems for democratic survival. Indeed, the very state weakness and elite divisions that lead insecure autocrats to accept democratization often plague new democracies. The dissatisfied elite outgroups behind autocratic coup cycles pose a similar threat within democracy, leading to either breakdown or compromises on policy and institutions to forestall challenges (Tusalem 2014). Similarly, economic crises that follow shocks can linger past democratization and erode democratic support (Gasiorowski 1995; Przeworski et al. 2000; Miller 2016). Post-shock transitions are also the least likely to have norms of elite cooperation and respect for elections. A positive for shocks is that instability surrounding the transition creates openings for popular mobilization and leverage over transitional terms. However, this is dangerous if it triggers elite opposition. Moreover, without electoral experience, popular movements often struggle to establish stable governance after transition, potentially triggering coups, autocratic elite comebacks, or declining support for democracy.

Unlike for democratization, domestic and foreign shocks may operate somewhat differently for democratic survival. First, pro-democratic international actors have played a much larger role in the foreign shocks, with this influence often continuing into democracy. Major democratic powers in the postwar and post-Soviet cases heavily invested in countries' democratic stability, in part for security reasons. In particular, many of these new democracies became enmeshed in democracy-dominated international institutions like NATO and the EU, after which an anti-democratic turn became more costly (Pevehouse 2005; Levitsky and Way 2010). Second, the international events preceding democratization discredited autocracy to a greater degree than domestic shocks. Especially for military regimes, defeat in war eradicated autocracies' claims to legitimacy. Similarly, Soviet failure badly damaged Marxism's appeal and produced crippling economic failures. The experiences disgraced a generation of autocratic leaders and led citizens to demand fundamental change (Dower 1999; Gunitsky 2017). The result was greater ideological support for democracy, compensating for the political instability.

In the empirical tests, I separate out democracies following domestic and foreign shocks. My clearest expectations concern electoral continuity and domestic shocks, with the relative place of foreign shocks, other transitions, and those following independence less clear. As in the prior two chapters, the hypothesis must be stated without reference to post-democratization events, requiring a comparison to all transitions with durable ruling parties rather than just the electoral continuity cases.

> *Hypothesis 11*: Democracies that transition from autocracies with durable ruling parties are more likely to survive and will be higher in democratic quality than democracies that transition following coups, civil wars, or assassinations.

## Empirical Results

### DESCRIPTIVE COMPARISON

This section examines how democracies perform following different transition types. We begin with two descriptive analyses of democratic survival, both using my qualitative paths coding. Table 9.1 divides democracies into the primary cases for each shock, electoral continuity, the outliers, and the 69 countries that were democratic at independence. The columns indicate the outcomes of each democratic spell. The first three columns count democracies that eventually broke down, dividing by whether democracy lasted 1–5 years, 6–20, or more. The final two columns count democracies that have not broken down, with ages below and above 20 years as of 2015.[2] I chose 20 years as

2. I generally use the democracy coding up to 2015 but count Turkey in 2016 as a breakdown.

**Table 9.1.** Democracy Outcomes by Transition Type

| Transition Type | Breakdown ≤ 5 Years | Breakdown 6–20 Years | Breakdown > 20 Years | Survival So Far | Survival > 20 Years |
|---|---|---|---|---|---|
| *Coup* | 15 | 18 | 6 | 6 | 10 |
| *Civil War* | 4 | 2 | | 10 | 2 |
| *Assassination* | | 1 | | | 1 |
| *Defeat in War* | 3 | 3 | 2 | | 8 |
| *Hegemon Withdrawal* | 1 | | | 1 | 7 |
| *Electoral Continuity* | 3 | 5 | 1 | 7 | 11 |
| *Other* | 2 | 3 | | 3 | 4 |
| *Independence* | 7 | 12 | 4 | 3 | 43 |

*Notes:* The table summarizes the durability of democracy by transition type (plus cases that were democratic at independence). The first three columns show the number of cases that broke down within specific age ranges. The next two show the number of cases that survive as of 2015, with ages below and above 20 years.

that's the median age for all democracies and a good marker of consolidation. For democracies under this age, the annual breakdown likelihood averages 3%. Above this age, it falls to under 0.5%. Thus, durability is increasing to the right, with the final column mostly representing consolidated democracies.

The stark difference across transition types is immediately clear. Two in three democracies at independence have never broken down, compared with about half of other democracies. This higher failure is heavily driven by coup cases, of which 71% have broken down and only 18% made it to the consolidated category.[3] In contrast, two-thirds of electoral continuity cases have not broken down and 41% have consolidated. Of the remaining categories, those following civil war and hegemonic withdrawal appear relatively stable, but this is complicated by how recent the former cases are and a small sample for the latter. Overall, we see an advantage for post-independence and electoral continuity cases, with some evidence of a divide between domestic and foreign shocks.

The second descriptive analysis is in Figure 9.1, which shows the Kaplan-Meier survival curves for democracies following domestic shocks, foreign shocks, electoral continuity, the outliers, and post-independence. This displays the fraction of democracies in each category surviving to a given age. We can clearly see that domestic shock cases do the worst, with barely 60% making it to 10 years. The outliers also do poorly. Electoral continuity cases again do best (especially for young democracies), although there's not a dramatic difference with foreign shocks or post-independence cases.

3. Of the 10 consolidated cases, all are in Latin America or Western Europe and thus benefited from pro-democratic regional linkage (Levitsky and Way 2010).

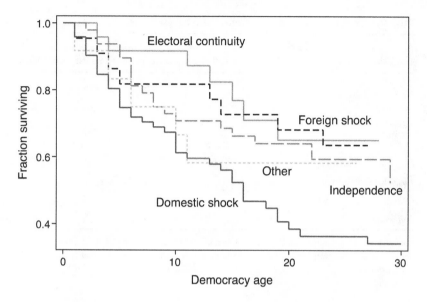

FIGURE 9.1. Kaplan-Meier survival curves. Fraction of democracies by transition type (or those democratic at independence) that survive to given age. Electoral continuity cases are generally the most durable and those following domestic shocks the least.

## EMPIRICAL SETUP

We now move to more rigorous testing of how the paths affect democratic survival and quality. To predict survival, I again use a dynamic logit model that controls for democracy age, making this a form of duration analysis. I test dummy variables for the transition types in a sample of democracies from 1800 to 2014, with up to 4,860 observations. Following the last two chapters, I categorize transitions using the quantitative data on domestic or foreign shocks in the five years before democratization, the presence of a durable ruling party at democratization, other transitions, and countries democratic at independence. I allow for overlaps between these categories and carry forward the coding as long as democracy survives. I use this data rather than my qualitative paths coding to avoid relying on my subjective evaluations and because electoral continuity is defined by a post-democratization event. Thus, electoral continuity cases' longer survival could simply reflect that they survived long enough for ruling parties to win power. However, I replicate the empirical findings using my paths coding, adding a correction for this issue.

I predict democratic quality using four continuous measures. Three are from V-Dem (Coppedge et al. 2018): the polyarchy index (covering elections and freedoms critical to contestation), liberal index (civil liberties, executive constraints, and the rule of law), and participatory index (civil society strength and local participation). The fourth is an average of Freedom House's (2016) civil liberties and political rights indices. All are scaled 0–1, with 1 more democratic. I test the same transitional dummy variables as for survival. The sample again covers democracies from 1800 to 2014, except the participation and Freedom House measures begin in 1900 and 1972, respectively. An important consideration is whether to control for the dependent variable's (DV's) level from autocracy, as this might predict transition type. I show results both with and without this lagged DV, taken from autocracy three years before democratization.[4] All models use OLS with robust standard errors.

Besides the lagged DV, controls are identical across the survival and quality tests. I keep the base model from the previous chapters, controlling for democracy age (as a cubic function), the fraction of regional democracies, previous democratic spells, average income, recent economic growth, population, and the year. Several further controls are considered below.

## DEMOCRATIC SURVIVAL

Figure 9.2 summarizes the results for democratic survival, showing the estimated differences in annual survival for four transition types. Democracies at independence are the reference category. Because young democracies are the most at risk, I show the results for all democracies and those 20 years or younger. For both samples, democracies following domestic shocks and those without shocks or parties (Other) are the least stable. Democracies with durable parties are the most stable but don't significantly differ from the independence or foreign shock cases.

Domestic shocks result in a 1.2% lower likelihood of survival overall and 2.2% lower for young democracies.[5] For perspective, the rate of democratic breakdown is only 1.8% for all democracies and 3% for young democracies. Further, this lower likelihood holds for the entire democratic spell. As a result, democratizing after a domestic shock compared to with a ruling party lowers a democracy's chances of making it past 20 years from 68% to 41%, a substantial effect. The Other category is the least stable, but this is based on a fairly small number of cases and is not matched by a similar finding for democratic quality. Foreign shock cases are more durable than their domestic counterparts, but the difference is not significant in either sample.

Among the controls, average income and regional democracy are strongly positive for democratic survival. For comparison, the estimated effect of moving the transition from domestic shock to party is equivalent to an additional half of a country's region being democratic or a shift in average income from that of modern-day Nigeria to Greece.

---

4. The three-year lag is to avoid picking up changes from the democratization process itself.

5. As before, this is based on holding the controls at their actual values and averaging across the sample.

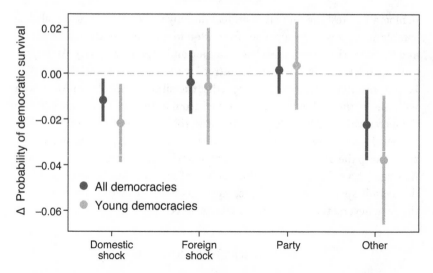

FIGURE 9.2. The paths and democratic survival. Estimated effects on democratic survival from type of democratization, varying by domestic shock, foreign shock, durable ruling party, and other. Results are shown for all democracies and those 20 years or younger. Reference category is countries democratic at independence. Bars = 95% CI.

## DEMOCRATIC QUALITY

Figure 9.3 summarizes the results predicting four measures of democratic quality, with and without a lagged DV from the autocratic period. For both tests, the Other transition category is the reference group. Democracy at independence is controlled for in the first set of tests but not shown. With the lagged DV, these democracies drop from the sample.

Results are consistent: for all eight variations, democracies following domestic shocks perform the worst and democracies transitioning with ruling parties perform the best. The estimated difference between the two on the polyarchy index is just over one-half a standard deviation of the index across democracies. For the liberal index, participation index, and Freedom House, the corresponding figures are 82%, 43%, and 40% of the standard deviations within democracy. This confirms Hypothesis 11. Unlike for survival, the foreign shock cases are significantly higher in quality than their domestic counterparts in every test. They perform similarly to the Other category, with the exception of foreign shocks' superior effects on participation.[6]

The caveat to the superior performance of transitions with ruling parties is their greater continuity from autocracy. Among post-1940 transitions, countries that democratized with durable ruling parties are about twice as likely as

---

6. Among the controls, higher average income always predicts higher quality. Regional democracy positively predicts each DV except for Freedom House. The year positively predicts the polyarchy and participation indices but negatively predicts Freedom House.

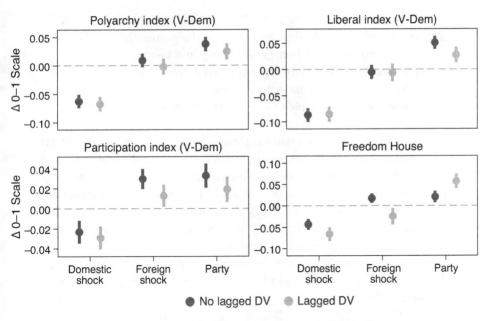

FIGURE 9.3. The paths and democratic quality. Estimated effects on four measures of democratic quality from type of democratization, varying by domestic shock, foreign shock, and durable ruling party. Results are shown with and without a lagged DV from three years before democratization. Reference category is no shock or party. Bars = 95% CI.

post-shock cases to have a former ruling party or dictator in power in a given year (46.3% vs. 27.1%). Similarly, 64.2% of the former group retain their constitutions from autocracy, compared to 29% of post-shock cases and 29.9% of other transitions (using Banks and Wilson 2017). The trade-off is a smoother transition with greater vestiges of autocratic power.

### ROBUSTNESS CHECKS

Results are very similar when using my paths coding to define the transitions instead of the quantitative measures. To avoid bias when predicting survival from electoral continuity, I limit the sample to *after* the party first gains power. Even with this correction, electoral continuity cases remain of similar durability as post-independence democracies and score significantly higher on the liberal index and Freedom House than the Other cases. Democracies following domestic shocks remain significantly worse across all measures.

A range of further controls are worth considering, especially those that might predict transition types. To examine the findings' robustness, I collected the controls included in the EBA tests in chapter 7 and the mediation tests in chapter 8. I dropped the variables already in the base model, that only apply to autocracies (e.g., autocratic regime type), and that measure democratic quality (to avoid post-treatment bias). This leaves 13 additional control sets: literacy, average education, oil dependence, natural resource dependence, equal resources across the population, gender equity in resources, recent economic crisis, military spending, state capacity, party system strength, state control of the economy, dummies for semi-presidentialism and presidentialism, and region dummies. I added each in turn to the models predicting democratic survival and quality.

In the original tests, the main significant findings were the negative effects of domestic shock transitions on survival and the four quality measures and the positive effects of party transitions on the quality measures. These findings proved highly robust to additional controls. Of the 117 new coefficients (9 findings across 13 additional control sets), all retain the same sign and 109 remain significant. For parties, 50 of 52 coefficients remain significant. This indicates strong robustness to potential confounders.

I also tested transitions following the Salvation, Reformer, and Regained Power patterns, both with and without simultaneously controlling for shocks and parties. The Salvation cases were consistently the least stable and lowest-quality democracies, whereas Reformer cases performed similarly to post-independence democracies. Finally, I tested for the presence of pro-democratic protest and international pressure before democratization. These have complex effects: protest has no effect on durability but predicts lower quality, while international pressure predicts higher durability and has mixed relationships with the quality measures.

## Conclusion

This chapter explored the aftereffects of the paths to democratization. Democratic transitions with established ruling parties are the most likely to survive and display the highest democratic quality across several measures. Transitions following domestic shocks (unfortunately, the most common type) are the most likely to break down and display the lowest quality. In comparison, those following *foreign* shocks are marginally more likely to survive and are higher in quality. Curiously, the transitions without shocks or parties are the least durable, but middling on quality. Finally, post-independence democracies are of similar durability and quality as the party cases.

This chapter did not attempt to canvass all of the paths' long-term effects. It may be that other aspects of democratic quality are negatively affected by electoral continuity or foreign shocks. Nevertheless, two implications of this chapter stand out. First, there is strong evidence that the paths do matter beyond the transition itself, broadening their significance. Second, the results point to electoral continuity as the most advantageous route to democracy, with implications for how we should promote democratization.

# CHAPTER TEN

# Conclusion

THIS BOOK PRESENTS a revisionist theory of democratization built on three central concepts: *power, context,* and *disruption.* Traditional views have focused in isolation on factors like societal preferences for democracy, protest, and economic structure. In contrast, I argue that they rarely matter outside of political contexts in which autocrats perceive they have little power to lose by democratizing. Further, these contexts nearly always follow major disruptions to the autocratic status quo. In more than 9 in 10 transitions since 1800, democratization followed a violent shock or featured a durable ruling party that faced some disruption to its hegemony but correctly anticipated success in democracy.

This chapter brings the book to a close by further exploring this theory's implications. After overviewing the key theoretical lessons on democratization, I discuss what the book implies for the predictors of democratization, future empirical work, and the most effective techniques for international democracy promotion and domestic opposition. I conclude by discussing democracy's uncertain future.

## *Theoretical Contributions*

In this section, I summarize the book's key conclusions regarding democratization. First, the book reimagines the underlying logic and process of democratization, contrasting sharply with prior work that neglects autocratic *power.* Second, the book stresses the significance of political *context* for understanding democratic transitions, with implications for both qualitative and quantitative research. Third, a singular lesson is how chaotic and surprising democratization can be, typically resulting from violent *disruption* and unintended consequences. This muddles the issue of who is responsible for transitions and frequently poses problems for democracy's survival.

## POWER LOGIC AND PROCESS OF DEMOCRATIZATION

This book's theory pivots around autocratic leaders' calculations about power. In nearly all democratic transitions, autocrats accept democratization because they perceive they have little to lose from regime change, either because they are already weak in autocracy or because they believe they will be strong in democracy. A range of evidence supports this, including case studies, the coding of final decisions to democratize, and direct quantitative tests. As shown in chapter 7, leaders and ruling parties facing greater insecurity in autocracy and ruling parties with a better chance of winning power in democracy are significantly more likely to democratize.

Yet contexts in which autocrats face little power loss from democratization are not the norm. Once an autocratic equilibrium is established, with leaders and elite supporters collaborating to control opponents, autocrats tend to be relatively secure and rarely tempted by democratic rewards. Rival autocratic elites can coercively topple such an equilibrium, but pro-democratic actors almost never do. As a result, democratization first requires a disruption to the status quo. When this combines with sufficient pro-democratic pressure, democratization becomes likely.

The patterns through which disruption and power calculations lead to democratization fall into two *paths*. In the shock path, democratization follows one of five major violent shocks (coups, civil wars, assassinations, defeat in war, and withdrawal of an autocratic hegemon), yielding insecure regimes that struggle to retain autocratic power. In the electoral continuity path, an established ruling party democratizes through elections and regains power in democracy, almost always following a trigger that disrupts party dominance. These two paths account for more than 90% of successful transitions. Both recent shocks and durable ruling parties significantly raise the likelihood of democratization. Without either, democratization occurs on average once every 356 years. With a durable party or recent shock, this likelihood increases by a factor of seven in the descriptive comparison (or 3.5–5 times in the quantitative tests).

At the simplest level, this offers an improved explanation of how democratization happens. Yet it also informs *why* democratization happens, focusing on autocratic power and how elite conflict erodes control. Importantly, very few of the pivotal disruptions were intended to produce democratization. Rather, they resulted from failed autocratic projects and elite rivalries. This perspective contrasts with traditional views of democratization as a function of societal attitudes about democracy, desires for economic rewards, or popular protest. These factors can contribute to pro-democratic pressure, but this primarily matters when the shift in power entailed by democratization is as small as possible.

## IMPORTANCE OF CONTEXT

An immediate implication of this framework is the importance of context in understanding democratization. Actors' choices and attitudes toward democracy, the relative strength and organization of pro- and anti-democratic groups, and even international pressure all intimately relate to the political context. A greater appreciation of this can help explain misunderstood cases and puzzling patterns in the literature. For instance, chapter 6 discussed how a lack of shocks or electoral parties can account for non-democratization in most autocracies, explaining failure in cases like the 1848 revolutions, the Arab Spring, and China. Chapter 8 showed that we can resolve why economic development has a weak relationship with democratization by recognizing the mediating role of shocks. In fact, most structural factors have stronger relationships with democratization after recent shocks or with durable ruling parties.

Similarly, the paths help explain why pro-democratic protest succeeds in some cases but not others. Both shocks and disrupted ruling parties provide openings for opposition groups and make them more likely to achieve regime change. Although the strength of these groups—whether social revolutionaries, opposition elites, or democrats—is also predicted by economic and political structure, their presence and success cannot be understood divorced from political context. As chapter 8 showed, without recent shocks or durable parties, pro-democratic activity is ineffectual for democratization. With either, pro-democratic activity is strongly predictive.

The importance of context extends to the aftermath of specific events, such as individual shocks. As chapters 3 and 4 discussed, the shocks have several commonalities, but each brings distinct features worth recognizing. Coups usually yield divided military factions and some of the worst instability and violence. Civil and foreign wars generally feature weak states and the most direct international involvement. Assassinations are highly specific in effect but can produce transformational changes through new leadership. Finally, hegemonic withdrawal displays its own character of trauma and ideological collapse. The same nuance applies to ruling parties shifting their attitudes toward democracy depending on how events weaken their hegemony or alter their beliefs about their democratic prospects.

Both qualitative and quantitative scholars of democratization should therefore pay close attention to political context. For case studies, the recent events shaping regime power and opposition openings are critical to understanding actors' choices and capabilities. For quantitative research, theories should take into account the near-universal presence of the paths around democratization. This includes testing how predictors interact with shocks and ruling parties, adding nuance and depth to the empirics.

## DEMOCRACY'S CHAOTIC ORIGINS

Democratization is rarely neat and tidy. Contradictions abound. Regime-shaking violence is intimately connected to democratization despite democracy being defined by peace. Autocratic parties frequently retain their influence into democracy despite the overthrow of dictators being central in democrats' minds. Moreover, transitions are rarely set in motion by actors intending to install democracy.

These tensions are less surprising when one considers that democratization is decided within autocracy, which is ruled by coercion, violence, fear, and duplicity. It is not so paradoxical that democratization takes on some characteristics of its setting. Moreover, when these tools of control are wielded effectively, autocracy can keep a stubborn grip, necessitating a serious rupture to shake the vipers loose from the bed. We thus get democratization from self-serving calculations of autocratic power, cycles of violence, and unexpected bursts of chaotic change.

How should this color our understanding of the democratization process? For one, it should inspire greater acceptance of disorder and autocratic continuity as common companions of successful democratization. Both can lead to nagging problems for democratic consolidation, as discussed in chapter 9, but often cannot be avoided. The same applies to concessions made to outgoing autocrats, such as compromises over institutional rules, amnesty, and policy (Dahl 1971; Przeworski 1991; Albertus and Menaldo 2018). This does not imply that shocks or satisfied autocrats must be considered inherently good, only necessary compromises to secure change.

The chaotic nature of democratization should also lead us to rethink how actors are held responsible for democracy. Autocratic actors' choices matter a great deal for democratization, but the most impactful choices are either attempts at grabbing power that are not intended to provide democratic openings or accessions to democracy for self-interested reasons. Pro-democratic actors (both reformers and civil society actors) also play critical roles in democratization, but their success usually depends on prior disruptions that they have little to do with. Thus, a lack of democratization does not necessarily spring from a failure of effort or skill among democrats. A bit of luck, or at least good timing, is needed too.

## *Implications*

This book's theory has several more tangible implications. I first discuss what the findings say about the key predictors of democratization. I then note some lessons for empirical testing, with recommendations for future work building on the book. Lastly, I discuss how foreign and domestic actors can most effectively spread democracy.

## PREDICTORS OF DEMOCRATIZATION

Debates over the relative importance of democratization's predictors have consumed the literature for decades. A handful of specific variables were discussed in chapter 8. Here, I discuss what the results say more broadly about the roles of international factors, protest, economic and political structure, and individual agency.

*International*: Numerous scholars emphasize the international sources of democracy, with debate about their importance relative to domestic characteristics (Huntington 1991; Whitehead 1996; Gleditsch and Ward 2006; Boix, Miller, and Rosato 2013). In this book, the clearest international influence appeared in the 29 total cases following defeat in war or hegemonic withdrawal. In addition, 6 cases featured foreign-sponsored coups and another 14 international mediation in civil wars. By my estimate, about 39% of on-path cases had foreign powers directly involved in the disruptive events. Adding in pro-democratic pressure following disruption, most transitions featured direct international involvement. This is on top of the diffuse effects stemming from regional contagion, normative diffusion, and so on. Thus, there is strong support for international factors as central to democratization.

*Protest*: It's a mistake to interpret this book as minimizing pro-democratic protest's significance. In fact, I found that 71% of all transitions had major pro-democratic protests, which were key to pushing autocratic leaders to accept democratization and to defeating alternative forms of regime change. Chapter 8 confirmed that protest is a strong contributor to democratization following shocks or with durable ruling parties. However, protests *by themselves*, independent of the right contexts, are usually ineffectual, explaining prominent failures like Tiananmen and most of the Arab Spring. Thus, protest is limited in what it can achieve alone, yet crucial to democratization on the whole.

*Structure vs. Agency*: An ongoing debate among political scientists concerns whether only some countries are "ready" for democracy or if it can take root anywhere if actors make the right decisions. What does this book imply about the relative importance of structure and individual agency? For starters, the findings demonstrate the central importance of regime strength, elite cohesion, and ruling party characteristics, which are all aspects of political structure. However, both structure *and* agency contribute to the disruptive events that transform this political context. In turn, both matter in the aftermath, with structure predicting the strength of pro-democratic activity and agency playing a large role through instigators of further shocks, reformers, opposition leaders, and strategic autocrats. Thus, the book's framework suggests the two elements are not easy to pry apart. Structure gives greater room for agency and the resulting choices can heighten or dampen the predictive value of structure.

What then does this book imply for democracy's reach? Can all countries realistically achieve democratization if actors make the right choices? The answer is a cautious yes. The very countries typically thought to not have the right conditions for democracy (low development and literacy, few democratic neighbors, high oil dependence, etc.) are also the most likely to experience shocks, providing openings for democratic change. When pro-democratic actors effectively mobilize in response, we see surprising transitions in seemingly inhospitable environments like Sudan, Sierra Leone, Liberia, and Nepal. In contrast, wealthier countries like Singapore, Mexico (until 2000), and Malaysia (until 2016) have had to wait out long periods of political stability. The downside for the former countries is they have to weather episodes of violence and face lower chances of democratic survival, but fledgling opportunities for freedom are better than none.

## EMPIRICAL TESTING AND FUTURE WORK

Previous empirical tests of democratization were missing a big piece of the puzzle by ignoring shocks and ruling parties. At minimum, scholars should take these seriously as potential confounders and moderators of variables' effects. I presented a new framework for testing structural factors that recognizes shocks and parties as first steps toward democratization, allowing scholars to predict these openings and capture their contextual effects. This can yield much greater nuance compared to the total effect alone.

Building on this framework, this book's empirical findings can be extended in several ways. First, chapter 8's findings on how structural factors are mediated and moderated by the paths are only a beginning. The most salient question is what predicts which transitions succeed and fail following shocks or with durable parties. Although I showed that favorable values on a handful of variables can make transition much more likely than not, the full range of predictive power remains unclear. Are there other structural elements that I've missed? Second, there is room to further disaggregate the shocks, such as different types of coups and other civil war resolutions. Similarly, autocratic ruling parties represent a diverse menagerie that could be further picked apart beyond my findings on multipartyism and winning chances in democracy. Bridging the empirical and conceptual, the question of the "right" set of shocks can also be debated.

It's also worth asking whether some previous findings on democratization are explained by the paths logic. For instance, there is debate as to whether the waves of democracy (see chapter 2) reflect contagion and democratic momentum or simply stem from common sources, such as geopolitical shifts and global economic crises (Weyland 2014; Houle, Kayser, and Xiang 2016; Gunitsky 2017). This book provides some evidence for interconnected shocks. The most significant modern global events—the two world wars and the

Soviet Union's fall—directly impacted about 35 total transitions. More generally, we could explain waves from shared increases in exposure to shocks and durable parties. Although there is no evidence that coups diffuse across borders (Miller, Joseph, and Ohl 2018), civil wars, other forms of instability, and autocratic elections and parties do (Miller 2020b). Thus, we can reinterpret the waves in terms of correlated disruptions and path conditions rather than a democratic zeitgeist. How much of the waves this accounts for I leave to future work.

There are also ample opportunities for scholars to expand on this book's theory and qualitative findings. Most generally, more can be done to integrate the book's framework with existing theories. Although my theory is revisionist in several respects, it's compatible with many theoretical approaches (such as the structural and actor-based schools) and points of emphasis. With my focus on defending my theory, I haven't spent much time on the outside looking in, that is, starting with an existing perspective and seeing how the book's framework can enrich it. For instance, scholarship on opposition organization, pacts, and international democracy promotion can find much to draw on. A promising avenue for future qualitative work is more explicit comparisons between successful and unsuccessful transitions. This book follows most of the democratization literature in focusing on successes, often because of a lack of appropriate control cases. Two types of comparison that I mainly examine quantitatively could be supplemented with further qualitative work. First, contrasts between protest movements with and without prior disruption could reinforce how protest success depends on existing regime weakness. Second, contrasts between successful and unsuccessful democratization after disruption could delve further into the interactive roles of agency and structure.

## DEMOCRACY PROMOTION AND OPPOSITION TACTICS

This brings us to the question of how to put this book's theory into action. How can international democracy promoters and domestic opponents best spread democracy? A common reaction I get to my argument is to ask whether democracy advocates should thus favor launching coups, wars, and assassinations in the world's dictatorships. This is not purely theoretical, as international actors have done exactly this (ostensibly to spread democracy) in countries like Guatemala, the Dominican Republic, and Iraq. Similarly, domestic democrats have supported coups in Bolivia, Portugal, Thailand, and elsewhere.

My answer to this is unhesitating: *No, pro-democracy advocates should not sponsor coups and other shocks to spread democracy.* True, if our only goal was to maximize next year's likelihood of democratization, this might make sense. However, a much better goal is democracy over the long term. As chapter 9 shows, shocks yield more fragile and lower-quality democracies. Although foreign shocks (wars and hegemonic withdrawals) are not the worst in this regard, very few of these were intentional democratic projects. Rather, the best barometer is the poor record of post-coup cases. Further, shocks are far from a guarantee of democratization and in most cases are more likely to feed into political instability, bloodshed, repression, and renewed authoritarianism. The human cost is not worth the increased chance of democratization. Even when domestic opponents believe that a coup will be pro-democratic, they should be cautious. Many more coup leaders promise this than actually follow through, and truly pro-democratic coups are extremely rare absent an earlier shock. Thus, this book does not imply that coups, wars, and assassinations are *good* even if they are causally related to democratization. They are rather double-edged events that pry open potential for regime change precisely because they trigger chaos and political instability.

So what are the lessons for democrats? First, even if shocks and other disruptions should not be instigated by democratic actors, they must still be recognized as opportunities. The best chances for democratization are rare, sudden, and entirely unplanned. Democrats must be ready to recognize these openings and apply maximal pressure when the time is right. When pursuing this, it is critical for regime opponents to understand leaders' calculations about power. The ultimate goal is to persuade autocratic decision makers to concede, meaning they must believe that autocracy can no longer be reliably maintained and that democracy is tolerable. It is particularly important for opponents to chip away at regime capacity by appealing to supporting elites, discouraging repression, and eroding the regime's economic resources. Displays of widespread support for democracy (through protest, strikes, elections, and other mobilization) help by convincing autocratic elites of the difficulty of reasserting control, deterring anti-democratic challengers, and shifting perceptions of regime invincibility.

Second, there is a path that democrats can push their country along without significant risk of bloodshed: electoral continuity. Although it may take slightly longer, this path is often peaceful and largely consensual and produces the highest-quality democracies. To encourage this path, pro-democratic actors should push for elections and party competition, even if highly imbalanced at first. Many autocracies have adopted these institutions expecting to retain control but later find their grip giving way. External leverage from democracies has been especially effective at incentivizing the adoption of autocratic elections and party competition (Miller 2020b). This does not mean meekly accepting unfairness in the electoral process. In fact, to make it to democratization, these party regimes must eventually be disrupted and then challenged effectively through elections. Thus, the encouragement of election adoption should go hand in hand with persistent pressure to make the elections as competitive as possible.

Championing the electoral continuity path also means accepting its implications. Parties will give in to democratization when they believe they can continue winning power within democracy, and most ruling parties do so. Thus, democrats who desire a clean slate devoid of the autocratic past will be disappointed. This is simply a necessary trade-off in pursuing democratization. A relatively consensual process requires autocrats to not lose too much, implying an acceptance of party continuity and other concessions. In contrast, a more complete transformation requires greater disruption and regime collapse, raising the specter of violence and disorder. For ardent democrats, these compromises are perhaps a bitter pill to swallow but a spur to long-term health. Over time, the concessions can be undone and ruling parties either fade away or become typical democratic parties. Freedom is worth the bitter taste.

## The Future of Democracy

Finally, what does this book imply for the future of global democracy? There is a great deal of agitation over the perceived stagnation (or even recession) in democracy over the last decade or two, a marked contrast to the democratic triumph of the 1990s (Fukuyama 2015; Freedom House 2016; Diamond 2019). Not only has the overall fraction of democracies barely budged since 2005, there has been notable erosion in the quality of several previously durable democracies, including Hungary, Poland, Brazil, Nicaragua, the Philippines, and the United States (Bermeo 2016; Waldner and Lust 2018; Ginsburg and Huq 2018).

One way to put current and future democracy into context is to see how the path conditions have changed over time, as they both provide openings for democratization and impact democratic stability. Figure 10.1 captures the trend, with the dark line showing the fraction of autocracies at high propensity to democratize either from a recent shock or a durable electoral ruling party. This has steadily trended up since the 1890s and is near a historic high, although little changed from the late 1960s. Not coincidentally, then, the entire Third Wave occurred in a period of high propensity to democratize. As a result, a large number of countries have recently experienced an opening for democratization. Since 2005, 66 of 83 autocracies in the sample faced a shock or durable party at some point.[1] These "primed" autocracies also have better socioeconomic conditions, more democratic neighbors, and stronger civil societies on average than their counterparts in the 1980s and 1990s. This provides reason for optimism in democracy's further expansion.

---

1. The 17 exceptions include 10 monarchies, plus Bangladesh, Belarus, China, Eritrea, Haiti, Iran, and Lebanon.

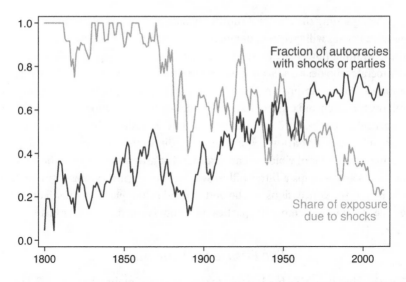

FIGURE 10.1. Changing causes of democratization. Fraction of autocracies at high propensity to democratize from any shock within the prior five years or a durable ruling party (dark line), plus the share of this "priming" due to shocks (light line). The latter splits the share for autocracies with both shocks and parties. Modern autocracies are near a historic high for democratic openings, but the share due to shocks has plummeted.

Why then has democracy stagnated? For one, actual democratization since 2005 lags a bit behind what this book's empirics predict (using Table 7.1, Model 2). Omitting microstates, there were 14 transitions from 2005 to 2015, whereas the model expected 20.4. This could represent a fundamental break or merely a temporary lull. It follows the democratic explosion of the 1990s and 11 transitions from 2000 to 2004, which swept up many of the most democracy-prone targets. Further, it must be kept in mind that the more democracy spreads, the more the rate of democratization needs to exceed that of breakdown to maintain democracy's global share.

The lighter line in Figure 10.1 shows the fraction of the priming due to shocks rather than durable parties. For autocracies with both, I split the credit. The centrality of shocks has plummeted since the 1950s, with a further decline in the 2000s. Among current autocracies, less than a quarter of the priming is from shocks, reflecting a general decline in coups and civil wars and the global spread of ruling parties and elections.[2] Chapter 7 also showed that the democratizing effect of parties slightly exceeds that of shocks post–Cold War, further magnifying their importance. As a result, since 1989, we've seen

2. Although less political violence is certainly a good thing, it can ironically hold back democratization when ruling parties are absent.

25 total electoral continuity cases and 35 total shock cases, as compared to a more than 5-to-1 ratio in favor of shocks before this.

This shift toward parties and away from shocks has several implications for democracy's future. First, it implies that recent and future democratizing countries should be relatively stable. For instance, none of the "democratic erosion" examples mentioned above are electoral continuity cases. About 70% of current democracies either democratized with durable electoral ruling parties or have been democratic from independence, the two conditions most conducive to high stability and democratic quality.[3] This is fertile ground for renewed democratic consolidation.

Second, the predominance of ruling parties implies that the structural factors predictive of democratization are changing. Recall that modernization variables (including economic development, literacy, and education) have a much stronger relationship with democratization after shocks but a nonsignificant or small relationship alongside ruling parties. The result is a general decline in the importance of economic modernization for democratization (see Boix, Miller, and Rosato 2013). What should *increase* in importance? Based on chapter 8, oil dependence, party strength, and institutions that constrain autocratic power should all grow in significance.

Third, much depends on the changing nature of electoral authoritarianism, including the political arms race between ruling party and opposition. As discussed in chapter 5, autocratic parties' styles of rule have changed over time and their durability has fluctuated with global events. If ruling parties can identify models of control that fend off disruption, leave them unconstrained by institutions, and keep oppositions weak, they will see no need to democratize. It is up to democratic actors to fight to prevent this. As a note of caution, there have been only 6 electoral continuity cases from 2000 to 2014, compared with 18 in the 1990s. Perhaps this signals a rising era of party dominance buttressed by new technologies and a friendlier international environment (Diamond 2019), or perhaps it's the eye of a popular hurricane, as recent opposition successes in Nigeria, Malaysia, Algeria, and Armenia may presage.

The spread of democracy since 1800 is one of the great transformations of human affairs in our history. Like most precious things, democracy is subject to theft, neglect, and faded luster over time. It can inspire false optimism, as in 1848 and much of the Arab Spring, and set the ideological stakes for world-shifting events like the world wars and the Soviet collapse. Whether it continues to spread or fades into history remains to be seen. Either way, I have hopefully persuaded you that any successes won't be from "miracles of nature" but from human conflict and ingenuity. If we do break from democracy's recent slump and see the values of political equality and freedom reinvigorated on the global stage, don't be shocked.

---

3. About the same fraction applies to democracies twenty years old or younger.

THIS APPENDIX INCLUDES the following:

- List of democratic transitions by paths
- Coding details
  - Suggested corrections for BMR democracy measure
  - Paths coding for shadow cases
  - Qualitative codings: Final *Decision Patterns*, pro-democratic pressure
  - Quantitative codings: Shocks, ruling parties, economic and political controls
- Case narratives, with qualitative categories

## *List of Democratic Transitions by Paths*

**Table A.1.** Categorization of Democratic Transitions, 1800–2014

---

**Domestic Shocks**

---

*Coup*

| | | |
|---|---|---|
| Greece 1864 | Cuba 1909 | Portugal 1911 |
| Greece 1926 | Spain 1931 | Chile 1934 |
| Cuba 1940 | Guatemala 1945 | Brazil 1946 |
| Ecuador 1948 | Costa Rica 1949 | Panama 1950 |
| Panama 1952 | Honduras 1957 | Argentina 1958 |
| Colombia 1958 | Guatemala 1958 | Venezuela 1959 |
| Burma 1960 | Turkey 1961 | Argentina 1963 |
| Peru 1963 | Dom. Rep. 1966 | Guatemala 1966 |
| Ghana 1970 | Argentina 1973 | Greece 1974 |
| Thailand 1975 | Portugal 1976 | Bolivia 1979 |
| Ecuador 1979 | Ghana 1979 | Nigeria 1979 |
| Peru 1980 | Bolivia 1982 | Honduras 1982 |
| Argentina 1983 | Thailand 1983 | Turkey 1983 |
| El Salvador 1984 | Guatemala 1986 | Sudan 1986 |
| Bangladesh 1991 | Suriname 1991 | Mali 1992 |
| Thailand 1992 | Niger 1999 | Lesotho 2002 |
| Ecuador 2003 | Comoros 2006 | Bangladesh 2009 |
| Honduras 2010 | Niger 2011 | Thailand 2011 |
| Fiji 2014 | | |

*Continued on next page*

**Table A.1.** (*continued*)

## Domestic Shocks

*Civil War*

| | | |
|---|---|---|
| Indonesia 1955 | Sudan 1965 | Lebanon 1971 |
| Nicaragua 1984 | The Philippines 1986 | Suriname 1988 |
| Sri Lanka 1991 | Mozambique 1994 | Albania 1997 |
| Croatia 2000 | Senegal 2000 | Serbia 2000 |
| Sierra Leone 2002 | Burundi 2005 | Liberia 2006 |
| Solomon Islands 2006 | Nepal 2008 | Pakistan 2008 |

*Assassination*

| | |
|---|---|
| Spain 1977 | Pakistan 1988 |

## Foreign Shocks

*Defeat in War*

| | | |
|---|---|---|
| France 1870 | Germany 1919 | Italy 1919 |
| Austria 1920 | Greece 1944 | San Marino 1945 |
| Austria 1946 | Italy 1946 | The Philippines 1946 |
| France 1946 | Japan 1952 | Honduras 1971 |
| Cyprus 1977 | Uganda 1980 | Grenada 1984 |
| Panama 1991 | | |

*Hegemonic Withdrawal*

| | | |
|---|---|---|
| Poland 1989 | Bulgaria 1990 | Hungary 1990 |
| Czechoslovakia 1990 | Mongolia 1990 | Romania 1991 |
| Albania 1992 | Lithuania 1992 | Latvia 1993 |

## Electoral Continuity

| | | |
|---|---|---|
| United Kingdom 1885 | Belgium 1894 | The Netherlands 1897 |
| Denmark 1901 | Chile 1909 | Sweden 1911 |
| Argentina 1912 | Uruguay 1919 | Colombia 1937 |
| Uruguay 1942 | South Korea 1988 | São Tomé and Príncipe 1991 |
| Benin 1991 | Cape Verde 1991 | Guyana 1992 |
| Niger 1993 | Madagascar 1993 | Guinea-Bissau 1994 |
| Malawi 1994 | Taiwan 1996 | Ghana 1997 |
| Indonesia 1999 | Mexico 2000 | Paraguay 2003 |
| Antigua and Barbuda 2004 | Zambia 2008 | The Maldives 2009 |

*Continued*

**Table A.1.** (*continued*)

## Other

*Protest/Opposition-Led*

| | | |
|---|---|---|
| France 1848 | South Korea 1960 | Nepal 1991 |
| Central African Rep. 1993 | Peru 2001 | Kenya 2002 |
| Georgia 2004 | | |

*Pacted/Regime-Led*

| | | |
|---|---|---|
| Peru 1956 | Brazil 1985 | Uruguay 1985 |
| Chile 1990 | South Africa 1994 | |

## Coding Details

### BMR SUGGESTED CORRECTIONS

I suggest the following fixes to Boix, Miller, and Rosato 2013 (BMR), with notes on how this changes the paths coding:

- France 1870 should be 1871 (still defeat in war)
- Chile 1934 should be 1932 (still coup)
- Cyprus 1977 should be 1976 (still defeat in war)
- Panama 1950/1952 should be 1956 (still coup from 1951, also assassination from 1955)
- Sri Lanka 1991 should be 1994 (still civil war, also assassination from 1993)
- Uruguay 1942 should be 1943 (still electoral continuity)
- Add Denmark 1945 (defeat in war, hegemonic withdrawal): After being conquered in Apr. 1940, Denmark collaborated as the Nazis' "model protectorate" with a functioning government and Crown, so (like France) it should be considered autocratic for 1940–42. After democratic parties won elections in Mar. 1943 and strikes began, military occupation ensued from Aug. 1943 to 1945.

### PATHS CODING FOR SHADOW CASES

Additional transitions that appear in other democracy data sets, as well as transitions omitted from the book's main list, present a useful out-of-sample test of this book's theory. For starters, I find 19 additional transitions in Polity (Marshall and Jaggers 2017) or CGV (Cheibub, Gandhi, and Vreeland 2010) that are not clearly contradicted by the other data set (e.g., no shift on Polity for a CGV transition).[1] Of these, 16 fit one of the paths: 9 following coups (Paraguay 1989/1992, Comoros 1990, Fiji 1992, Nigeria 1999, Guinea-Bissau 2004/2005,

---

1. Five of these are Polity transitions outside of CGV's sample.

Mauritania 2007, Thailand 2008, Guinea-Bissau 2014, Madagascar 2014), 2 after civil wars (Sierra Leone 1996, Guinea-Bissau 2000), 3 after defeat in war (Spain 1900, Serbia 1919, Iraq 2014), and 2 electoral continuity cases (Denmark 1911, Congo-Brazzaville 1992). The remaining 3 are elite-led (The Netherlands 1917) or protest-led (Kyrgyzstan 2005 and 2010). We can go further and look at any case of democratization that appears in either Polity or CGV. This adds 23 Polity cases, 22 of which fit one of the paths,[2] and 8 CGV cases, 6 of which fit one of the paths.[3]

This pattern of agreement also holds for other potential transitions not included in this book's sample. Among the two post-2014 transitions, Nigeria 2015 (electoral continuity) appears likely to qualify and Tunisia 2015 (protest-led) does not, although it bears resemblance to the electoral continuity path if Nidaa Tounes is considered a continuation of ruling party interests. Of the four cases that quickly democratized after independence, three fit: Ireland 1922 (defeat in war, civil war, assassination), Pakistan 1950 (civil war, defeat in war), and Gambia 1972 (electoral continuity).[4] Finally, there are three cases where democracy was immediately installed in a new country closely associated with an autocratic predecessor. If the country change is ignored and this is treated as democratization, all three fit the paths: West Germany 1945 (defeat in war), Pakistan 1972 (civil war, coup), and Russia 1991 (electoral continuity).

In total, 51 of 59 (86.4%) shadow cases fit one of the paths, about the same success rate as the main BMR cases. The additional cases correspond to the following primary types: 17 coup, 14 electoral continuity, 12 civil war, 7 defeat in war, and 1 assassination. In sum, the success of the main sample's categorization does not depend on the BMR sample of transitions.

## QUALITATIVE CODING

The qualitative codings were derived from the case narratives, which in turn draw on a large range of sources. Several codings were described in the text, including the motives for the initial shocks, the intentions of coup plotters,

2. These are Belgium 1853 (EC), Colombia 1867 (civil war), Costa Rica 1875 (coup), UK 1880 (EC), Norway 1898 (EC), Czechoslovakia 1945 (defeat in war), Turkey 1946 (EC), Uruguay 1952 (EC), Syria 1954 (coup), Pakistan 1956 (civil war, assassination), Laos 1957 (defeat in war), Dominican Republic 1962 (assassination, coup), Cyprus 1968 (civil war), Turkey 1973 (coup), Dominican Republic 1978 (EC), Nicaragua 1990 (civil war, EC), Haiti 1990 (coup), Lesotho 1993 (coup), Haiti 1994 (coup), Guatemala 1996 (civil war), Russia 2000 (civil war), and Malaysia 2008 (EC). Zambia 1991 does not fit.

3. These are Thailand 1979 (coup), Cyprus 1983 (EC), Bangladesh 1986 (coup), Burundi 1993 (civil war, coup), Sierra Leone 1998 (civil war, coup), and Kenya 1998 (EC). Ghana 1993 (near-miss for EC) and Bhutan 2007 (near-miss for civil war) do not fit.

4. The exception is Luxembourg 1890, a highly unusual case that was still controlled by the Dutch monarchy. When King William III died in 1890, control transitioned to his seventeenth cousin (his closest male heir), who took no interest in politics and thus accepted a constitutional monarchy.

and details on civil war settlements (see chapter 3). More detail is warranted for two important qualitative codings:

*Final decisions to democratize*: This codes for the circumstances of the final autocratic decision maker's choice to democratize. As a first step, I identified the last autocratic executive or ruling body (e.g., a ruling party or junta). This excludes rulers put into place by a democratization process, such as a caretaker executive, power-sharing coalition, or constitutional convention tasked with preparing the transition. It also excludes figurehead kings and puppet presidents. This final autocrat must be the primary decision maker in allowing democratization.

For Regained Power, I tracked whether this final decision maker gained power in the following democratic spell. In three cases, I allowed this to occur in a future spell separated from the immediately following one by a single-year break. This counts either the supreme autocrat, the ruling party, or senior members of ruling juntas, as applicable. Regained power requires control of either the executive or legislature (for former ruling parties). Again, caretaker executives, figurehead kings, and transitional power-sharing governments are not counted.

The Reformer coding requires a new executive to take power after a prior shock or trigger. For electoral continuity, this can include winners of contested autocratic elections. It also includes foreign powers if they take effective control. Reformers do not include caretaker executives (when it is clear that their assumption of power constitutes the previous ruler's decision to democratize), winners of democratic elections, or instigators of the initial shocks. Reformers must then quickly and deliberately shift the country to democracy, with no attempt to entrench their autocratic rule. Evidence of pro-democratic beliefs is supportive of this determination but neither necessary nor sufficient.

The Salvation coding focuses on the moment that the final autocrat decides to accept democratization. Prior decisions may have *led* to this moment (e.g., Pinochet's choice to use minimal repression in Chile's 1988 plebiscite), but the central moment is when the ruler finally concedes (e.g., Pinochet's choice to accept the plebiscite results and democratic elections in 1989). For Salvation, this choice must occur amid significant *elite* threats that imply the executive is insecure regardless of decisions about repression. Cases with a generally united regime against popular opposition (e.g., South Korea 1960) are not counted.

*Pro-democratic pressure*: I code for the presence of two forms of major pro-democratic pressure *after* shocks or triggers: pro-democratic protest and international pressure. All transitions involve some popular dissent, so the protest coding relies on judgments in the case literature that organized public opposition was pro-democratic, large in number and scope, and played a meaningful role in the transition. Seventy-one percent of all transitions qualify. For international pressure, this requires a foreign power or organization exerting direct pro-democratic pressure (e.g., threatening to withdraw aid) or their direct involvement in the transition (e.g., the United States in Japan

1952). Diffuse influence (e.g., normative emulation or linkage) is not counted. Thirty-seven percent of all transitions qualify.

## QUANTITATIVE CODING

I describe below the procedures used to code comprehensive data on shocks, ruling parties, and other political and economic variables. The aim was to construct as complete a data set as possible for all autocracies from 1800 to 2013. The data end in 2013 since the last transition year I'm predicting is 2014 and all predictors are lagged. Unless noted otherwise, the main variables cover a total of 11,489 observations. This omits microstates but captures 132 of the democratic transitions. The data set is available on my personal website (sites .google.com/site/mkmtwo).

Repeatedly used data sets are summarized as follows: Archigos (Goemans, Gleditsch, and Chiozza 2016), PIPE (Przeworski 2013), CNTS (Banks and Wilson 2017), COW (Correlates of War Project 2010a), and V-Dem (Coppedge et al. 2018).

### Shocks Coding

*Coups*: For 1950–2013, I used majority agreement among Archigos, Powell and Thyne (2011), and Marshall and Marshall (2018). For pre-1950, I first used Archigos. For missing data pre-1950, I used PIPE. For remaining missing data pre-1950, I used CNTS. Remaining missing data were self-coded, with 19 coup years found. Result is 412 coup years.

*Civil Wars*: To define civil war, I used COW for 1816–2007, UCDP (2017) for post-2007, and self-coded 1800–1815 (no cases). I checked any cases still ongoing in 2007 to avoid data mismatch, corrected ending dates for four cases, removed two cases (which clearly involved fights for democracy), and added three cases. Result is 786 civil war years.

*Assassinations*: I began with Archigos and the 37 assassinations recorded in Jones and Olken 2009. I then scrutinized additional cases listed in Iqbal and Zorn 2006, Marshall and Marshall 2018, and Wikipedia's "list of assassinations." After ensuring these were killings of heads of state or government and removing those synonymous with coups, this added 39 cases. Result is 82 assassination years.

*Defeats in War*: To define war, I began with COW for 1816–2007, which requires 1,000 deaths in some year of the conflict. I removed cases where an ally of a main combatant was involved but didn't suffer 100 battle deaths in any year. I used UCDP 2017 for post-2007 and self-coded prior years. I coded the Napoleonic Wars as 5 separate wars and added 5 others. War outcomes were taken from COW and my coding for remaining cases. Defeat was dated to the end of military occupation if applicable. Result is 145 years with a defeat in war.

*Hegemonic Withdrawals*: This counts Soviet-dominated countries in 1989 and Nazi-dominated countries in 1944.

*Shocks*: The main variable tested in the text is whether any of these five shocks occurred in the five-year window ending the current year.

### Electoral and Party Variables

*Electoral*: Electoral regimes were coded from the LIED data set (Skaaning, Gerring, and Bartusevicius 2015), with recoding for shifts to elections one or two years prior to BMR transitions (which reflect different timing for democratization). For missing values, cases in state collapse were set to 0 and the remainder were self-coded.

*Ruling Parties and Durability*: The key variable *Durable Ruling Party* requires an electoral ruling party in power for 4+ years. Country-years with elections were checked for the presence of ruling parties, using Miller 2020a for post-1940 and self-coding for prior years (aided by Anckar and Frederiksson 2018, V-Dem, and PIPE). Ruling parties must be either the supreme power or used as significant vehicles of power by the executive. For constitutional monarchies, parties must have been allowed to form governments and have dominant legislative power. Cases under external hegemonic control or occupation were not counted. Cases were then checked to ensure durable party control without turnover or regime change, using Miller 2020a for post-1940 and self-coding for prior years.

*Multiparty Electoral*: Multipartyism was coded from the LIED data set (Skaaning, Gerring, and Bartusevicius 2015), with self-coding for missing values.

### Other Political Variables

*Other War Outcomes*: Coded same as for defeats.

*Civil War Outcomes*: I began with COW's coding for stalemates, rebel wins, and government wins. I self-coded UCDP's cases and other additional civil wars, then corrected three COW codings (Mozambique, Angola, Sierra Leone).

*Leader Change*: Executive turnovers, which were further divided into regular and irregular turnovers, were coded from Archigos. Missing values were then filled in by PIPE and CNTS. Finally, any coups or ousters from below were counted as irregular turnovers.

*Leader Tenure*: For executive tenure, I used Archigos for 1875–2013 and PIPE for remaining values, ensuring consistency for adjoining years.

*Authoritarian Regime Change*: This uses Geddes, Wright, and Frantz's (2018) measure of regime failure for 1946–2010. For missing values, I use Mattes, Leeds, and Matsumura's (2016) measure of major coalition change. Remaining missing values were proxied by irregular turnover in Archigos and PIPE, omitting cases of assassination or intermilitary shuffling. I then self-coded cases for 2011–13.

*Authoritarian Regime Type*: This codes autocracies into military, monarchy, other, party, and personalist. I began by using Geddes, Wright, and Frantz

2018 for 1946–2010, supplemented by a recoding of Anckar and Frederiksson 2018 for missing data. I self-coded remaining missing data and any post-2010 values that differed with Geddes, Wright, and Frantz's (2018) last value.

*State Collapse*: This counts state collapse if Polity (Marshall and Jaggers 2017) codes for state failure, disintegration, or interruption; PITF (Marshall, Gurr, and Harff 2019) codes for adverse regime change with substantial or total state failure; or the country is under military occupation (extending PIPE with Polity, V-Dem, and self-coding).

*Protest-Led Ousters*: This uses the Archigos measure of turnovers from below, not including by rebels. Further cases of regime failure in Nardulli et al. 2013 (not counting traditional coups) and Geddes, Wright, and Frantz 2018 (from popular protest) were added if deemed to be protest-led ousters.

*Revolution*: This uses the Archigos measure of rebel-led turnover. Further cases of rebel-led turnover in Nardulli et al. 2013 and Geddes, Wright, and Frantz 2018 were added, as well as cases of rebel victory in civil war (from above) that coincided with irregular turnovers in Archigos. Finally, I hand-coded cases from 1800 to 1814.

*Military Size and Spending*: Both military size (as % of population) and spending (as % of GDP) use Correlates of War Project 2010b, with missing values replaced by World Bank 2017 and then CNTS.

### Economic Variables

For each of these variables, I combine multiple data sets to maximize coverage. For several, one data set covers earlier years and another later years. To avoid jumps at the crossover between series, I adjust consecutive series by a country-specific constant calculated from three overlapping years.

*Average Income and Growth*: Average income is captured as natural-logged GDP/capita (in real 2000 dollars). The data begin with Haber and Menaldo 2011, then fill in missing values from World Bank 2017 and Gapminder 2018. Economic growth is the two-year average percentage change in average income.

*Inflation*: This combines inflation data from World Bank 2017 for 1961–2013 and from V-Dem (Clio Infra data) and Reinhart and Rogoff 2011 for prior years.

*Inequality*: This proxies inequality as the Gini index. I take World Bank 2017, then replace missing values with an average of Galbraith and Kum 2003 and UNU-WIDER 2005.

*Oil and Resource Dependence*: Oil dependence (as % of GDP) is calculated from Ross's (2013) oil revenue/capita data, with missing values replaced by Haber and Menaldo 2011, and then divided by GDP/capita. Similarly, total natural resource dependence uses World Bank 2017 for 1970–2013 and Haber and Menaldo 2011 for prior years.

*Population*: This is taken from Gapminder 2018, with missing values replaced by CNTS for 1815–1939 and Heston, Summers, and Aten 2011 for later years.

*Urbanization*: This captures the urban population %, using World Bank 2017 for 1960–2013 and Correlates of War Project 2010b for prior years.

*Literacy and Education*: Literacy (as % of population) is taken from CNTS for 1830–2004 and World Bank 2017 for missing and later years. Remaining missing data were replaced by UNESCO 2015. Education (as average schooling years among population 15+) is taken from V-Dem, with missing values replaced by Lee and Lee 2016 and then World Bank 2017.

*External Dependence on Democracies*: This uses measures of trade, military, and aid dependence on external democracies from Miller 2020b.

*Fixed Characteristics*: Colonial history was self-coded to track British colonial history, other colonial history, and none. Religion is captured by fractions of the population that are Christian, Muslim, and non-religious. I use Brown and James 2018, with missing values replaced by Maoz and Henderson 2013. Ethnolinguistic fractionalization is measured with Roeder 2001, with missing values from Alesina et al. 2003.

## Case Narratives

For each transition, I indicate the primary path category, divided into the shocks (Coup, Civil War, Assassination, Defeat in War, and Hegemonic Withdrawal), Electoral Continuity, and None. The shock cases all occur shortly after one of the listed shocks, generally within a few years. Electoral Continuity requires an established ruling party to democratize through elections and win power in democracy. I also indicate whether the case qualifies for a *Secondary Category* deemed less causally significant.

*Decision Pattern* indicates the coding for the final autocrat's decision to democratize, divided into Salvation (concession due to insecurity from elite opposition), Reformer (a reformer takes power following a shock or party disruption and deliberately installs democracy), Regained Power (the final autocrat or party regains power in democracy), and None. Overlaps are allowed with Regained Power.

A narrative drawn from various sources follows, providing a concrete sequence of events leading to democratization and contextualizing the qualitative codings. I also frequently make note of political violence and autocratic parties' electoral records after democratization. The list of transitions is taken from BMR, which typically dates the transition to when election winners sit. The sources used for the narratives and codings are in an online appendix, available on my personal website (sites.google.com/site/mkmtwo). This also includes narratives for the cases covered in the book's text, which are omitted here.

### ALBANIA 1992

*Primary Category*: Hegemonic Withdrawal
*Secondary Category*: Electoral Continuity
*Decision Pattern*: Regained Power

Hoxha retires, 1983, and dies, 1985 ∘ Partial reforms under Alia ∘ Revolts met by further liberalization, 1989–90 ∘ Legalization of opposition following student protests, with Sali Berisha acting as mediator, Dec. 1990 ∘ Democratic Party founded by students and intellectuals, Dec. 1990 ∘ Major protests and miners' strikes, 1990–91 ∘ Aid pressure by United States, 1991 ∘ Protesters tear down Hoxha statue in capital, Feb. 1991 ∘ Alia appoints Nano as prime minister to organize opening, Feb. 1991 ∘ Constituent elections won by Communists, renamed as Party of Labor, Mar.–Apr. 1991 ∘ Alia chosen as first president, Apr. 1991 ∘ Protests and burning of Labor offices, Apr. 1991 ∘ General strike and economic crisis cause Nano to resign, leading to coalition government, June 1991 ∘ Party of Labor changes ideology and name to Socialist Party, with Nano as leader, June 1991 ∘ Major protests and riots amid economic and food crisis, May–Dec. 1991 ∘ Alia commits to new elections to maintain coalition, but it collapses and Socialist prime minister resigns, Dec. 1991 ∘ Democrats win legislative elections under Berisha, Mar. 1992 ∘ Nano arrested for corruption and Alia imprisoned for abuses of power, 1993 ∘ Socialists win power and Nano made prime minister after brief democratic breakdown, 1997

## ALBANIA 1997

*Primary Category*: Civil War
*Decision Pattern*: Salvation, Regained Power

Democrats reelected in flawed elections, 1996 ∘ National pyramid schemes collapse, with claims of government culpability, leading to rioting and collapse of state, Feb. 1997 ∘ Prime minister resigns and south falls to rebels and Socialist forces, with ~2,000 killed, Mar. 1997 ∘ UN force enters, Apr. 1997 ∘ Italy and OSCE broker transitional government and election plan ∘ Elections won by Socialists, with Democrats falling to 24/155 seats, June 1997 ∘ New constitution, 1998 ∘ Disputed reelection, 2001 ∘ Electoral turnover back to Berisha in third presidential election, 2005

## ANTIGUA AND BARBUDA 2004

*Primary Category*: Electoral Continuity
*Decision Pattern*: Regained Power

Dominant party ALP wins elections, 1976–1999 ∘ General strike over corruption and arms-smuggling scandal convinces Prime Minister Vere Bird to promise to give up power, 1992 ∘ Power passes to prime minister's son Lester, 1994 ∘ Irregular elections prompt creation of election commission, 1999 ∘ Opposition UPP wins on anti-corruption platform, 2004 ∘ ALP remains second-largest party, winning 47% of seats, 2009 ∘ ALP wins 14 of 17 seats, 2014

## ARGENTINA 1912

*Primary Category*: Electoral Continuity
*Decision Pattern*: Reformer, Regained Power

Major expansion of middle and working classes from 1880s ∘ Following similar revolts in 1890 and 1893, mass protests led by middle-class Radical Civic
Union (UCR) and radical labor call for political reform, 1905 ∘ Dominant
conservative PAN fractures in response to reformer de la Torre, 1908 ∘ PAN's
Sáenz Peña elected president as progressive opposed to fraudulent electoral
system, 1910 ∘ Sáenz Peña implements male suffrage, secret ballot, and fraud
protections, responding to unrest from UCR and urban worker organization,
1912 ∘ Sáenz Peña and conservatives reassured by expectation that status quo
would be maintained and UCR could not win elections ∘ PAN retains plurality
in free 1912 elections, but major boost for liberals ∘ PAN formally splits into
Conservative faction and DPP under de la Torre ∘ UCR wins first legislative
elections after suffrage law fully in effect, 1914, and presidency, 1916 ∘ UCR
remains dominant until 1931

## ARGENTINA 1958

*Primary Category*: Coup
*Decision Pattern*: Salvation

Military coup, 1943 ∘ Gen. Juan Perón elected president with populist platform, 1946, and reelected, 1951 ∘ Failed coups, 1951 and 1955 ∘ Conflict with
Church, opposition, and military leads to air bombing of pro-Perón rally, then
military coup, 1955 ∘ Initial coup leader considered too Perónist and deposed
by military faction under Aramburu two months later ∘ Attempted coup by
Perónist generals, 1956, but defeated and 27 officers executed ∘ Total ban
passed on Perónism and mentioning Perón's name, 1956 ∘ Aramburu steals
Eva Perón's corpse and ships it to Italy ∘ General strikes, 1957 ∘ Constituent
elections, with 25% blank ballots indicating Perónist support, July 1957 ∘ With
Perónist parties banned, presidential election won by Frondizi with Perónist
support, Feb. 1958

## ARGENTINA 1963

*Primary Category*: Coup
*Decision Pattern*: None

Perón-supported Frondizi wins presidency, 1958 ∘ Conflict between president
and Perónist factions, military ∘ Growth of fascist urban guerrilla movement,
1960 ∘ Newly legal Perónist candidates win local elections, 1962 ∘ Military

coup, installing civilian head of Senate, 1962 ∘ Perónists again banned ∘ Military revolt over degree of legal participation of Perónist parties, with hardline faction favoring longer military rule overruled ∘ 1963 elections with ban on Perónists and Communists won by Illia, who becomes unpopular and deposed, 1966

## ARGENTINA 1973

*Primary Category*: Coup
*Secondary Category*: Civil War
*Decision Pattern*: Salvation

Illia ousted by military coup under Onganía, installing new bureaucratic authoritarian political order, 1966 ∘ Tense cooperation with labor sectors allied with Perón ∘ Growth of left-wing guerrilla groups, with Montoneros, FAL, and ERP launching urban guerrilla attacks and kidnappings, 1969 ∘ Military fracture begins, 1969 ∘ Student protests and violence against striking workers in Cordobazo, May 1969 ∘ Montoneros kill former president Aramburu, June 1970 ∘ Military coup replaces Onganía, June 1970, then Lanusse coups, Mar. 1971 ∘ Attempted coup, 1971 ∘ Lanusse develops plan to return to civilian rule ∘ Amid Perónist protests, elections held, with Perónist stand-in Cámpora elected president, Mar. 1973 ∘ Cámpora resigns to allow Perón to resume power, July 1973

## ARGENTINA 1983

*Primary Category*: Coup
*Secondary Categories*: Civil War, Defeat in War
*Decision Pattern*: Salvation

See pages 86–87.

## AUSTRIA 1920

*Primary Category*: Defeat in War
*Decision Pattern*: Reformer

Treaty leads empire to dissolve and territory ceded, Nov. 1918 ∘ Emperor Charles I accepts self-determination of Austria and republic declared, initially called German-Austria and led by Chancellor Renner, Nov. 1918 ∘ Provisional assembly meets, 1918–19 ∘ Full-suffrage constituent assembly elections, Feb. 1919 ∘ New constitution adopted, Oct. 1919 ∘ Initial plan to ally with Germany vetoed by Allies, leading to independent country ∘ New constitution and elections, Oct. 1920 ∘ Elections won by Christian Social Party, which retains power until breakdown under Dollfuss, 1933

# AUSTRIA 1946

*Primary Category*: Defeat in War
*Secondary Category*: Hegemonic Withdrawal
*Decision Pattern*: Reformer

Dollfuss self-coups and bans Communists and Nazis, 1933 ∘ Rise of Father-land Front from paramilitary group, which allies with Dollfuss, 1933 ∘ Dollfuss assassinated by Nazis and Schuschnigg takes over, 1934 ∘ Schuschnigg tries to resist Nazi control but fails ∘ Preempting planned plebiscite, Germany takes control in Anschluss, with Seyss-Inquart imposed as leader, 1938 ∘ Union with Germany, 1938 ∘ Austria conquered by Allies, Mar.–Apr. 1945 ∘ Empowered by Soviets, Karl Renner declares independence and sets up transitional govern-ment, Apr. 1945 ∘ Christian-democratic Austrian People's Party (ÖVP) founded, Apr. 1945 ∘ Occupation forces divide control into American, French, British, and Soviet zones, July 1945 ∘ Legislative elections (with Nazis banned from voting) won by ÖVP, which forms grand coalition and votes in Renner as presi-dent, Nov. 1945 ∘ Occupation fully ends, 1955 ∘ ÖVP and social-democratic SPÖ coalition in power until 1966 ∘ ÖVP in power 1945–70, 1986–present

# BANGLADESH 1991

*Primary Category*: Coup
*Decision Pattern*: Salvation

Independence after war with Pakistan, 1971 ∘ Economic and civil disorder prompt assassination of Mujib, 1975 ∘ Military coup, followed by political chaos, 1975 ∘ Rahman gains power, dissolves parliament, and establishes martial law ∘ Rahman wins elections, 1978, then lifts ban on parties, 1979 ∘ Rahman assassinated by military elements, 1981 ∘ Military coup installs Gen. Ershad, 1982 ∘ Ershad wins referendum, 1985, then creates ruling Jatiya Party and wins flawed legislative elections, 1986 ∘ Ershad wins boycotted presiden-tial election and lifts martial law, 1986 ∘ Major strikes and opposition parties call for reforms, 1987 ∘ Political crisis leads Ershad to dissolve parliament and hold boycotted elections, 1988 ∘ Mass strikes and protests lead Ershad to offer concessions and then resign after losing army support, Dec. 1990 ∘ Caretaker presidency goes to Supreme Court Chief Justice Ahmed, who arrests Ershad ∘ Free elections won by Khaleda Zia (widow of Rahman), Feb. 1991 ∘ Jatiya Party wins just over 10% of seats and remains minor party ∘ Change to parlia-mentary system ∘ Ahmed later selected as president, 1996–2001

# BANGLADESH 2009

*Primary Category*: Coup
*Decision Pattern*: None

Khaleda Zia's BNP and Sheikh Hasina's Awami League alternate power after 1991 ∘ BNP wins elections, 2001 ∘ Protests over neutrality of caretaker government required around elections, 2006 ∘ Awami League announces election boycott, Jan. 2007 ∘ Military coup, Jan. 2007 ∘ Transitional government under economist installed, elections postponed, civil liberties restricted, and mass arrests used to fight corruption, 2007 ∘ Electoral system overhaul ∘ Party leaders released from jail and new elections, Dec. 2008, with Hasina winning prime minister position, Jan. 2009

## BELGIUM 1894

*Primary Category*: Electoral Continuity
*Decision Pattern*: Regained Power

Politics before 1890s dominated by Catholics and Liberals ∘ Catholics' Beernaert becomes prime minister, 1884 ∘ Belgian Workers' Party founded, 1885, then Progressive Party breaks from Liberals, 1887 ∘ Major strikes start, 1892 ∘ Government rejects universal male suffrage, provoking general strike called by BWP that turns violent and is met by government violence, Apr. 1893 ∘ Demonstration grows to ~50,000 and continues for a week ∘ Government fears revolution and relents with plural-vote system and universal compulsory suffrage for men over twenty-five, 1893 ∘ Beernaert supports reforms but resigns when proportional representation proposal rejected, Mar. 1894 ∘ Catholics win legislative elections with over two-thirds of seats, Oct. 1894, then retain majority until 1919

## BENIN 1991

*Primary Category*: Electoral Continuity
*Decision Pattern*: Regained Power

President Mathieu Kérékou leads ruling party PRPB, which renounces Marxism in 1989 ∘ Economic crisis and IMF adjustment program lead to unrest and pressure from French, 1989 ∘ Party conference, Dec. 1989, decides to legalize opposition parties and allow national conference, which declares itself sovereign and strips Kérékou of most power, 1990 ∘ National conference assumes legislative power and sets up elections, 1990 ∘ Referendum passes constitution, Dec. 1990 ∘ Legislative elections produce fragmented assembly, Feb. 1991 ∘ Kérékou breaks from PRPB and loses presidential election to Soglo, Mar. 1991 ∘ PRPB disbands in 1990 and changes to UFP, which doesn't contest 1991 election, then joins coalition that wins 1.5% of vote, 1995 ∘ Democratic parties win legislative pluralities in 1991, 1995, and 1999 ∘ Kérékou wins presidential elections as independent, 1996, and as nominee of FARD-Alafia, 2001

## BOLIVIA 1979

*Primary Category*: Coup
*Decision Pattern*: Salvation

See pages 88–90.


## BOLIVIA 1982

*Primary Category*: Coup
*Decision Pattern*: Salvation

See pages 88–90.


## BRAZIL 1946

*Primary Category*: Coup
*Decision Pattern*: Regained Power

See page 78.


## BRAZIL 1985

*Primary Category*: None (Regime-Led)
*Decision Pattern*: None

See pages 169–70.


## BULGARIA 1990

*Primary Category*: Hegemonic Withdrawal
*Secondary Category*: Electoral Continuity
*Decision Pattern*: Reformer, Regained Power

Protests repressed, Oct.–Nov. 1989 ∘ Leader Zhivkov removed with Soviet support over repression and intended expulsion of minority Turks, then reformer Mladenov installed, Nov. 1989 ∘ Opposition forms Union of Democratic Forces and organizes protests, Nov. 1989 ∘ Concession on elections and talks with opposition, Jan.–May 1990 ∘ Communists renamed to Bulgarian Socialist Party, Apr. 1990 ∘ BSP wins free elections, June 1990, but knocked out of power by protests, Dec. 1990 ∘ Caretaker government installed until new elections ∘ BSP narrowly loses elections, Oct. 1991, then regains power, Dec. 1994

## BURMA 1960

*Primary Category*: Coup
*Secondary Category*: Civil War
*Decision Pattern*: Regained Power

Independence after World War II, with U Nu as prime minister, 1948 ∘ Numerous insurgencies (including Communists, Karen secessionists, and Rohingya secessionists) and presence of KMT from China ∘ Gen. Ne Win made head of military, 1949, and successfully limits insurgencies, 1949–50 ∘ Political dominance by AFPFL, but 1956 elections close and party splits, June 1958 ∘ Surrender of several insurgent groups, 1958 ∘ Given fears of insurgencies and Communists gaining parliamentary power, U Nu asks Ne Win to take control in caretaker government, Oct. 1958 ∘ Communists purged ∘ New elections won by "Clean AFPFL" under U Nu, Feb. 1960 ∘ Military coup by Ne Win, Mar. 1962

## BURUNDI 2005

*Primary Category*: Civil War
*Decision Pattern*: Salvation

See pages 110–11.

## CAPE VERDE 1991

*Primary Category*: Electoral Continuity
*Decision Pattern*: Regained Power

See page 165.

## CENTRAL AFRICAN REPUBLIC 1993

*Primary Category*: None (Protest-Led)
*Decision Pattern*: Salvation

See page 172.

## CHILE 1909

*Primary Category*: Electoral Continuity
*Decision Pattern*: Regained Power

Government eliminates property requirements to vote, but system still allows landowners to control rural votes, 1874 ∘ Suffrage explicitly restricted to male literates, 1885 ∘ Rebellion, with split of military, overthrows Balmaceda, 1891

∘ Politics dominated by local bosses and clientelism ∘ Close election, 1896 ∘ Growth of urban parties and labor organization, 1900 ∘ Conservatives in coalition dominate Congress, 1891–1918 ∘ Due to spread of literacy, suffrage threshold of half of men estimated to be reached, 1909 ∘ Secret ballot, 1958, and universal suffrage, 1970

## CHILE 1934*

*[*Should be 1932]*

*Primary Category*: Coup
*Decision Pattern*: Salvation

Right-wing coup, 1924 ∘ Countercoup returns presidency to Alessandri, who ratifies reform program and increases presidential powers in plebiscite, 1925 ∘ Brutal repression of strike, 1925 ∘ Alessandri resigns, 1925 ∘ Ibáñez becomes military leader, pledging allegiance to Germany, 1927 ∘ Coup plots and economic protests lead him to resign, July 1931 ∘ Interim president Montero defeats Alessandri in presidential election, Oct. 1931 ∘ Navy rebellion put down, Dec. 1931 ∘ National Socialist movement organized, Apr. 1932 ∘ Coup led by civilian socialists, June 1932, but military takes over and empowers Gen. Blanche, Sept. 1932 ∘ Despite Blanche's opposition, a military mutiny led by Gen. Vignola forces elections ∘ Alessandri elected president, Oct. 1932 ∘ Rural rebellion in Ranquil violently crushed, 1934 ∘ Alessandri resigns after quashing Nazi insurrection, 1938 ∘ Ibáñez elected president, 1952

## CHILE 1990

*Primary Category*: None (pact)
*Decision Pattern*: None

Marxist Salvador Allende wins election, 1970, and institutes program of nationalization and land reform ∘ With U.S. support, Augusto Pinochet coups, Sept. 1973 ∘ Extensive repression, with ~3,000 killings in first days, purge of public administration and universities, ~100,000 forced into exile, all parties dissolved, and curfew enforced for next decade ∘ Successful move to free-market economy, 1975– ∘ Pinochet institutionalizes autocracy from 1977 ∘ Plebiscite supports Pinochet, 1978 (with Yes box featuring Chilean flag and No a black rectangle) ∘ Under international pressure, new constitution approved in unfree plebiscite with eight-year term for Pinochet, 1980 ∘ Economic collapse and protests, 1982 ∘ Moderate opposition begins to coalesce, forming party-based Democratic Alliance, Aug. 1983, but Communists turn to violence ∘ Slight liberalization by regime in dialogue with opposition, Aug. 1983 ∘ Labor and urban protests met with repression, 1983–85 ∘ 11 parties sign accord agreeing to gradual transition through engagement, Aug. 1985 ∘ After large arms stockpile found, failed assassination attempt against Pinochet by Communists, 1986 ∘ Parties legalized, 1987 ∘ Confident of victory in reelection plebiscite, Pinochet lessens repression, 1988 ∘ Opposition organizes and defeats plebiscite with 56% of vote, pushing pro-Western message, Oct. 1988 ∘ Pinochet attempts to nullify result, but officers refuse ∘ Agreement with regime affirmed with constitutional referendum, July 1989 ∘ Elections won by Aylwin and broad center-left coalition (Concertación), Dec. 1989, which dominates politics and controls presidency to 2010 ∘ Coalition takes power, 1990 ∘ Pinochet stays as head of army until 1998 and appoints 14 of 17 Supreme Court justices in final autocratic year ∘ Aylwin cautiously challenges authoritarian vestiges, with gradual reforms continuing to 2005

## COLOMBIA 1937

*Primary Category*: Electoral Continuity
*Decision Pattern*: Reformer, Regained Power

Union growth, strikes, and social tensions, 1920s ∘ Bloody repression of peasant strike, leaving 1,400 dead, 1929 ∘ Liberals win presidential election after long rule by Conservatives, 1930 ∘ Liberals win legislative elections, 1931 and 1933 ∘ Both parties split between moderates and radicals ∘ Liberals' López Pumarejo elected president, 1934 ∘ Extensive New Deal–inspired reforms under López Pumarejo in agriculture, right to education, progressive taxes, labor rights, and trade ∘ Universal male suffrage, 1936 ∘ Boycotted elections, but victory by anti-López Liberals, 1937 ∘ Liberals' Santos wins presidency unopposed, triggering turn to right, 1938 ∘ Liberals win first contested legislative election, 1939, then keep legislature until 1951 and presidency until 1946

## COLOMBIA 1958

*Primary Category*: Coup
*Secondary Category*: Civil War
*Decision Pattern*: Reformer, Regained Power

See pages 85–86.

## THE COMOROS 2006

*Primary Category*: Coup
*Secondary Category*: Civil War
*Decision Pattern*: Regained Power

See pages 87–88.

## COSTA RICA 1949

*Primary Category*: Coup
*Secondary Category*: Civil War
*Decision Pattern*: Reformer, Regained Power

Politics dominated by Calderón, president from 1940 to 1944 ∘ After limited liberal reforms, ally Picado wins election, 1944 ∘ Picado allies with Communists and faces unrest and strikes, which are met with widespread violence ∘ Conservative faction of Calderón's party breaks away ∘ José Figueres founds party and organizes anti-Calderón insurgent force, 1945 ∘ Government wins legislative election, 1946 ∘ Police fire on crowd, provoking national strike, July 1947 ∘ Ulate defeats Calderón in 1948 election, confirmed by electoral commission, but results annulled by congress over fraud claims, Mar. 1948 ∘ Violent outbreak and Ulate imprisoned ∘ Figueres begins civil war with coalition of right-wingers and social democrats against Picado government ∘ Figueres wins with support of Guatemala and United States, with ~2,000 deaths, Apr. 1948 ∘ Pact gives Picado government safe passage, with separate agreement between Figueres and Ulate allowing Figueres to rule before elections ∘ Figueres rules through junta for eighteen months, rewrites constitution, abolishes army, and implements clean elections with universal suffrage ∘ Figueres returns power to Ulate and party loses legislative election, 1949 ∘ Calderón twice tries to invade from Nicaragua but fails, 1950s ∘ Figueres breaks with Ulate and founds new National Liberation Party, 1951 ∘ Figueres wins presidency, 1953, with PLN winning 9 of 15 general elections from 1953 to 2018

## CROATIA 2000

*Primary Category*: Civil War
*Secondary Category*: Electoral Continuity
*Decision Pattern*: Regained Power

Croatia declares independence from Yugoslavia, 1991 ∘ President Tuđman's ethnic cleansing contributes to war between Serbs and Croats, 1991–95 ∘ Ceasefire with international intervention, 1992 ∘ War won by Croatia after major offensive, 1995, resulting in Erdut Agreement providing transitional period of control until 1998 for some territory ∘ Regime supports Croats within Bosnia in war, 1992–95, then supports Kosovo in war, 1998–99 ∘ Ruling party HDZ refuses to recognize opposition party victories in local elections (Zagreb crisis), 1995 ∘ Major protests, 1998 ∘ Tuđman dies, sparking succession crisis, 1999 ∘ HDZ replaced in elections despite favorable rule changes and gerrymandering, Jan.–Feb. 2000 ∘ Change to parliamentary system ∘ Legislative elections won by HDZ under Sanader, 2003

## CUBA 1909

*Primary Category*: Coup
*Decision Pattern*: Reformer

After Spanish-American War, Platt Amendment establishes U.S. dominance over Cuba, 1901 ∘ Independence and Tomás Palma elected, 1902 ∘ Palma reelected over Gen. Gómez, but opposition Liberals boycott polls and claim fraud, Dec. 1905 ∘ Legislature affirms election and Liberals walk out, Apr. 1906 ∘ Military revolt produces disordered insurgency, partly aimed at getting United States to intervene and hold fair elections, Aug. 1906 ∘ Palma arrests Liberal leaders, but this triggers further opposition ∘ Palma calls for U.S. intervention to stop rebels and possibly lead to annexation, insisting on resigning rather than rerunning elections ∘ Fearing a guerrilla war and economic collapse, United States accepts Palma's resignation and takes control in provisional government under War Secretary Taft, Sept. 1906 ∘ 6,000 troops occupy posts around island ∘ United States rewrites electoral law and creates new Cuban army ∘ Palma dies, 1908 ∘ Gómez wins Nov. 1908 election ∘ Power handed over Jan. 1909, and troops withdraw, Mar. 1909

## CUBA 1940

*Primary Category*: Coup
*Decision Pattern*: Regained Power

See pages 168–69.

## CYPRUS 1977*

*[\*Should be 1976]*

*Primary Category*: Defeat in War
*Secondary Categories*: Coup, Civil War
*Decision Pattern*: Reformer

Independence gained, with violence between ethnic Greeks (who want union with Greece) and Turks, 1960 ∘ Turkish Cypriots removed from government and organize separately, 1963 ∘ UN peacekeeping force enters, 1964 ∘ Archbishop/President Makarios III reelected, 1968 ∘ Country partitions and guerrilla activities supported by Greece increase, 1971 ∘ Makarios wins uncontested presidential election, 1973 ∘ Insurgent leader dies, 1974 ∘ Greek junta removes Makarios with cooperation of Cypriot National Guard and pro-Greek paramilitary EOKA B after he demands removal of Greek military officers, July 1974 ∘ Pro-Greek politician and 1950s EOKA member Sampson made president

◦ Turkey invades, July 1974 ◦ Sampson ousted after eight days and power given to caretaker Clerides, July 1974 ◦ Greek junta collapses and direct war avoided ◦ Turkey takes over 40% of country, devastating economy and setting up separate government ◦ Brokered cease-fire, Aug. 1974 ◦ Makarios returns, Dec. 1974, but dies, 1977 ◦ Legislative elections, Sept. 1976

## CZECHOSLOVAKIA 1990

*Primary Category*: Hegemonic Withdrawal
*Decision Pattern*: None

Hard-liner Husák replaced by moderate Jakeš, Dec. 1987 ◦ Student protests begin, Aug. 1988 ◦ Major protests after students suppressed violently, Nov.–Dec. 1989 ◦ Dissidents led by Václav Havel and other Charter 79 members begin negotiating with government as Civic Forum ◦ Jakeš resigns and replaced by reformer Urbánek, late Nov. 1989 ◦ Communists relinquish power and appoint non-Communist government, with Dubček (reformist Communist leader who triggered Prague Spring) as speaker of federal parliament and Havel as president, Dec. 1989 ◦ Elections won by Civic Forum, June 1990 ◦ Havel and Dubček kept in positions, with Dubček remaining until death, 1992 ◦ After getting 13% of legislative vote in election, Communists fragment, with main factions becoming federation of two regional parties, Nov. 1990 ◦ Federation dissolves, 1992 ◦ Parties evolve into SDL' in Slovakia (getting 15% of vote in 1992) and KSČM in Czech Republic (getting 14% of vote in 1992), which remain minor parties

## DENMARK 1901

*Primary Category*: Electoral Continuity
*Decision Pattern*: Regained Power

Constitutional monarchy with universal male suffrage but king as executive, 1849 ◦ Peasant/urban coalition gains power in lower house of legislature ◦ Shift of working class from right to left ◦ Reform increases power of upper house, with appointed and indirectly elected members ◦ Venstre Reform Party wins lower house elections from 1895 and majority of seats from 1898, but king denies chance to form government ◦ Secret ballot passed, Jan. 1901 ◦ VRP wins overwhelming majority in election, Apr. 1901 ◦ Christian IX reluctantly allows center-left to form cabinet, replacing conservative government from upper house and starting tradition of parliamentary majority government ◦ VRP's Deuntzer sits as Council president, July 1901 ◦ VRP wins elections until 1909 ◦ Universal suffrage, 1914

## DOMINICAN REPUBLIC 1966

*Primary Category*: Coup
*Secondary Category*: Assassination
*Decision Pattern*: Salvation

See pages 49, 71, and 118.

## ECUADOR 1948

*Primary Category*: Coup
*Secondary Category*: Defeat in War
*Decision Pattern*: Salvation

Coup ousts Velasco Ibarra, 1935 ∘ Intramilitary coup, 1937 ∘ Fraudulent election defeats Velasco, followed by repression under Arroyo, 1940 ∘ Costly war with Peru, 1941–42, with Peru's occupation ending after international mediation ∘ Widespread opposition to war outcome and inflation ∘ Uprising leads to military handing power to Velasco, who promises leftist turn, 1944 ∘ Velasco repudiates constitution and closes assembly, 1945, then passes new constitution, declares himself dictator, and turns rightward, 1946 ∘ Military coups, 1947 ∘ Three turnovers of power before Plaza wins presidential election, 1948 ∘ Velasco later wins in democracy, 1952

## ECUADOR 1979

*Primary Category*: Coup
*Decision Pattern*: Salvation

Coups, 1961 and 1963 ∘ Junta broken by popular revolt, 1966 ∘ Elections narrowly won by Velasco Ibarra, 1968 ∘ Velasco self-coups, 1970 ∘ Military coup by Lara, stopping presidential election likely to be won by populist CFP leader Bucaram, 1972 ∘ Failed attempts at economic reform and partial oil nationalization, opposed by business ∘ Failed military coup, 1975 ∘ Economic crisis and general strike, Nov. 1975 ∘ Successful military coup, supported by Right against pro-labor reforms, 1976 ∘ Junta representing three armed services promises return to civilian rule to avoid military fracture but pursues slow process designed to control outcome ∘ Constitutional referendum, Jan. 1978, presidential election first round, July 1978, and second round, Apr. 1979 ∘ Military disqualifies Bucaram, but CFP's Roldós wins presidency ∘ Military allows inauguration due to U.S. pressure and clear mandate but extracts concessions, including amnesty ∘ Roldós dies, 1981

## ECUADOR 2003

*Primary Category*: Coup
*Decision Pattern*: Reformer

Bucaram wins 1996 election but faces allegations of corruption ○ With popular support, Congress ousts him, charging mental incompetence ○ Popular pressure leads to constitutional assembly, 1997 ○ Elections won by Mahuad of DP, 1998 ○ Treaty with Peru viewed as unfavorable by military, Oct. 1998 ○ Economic crisis prompted by dollarization and neoliberal reforms ○ Indigenous group marches on Quito and demands Mahuad ouster, supported by junior military officers under Col. Gutierrez, who let protesters take over parliament, Jan. 2000 ○ Officers declare junta ○ United States and senior military command oppose leaders, dissolve junta, and install Vice President Noboa as president, with little public opposition, Jan. 2000 ○ Gutierrez imprisoned but wins presidential election over banana tycoon, Nov. 2002, and takes power, Jan. 2003 ○ Gutierrez illegally dissolves Supreme Court, 2005 ○ Protests and military opposition oust Gutierrez, giving power to vice president, Apr. 2005

## EL SALVADOR 1984

*Primary Category*: Coup
*Secondary Category*: Civil War
*Decision Pattern*: Salvation, Regained Power

Army blocks election victory of PDC's Duarte, beats, and deports him, 1972 ○ Failed coup supporting Duarte, 1972 ○ Extreme instability through 1970s, with left-wing insurgency and government-sponsored rural counterinsurgency ○ Stolen election helps shift Left toward armed opposition, 1977 ○ Death squads and violence against protesters ○ Mass strikes repressed, Mar. 1979 ○ Extensive anti-government violence and president's brother killed, Sept. 1979 ○ Reformist coup sets up fractured junta combining military and civilians, Oct. 1979 ○ New conservative junta in alliance with PDC, Jan. 1980 ○ Mass protest in capital, Jan. 1980 ○ Forced land redistribution begins, Mar. 1980 ○ Junta reshuffle brings in Duarte, Mar. 1980 ○ Archbishop Romero assassinated, Mar. 1980 ○ Five left-wing groups form FMLN, which unites with Communists, Oct. 1980 ○ Junta leader Majano escapes assassination attempt and flees, Dec. 1980

Hard-liner junta installed, led by Duarte, first civilian president in forty-nine years, Dec. 1980 ○ Violence kills ~22,000, 1980 ○ Land reform and nationalization to win peasant loyalty ○ Failed coup plot by death-squad leader D'Aubuisson, Jan. 1981 ○ Insurgency begins with FMLN offensive, Jan. 1981 ○ United States expands military assistance ○ D'Aubuisson and government found conservative ARENA party, with support from business elites, Sept. 1981 ○ Military kills over 1,000 civilians in El Mozote, Dec. 1981 ○ Under U.S. pressure, junta holds constituent elections, Mar. 1982 ○ PDC wins plurality, but ARENA forms coalition with former ruling party PCN ○ Facing U.S. threat of aid shutoff, banker Magaña chosen as president by assembly, over ARENA's wishes, Apr. 1982 ○ Right-wing parties sign Pact of Apaneca agreeing on election plan and intention to end war, Aug. 1982 ○ Assembly blocks land reforms,

1982 ◦ Duarte cedes power to focus on party-building, 1982 ◦ Parties agree on constitution, Dec. 1983 ◦ Presidential election votes in U.S.-favored Duarte over D'Aubuisson, May 1984 ◦ FMLN shifts to irregular tactics ◦ Against U.S. and military wishes, Duarte negotiates with rebels, but talks fail, Nov. 1984 ◦ Legislative elections won by PDC, Mar. 1985 ◦ ARENA wins legislature, 1988, and controls presidency, 1989–2009 ◦ FMLN signs peace agreement and becomes political party, 1992

## FIJI 2014

*Primary Category*: Coup
*Decision Pattern*: Regained Power

Attempted civilian coup by businessman and nationalists, who hold Prime Minister Chaudhry and most of cabinet hostage for two months, 2000 ◦ After president tries to take power, military under Bainimarama coups and installs interim prime minister Qarase, 2000 ◦ Supreme Court invalidates move, but legal workaround keeps Qarase and calls for elections, 2001 ◦ Qarase and United Fiji Party win 2001 elections, judged free ◦ Rising tensions between civilians and military over lenient treatment of 2000 coup plotters, 2005 ◦ Qarase reelected, 2006 ◦ Citing corruption and racist policies against Indo-Fijians, Bainimarama launches bloodless coup after Qarase refuses to prosecute leaders of 2000 coup, Dec. 2006 ◦ Bainimarama appointed prime minister, 2007 ◦ After courts declare 2006 coup illegal, Bainimarama steps down, Apr. 2009 ◦ President Iloilo takes power, dismisses all judges, abrogates constitution, and reinstates Bainimarama within twenty-four hours, Apr. 2009 ◦ Bainimarama pushes to eliminate racial classifications in electoral law, outlined in People's Charter ◦ Elections repeatedly delayed from initial schedule in 2009, but Bainimarama commits to elections in 2014 ◦ New constitution eliminates ethnic quotas and unelected upper house, 2013 ◦ Elections won by Bainimarama's new FijiFirst party, 2014

## FRANCE 1848

*Primary Category*: None (Protest-Led)
*Decision Pattern*: None

Reform movement grows amid economic crisis and increasing inequality, organized around banquets designed to skirt anti-association laws, 1847 ◦ Banquets outlawed, Feb. 1848 ◦ Mass protests lead to defections from National Guard and lead King Louis Philippe to dismiss minister Guizot ◦ Repression accelerates broad revolt that removes king, Feb. 1848 ◦ Liberal opposition comes to power in Second Republic, votes in universal male suffrage and right-to-work laws ◦ April constituent assembly elections relatively conservative, leading to attempted overthrow of assembly, May 1848 ∘ Workers' revolt protesting closure of work program violently suppressed by Cavaignac with 100,000+ soldiers, June 1848 ∘ Conservatives choose Cavaignac as head of state, June 1848 ∘ Presidential elections install Napoleon III, Dec. 1848 ∘ Self-coup, 1851

## FRANCE 1870*

### [*Should be 1871]

*Primary Category*: Defeat in War
*Decision Pattern*: Reformer

See page 132.

## FRANCE 1946

*Primary Category*: Defeat in War
*Secondary Category*: Hegemonic Withdrawal
*Decision Pattern*: Reformer

After Reynaud resigns as prime minister rather than sign armistice, Pétain forms government at Vichy and is granted emergency powers, June 1940 ∘ Laval takes over as prime minister, Apr. 1942 ∘ Vichy government loses independence, Nov. 1942 ∘ Liberation by Allies, 1944 ∘ Charles de Gaulle, head of proclaimed government-in-exile, returns to Paris, Aug. 1944, then is made leader, Sept. 1944 ∘ De Gaulle forms three-party alliance with Communists, socialists, and Christian Democrats ∘ Legislative/constituent elections won by alliance, Oct. 1945 ∘ De Gaulle resigns, Jan. 1946 ∘ Constitutional referendum voted down, May 1946 ∘ Second constituent elections, June 1946, then constitution approved in referendum, Oct. 1946 ∘ Legislative election won by Communists and alliance, Nov. 1946 ∘ Opposition to Communist prime minister leads to socialist Blum as leader ∘ Alliance breaks up and socialists and Christian Democrats form Third Force coalition

## GEORGIA 2004

*Primary Category*: None (Protest-Led)
*Decision Pattern*: None

See pages 176–77.

## GERMANY 1919

*Primary Category*: Defeat in War
*Decision Pattern*: Reformer

Wide suffrage but unequal voting rights and limited parliamentary power ∘ World War I weakens government and increases worker leverage ∘ Kaiser pushes for new government and electoral reform to appeal to Allies and to spread responsibility for postwar outcome, Oct. 1918 ∘ Naval revolts spread mass unrest, Oct. 1918 ∘ Republic proclaimed, Kaiser Wilhelm II flees, and armistice agreed, Nov. 1918 ∘ Chancellor resigns and hands power to Social Democratic Party under Ebert, who opts for republic in alliance with army ∘ Communist uprising crushed, Jan. 1919 ∘ Full-suffrage national assembly elections won by SPD and centrists, Jan. 1919 ∘ Assembly approves Treaty of Versailles and Weimar Constitution, July 1919 ∘ New elections transition power to Reichstag, June 1920 ∘ Ebert as chancellor, then president, 1918–25

## GHANA 1970

*Primary Category*: Coup
*Decision Pattern*: Salvation

Independence, 1957, and republic formed, 1960 ∘ Nkrumah made president for life and represses opponents, 1961 ∘ Opposition parties outlawed, 1964 ∘ Opposed to Nkrumah rule, military policy, and corruption, military coups jointly with police while Nkrumah is visiting China, promising turn to democracy, Feb. 1966 ∘ Junta organizes as National Liberation Council, Feb. 1966 ∘ Junta abolishes legislature, suspends constitution, implements IMF structural adjustment policies, and ends turn toward USSR ∘ Delayed restoration of civilian government and aborted coup attempt, 1967 ∘ Internal turmoil in junta over ethnic politics ∘ Parties legalized, but Nkrumah's CPP banned, 1968 ∘ Head of junta forced to resign over bribery scandal, 1969 ∘ Appointed constitutional assembly and elections, 1969 ∘ New prime minister Busia a long-time opponent of Nkrumah and supported by junta

## GHANA 1979

*Primary Category*: Coup
*Decision Pattern*: Reformer

Violence against unions by Busia government ∘ Military coup over defense budget cuts and leadership changes, 1972 ∘ Ruling council reverses fiscal policies ∘ Political consolidation over government and change into Supreme Military Council, 1975 ∘ Nonviolent protests, 1977 ∘ Military proposes non-party-based power-sharing with civilians (UNIGOV), passed narrowly by referendum, 1978 ∘ Opposed junta officers led by Akuffo launch coup and promise transition to elected government, 1978 ∘ Parties legalized under protest pressure, Jan. 1979 ∘ Constitutional draft created, May 1979 ∘ Junior officer coup initially fails, May 1979, but new supporters led by Jerry Rawlings and

AFRC movement succeed, June 1979 ◦ Former military leaders (including three former heads of state) executed, but elections continue as planned, with civilian government inaugurated, Sept. 1979 ◦ AFRC continues as watchdog ◦ Corruption and conflict with labor erodes government support and Rawlings leads coup promising "people's revolution" with local governance, 1981

## GHANA 1997

*Primary Category*: Electoral Continuity
*Decision Pattern*: Regained Power

See pages 163–64.

## GREECE 1864

*Primary Category*: Coup
*Decision Pattern*: Reformer, Regained Power

Military coup against unpopular King Otto of Bavaria forces semi-democratic constitution, 1843 ◦ Greece blockaded by British during Crimean War, 1854 ◦ Protest and political opposition against Otto resurges, 1859 ◦ Attempted assassination of queen, 1861 ◦ Otto dismisses prime minister, provoking student/ political/military rebellion, implicitly supported by major European powers ◦ King flees, 1862 ◦ Interim government under three revolutionaries from 1821 war of independence ◦ Greek choice for new king (Queen Victoria's second son, Prince Alfred) vetoed by Great Powers ◦ Austria's Maximilian refuses Britain's offer to become king, 1863, instead becoming emperor of Mexico ◦ At behest of Britain, Danish prince becomes King George I, 1863 ◦ With king's support, new constitution adopted with weaker monarchy and universal male suffrage, 1864

## GREECE 1926

*Primary Category*: Coup
*Secondary Category*: Defeat in War
*Decision Pattern*: Reformer

Continuous war involving Ottomans, World War I, and Turkey, 1912–22 ◦ Prime Minister Venizelos supports Allies, but King Constantine favors neutrality, leading to sharp division of authority ◦ King flees, 1917 ◦ Venizelos rules supreme and sets up puppet King Alexander (second son of Constantine) ◦ Venizelos continues territorial war with Turkey, 1919 ◦ Alexander dies from monkey bite, adding to instability, Oct. 1920 ◦ Venizelos loses elections, Nov. 1920, faces assassination attempt, and flees ◦ King Constantine returns and wins referendum, Nov. 1920 ∘ Defeat by Turkey and refugee crisis, 1922 ∘ Pro-Venizelos military revolt forces king to flee again, 1922 ∘ Assembly elections, 1923 ∘ Failed royalist coup, 1923 ∘ Republic declared and supported by plebiscite, 1924 ∘ General coups and rules for a year, 1925 ∘ Countercoup by another general restores republic and holds elections, 1926 ∘ Venizelos returns and wins major electoral victory, 1928

## GREECE 1944

*Primary Category*: Defeat in War
*Decision Pattern*: Reformer

Metaxas coups with support of King George II, 1936 ∘ Greeks defend against Italian invasion, 1940 ∘ Metaxas dies, 1941 ∘ Germany conquers country, producing multiple resistance movements, 1941 ∘ German forces withdraw and UK-backed government-in-exile returns, Oct. 1944 ∘ Tensions develop among government and pro- and anti-Communist militias, with agreement to represent them in government ∘ Government uses violence against Communist rally, Dec. 1944 ∘ Treaty with Communists, Feb. 1945 ∘ Elections boycotted by Communists, 1946 ∘ Eruption into civil war, 1946–49

## GREECE 1974

*Primary Category*: Coup
*Decision Pattern*: Salvation

Right-wing military coup dismisses Papandreou, dissolving parties and civil liberties, 1967 ∘ Failed countercoup by king, Dec. 1967 ∘ Junta leader Papadopoulos pushes for liberalization but prevented by hard-liners ∘ Naval coup narrowly suppressed, May 1973, convincing Papadopoulos to announce transition to parliamentary government, June 1973 ∘ Papadopoulos appoints Markezinis as civilian prime minister, Sept. 1973 ∘ Student protests repressed, partly influencing hard-liner military coup (Colonels' regime) under Ioannides, who tries to consolidate power, Nov. 1973 ∘ Oil in Aegean discovered, with heightened tensions with Turkey over oil rights, Feb. 1974 ∘ Junta attempts to assassinate Makarios in Cyprus and organizes coup ∘ Greek support collapses after interference in Cyprus almost leads to war with Turkey, July 1974 ∘ Joint Chiefs reassert power and decide to concede to democracy, tapping Karamanlis as interim prime minister, July 1974 ∘ Karamanlis returns to Greece ∘ Standoff with military over tank presence in Athens and military relents, Aug. 1974 ∘ Karamanlis wins elections, Nov. 1974 ∘ 1974 referendum leads to abolition of monarchy and new constitution, 1975 ∘ Prosecution of junta members and failed coup, Feb. 1975

## GRENADA 1984

*Primary Category*: Defeat in War
*Secondary Category*: Coup
*Decision Pattern*: Reformer

See page 129.

## GUATEMALA 1945

*Primary Category*: Coup
*Decision Pattern*: Salvation, Regained Power

General strike, student protests, and military defections lead to abdication of repressive Gen. Ubico (president since 1931), June 1944 ∘ Ubico-chosen junta takes over, led by Ponce Vaides ∘ Soldiers hold congress at gunpoint and force them to appoint Ponce president, July 1944 ∘ Stolen election and civil unrest led by professor Arévalo prompt another coup (October Revolution) led by exiled Captain Árbenz and Colonel Arana, who storm National Palace, Oct. 1944 ∘ New junta allows legislative elections (limited to literate men), Nov. 1944, and presidential elections, Dec. 1944, which are won by Arévalo and leftist PAR coalition ∘ Arana opposes elections and Arévalo's win but relents after being made head of armed forces, 1945 ∘ New democratic constitution expands suffrage and gives more power to legislature, Mar. 1945 ∘ Arévalo survives about twenty coup attempts from 1945 to 1950 ∘ Arévalo hurt in car accident but quickly recovers, Dec. 1945 ∘ Arana prevented from leading coup by PAR's promised support for his 1950 presidential campaign ∘ Arana threatens coup if Defense Minister Árbenz's faction not purged, leading to bloody retaliation by Árbenz and Arana's death while resisting arrest, July 1949 ∘ Presidency won by Árbenz, 1950 ∘ Coup, 1954, ending 1944–54 opening known as Ten Years of Spring

## GUATEMALA 1958

*Primary Category*: Coup
*Secondary Category*: Assassination
*Decision Pattern*: Salvation, Regained Power

Numerous coup attempts during Arévalo presidency, 1945–51 ∘ Presidential election won by former coup leader Árbenz over Gen. Ydigoras, Nov. 1950 ∘ Agrarian reform law tries to empower local workers, 1952 ∘ Victory for leftist parties in legislative elections, Jan. 1953 ∘ Failed United Fruit-sponsored rebellion, Mar. 1953 ∘ U.S.-supported invasion led by exiled Col. Castillo Armas to oppose land reform and communism, ending in coup ousting Árbenz,

June 1954 ∘ Successor Diaz ousted by military after two days ∘ Monzon hands power to Castillo Armas under pressure from United States, July 1954 ∘ Indians disenfranchised, constitution suspended, and mass repression, July 1954 ∘ Snap elections and plebiscite, Oct. 1954 ∘ Castillo Armas founds MLN as junta party, which wins uncontested Dec. 1955 legislative elections ∘ Coup attempts, Jan. 1956 and June 1957 ∘ Castillo Armas assassinated by member of presidential guard, July 1957 ∘ Series of interim presidents ∘ Ydigoras loses fraudulent presidential election to MLN candidate, triggering protest, Oct. 1957 ∘ Military coup annuls election and junta agrees to hand over power given opposition to longer rule, Oct. 1957 ∘ Ydigoras wins fairer election over MLN candidate, Jan. 1958 ∘ MLN wins legislative plurality in three-party coalition, 1961 ∘ MLN allies with future military party PID to win presidency, 1970 and 1974

## GUATEMALA 1966

*Primary Category:* Coup
*Secondary Category:* Civil War
*Decision Pattern:* Regained Power

Election of Ydigoras after assassination of Castillo Armas, 1958 ∘ Failed military coup, Nov. 1960 ∘ Leftist officers from coup attempt form rebel group MR-13 (after date of revolt), then join left-wing guerrillas in multifront insurgency called Rebel Armed Forces (FAR), 1962 ∘ Failed air force coup, Nov. 1962 ∘ Ydigoras ousted in coup by Defense Minister Peralta, Mar. 1963 ∘ Peralta establishes ruling party PID, 1963 ∘ Major counterinsurgency operations start, 1964 ∘ Limited constituent elections, with 60 of 80 seats appointed by military, May 1964 ∘ United States starts advising on counterinsurgency, 1965 ∘ New constitution with universal suffrage ratified, Sept. 1965 ∘ Opposition leader and 1958 election loser Méndez found dead (shot through heart in claimed suicide), shifting candidacy to brother, Oct. 1965 ∘ Pact gives military broad powers and veto over policy, 1966 ∘ Center-left civilian Méndez wins presidential election on pro-democracy platform, Mar. 1966 ∘ FAR kills U.S. ambassador, 1968 ∘ PID wins legislature and presidency in coalition, 1970 ∘ Peralta runner-up in 1978 presidential election ∘ Peace agreement, 1996

## GUATEMALA 1986

*Primary Category:* Coup
*Secondary Category:* Civil War
*Decision Pattern:* Reformer

Repressive rule of Gen. Lucas, 1978–82 ∘ Counterinsurgency campaign against indigenous Mayan and peasant groups (including remnant of FAR) ∘ ~5,000 killed by government, 1980 ∘ Leftist groups join umbrella organization

URNG, Feb. 1982 ∘ Lucas's hand-picked successor Gen. Guevara declared winner of fraudulent election, triggering protests, Mar. 1982 ∘ Military coup in response, Mar. 1982 ∘ Three-man junta led by Gen. Montt, who favors opening but increases violence against URNG, killing tens of thousands of Indian citizens and causing refugee crisis ∘ Economic crisis ∘ Montt takes sole power, June 1982 ∘ Montt faces repeated coup attempts and delays plan for elections until 1986, 1983 ∘ Coup led by Defense Minister Mejía, opposing religiosity of Montt and corruption, Aug. 1983 ∘ Under U.S. pressure, managed turn to democracy with constituent assembly elections, July 1984 ∘ Democratic constitution, May 1985 ∘ General election, Nov. 1985 ∘ Civilian president Cerezo takes office with promise not to pursue land reform or prosecute military, 1986 ∘ Coup attempt, with Cerezo agreeing to cancel talks with URNG, May 1988 ∘ Peace agreement, 1996

### GUINEA-BISSAU 1994

*Primary Category*: Electoral Continuity
*Decision Pattern*: Regained Power

João Vieira leads coup, 1980 ∘ Single-party assembly reconstituted, with Vieira head of ruling PAIGC, 1984 ∘ Opposition parties legalized amid economic problems and international pressure, 1991 ∘ Coup plots, 1983, 1985, and 1993 ∘ Protracted transitional process controlled by regime, 1991–94 ∘ Vieira and PAIGC win competitive elections, July 1994 ∘ Civil war, 1998–99, and coup ousts Vieira, 1999 ∘ Coup, 2003 ∘ Vieira elected, 2005, then assassinated by military, 2009 ∘ PAIGC remains largest party in assembly as of 2020

### GUYANA 1992

*Primary Category*: Electoral Continuity
*Decision Pattern*: Reformer, Regained Power

See page 167.

### HONDURAS 1957

*Primary Category*: Coup
*Decision Pattern*: Reformer

Gálvez elected, 1949, continuing economic modernization and pivoting to increase press freedom and pro-labor legislation ∘ Widespread anti–United Fruit strikes, May 1954 ∘ Gálvez supports coup/invasion in Guatemala, June 1954 ∘ Ruling party splits and opposition leader Villeda gains plurality in presidential election but not enough to win, Oct. 1954 ∘ Constitutional crisis when pro-regime parties boycott assembly to pick president, Nov. 1954

○ Gálvez cedes power to Vice President Lozano and leaves country for medical care, Nov. 1954 ○ Lozano grabs power in self-coup, suspending legislature and postponing new elections, Dec. 1954 ○ Female suffrage extended by decree, Jan. 1955 ○ Lozano organizes PUN party, Oct. 1955 ○ Opposition repressed, followed by failed coup, Aug. 1956 ○ PUN wins boycotted constituent elections, Oct. 1956 ○ Military coup, supported by Gálvez's son (a major), who joins three-person junta headed by Rodríguez, Oct. 1956 ○ Rodríguez resigns under pressure from Minister of Defense López, July 1957 ○ Liberals win constituent elections, Sept. 1957 ○ Villeda appointed president after making secret deal with military, Nov. 1957 ○ New constitution with significant reserve powers for military, Nov. 1957 ○ Failed coup, Feb. 1959 ○ Coup by López, 1963

## HONDURAS 1971

*Primary Category*: Defeat in War
*Secondary Category*: Coup
*Decision Pattern*: Salvation, Regained Power

See pages 132–33.

## HONDURAS 1982

*Primary Category*: Coup
*Decision Pattern*: Reformer

Military coup by López against unpopular power-sharing government supported by labor, Dec. 1972 ○ Damaging hurricane destroys majority of agricultural land, 1974 ○ Coup by Melgar and dissident officers over corruption scandal involving United Fruit bribes, Apr. 1975 ○ Continued conflict over land reform ○ Coup attempt, Oct. 1977 ○ Drop in support over electoral delays, corruption, and drugs leads to right-wing coup by military leadership, promising return to civilian rule, Aug. 1978 ○ Constituent elections narrowly won by Liberals (PLH), Apr. 1980 ○ Liberals accept coup leader Paz as interim president, July 1980 ○ Officer purge, Aug. 1980 ○ Peaceful protest as Paz suggests delaying elections, Sept. 1981 ○ Deal between military and major parties allowing elections in exchange for military autonomy and veto power over cabinet, Oct. 1981 ○ Elections won by PLH, Nov. 1981 ○ New constitution goes into force, Jan. 1982 ○ Military maintains significant control, benefits from U.S. aid buildup, and represses civil society groups

## HONDURAS 2010

*Primary Category*: Coup
*Decision Pattern*: None

Turnover to Liberals' Manuel Zelaya in presidential election, Nov. 2005 ∘ Zelaya plans constitutional referendum to allow presidential reelection, June 2009 ∘ Referendum judged unconstitutional by most in government, including Supreme Court, but no clear procedure for impeachment ∘ Military coup removes Zelaya on morning of poll, June 2009 ∘ Zelaya flown abroad, Congress votes to officially remove, and Speaker Micheletti sworn in as president ∘ Various civil liberties suspended after Zelaya returns to country, Sept. 2009 ∘ Internationally brokered agreement to return Zelaya to presidency breaks down ∘ Scheduled presidential election won by Lobo, Nov. 2009, who is inaugurated, Jan. 2010 ∘ Zelaya exiled to Dominican Republic but returns, 2011

## HUNGARY 1990

*Primary Category*: Hegemonic Withdrawal
*Secondary Category*: Electoral Continuity
*Decision Pattern*: Reformer, Regained Power

Kádár as Communist Party leader from 1956, favoring relative economic openness ∘ Acceptance of pluralist elite factions widespread by 1980s, with Pozsgay faction supporting pluralism with Communist control ∘ Freer vote choice allowed in legislative elections, 1985 ∘ Kádár resigns, leading to moderate leader Grósz, May 1988 ∘ Grósz tries to slow major changes pushed by Pozsgay and Prime Minister Németh ∘ Softening of laws followed by Pozsgay's revision of view of 1956 revolution, Jan. 1989 ∘ Mass protests, Mar. 1989 ∘ Nascent parties and opposition groups form Opposition Round Table (EKA), Mar. 1989 ∘ Preliminary talks with dissidents, Mar.–Apr. 1989 ∘ Border fence with Austria dismantled, May 1989 ∘ Reburial of reformer Nagy, June 1989 ∘ Communists form four-person collective leadership in which Grósz is outvoted by reformers, June 1989 ∘ After protests, Round Table talks agree on power-sharing deal, June–Sept. 1989 ∘ Communists become Hungarian Socialist Party (MSZP) and accept multiparty legislature and direct presidential elections, Oct. 1989 ∘ Grósz pushed out of leadership and forms hard-liner successor party ∘ Elections, Mar.–Apr. 1990 ∘ Opposition Hungarian Democratic Forum wins plurality but fails at economic reforms ∘ ∼ 100,000 Soviet troops leave Hungary, 1990–91 ∘ Socialists win legislature, 1994

## INDONESIA 1955

*Primary Category*: Civil War
*Secondary Category*: Electoral Continuity
*Decision Pattern*: Reformer, Regained Power

Independence declared by Sukarno and Hatta, 1945 ∘ Initial plans for 1946 elections delayed ∘ After bloody revolution, Netherlands recognizes independence in peace deal, 1949 ∘ Several breakaway regions and Communist rebellion, 1948–50 ◦ Declaration of breakaway Islamic regions in South Maluku and Central Java, 1950, and Aceh, 1953, but repressed ◦ Unitary republic established under Sukarno, 1950 ◦ Failed coup, 1950 ◦ Military opposition and shakeup after dissident officers organize protest, Oct. 1952 ◦ First parliamentary and constituent assembly elections narrowly won by Sukarno's PNI, with 28 parties gaining seats, 1955 ◦ Suharto dissolves constituent assembly in self-coup, 1959

## INDONESIA 1999

*Primary Category*: Electoral Continuity
*Decision Pattern*: Reformer, Regained Power

Coup against Sukarno, followed by mass purge, 1965 ◦ Suharto rules based on pact between Golkar party and military ◦ Regular elections from 1973, but only parties allowed are Golkar, Islamic PPP, and PDI ◦ Bloody insurrection and annexation of East Timor, 1975–99, including massacre of protestors, 1991 ◦ Insurgency in Aceh, 1976–2005 ◦ Partial opening (*keterbukaan*) of speech and media, early 1990s ◦ Under Megawati, PDI begins pro-democratic stance and party fractures, 1996 ◦ Suharto allows crackdown, 1996 ◦ Golkar wins legislative election with 68% of vote, 1997 ◦ Major economic crisis begins and IMF aid package accepted with promised reforms, 1997 ◦ Suharto suffers mild stroke, Dec. 1997 ◦ Assembly election of Suharto and appointment of aide B. J. Habibie as vice president, Mar. 1998 ◦ Widespread protests and riots with over 1,000 killed and students fired upon, May 1998 ◦ Mass cabinet resignations, May 1998 ◦ Military splits, withdraws support of Suharto, and allows students to occupy parliament, forcing Suharto's resignation and succession by Habibie, May 1998

Habibie establishes civilian control of military and stops military coup plot by Suharto's son-in-law, May 1998 ◦ Habibie has little support but faces divided opposition and no calls for resignation among opposition parties ◦ Habibie releases political prisoners, frees press, legalizes parties, creates independent electoral commission, severs Golkar-military link, and pushes up elections from 2003 to 1999, June 1998 ◦ Consultative assembly opts for opening, Nov. 1998 ◦ Shift to take military out of politics, with national police and armed forces separated, 1999 ◦ Decentralization law, May 1999 ◦ Legislative election won by Megawati's PDI-P, June 1999 ◦ Referendum for Timorese independence followed by violence and international peacekeeping force, Aug. 1999 ◦ Habibie loses no-confidence vote, then chooses not to contest presidential election, Oct. 1999 ◦ Wahid elected president by assembly, Nov. 1999 ◦ Golkar places second with 26% of seats in 1999, then successfully supports Wahid for president ◦ Wahid sets up coalition cabinet but gets impeached and replaced by Megawati, 2001 ◦ Golkar wins legislative plurality with 23% of seats but joins losing coalition for Megawati as president, 2004 ◦

President Yudhoyono picks head of Golkar as vice president, bringing it into ruling coalition, 2004 ∘ Golkar wins legislative plurality but again defeated for president, 2009

## ITALY 1919

*Primary Category*: Defeat in War
*Decision Pattern*: Regained Power

Breaking prior treaty, Italy joins with Allies in World War I, 1915 ∘ Italy routed at Caporetto, leading to Orlando's rise as prime minister, Oct. 1917 ∘ Italy regains territory from Austria until armistice, Nov. 1918 ∘ Fascist Party founded in Milan, Mar. 1919 ∘ Italy loses territorial acquisitions in Versailles treaty, leading Orlando to resign, June 1919 ∘ Revolts and strikes spread following unfavorable conclusion of war ("mutilated victory"), 1919–20 (Biennio Rosso) ∘ Political reforms instituting expanded suffrage, proportional representation, and cleaner elections, Aug. 1919 ∘ Nationalist leader d'Annunzio takes over Fiume region, Sept. 1919 ∘ General elections won by Socialists, with Radical Party leader Nitti remaining prime minister, Nov. 1919 ∘ Widespread violence grows, leading to acceptance of Fascists and Mussolini's appointment as prime minister by king, Oct. 1922

## ITALY 1946

*Primary Category*: Defeat in War
*Secondary Categories*: Coup, Hegemonic Withdrawal
*Decision Pattern*: Reformer

See page 139.

## JAPAN 1952

*Primary Category*: Defeat in War
*Decision Pattern*: Reformer

See pages 130–31.

## KENYA 2002

*Primary Category*: None (Protest-Led)
*Decision Pattern*: None

Jomo Kenyatta dies and Daniel arap Moi succeeds to lead fragmented party, 1978 ∘ Failed coup, 1982 ∘ Moi rules autocratically under single-party KANU and consolidates power in Kalenjin tribe ∘ Forum for Restoration of

Democracy launched but repressed, 1991 ∘ Multiparty legalization under foreign aid pressure, 1991 ∘ Moi wins presidential election after opposition ethnic split and use of state violence and state media, Dec. 1992 ∘ ~1,000 dead in ethnic fighting surrounding election ∘ Economic reforms, 1993 ∘ Ethnic violence by government against Kikuyu, 1993–∘ Mass protests and international pressure force bargain between KANU and opposition over electoral rules, 1997 ∘ Narrow KANU reelection, with further strategic use of ethnic violence and party fracture, 1997 ∘ Hundreds of thousands displaced in 1992 and 1997 ∘ Opposition leader Odinga joins KANU, 2002 ∘ Unable to defeat term limits, Moi picks successor Uhuru Kenyatta but faces party split over ethnic politics ∘ Defectors (including Odinga) form new party and then NaRC coalition, Oct. 2002 ∘ KANU loses badly to NaRC coalition and Kibaki, Dec. 2002 ∘ Coalition frays and constitutional referendum defeated, 2005 ∘ Disputed election, 2007, followed by extensive violence and power-sharing agreement, 2008 ∘ KANU splits after 2002 and factions join coalitions, one with Kibaki

## LATVIA 1993

*Primary Category*: Hegemonic Withdrawal
*Decision Pattern*: Reformer, Regained Power

Mass demonstrations calling for independence and democracy, 1987–88 ∘ Baltic Way protest, Aug. 1989 ∘ Popular Front elected to Supreme Soviet and calls for independence, 1990 ∘ Popular Front elects Prime Minister Godmanis, who serves 1990–93 ∘ Independence supported by Communist head Gorbunovs, but division develops between pro-Soviet and pro-Latvian independence sides ∘ Fight at "Barricades" against pro-Soviet forces, Jan. 1991 ∘ Approval of independence and democracy in referendum, Mar. 1991 ∘ After failed Soviet coup, Latvia announces independence, Aug. 1991 ∘ Communists banned and fail to reform as successful party ∘ Gorbunovs serves as president, 1991–93, then speaker of House, 1993–95 ∘ First legislative election won by Latvian Way, 1993 ∘ Godmanis later serves as prime minister, 2007–9

## LEBANON 1971

*Primary Category*: Civil War
*Decision Pattern*: Salvation

After 1958 insurrection, relative calm in early 1960s ∘ Palestinian refugees surge after 1967 Arab-Israeli War, 1967–∘ Use of Lebanon as stage for attacks into Israel, 1968–∘ Attack by Israel on Beirut airport, 1968 ∘ Fight with Palestinian groups and agreement giving PLO autonomy brokered by Nasser, 1969 ∘ PLO effectively takes over south of Lebanon ∘ Maronite militias continue fight against PLO ◦ More refugees from Jordan's 1970 civil war ◦ Clashes with guerrillas and general strike, 1970 ◦ Growing connections between guerrillas and leftist and Muslim elements in Lebanon ◦ New president chosen by one-vote margin, 1970 ◦ House Speaker delays confirmation over required margin, but relents ◦ Assembly elections, 1972 ◦ Wider civil war breaks out, 1975

## LESOTHO 2002

*Primary Category*: Coup
*Decision Pattern*: Salvation, Regained Power

Coup exiles king, 1990 ◦ Military appoints constituent assembly but met with protests, 1990 ◦ Military coup, 1991 ◦ New constitution removes authority from king, 1993 ◦ Multiparty elections won by opposition BCP ◦ Mutinies within military, 1994 ◦ King and parts of military lead coup but quickly return power, 1994 ◦ Police mutiny, 1997 ◦ Breakaway faction of BCP called LCD dominates May 1998 election, winning 79 of 80 seats ◦ Widespread violent protests, Aug. 1998 ◦ Junior military mutiny ousts army chief, leading government to request peacekeeping troops from Botswana and South Africa, which enter Sept. 1998 ◦ Interim pact agrees on new elections, Nov. 1998 ◦ Troops withdraw, 1999 ◦ Electoral system changed and new elections result in LCD win, with significant opposition representation, 2002

## LIBERIA 2006

*Primary Category*: Civil War
*Decision Pattern*: Reformer

Civil war, 1989–96, with Taylor overthrowing Doe ◦ Taylor elected president, 1997 ◦ Insurgencies, 1997–99 ◦ Civil war, 1999–2003, with 150,000+ killed ◦ LURD rebels in north, a loose coalition organized around opposition to Taylor and supported by Guinea ◦ Second Ivory Coast–supported rebel group MODEL emerges in south, 2003 ◦ Rebels control most of country and shell Monrovia, mid-2003 ◦ Taylor exiled, Aug. 2003 ◦ Accra peace agreement with power-sharing deal and transitional government agreed with international mediation, Aug. 2003 ◦ Transitional government, 2003–5 ◦ LURD and MODEL disband ◦ Fractured legislative elections, Oct. 2005 ◦ Ex–finance minister Sirleaf elected president in second round, Nov. 2005, then reelected, 2011

## LITHUANIA 1992

*Primary Category*: Hegemonic Withdrawal
*Secondary Category*: Electoral Continuity
*Decision Pattern*: Reformer, Regained Power

Nationalist, pro-independence protests begin, organized as Reform Movement of Lithuania (Sąjūdis), 1988 ∘ Communists under Brazauskas break from USSR's Communist Party, Dec. 1989 ∘ Independent, Sąjūdis-supported candidates win Supreme Soviet election, Feb. 1990 ∘ Independence declared, Mar. 1990 ∘ Violent Soviet crackdown met with resistance, Jan. 1991 ∘ International recognition given after failed Soviet coup, Aug. 1991 ∘ Communists, renamed as Democratic Labour, win legislative election, Nov. 1992 ∘ Sąjūdis splits and right wing forms competitive Homeland Union ∘ Brazauskas serves as president, 1993–98, then prime minister, 2001–6

## MADAGASCAR 1993

*Primary Category*: Electoral Continuity
*Decision Pattern*: Regained Power

See pages 172–74.

## MALAWI 1994

*Primary Category*: Electoral Continuity
*Decision Pattern*: Regained Power

Single-party state under Hastings Banda and MCP, 1966 ∘ Beginning of civil society and religious opposition, 1992 ∘ Banda begins negotiations with opposition, Oct. 1992 ∘ Domestic protests and church and international pressure after crackdown lead to national council and constitutional referendum, with vote supporting multiparty democracy, June 1993 ∘ Muluzi defects from MCP ∘ Army opposes plan to transfer power to Banda ally, 1993 ∘ Army cracks down on regime-allied paramilitary Malawi Young Pioneers, signaling support for transition, Nov. 1993 ∘ Free elections defeat Banda and elect UDF's Muluzi, May 1994 ∘ UDF reelected, 1999 ∘ MCP remains strongest opposition party and usual runner-up for presidency, then wins legislative plurality, 2004

## THE MALDIVES 2009

*Primary Category*: Electoral Continuity
*Decision Pattern*: Regained Power

Gayoom rises to power, 1978 ∘ Coup attempt, 1988 ∘ Riots, 2003 ∘ Protests in capital, 2004 ∘ Reforms promised and constitutional assembly elected, 2004 ∘ Tsunami with damage to ~62% of GDP, Dec. 2004 ∘ First multiparty elections won by Gayoom's DRP, 2005 ∘ Moderates allowed to form government, but continued crackdowns against opposition MDP ∘ Dissident Nasheed arrested, prompting protests that are repressed, Aug. 2005 ∘ Failed assassination

attempt, with president saved by Boy Scout, 2008 ∘ Under protest, new constitution passed, Aug. 2008 ∘ First competitive presidential election won
by MDP's Nasheed in second round after three officials defect from DRP,
Oct. 2008 ∘ Expanded civil liberties, 2009 ∘ Gayoom's DRP narrowly wins
seat plurality in reasonably fair legislative election despite getting fewer votes,
2009 ∘ Gayoom resigns from politics, 2010, but returns as leader of new party
PPM, 2011 ∘ After resigning in claimed coup and getting imprisoned for terrorism, Nasheed loses 2013 election to PPM's Yameen, Gayoom's half brother

## MALI 1992

*Primary Category*: Coup
*Secondary Category*: Civil War
*Decision Pattern*: Regained Power

See page 78.

## MEXICO 2000

*Primary Category*: Electoral Continuity
*Decision Pattern*: Regained Power

See pages 150 and 156–57.

## MONGOLIA 1990

*Primary Category*: Hegemonic Withdrawal
*Secondary Category*: Electoral Continuity
*Decision Pattern*: Reformer, Regained Power

Communist Party (MPRP) leader ousted and Batmönkh rises to power,
1984 ∘ Signals of support for liberalization within Party, 1988 ∘ Starting
with youth, mass protests spread around center of capital, demanding free
elections, economic reforms, and free press, Dec. 1989–Mar. 1990 ∘ Regime
offers gradual liberalization, but opposition rejects, Dec. 1990 ∘ Protests
rise to 20,000-strong, Jan. 1990 ∘ Opposition illegally forms political parties, Feb. 1990 ∘ Hunger strike in central square, followed by national strikes,
Mar. 1990 ∘ MPRP head and Politburo resign after hard-liners agree not to
use force, Mar. 1990 ∘ Reformers under Ochirbat legalize opposition, agree to
roundtable talks, and allow elections ∘ MPRP wins over 80% of seats in free
elections and Ochirbat becomes president, July 1990 ∘ New constitution agreed
on, 1991 ∘ MPRP reelected, 1992 ∘ Opposition wins first presidential election
after Ochirbat defects 1993 ∘ Opposition coalesces and wins 1996 election

## MOZAMBIQUE 1994

*Primary Category*: Civil War
*Secondary Category*: Electoral Continuity
*Decision Pattern*: Regained Power

See page 110.

## NEPAL 1991

*Primary Category*: None (Protest-Led)
*Decision Pattern*: None

King Mahendra launches coup, 1960, and establishes party-less *panchayat* system, 1962 ∘ Civil disobedience campaign by Nepali Congress movement, 1985 ∘ Diplomatic dispute with India leads to virtual economic blockade, 1988–90 ∘ Nepali Congress organizes mass rallies under Jan Andolan (People's Movement) banner, joined by Communists, Jan. 1990 ∘ Student protests met with violence, Feb. 1990 ∘ Lawyers and government workers protest, Mar. 1990 ∘ General strike and mass pro-democracy protests, Apr. 1990 ∘ Large rally of ~200,000 in capital met with violence, with ~150 killed, Apr. 1990 ∘ King reacts by legalizing political parties and creating constitutional commission, Apr. 1990 ∘ Constitution establishing multiparty democracy passed, Nov. 1990 ∘ First parliamentary elections won by Nepali Congress, with Communists also getting significant support, May 1991

## NEPAL 2008

*Primary Category*: Civil War
*Secondary Categories*: Coup, Assassination
*Decision Pattern*: Reformer

Communist Party begins revolution, producing civil war, 1996–2006, with ~18,000 killed ∘ Crown Prince Dipendra goes on shooting spree and kills members of royal family, including king and himself, 2001 ∘ King's brother Gyanendra becomes king and illegally dissolves government in face of rebellion, 2002, then again, 2005, assuming direct power ∘ Politicians and press repressed ∘ Flawed local elections and military setbacks bring mass protests and general strike, forcing king to reinstate parliament, Apr. 2006 ∘ Parliament curtails king's powers, May 2006 ∘ Comprehensive Peace Accord signed with Maoists, Nov. 2006 ∘ Coalition including Maoists agrees to abolish monarchy and establish republic, Dec. 2007 ∘ Constituent elections won by Maoists, with Nepali Congress placing second, Apr. 2008 ∘

Assembly formally abolishes monarchy, May 2008 ∘ Maoist government falls and replaced by coalition led by opposed Communist leader, May 2009 ∘ Assembly fails to draft new constitution, triggering elections won by Nepali Congress, Nov. 2013 ∘ New constitution and assembly transformed into parliament, 2015

## THE NETHERLANDS 1897

*Primary Category*: Electoral Continuity
*Decision Pattern*: Reformer, Regained Power

Constitutional monarchy with supreme elected parliament, 1848 ∘ Limited suffrage extension to about one-fourth of men, 1887 ∘ Elections won by Liberal Union, 1891 and 1894 ∘ Parties split on suffrage extension proposed by Minister of Interior Tak van Poortvliet, which is rejected, 1894 ∘ Röell becomes prime minister and supports suffrage, 1894 ∘ New minister of interior Van Houten's suffrage law doubles number of voters, 1896 ∘ Liberals win general election, 1897, then keep plurality until 1909 ∘ Universal male suffrage, 1917

## NICARAGUA 1984

*Primary Category*: Civil War
*Decision Pattern*: Regained Power

See pages 104–7.

## NIGER 1993

*Primary Category*: Electoral Continuity
*Decision Pattern*: Regained Power

Kountché leads military coup, 1974 ∘ Failed coups, 1975 and 1976 ∘ Increased civilian representation, 1981–84 ∘ Kountché dies, 1987 ∘ Successor Saibou wins as sole presidential candidate, running under new MNSD party, 1989 ∘ Saibou liberalizes system, but demands persist ∘ Tuareg rebellion starts, 1990 ∘ Strikes and protests, 1990 ∘ Parties and independent organizations allowed, with national constitutional conference that regime fails to control, 1991 ∘ Saibou loses position as party leader and is barred from running in new elections, 1991 ∘ Transitional government, 1991–93 ∘ MNSD places first in legislative elections, but coalition blocks party from power, Feb. 1993 ∘ MNSD's Tandja places second in presidential election won by Ousmane in second round, Mar. 1993 ∘ MNSD wins legislative election and installs prime minister, 1995 ∘ Coup, 1996

## NIGER 1999

*Primary Category*: Coup
*Secondary Category*: Assassination
*Decision Pattern*: Reformer

Tuareg rebellion, 1990–95 ∘ Ousmane ousted in coup, Jan. 1996 ∘ New constitution, May 1996 ∘ Coup leader Maïnassara sets up UNIRD party and wins fraudulent presidential election over Ousmane, July 1996, and legislative election, Nov. 1996 ∘ Repeated protests and strikes ∘ Disputed local elections, Feb. 1999 ∘ Maïnassara assassinated during military coup by Wanké while attempting to flee country, Apr. 1999 ∘ Constitutional referendum and amnesty for coup leaders, July 1999 ∘ Quick move to elections, with presidency won by MNSD's Tandja after Ousmane pledges support in second round, Oct.–Nov. 1999 ∘ Coalition between Ousmane and MNSD wins legislative elections, Nov. 1999

## NIGER 2011

*Primary Category*: Coup
*Decision Pattern*: Reformer

Tandja fairly reelected, 2004 ∘ Fighting with Tuareg rebels, 2007–9 ∘ Protests and institutional opposition to plan to overturn Tandja's term limits in referendum, May–June 2009 ∘ Tandja dissolves National Assembly in May, then initially agrees to rescind plan after court rules it unconstitutional, June ∘ Self-coup overturns democracy and Tandja assumes emergency powers, June 2009 ∘ Boycotted referendum, Aug. 2009 ∘ Boycotted legislative elections, Oct. 2009 ∘ Protests after talks with opposition break down, Feb. 2010 ∘ United States and European Union withdraw aid ∘ Military coup, Feb. 2010 ∘ One-year transition plan adopted and legal actions against opposition dropped ∘ Constitutional referendum, Oct. 2010 ∘ Fair elections won by opposition PNDS and Issoufou, Jan. 2011 ∘ Failed coup attempt, 2011

## NIGERIA 1979

*Primary Category*: Coup
*Secondary Categories*: Civil War, Assassination
*Decision Pattern*: Reformer

See page 120.

## PAKISTAN 1988

*Primary Category*: Assassination
*Decision Pattern*: Reformer

See pages 117–18.

## PAKISTAN 2008

*Primary Category*: Civil War
*Decision Pattern*: None

Coup by Pervez Musharraf, 1999 ∘ Referendum and national assembly elections, 2002 ∘ Musharraf elected president through electoral college, while remaining non-partisan, 2004 ∘ Stemming from War on Terror, violence against Islamic militants begins, causing opposition from tribal groups, 2004 ∘ ~40,000 killed in fighting from 2004 ∘ Several militant groups ally as Pakistani Taliban, 2007 ∘ Musharraf sacks Chief Justice, prompting lawyer protests, Mar. 2007 ∘ Bloody standoff at Red Mosque in capital, July 2007 ∘ Nawaz Sharif returns but is arrested and exiled, Sept. 2007 ∘ Musharraf elected to second presidential term, announcing he would extend rule past previous agreement, Oct. 2007 ∘ Musharraf retires from army to allow presidential rule, Nov. 2007 ∘ Sharif returns again, Nov. 2007 ∘ Bhutto returns for 2008 elections, Oct. 2007, but is assassinated, Dec. 2007 ∘ Central Asian groups join conflict, 2008 ∘ Elections won by anti-Musharraf PPP, Feb. 2008, forming coalition and impeaching Musharraf, who resigns, Aug. 2008 ∘ Musharraf supporter PML-Q distant second place ∘ Presidential election won by PPP's Zardari, Sept. 2008 ∘ Sharif's PML-N wins 2013 elections

## PANAMA 1950*

*[*Should be 1956]*

*Primary Category*: Coup
*Decision Pattern*: Salvation, Regained Power

See page 81.

## PANAMA 1952*

*[*Should be 1956]*

*Primary Category*: Coup
*Decision Pattern*: Regained Power

See pages 81–82.

## PANAMA 1991

*Primary Category*: Defeat in War
*Decision Pattern*: Reformer

See page 129.

## PARAGUAY 2003

*Primary Category*: Electoral Continuity
*Decision Pattern*: Salvation, Regained Power

Stroessner overthrown in coup, Feb. 1989 ∘ Opposition legalized and coup leader Rodríguez wins presidential election as Colorado Party head, May 1989 ∘ Democratic constitution passed, 1992 ∘ Colorados reelected, with threat of coup if voted out, 1993 ∘ Popular reaction successfully stops attempted coup by Gen. Lino Oviedo, 1996 ∘ Oviedo gets Colorado presidential nomination, but Supreme Court disallows run and Oviedo is jailed for coup attempt, 1998 ∘ Running mate Cubas wins and frees Oviedo, which is deemed unconstitutional, 1998 ∘ Cubas refuses to return Oviedo to jail, then is impeached after assassination of vice president and Oviedo rival, 1999 ∘ Cubas resigns after protests and opponent Macchi becomes president, 1999 ∘ Failed coup, 2000 ∘ Failed impeachment, 2001 ∘ Faction splits from Colorados, 2002 ∘ Colorado's Duarte wins election, 2003 ∘ Macchi imprisoned for fraud, 2006 ∘ Colorados defeated in elections after sixty-one years in power, with Oviedo also losing as head of ex-Colorado faction, 2008

## PERU 1956

*Primary Category*: None (Regime-Led)
*Decision Pattern*: Salvation, Regained Power

See pages 177–78.

## PERU 1963

*Primary Category*: Coup
*Decision Pattern*: Reformer

Prado elected, 1956 ∘ Odría returns and forms party, 1961 ∘ APRA's de la Torre narrowly wins June 1962 presidential election but not with sufficient one-third of vote, sending election to congress ∘ Military signals opposition to letting APRA win and pushes Prado to rerun election under pretense of electoral fraud, July 1962 ∘ De la Torre makes deal with former dictator Odría to make Odría president and APRA dominant in legislature ∘ Military coup by Gen. Pérez Godoy, July 1962 ∘ Strongly negative international reaction ∘ Pérez Godoy initially promises clean elections, 1962, then tries to prevent them but cannot retain military support ∘ Pérez Godoy transfers power to Gen. Lindley, Mar. 1963 ∘ Land invasions by Indian peasants, mid-1963 ∘ Elections won by 1956 runner-up, AP's Belaúnde, June 1963 ∘ Odría forms strong opposition coalition with APRA ∘ Military coup, 1968

## PERU 1980

*Primary Category*: Coup
*Decision Pattern*: Salvation

Belaúnde violently represses peasant guerrilla movement, 1965 ∘ Coup by Gen. Velasco, 1968 ∘ Ambitious reform designed to break power of oligarchs and develop rural areas, with land redistribution to peasants, industry nationalization, and social welfare expansion ∘ Party-less bureaucratic authoritarianism becomes increasingly personalized ∘ Dismissal of admiral generates opposition from navy, 1974 ∘ Velasco in poor health and economic growth plummets ∘ Police strike and student protests, 1975 ∘ Conservative military coup under Bermúdez, opposed to economic trajectory and role of military in politics, Aug. 1975 ∘ Bermúdez tempers reforms and combats inflation, with shift against labor ∘ Economic stabilization package leads to protests, 1976 ∘ Bermúdez signals willingness to end military government, Jan. 1977 ∘ Large general strike, July 1977, triggering state of emergency ∘ Military divisions grow ∘ Bermúdez presents Plan Túpac Amaru, offering four-year transition to democracy conditional on keeping reforms, Oct. 1977 ∘ Major strike, May 1978 ∘ Constituent elections, June 1978 ∘ New constitution, extending vote to illiterates, 1979 ∘ APRA leader de la Torre dies, Aug. 1979 ∘ Shining Path begins violent campaign, May 1980 ∘ Belaúnde elected president, May 1980

## PERU 2001

*Primary Category*: None (Protest-Led)
*Decision Pattern*: None

APRA wins elections, in first democratic power exchange in forty years, 1985 ∘ President García nationalizes banks, 1987, then faces hyperinflation and major insurgencies, 1988–90 ∘ Shining Path assassinates ~80 mayors and targets electoral candidates, 1989 ∘ Alberto Fujimori elected president over Llosa, June 1990 ∘ Fujimori combats inflation, but gridlock develops with legislature ∘ Fujimori dissolves Congress in self-coup, Apr. 1992 ∘ Shining Path leader captured, Sept. 1992 ∘ Aborted coup plot, Nov. 1992 ∘ Fujimori's Cambio 90 wins constituent elections, Nov. 1992 ∘ Fujimori passes successful liberal economic reforms and fights insurgent groups, with serious atrocities by both sides ∘ Shining Path broken ∘ New constitution allowing presidential reelection narrowly approved in referendum, Oct. 1993 ∘ Border skirmish with Ecuador, Jan. 1995 ∘ Fujimori reelected president and Cambio 90 gains legislative majority, Apr. 1995 ∘ Hostage crisis with MRTA, 1996–97 ∘ Overruling popular opposition, Supreme Court allows Fujimori to run for third term, 1998 ∘ Military head Hermoza forced out, increasing power of intelligence head Montesinos, Aug. 1998 ∘ National strike, May 1999

Abusing state resources and likely committing fraud, Fujimori leads in first round of presidential vote but misses majority, Apr. 2000 ∘ Opponent Toledo withdraws from second round in protest, May 2000 ∘ International opposition and numerous disordered protests ∘ Scandal erupts with video of Montesinos bribing opposition legislator, Sept. 2000 ∘ Within forty-eight hours, Fujimori calls for new elections without him and abolition of intelligence agency ∘ Montesinos breaks with Fujimori and flees to Panama, Sept. 2000 ∘ Fujimori announces resignation while in Japan, but this is rejected and Fujimori is impeached for "moral incapacity," Nov. 2000 ∘ Congress head Paniagua made provisional president, Nov. 2000, and fires Montesinos-connected military heads ∘ New elections won by Toledo, Apr.–June 2001 ∘ Montesinos arrested, June 2001 ∘ Fujimori's Cambio 90 and Peru 2000 coalition not competitive, but Fujimorista successor parties are more successful ∘ Fujimori's daughter narrowly loses presidency, 2011 and 2016, with Popular Force gaining legislative plurality, 2016

## THE PHILIPPINES 1946

*Primary Category*: Defeat in War
*Decision Pattern*: Reformer

Brief independence, 1899–1901 ∘ "Colonial democracy" under United States, with legislative elections from 1907 ∘ Following 1934 U.S. law establishing transition to full independence, Philippine Commonwealth created with elected president and bicameral Congress, 1935 ∘ United States retains control over foreign policy, but Philippines controls domestic affairs ∘ Development of stable two-party system with Nacionalistas and Liberals ∘ Japanese occupation, 1942–45 ∘ Full independence and elections, 1946 ∘ Huk resistance (begun as anti-Japanese army) restarts, 1946

## THE PHILIPPINES 1986

*Primary Category*: Civil War
*Decision Pattern*: Salvation

See pages 112–14.

## POLAND 1989

*Primary Category*: Hegemonic Withdrawal
*Secondary Category*: Electoral Continuity
*Decision Pattern*: Regained Power

See pages 137–39.

## PORTUGAL 1911

*Primary Category*: Coup
*Decision Pattern*: Regained Power
*Secondary Category*: Assassination

See pages 78–79.

## PORTUGAL 1976

*Primary Category*: Coup
*Decision Pattern*: Reformer, Regained Power

See pages 90–96.

## ROMANIA 1991

*Primary Category*: Hegemonic Withdrawal
*Decision Pattern*: Reformer

Major protests ended in Braşov, 1987 ∘ Letter of the Six indicates opposition to Ceauşescu from top members of Communist Party, Mar. 1989 ∘ Major civil unrest starts in Timioara over eviction of priest, Dec. 1989 ∘ Security forces initially agree to fire on crowds but switch sides when defense minister found dead ∘ Crowd storms Central Committee building in Bucharest during speech by Ceauşescu, who flees for his life ∘ Ceauşescu captured and killed after being convicted of genocide, Dec. 1989 ∘ Disordered fighting costs ~1,000 lives ∘ National Salvation Front under Iliescu takes power, with Communist representation, Dec. 1989 ∘ FSN reneges on promise to not organize as party, prompting mass resignations of ex-Communists, Feb. 1990 ∘ Opposing violent protests by opponents of FSN and pro-FSN miners, Jan.–Feb. 1990 ∘ Provisional multiparty coalition rules until election, Feb.–May 1990 ∘ Mass student demonstration opposing ex-Communist participation in elections, growing to 50,000, Apr. 1990 ∘ Elections won by FSN, May 1990 ∘ Student protests put down violently by miners, June 1990 ∘ Suspension of Western aid, 1990–91 ∘ New constitution by referendum, Dec. 1991 ∘ FSN fractures, 1992 ∘ Economic crisis and international pressure lead to clean election and turnover, 1996

## SAN MARINO 1945

*Primary Category*: Defeat in War
*Secondary Category*: Hegemonic Withdrawal
*Decision Pattern*: Salvation

See pages 139–40.

## SÃO TOMÉ AND PRÍNCIPE 1991

*Primary Category*: Electoral Continuity
*Decision Pattern*: Regained Power

See pages 166–67.


## SENEGAL 2000

*Primary Category*: Civil War
*Decision Pattern*: None

Opposition allowed by ruling Socialist Party (PS) under Senghor, but only in highly constrained parties, 1976 ∘ Senghor retires and Diouf becomes president, 1981 ∘ Fuller liberalization, 1981 ∘ Senegal joins with Gambia to form Senegambia, 1982, but union falls apart, 1989 ∘ Separatist movement in Casamance from 1982, with insurgency from 1990, led by Christian Jolo people organized as MFDC ∘ ~5,000 killed from 1982 ∘ External support for rebels from Guinea-Bissau and Gambia ∘ Protests and electoral reforms after flawed 1988 election ∘ Diouf defeats Wade in 1993 presidential election, followed by opposition arrests ∘ Several party defections, with decline of clientelist network and local religious support ∘ Repeated cease-fires and outbreaks of violence in Casamance, 1997–2001 ∘ Diouf gets term limits abolished, 1998, but defeated by Wade in election, Mar. 2000 ∘ New constitution, Jan. 2001 ∘ PS wins 17% of vote in legislative elections won by Wade's PDS, Apr. 2001 ∘ Peace agreement in Casamance, 2004 ∘ Wade reelected, 2007 and 2012, with PS uncompetitive


## SERBIA 2000

*Primary Category*: Civil War
*Secondary Category*: Defeat in War
*Decision Pattern*: Salvation

See pages 101–2.


## SIERRA LEONE 2002

*Primary Category*: Civil War
*Secondary Category*: Coup
*Decision Pattern*: Reformer, Regained Power

See pages 98 and 108–9.

## SOLOMON ISLANDS 2006

*Primary Category*: Civil War
*Decision Pattern*: Salvation

Ethnic civil war breaks out in Guadalcanal between Isatabu Freedom Movement, Malaita Eagle Force, and government, 1999, with death or serious injury to ~30,000 ◦ Peace accord breaks down with new violence, June 2000 ◦ MEF seizes parliament and kidnaps co-ethnic Prime Minister Ulufa'alu, who agrees to resign in exchange for release, June 2000 ◦ Legislature elects Sogavare as new prime minister, June 2000 ◦ More successful peace agreements, Oct. 2000 and Feb. 2001, but sporadic chaos ◦ Kamekaza becomes prime minister after new election, Dec. 2001 ◦ International peacekeeping force enters, 2003 ◦ Elections defeat ruling PAP, Apr. 2006 ◦ Prime minister's attempt to form government met by riots (targeting Chinese minority and accusing leader of taking Chinese bribes and buying votes), forcing him to step down, Apr. 2006 ◦ New prime minister Sogavare leads grand coalition government ◦ Sogavare loses no-confidence vote, Dec. 2007 ◦ PAP collapses by 2010 ◦ Peacekeepers withdraw, 2013 ◦ Sogavare re-ascends to prime minister, 2014–17, 2019–present

## SOUTH AFRICA 1994

*Primary Category*: None (Pact)
*Decision Pattern*: None

See pages 170–71.

## SOUTH KOREA 1960

*Primary Category*: None (Protest-Led)
*Decision Pattern*: None

See page 56.

## SOUTH KOREA 1988

*Primary Category*: Electoral Continuity
*Decision Pattern*: Regained Power

See pages 164–65.

## SPAIN 1931

*Primary Category*: Coup
*Decision Pattern*: Salvation

Coup by Primo Rivera, 1923 ◦ Internal conflict with military from 1925 ◦ Republican movement among intellectuals and students ◦ Coup attempt, 1926 ◦ Rivera creates weak party and assembly, 1927 ◦ Protests, 1929 ◦ New constitution written, 1929, and plebiscite intended, 1930 ◦ Economic crisis begins, 1930 ◦ Student protests, coup plot, and pressure from military and King Alfonso XIII lead Rivera to resign, Jan. 1930 ◦ Republican coup plot, 1930 ◦ King appoints General Berenguer, who tries softer dictatorship, but cannot maintain order and resigns, Feb. 1931 ◦ Facing military opposition and municipal elections favoring republicanism, king flees and Second Republic declared, Apr. 1931 ◦ General election, June 1931

### SPAIN 1977

*Primary Category*: Assassination
*Secondary Category*: Civil War
*Decision Pattern*: Reformer, Regained Power

See pages 118–20.

### SRI LANKA 1991*

*[\*Should be 1994]*

*Primary Category*: Civil War
*Secondary Category*: Electoral Continuity
*Decision Pattern*: Regained Power

United National Party wins elections, 1977, then passes new constitution ◦ Communal riots against Tamils, with neglect by government, 1983 ◦ Civil war between government and Tamil Tigers (LTTE) begins, 1983, then intensifies, 1987 ◦ Failed peace agreement, 1987 ◦ Attempted coup, 1987 ◦ Indian intervention after switching support to government, 1987–90 ◦ Marxist group JVP leads bloody insurrection but defeated, costing ~60,000 lives, 1987–90 ◦ Election brings UNP's Premadasa to power, 1989, and he asks India's forces to leave, 1990 ◦ UNP split, 1991 ◦ Premadasa assassinated by LTTE suicide bomber, May 1993 ◦ UNP performs poorly in provincial elections, Mar. 1994 ◦ President Wijetunga calls for national elections six months early, June 1994 ◦ Narrow legislative electoral turnover to People's Alliance, Aug. 1994 ◦ UNP's presidential candidate assassinated by LTTE, Oct. 1994 ◦ People's Alliance's Kumaratunga defeats candidate's widow in presidential election, Nov. 1994 ◦ UNP wins legislative election, 2001 ◦ Cease-fire in Tamil struggle, 2001, but war resumes, 2005

## SUDAN 1965

*Primary Category*: Civil War
*Secondary Category*: Coup
*Decision Pattern*: Salvation

Insurgency begins in south, 1955 ∘ Independence declared, 1956 ∘ After federal structure rejected, southern army officers revolt, sparking civil war, 1955–72 ∘ Coup by Abboud, 1958 ∘ Three failed military countercoups, 1959 ∘ High instability and cultural/religious repression ∘ Southern revolt renewed, 1963 ∘ Opposition over civil war, economy, and education policies lead to strikes and riots in October Revolution of 1964 ∘ Opposition organizes as UNF with support of military factions ∘ Transition to civilian coalition government, 1964 ∘ Fragmented elections, 1965 ∘ Coup, 1969

## SUDAN 1986

*Primary Category*: Coup
*Secondary Category*: Civil War
*Decision Pattern*: Salvation

See page 83.

## SURINAME 1988

*Primary Category*: Civil War
*Secondary Category*: Coup
*Decision Pattern*: Regained Power

Independence, 1975 ∘ Military coup led by Dési Bouterse, 1980 ∘ Four attempted coups, 1980–82 ∘ Massacre of opposition politicians, 1982 ∘ Crisis from cutoff of Dutch aid, leading to protests, 1982 ∘ Ban on opposition parties lifted and constitutional convention called, 1985 ∘ Insurgency by Maroons (former escaped slaves living in interior) begins over resettlement, led by Bouterse's former bodyguard Ronnie Brunswijk, 1986 ∘ Army response destroys villages and forces thousands to flee, with ~500 deaths in population of ~400,000 ∘ New constitution supported in referendum and elections follow, with Bouterse remaining in charge of military, 1987 ∘ Civilian president Shankar elected by assembly, 1988 ∘ Bouterse-founded NDP performs poorly in 1987 but grows stronger, with Bouterse elected president, 2010

## SURINAME 1991

*Primary Category*: Coup
*Secondary Category*: Civil War
*Decision Pattern*: Regained Power

Military coup over telephone by Dési Bouterse, opposing the 1989 Kourou Accord peace agreement with Maroons, Dec. 1990 ∘ Bouterse continues war ∘ Strong pressure for elections from United States, Netherlands, and Venezuela ∘ General election brings Bouterse opponent to power and reduces military power, May 1991 ∘ Peace accord with Maroons, exchanging amnesty for weapons surrender, 1992 ∘ Bouterse's NDP builds strength, placing at least second in every election from 1991 to 2020, leading governing coalitions, 1996 and 2010, and winning majority, 2015 ∘ Bouterse wins presidency, 2010

## SWEDEN 1911

*Primary Category*: Electoral Continuity
*Decision Pattern*: Reformer, Regained Power

Increased taxes prompt call for extension of franchise, 1901 ∘ General strike, 1902 ∘ Liberals win elections, 1905 ∘ Suffrage extension passed by one chamber but rejected by other, with disagreement over electoral system and size of extension, 1906 ∘ Liberals resign and right-wing General Electoral League's Lindman becomes prime minister, 1906 ∘ Lindman supports lower-house male suffrage in combination with proportional representation and passes it despite his party's opposition, 1907 ∘ King dies, 1907 ∘ GEL loses plurality, 1908, but Lindman retains position through 1911 ∘ Protests and general strike, 1909 ∘ Leftists win first full-suffrage election, 1911, but GEL regains plurality, 1914 ∘ Full suffrage in both houses and elimination of plural voting, 1918 ∘ Lindman regains prime ministership, 1928

## TAIWAN 1996

*Primary Category*: Electoral Continuity
*Decision Pattern*: Reformer, Regained Power

See pages 1–2 and 163.

## THAILAND 1975

*Primary Category*: Coup
*Decision Pattern*: Reformer

Military government wins elections but faces growing opposition from Assembly, military, students, insurgents, and peasants, 1969 ∘ Self-coup by senior military leader and Prime Minister Thanom Kittikachorn, 1971 ∘ Thanom bans all parties and cracks down on Communist insurgents, with ~200 killed, 1972 ∘ New appointed Assembly in 1972 and economic grievances inspire student protests, May 1973 ∘ Troops open fire on students and king calls on Thanom to resign, Oct. 1973 ∘ Thanom flees country and king appoints new prime minister, Oct. 1973 ○ New constitution, 1974 ○ Introduction of numerous parties and fractured elections, 1975

## THAILAND 1983

*Primary Category*: Coup
*Decision Pattern*: Reformer, Regained Power

U.S. military pulls out 27,000 troops, 1975–76 ○ Communist fears and major insurgency lead right-wing militants to attack students, 1975–76 ○ Insurgency attracts students and grows to 6,000–8,000 fighters ○ Thanom returns to country and inspires student protests, 1976 ○ Bloody assault by right-wing groups in Thamassat University Massacre and military coups immediately afterward, 1976 ○ Civilian leader installed as prime minister but rules harshly and promises long delay before elections ○ Leader replaced in coup by Gen. Kriangsak, 1977 ○ Kriangsak calls for limited freedoms, a more democratic constitution, and new elections, 1979 ○ Economic protests by politicians and students lead Kriangsak to resign and Gen. Prem to take over, 1980 ○ Prem supports democratic moves and amnesty for communist insurgents, prompting coup attempt that takes over capital, Apr. 1981 ○ King and regional military commanders support Prem and capital retaken ○ Four assassination attempts on Prem, 1982 ○ State weakness compounded by opposition from civilian government and military factions ○ Loss of power for military under new constitution ○ Fractured elections with Prem retaining position as prime minister, 1983

## THAILAND 1992

*Primary Category*: Coup
*Decision Pattern*: Reformer

Prem reelected, 1983 and 1986 ○ Amnesty given to communist insurgents ○ Gen. Chatichai elected and tries to shift power from military to elected officials, 1988 ○ Opposition to liberalization and economic rivalry between military factions leads to coup, Feb. 1991 ○ Junta founds pro-military Justice Unity Party ○ Mass protest defused by king and coup leader Suchinda's promise not to become prime minister, Nov. 1991 ○ New constitution passed with elections and military control over Senate and prime minister, Mar. 1992 ○ Coalition appoints Suchinda as prime minister, Apr. 1992 ○ Massive protests with march on Suchinda's house confronted violently, killing 60+ protestors (Black May), May 1992 ○ King calls meeting with junta head and protest leader, reprimanding both on television, May 1992 ○ King's intervention leads Suchinda to resign, May 1992 ○ New elections won by Democrat Party, Sept. 1992 ○ New democratic constitution establishes Supreme Court and strengthens parties, 1997

## THAILAND 2011

*Primary Category*: Coup
*Secondary Category*: Civil War
*Decision Pattern*: None

Thaksin Shinawatra comes to power on populist platform, 2001 ◦ Major insurgency in Southern Patani region among ethnic minorities, allied with radical Islamic groups and separatists, 2004– ◦ Estimated ~4,500 dead from 2004 to 2011 ◦ Thaksin reelected overwhelemingly, 2005 ◦ Protests over business deal favoring Thaksin's family, 2006 ◦ Parliament dissolved and new elections announced, Feb. 2006 ◦ Flawed, boycotted elections, Apr. 2006, later invalidated by courts ◦ King-supported military coup preempts new elections, Sept. 2006 ◦ New constitution, 2007 ◦ Flawed general election won by Thaksin partisans organized as PPP, Dec. 2007 ◦ Prime minister dismissed by courts for hosting cooking show, Sept. 2008 ◦ Mass protests and state of emergency, Sept. 2008, ended when court dissolves PPP and two other governing parties for election fraud, 2008 ◦ Opposition Democrats take over and face protests and street violence, 2009–10 ◦ Bloody fighting in Bangkok, with 80+killed, 2010 ◦ Curbs on civil liberties ◦ Defying military warnings, new elections won by PPP leaders in renamed party led by Thaksin's sister, 2011 ◦ High polarization, violence, and repression of free speech, 2012–14 ◦ Military coup, 2014 ◦ Attempts at talks with rebel group BRN-C, Apr. 2017

## TURKEY 1961

*Primary Category*: Coup
*Decision Pattern*: Regained Power

Democratic Party (DP) defeats ruling party CHP, 1950 ◦ DP reelected after confiscating CHP's assets, 1954 ◦ Support falls and DP becomes increasingly autocratic, with censorship laws and use of army to repress opponents ◦ Military opposition to treatment of officers and economic problems ◦ DP establishes parliamentary commission to repress opposition and press, 1960 ◦ Military coup led by Col. Türkeş, opposing perceived lack of respect for military officers, May 1960 ◦ Junta punishes DP leaders and forms National Unity Committee under Gen. Gürsel ◦ Türkeş pushes for military rule under new party, but committee opposes and plans transition ◦ Major purge of military leadership, with Türkeş sent abroad ◦ Constitutional referendum, July 1961 ◦ Former DP prime minister Menderes hanged, Sept. 1961 ◦ Military establishes powerful allied Constitutional Court that can ban parties and veto legislation ◦ General elections, Oct. 1961 ◦ Gürsel kept as president by new legislature and he names Atatürk protege İnönü as prime minister ◦ Türkeş emerges as major right-wing nationalist figure in late 1960s, heading Grey Wolves movement

## TURKEY 1983

*Primary Category*: Coup
*Secondary Category*: Civil War
*Decision Pattern*: None

See pages 82 and 84.

## UGANDA 1980

*Primary Category*: Defeat in War
*Secondary Category*: Coup
*Decision Pattern*: Salvation

Military coup by Idi Amin overthrows independence leader Obote, 1971 ∘ Economic decline, mass repression, and government-sponsored terror widespread ∘ Expulsion of Asian minority, 1972 ∘ Military mutiny fails and supporters flee to Tanzania, 1978 ∘ Border war with Ugandan exiles (UNLF) in Tanzania, leading to invasion by Uganda and counterinvasion by Tanzania, 1978 ∘ Despite Libyan support, Uganda loses and Amin flees, Apr. 1979 ∘ Academic Lule serves as interim president but is quickly removed in dispute over presidential powers, June 1979 ∘ UNLF installs Binaisa, but coup by military commission replaces him with Muwanga, May 1980 ∘ After shifting electoral rules, elections won by Obote, Dec. 1980 ∘ Ugandan Bush War led by Museveni develops over election and alienation of southern groups, 1981–86 ∘ Military coup, 1985 ∘ Museveni takes power, 1986

## UNITED KINGDOM 1885

*Primary Category*: Electoral Continuity
*Decision Pattern*: Reformer, Regained Power

See pages 160–61.

## URUGUAY 1919

*Primary Category*: Electoral Continuity
*Decision Pattern*: Reformer, Regained Power

Colorado's Batlle becomes president, 1903 ∘ Batlle defeats Blancos revolt, ending cycle of civil wars, 1904 ∘ Batlle reelected after studying political reform in Europe, 1911 ∘ Batlle passes social reform program, with unemployment insurance, pensions, and free high school, 1910s ∘ Batlle proposes changing presidency to nine-member executive, causing party split, 1913 ∘ Colorado's Viera becomes president and opposes reforms, 1915 ∘ Colorados vote for universal suffrage for constituent elections, 1915, leading to constitutional assembly dominated by Blancos, 1916 ∘ Blancos take lead pushing for electoral reform and form pact with non-Batlle Colorados in legislature to approve secret ballot and universal male suffrage in new constitution ∘ Reforms approved by referendum, 1917 ∘ Blancos adopt form of collegiate executive in deal to get Batlle faction support and to prevent Batlle run in 1919 ∘ Blancos win plurality in 1919 elections but combined factions of Colorados larger ∘ Colorados keep presidency and Blancos continue to win plurality until 1928

## URUGUAY 1942*

### [*Should be 1943]

*Primary Category*: Electoral Continuity
*Decision Pattern*: Regained Power

Opposition of conservatives and business lead to dilution of Batlle's reforms ∘ Batlle dies, 1929 ∘ Colorado's Terra wins presidential election, 1930 ∘ Terra pushes for constitutional reform but faces legislative stalemate, 1933 ∘ Impeachment attempt, Feb. 1933 ∘ Terra self-coups, dissolving assembly and ruling by decree, Mar. 1933 ∘ New constitution and flawed elections, 1933 and 1934 ∘ Uprisings, 1935 ∘ Elections bring in Colorado's Baldomir, 1938 ∘ Protests from labor and Nationals lead Baldomir to promise return to democracy ∘ Baldomir dissolves assembly in quasi-coup, Feb. 1942 ∘ Elections vote in Colorado's Amézaga and approve democratic constitution, Nov. 1942 ∘ Amézaga sits, Mar. 1943

## URUGUAY 1985

*Primary Category*: None (Pact)
*Decision Pattern*: None

Bordaberry elected president but faces economic and military crises, 1971 ∘ Defeat of Tupamaros guerrilla movement, 1972 ∘ Military encourages Bordaberry to dissolve assembly and rule by decree, 1973 ∘ Extensive repression, with unions and leftist Broad Front outlawed, 1973–80 ∘ Bordaberry forced to resign, 1976 ∘ Elections and parties eliminated, 1977 ∘ Autocratic constitution with military veto put to plebiscite, which citizens vote down 57–43%, 1980 ∘ Coup leader Alvarez assumes presidency, 1981 ∘ Non-left parties legalized, 1982 ∘ Primary elections demonstrate opposition to military, 1982 ∘ Economic crisis and massive demonstrations, 1983 ∘ Military convinced they need to exit and negotiations begin, 1983 ∘ Mass general strike, 1984 ∘ Naval Club Pact between military and parties (excluding Blancos, who insist on military entirely leaving politics) signed, Aug. 1984 ∘ Pact agrees to elections, allowance of Left, a few candidates disqualified, and small advisory role for military

∘ Elections won by Colorados and Sanguinetti, 1984 ∘ Colorados take power, 1985 ∘ Controversial amnesty law passed, 1986

## VENEZUELA 1959

*Primary Category*: Coup
*Decision Pattern*: Salvation

Democratic Action (AD) organizes working class from 1930s ∘ Coup with AD support, 1945 ∘ AD wins elections, 1947 ∘ Anti-AD coup, 1948 ∘ Coup leader assassinated, 1950 ∘ Military party organized, 1951 ∘ Constituent election results ignored after democratic opposition wins and junta leader Perez declared president, 1952 ∘ Intense repression combined with corruption and use of oil revenues ∘ Opposition organizes revolutionary force and military opposition grows over corruption and military promotion policies ∘ Elections preempted in favor of plebiscite, with fraudulent result announced, Dec. 1957 ∘ Leaders of main parties and business elites meet in New York City to plot to oust Perez, Dec. 1957 ∘ Air Force bombs capital, Dec. 1957–Jan. 1958 ∘ After attempted coup on Jan. 1, 1958, Perez dismisses cabinet and fires military leaders ∘ Protests, strikes, and naval revolt lead army to defect and Perez flees, Jan. 1958 ∘ With military fractured, junta forced to agree to elections ∘ Opposition parties sign Pact of Punto Fijo agreeing to respect election result and committing to democracy ∘ Elections won by AD and Betancourt, Dec. 1958 ∘ Anti-regime insurgency by excluded groups defeated, 1960s

## ZAMBIA 2008

*Primary Category*: Electoral Continuity
*Decision Pattern*: Regained Power

Mass protests over economic issues and failed coup, 1990 ∘ Defections from ruling party, 1990 ∘ Dictator Kaunda allows elections won by union leader Chiluba and opposition MMD, with former single-party UNIP a distant second, 1991 ∘ MMD rules autocratically and UNIP is repressed after revelation of plans for violence and protest, 1993 ∘ MMD wins boycotted elections after law disallows Kaunda from running, 1996 ∘ Failed coup, 1997 ∘ Chiluba accepts term limits after protests and MMD narrowly wins flawed elections with Mwanawasa as president, 2001 ∘ Abuse of power in selecting House speaker, 2002 ∘ Mwanawasa allows Chiluba to be prosecuted for corruption, 2003 ∘ Mwanawasa reelected, with MMD getting legislative plurality, 2006 ∘ Mwanawasa leaves office due to poor health and dies, Aug. 2008 ∘ Presidential election won narrowly by MMD's Banda, Oct. 2008 ∘ Elections won by Sata and PF over Banda and MMD, 2011

CITATIONS

Abente-Brun, Diego. 2009. Paraguay: The unraveling of one-party rule. *Journal of Democracy* 20(1): 143–56.

Abrahams, Fred C. 2015. *Modern Albania: From Dictatorship to Democracy in Europe*. New York: New York University Press.

Accornero, Guya. 2013. Contentious politics and student dissent in the twilight of the Portuguese dictatorship: Analysis of a protest cycle. *Democratization* 20(6): 1036–55.

Acemoglu, Daron, Simon Johnson, James A. Robinson, and Pierre Yared. 2009. Reevaluating the modernization hypothesis. *Journal of Monetary Economics* 56(8): 1043–58.

Acemoglu, Daron, and James A. Robinson. 2006. *Economic Origins of Dictatorship and Democracy*. Cambridge: Cambridge University Press.

Ackerman, Peter, and Jack Duvall. 2000. *A Force More Powerful: A Century of Nonviolent Conflict*. New York: Palgrave.

Ackroyd, Peter. 2011. *Foundation: The History of England from Its Earliest Beginnings to the Tudors*. New York: St. Martin's Press.

———. 2014. *Rebellion: The History of England from James I to the Glorious Revolution*. New York: St. Martin's Press.

Adesnik, A. David, and Sunhyuk Kim. 2013. South Korea: The puzzle of two transitions. In Stoner and McFaul 2013, 266–89.

Aguilar, Luís E. 1993. Cuba, c. 1860–c. 1930. In *Cuba: A Short History*, ed. Leslie Bethell, 21–55. Cambridge: Cambridge University Press.

Ahmad, Feroz. 1977. *The Turkish Experiment in Democracy, 1950–1975*. Boulder, CO: Westview Press.

Aidt, Toke S., and Raphaël Franck. 2015. Democratization under the threat of revolution: Evidence from the Great Reform Act of 1832. *Econometrica* 83(2): 505–47.

Aidt, Toke S., and Peter S. Jensen. 2014. Workers of the world, unite! Franchise extensions and the threat of revolution in Europe, 1820–1938. *European Economic Review* 72: 52–75.

Aidt, Toke S., and Gabriel Leon. 2016. The democratic window of opportunity: Evidence from riots in sub-Saharan Africa. *Journal of Conflict Resolution* 60(4): 694–717.

Albertus, Michael. 2019. The fate of former authoritarian elites under democracy. *Journal of Conflict Resolution* 63(3): 727–59.

Albertus, Michael, and Victor Gay. 2017. Unlikely democrats: Economic elite uncertainty under dictatorship and support for democratization. *American Journal of Political Science* 61(3): 624–41.

Albertus, Michael, and Victor Menaldo. 2012. Coercive capacity and the prospects for democratization. *Comparative Politics* 44(2): 151–69.

———. 2018. *Authoritarianism and the Elite Origins of Democracy*. Cambridge: Cambridge University Press.

Alden, Chris. 2001. *Mozambique and the Construction of the New African State: From Negotiations to Nation Building*. London: Palgrave.

Alemán, José, and David D. Yang. 2011. A duration analysis of democratic transitions and authoritarian backslides. *Comparative Political Studies* 44: 1123–51.

Alesina, Alberto, Arnaud Devleeschauwer, William Easterly, Sergio Kurlat, and Romain Wacziarg. 2003. Fractionalization. *Journal of Economic Growth* 8(2): 155–94.

Alesina, Alberto, and David Dollar. 2000. Who gives foreign aid to whom and why? *Journal of Economic Growth* 5(1): 33–63.

Alexander, Robert. 1973. *Latin American Political Parties*. New York: Praeger.

———. 1982. *Bolivia: Past, Present, and Future of Its Politics*. New York: Praeger.

Ali, S. Mahmud. 2010. *Understanding Bangladesh*. New York: Columbia University Press.

Allen, Philip M. 1995. *Madagascar: Conflicts of Authority in the Great Island*. Boulder, CO: Westview Press.

Ameringer, Charles D. 2000. *The Cuban Democratic Experience: The Auténtico Years, 1944–1952*. Gainesville: University Press of Florida.

Anckar, Carsten, and Cecilia Frederiksson. 2018. *Political Regimes of the World Dataset*. Åbo Akademi University.

Andersen, David, Jørgen Møller, Lasse Lykke Rørbæk, and Svend-Erik Skaaning. 2014. State capacity and political regime stability. *Democratization* 21(7): 1305–25.

Anderson, G. Norman. 1999. *Sudan in Crisis: The Failure of Democracy*. Gainesville: University Press of Florida.

Anderson, Perry. 1974. *Lineages of the Absolutist State*. London: NLB.

Anderson, Thomas P. 1981. *The War of the Dispossessed: Honduras and El Salvador, 1969*. Lincoln: University of Nebraska Press.

———. 1988. *Politics in Central America: Guatemala, El Salvador, Honduras, and Nicaragua*. Rev. ed. New York: Praeger.

Andrew, Christopher. 1995. *For the President's Eyes Only: Secret Intelligence and the American Presidency from Washington to Bush*. New York: HarperCollins.

Anene, John N. 2000. Military elites and democratization: Ghana and Nigeria. *Journal of Political and Military Sociology* 28(2): 230–45.

Ansell, Ben, and David Samuels. 2014. *Inequality and Democratization: An Elite-Competition Approach*. Cambridge: Cambridge University Press.

AP. 1943. Republic of San Marino ousts its fascist council. August 4.

———. 1949. Panama police say ex-President Arias again heads country. November 25.

———. 1988. Pakistan points to sabotage in Zia crash. October 17.

———. 1995. Soldier emerges as leader after Comoros coup. October 2.

———. 1997. Indian Ocean islands racked by secession. September 7.

Applebaum, Anne. 2012. *Iron Curtain: The Crushing of Eastern Europe, 1944–56*. London: Penguin.

Ardón, Patricia. 1999. *Post-War Reconstruction in Central America: Lessons from El Salvador, Guatemala, and Nicaragua*. Oxfam GB.

Arendt, Hannah. 1963. *On Revolution*. Viking Press.

Armacost, Michael H. 1987. Philippine aspirations for democracy. In Binnendijk 1987, 296–305.

Arnulfo again. 1949. *Time Magazine*, December 5.

Arriagada, Genaro. 1988. *Pinochet: The Politics of Power*. Boston: Unwin Hyman.

Arusha Accords. 2000. Arusha peace and reconciliation agreement for Burundi. peacemaker .un.org/node/1207.

Ash, Timothy Garton. 1990. *The Magic Lantern: The Revolution of '89 Witnessed in Warsaw, Budapest, Berlin, and Prague*. New York: Random House.

Aspinall, Edward, and Marcus Mietzner. 2013. Indonesia: Economic crisis, foreign pressure, and regime change. In Stoner and McFaul 2013, 144–67.

Astiz, Carlos A. 1969. *Pressure Groups and Power Elites in Peruvian Politics*. Ithaca: Cornell University Press.

Athey, Susan, and Guido W. Imbens. 2006. Identification and inference in nonlinear difference-in-differences models. *Econometrica* 74(2): 431–97.

Atkinson, William C. 1960. *A History of Spain and Portugal*. Baltimore: Penguin Books.

Ayangafa, Chrysantus. 2008. Situation critical: The Anjouan political crisis. Working paper, Pretoria, Institute for Security Studies.

Aydin-Düzgit, and Yaprak Gürsoy. 2013. Turkey: The counterintuitive transition of 1983. In Stoner and McFaul 2013, 290–315.

Baker, Bruce. 1998. The class of 1990: How have the autocratic leaders of sub-Saharan Africa fared under democratisation? *Third World Quarterly* 19(1): 115–27.

Banks, Arthur S., and Kenneth A. Wilson. 2017. *Cross-National Time-Series Data Archive*. Databanks International, Jerusalem, Israel. www.cntsdata.com.

Barker, Elisabeth. 1973. *Austria, 1918–1972*. London: Macmillan.

Baron, Reuben M., and David A. Kenny. 1986. The moderator-mediator variable distinction in social psychological research: Conceptual, strategic, and statistical considerations. *Journal of Personality and Social Psychology* 51(6): 1173–82.

Barracca, Steven. 2007. Military coups in the post-cold war era: Pakistan, Ecuador and Venezuela. *Third World Quarterly* 28(1): 137–54.

Barro, Robert J. 1999. Determinants of democracy. *Journal of Political Economy* 107: 158–83.

Baturo, Alexander. 2017. Democracy, development, and career trajectories of former political leaders. *Comparative Political Studies* 50(8): 1023–54.

Bayer, Markus, Felix S. Bethke, and Daniel Lambach. 2016. The democratic dividend of nonviolent resistance. *Journal of Peace Research* 53(6): 758–71.

Bayer, Resat, and Matthew Rupert. 2004. Effects of civil wars on international trade, 1950–92. *Journal of Peace Research* 41(6): 699–713.

BBC News. 2001. Prince blamed for Nepal massacre. June 14.

———. 2012. Tunisia's Ben Ali sentenced over protesters' deaths. June 13.

Bearak, Barry. 2009. Madagascar political rivals agree to power-sharing deal. *New York Times*, August 9.

Beard, Mary. 2015. *SPQR: A History of Ancient Rome*. New York: Liveright Publishing.

Beaulieu, Emily. 2014. *Electoral Protest and Democracy in the Developing World*. Cambridge: Cambridge University Press.

Belkin, Aaron, and Evan Schofer. 2003. Toward a structural understanding of coup risk. *Journal of Conflict Resolution* 47(5): 594–620.

Bell, John Patrick. 1971. *Crisis in Costa Rica: The 1948 Revolution*. Austin: University of Texas Press.

Bellin, Eva. 2000. Contingent democrats: Industrialists, labor, and democratization in late-developing countries. *World Politics* 52: 175–205.

———. 2004. The robustness of authoritarianism in the Middle East: Exceptionalism in comparative perspective. *Comparative Politics* 36(2): 139–57.

Berg-Schlosser, Dirk, and Rainer Siegler. 1990. *Political Stability and Development: A Comparative Analysis of Kenya, Tanzania, and Uganda*. Boulder, CO: Lynne Rienner.

Berman, Sheri. 2007. How democracies emerge: Lessons from Europe. *Journal of Democracy* 18(1): 28–41.

Bermeo, Nancy. 1986. *The Revolution within the Revolution: Workers' Control in Rural Portugal*. Princeton: Princeton University Press.

———. Sacrifice, sequence, and strength in successful dual transitions: Lessons from Spain. *Journal of Politics* 56(3): 601–27.

———. 1997. Myths of moderation: Confrontation and conflict during democratic transitions. *Comparative Politics* 29(3): 305–22.

———. 2003a. *Ordinary People in Extraordinary Times: The Citizenry and the Breakdown of Democracy*. Princeton: Princeton University Press.

———. 2003b. What the democratization literature says—or doesn't say—about postwar democratization. *Global Governance* 9(2): 159–77.

———. 2007. War and democratization: Lessons from the Portuguese experience. *Democratization* 14(3): 388–406.

———. 2010a. Armed conflict and the durability of electoral democracy. In Kier and Krebs 2010, 67–94.

———. 2010b. Interests, inequality, and illusion in the choice for fair elections. *Comparative Political Studies* 43: 1119–47.

———. 2016. On democratic backsliding. *Journal of Democracy* 27(1): 5–19.

Bernhard, Michael. 1993. *The Origins of Democratization in Poland*. New York: Columbia University Press.

Bernhard, Michael, Allen Hicken, Christopher Reenock, and Staffan I. Lindberg. 2020. Parties, civil society, and the deterrence of democratic defection. *Studies in Comparative International Development* 55: 1–26.

Berridge, Willow J. 2015. *Civil Uprisings in Modern Sudan: The "Khartoum Springs" of 1964 and 1985*. London: Bloomsbury Publishing.

Besley, Timothy, Torsten Persson, and Marta Reynal-Querol. 2013. Political instability and institutional reform: Theory and evidence. Working paper.

Biberaj, Elez. 1999. *Albania in Transition: The Rocky Road to Democracy*. Boulder, CO: Westview Press.

Binnendijk, Hans, ed. 1987. *Authoritarian Regimes in Transition*. Washington, DC: Center for the Study of Foreign Affairs, U.S. Department of State.

Binningsbø, Helga Malmin. 2013. Power sharing, peace and democracy: Any obvious relationships? *International Area Studies Review* 16(1): 89–112.

Bitar, Sergio, and Abraham F. Lowenthal, eds. 2015. *Democratic Transitions: Conversations with World Leaders*. Baltimore: Johns Hopkins University Press.

Blaydes, Lisa. 2011. *Elections and Distributive Politics in Mubarak's Egypt*. Cambridge, Cambridge University Press.

Blum, William. 2003. *Killing Hope: U.S. Military and CIA Interventions Since World War II*. Zed Books.

Bodea, Cristina, Ibrahim Elbadawi, and Christian Houle. 2017. Do civil wars, coups and riots have the same structural determinants? *International Interactions* 43(3): 537–61.

Boix, Carles. 2003. *Democracy and Redistribution*. Cambridge, Cambridge University Press.

———. 2011. Democracy, development, and the international system. *American Political Science Review* 105(4): 809–28.

Boix, Carles, Michael Miller, and Sebastian Rosato. 2013. A complete data set of political regimes, 1800–2007. *Comparative Political Studies* 46(12): 1523–54.

Boix, Carles, and Susan Stokes. 2003. Endogenous democratization. *World Politics* 55: 517–49.

Bonner, Raymond. 1986. What will happen after the Philippines election? Civil war is likely. *New York Times*, January 12.

Booth, John A. 1990. Nicaragua: Revolution under siege. In *Latin American Politics and Development*, ed. Howard J. Wiarda and Harvey F. Kline, 467–82. Boulder, CO: Westview Press.

Borowiec, Andrew. 2000. *Cyprus: A Troubled Island*. Westport, CT: Praeger.

Brancati, Dawn. 2014. Pocketbook protests: Explaining the emergence of pro-democracy protests worldwide. *Comparative Political Studies* 47(11): 1503–30.

Bratton, Michael, and Nicolas van de Walle. 1997. *Democratic Experiments in Africa: Regime Transitions in Comparative Perspective*. Cambridge: Cambridge University Press.

Brooke, James. 1988. Marxist ideal loses allure for Sao Tome. *New York Times*, March 14.

Brown, Davis, and Patrick James. 2018. The religious characteristics of states: Classic themes and new evidence for international relations and comparative politics. *Journal of Conflict Resolution* 62(6): 1340–76.

Brown, Fred. 1987. Creating the environment for a transition. In Binnendijk 1987, 312–16.

Brown, Stephen. 2011. "Well, what can you expect?": Donor officials' apologetics for hybrid regimes in Africa. *Democratization* 18(2): 512–34.

Brownlee, Jason. 2007. *Authoritarianism in an Age of Democratization.* Cambridge: Cambridge University Press.

Bunce, Valerie. 2000. Comparative democratization: Big and bounded generalizations. *Comparative Political Studies* 33: 703–34.

———. 2003. Rethinking recent democratization: Lessons from the Postcommunist experience. *World Politics* 55: 167–92.

Bunce, Valerie, Michael McFaul, and Kathryn Stoner-Weiss, eds. 2010. *Democracy and Authoritarianism in the Postcommunist World.* Cambridge: Cambridge University Press.

Bunce, Valerie J., and Sharon L. Wolchik. 2006. Favorable conditions and electoral revolutions. *Journal of Democracy* 17(4): 5–18.

———. 2010. Defeating dictators: Electoral change and stability in competitive authoritarian regimes. *World Politics* 62(1): 43–86.

———. 2011. *Defeating Authoritarian Leaders in Postcommunist Countries.* Cambridge: Cambridge University Press.

Burkhart, Ross, and Michael Lewis-Beck. 1994. Comparative democracy: The economic development thesis. *American Political Science Review* 88: 903–10.

Burt, Jo-Marie. 2007. *Political Violence and the Authoritarian State in Peru: Silencing Civil Society.* New York: Palgrave Macmillan.

Bush, Sarah Sunn. 2015. *The Taming of Democracy Assistance: Why Democracy Promotion Does Not Confront Dictators.* Cambridge: Cambridge University Press.

Cabrita, João M. 2000. *Mozambique: The Tortuous Road to Democracy.* New York: Palgrave Macmillan.

Calhoun, C. H. 1951. Protests swaying Panama president. *New York Times,* May 9.

Callahan, William A. 1998. *Imagining Democracy: Reading "The Events of May" in Thailand.* Singapore: Institute of Southeast Asian Studies.

Capoccia, Giovanni, and Daniel Ziblatt. 2010. The historical turn in democratization studies: A new research agenda for Europe and beyond. *Comparative Political Studies* 43: 931–68.

Carothers, Thomas. 1999. *Aiding Democracy Abroad: The Learning Curve.* Washington, DC: Carnegie Endowment for International Peace.

Carrión, Julio F., ed. 2006. *The Fujimori Legacy: The Rise of Electoral Authoritarianism in Peru.* University Park: Pennsylvania State University Press.

Carstairs, Andrew McLaren. 2010. *A Short History of Electoral Systems in Western Europe.* New York: Routledge.

Cartledge, Paul. 2016. *Democracy: A Life.* Oxford: Oxford University Press.

Casar, María Amparo. 1995. The 1994 Mexican presidential elections. Institute of Latin American Studies, Occasional Papers #8.

Case, William. 2011. Electoral authoritarianism and backlash: Hardening Malaysia, oscillating Thailand. *International Political Science Review* 32(4): 438–57.

Casper, Gretchen. 2000a. The benefits of difficult transitions. *Democratization* 7(3): 46–62.

———. 2000b. From confrontation to conciliation: The Philippine path toward democratic consolidation. In *Pathways to Democracy: The Political Economy of Democratic Transitions,* ed. James F. Hollifield and Calvin Jillson, 147–59. New York: Routledge.

Casper, Gretchen, and Michelle M. Taylor. 1996. *Negotiating Democracy: Transitions from Authoritarian Rule*. Pittsburgh: University of Pittsburgh Press.

Caudill, Steven B. 1988. Practitioners corner: An advantage of the linear probability model over probit or logit. *Oxford Bulletin of Economics and Statistics* 50(4): 425–27.

Cederman, Lars-Erik, Kristian Skrede Gleditsch, and Simon Hug. 2013. Elections and ethnic civil war. *Comparative Political Studies* 46(3): 387–417.

Celestino, Mauricio Rivera, and Kristian Skrede Gleditsch. 2013. Fresh carnations or all thorn, no rose? Nonviolent campaigns and transitions in autocracies. *Journal of Peace Research* 50: 385–400.

Cervellati, Matteo, Piergiuseppe Fortunato, and Uwe Sunde. 2014. Violence during democratization and the quality of democratic institutions. *European Economic Review* 66: 226–47.

Chacha, Mwita, and Jonathan Powell. 2017. Economic interdependence and post-coup democratization. *Democratization* 24(5): 819–38.

Chadda, Maya. 2000. *Building Democracy in South Asia: India, Nepal, Pakistan*. Boulder, CO: Lynne Rienner.

Chao, Linda, and Ramon H. Myers. 1998. *The First Chinese Democracy: Political Life in the Republic of China on Taiwan*. Baltimore: Johns Hopkins University Press.

Cheeseman, Nic. 2010. African elections as vehicles for change. *Journal of Democracy* 21(4): 139–53.

Cheibub, José Antonio, Jennifer Gandhi, and James Raymond Vreeland. 2010. Democracy and dictatorship revisited. *Public Choice* 143: 67–101.

Cheng, Tun-jen. 2008. Embracing defeat: The KMT and the PRI after 2000. In Friedman and Wong 2008, 127–47.

Chenoweth, Erica, and Orion A. Lewis. 2013. Unpacking nonviolent campaigns: Introducing the NAVCO 2.0 dataset. *Journal of Peace Research* 50(3): 415–23.

Chenoweth, Erica, and Maria J. Stephan. 2011. *Why Civil Resistance Works: The Strategic Logic of Nonviolent Conflict*. New York: Columbia University Press.

Chenoweth, Erica, and Jay Ulfelder. 2017. Can structural conditions explain the onset of nonviolent uprisings? *Journal of Conflict Resolution* 61(2): 298–324.

Chilcote, Ronald H. 2010. *The Portuguese Revolution: State and Class in the Transition to Democracy*. Lanham, MD: Rowman & Littlefield.

Chin, John J. 2015. Military coups, regime change, and democratization. Working paper, Princeton University.

Clark, Andrew F. 1995. From military dictatorship to democracy: The democratization process in Mali. *Journal of Third World Studies* 12(1): 201–22.

Cleaves, Peter S., and Henry Pease García. 1983. State autonomy and military policy making. In *The Peruvian Experiment Reconsidered*, ed. Cynthia McClintock and Abraham F. Lowenthal, 209–44. Princeton: Princeton University Press.

Close, David. 1985. The Nicaraguan elections of 1984. *Electoral Studies* 4(2): 152–58.

Close, David, Salvador Martí i Puig, and Shelley A. McConnell, eds. 2012. *The Sandinistas and Nicaragua since 1979*. Boulder, CO: Lynne Rienner.

Cohen, Lenard J. 2001. *Serpent in the Bosom: The Rise and Fall of Slobodan Milosevic*. Boulder, CO: Westview Press.

Cohn, Samuel K., Jr. 2006. *Lust for Liberty: The Politics of Social Revolt in Medieval Europe, 1200–1425*. Cambridge, MA: Harvard University Press.

Colgan, Jeff. 2015. Oil, domestic conflict, and opportunities for democratization. *Journal of Peace Research* 52(1): 3–16.

Collier, David, Henry E. Brady, and Jason Seawright. 2004. Sources of leverage in causal inference: Toward an alternative view of methodology. In *Rethinking Social Inquiry:*

*Diverse Tools, Shared Standards*, ed. David Collier and Henry E Brady, 229–66. Lanham, MD: Rowman & Littlefield.

Collier, Paul. 1999. On the economic consequences of civil war. *Oxford Economic Papers* 51(1): 168–83.

——. 2009. *Wars, Guns, and Votes: Democracy in Dangerous Places*. New York: HarperCollins.

Collier, Ruth Berins. 1999. *Paths toward Democracy: The Working Class and Elites in Western Europe and South America*. Cambridge: Cambridge University Press.

Collins, Robert O. 2008. *A History of Modern Sudan*. Cambridge: Cambridge University Press.

Colomer, Josep M. 1991. Transitions by agreement: Modeling the Spanish way. *American Political Science Review* 85(4): 1283–1302.

——. 2000. *Strategic Transitions: Game Theory and Democratization*. Baltimore: Johns Hopkins University Press.

Commonwealth Secretariat. 2004. Antigua and Barbuda general election: The report of the Commonwealth expert team. Westminster, UK: Commonwealth of Nations.

Conaghan, Catherine M. 2005. *Fujimori's Peru: Deception in the Public Sphere*. Pittsburgh: University of Pittsburgh Press.

Coppedge, Michael, John Gerring . . . Daniel Ziblatt. 2018. *V-Dem Dataset, Version 8*. Varieties of Democracy (V-Dem) Project.

Cornelius, Wayne A. 1986. The Nicaraguan elections of 1984: A reassessment of their domestic and international significance. In *Elections and Democratization in Latin America, 1980–85*, ed. Paul W. Drake and Eduardo Silva, 61–72. San Diego: Center for Iberian and Latin American Studies, University of California.

Correlates of War Project. 2010a. *COW Wars, Version 4.0, 1816–2007*. www.correlatesofwar.org.

——. 2010b. *National Material Capabilities Dataset, Version 4.0*. www.correlatesofwar.org.

Covell, Maureen. 1987. *Madagascar: Politics, Economics and Society*. London: Frances Pinter.

Coyne, Christopher J. 2008. *After War: The Political Economy of Exporting Democracy*. Stanford: Stanford University Press.

Cribb, Robert. 1986. A revolution delayed: The Indonesian republic and the Netherlands Indies, August–November 1945. *Australian Journal of Politics & History* 32(1): 72–85.

Croissant, Aurel, David Kuehn, and Tanja Eschenauer. 2018. Mass protests and the military. *Journal of Democracy* 29(3): 141–55.

Crosette, Barbara. 1988. After Zia, Pakistan takes well to politics. *New York Times*, November 12.

——. 1990. Revolution brings Bangladesh hope. *New York Times*, December 9.

——. 1991. General's widow wins Bangladesh vote. *New York Times*, March 1.

Cunningham, Hugh. 2001. *The Challenge of Democracy: Britain, 1832–1918*. London: Pearson Education Limited.

Curtis, Glenn E., ed. 1994. *Georgia: A Country Study*. Washington, DC: Library of Congress.

Dahl, Robert A. 1971. *Polyarchy: Participation and Opposition*. New Haven: Yale University Press.

Dahlum, Sirianne, Carl Henrik Knutsen, and Tore Wig. 2019. Who revolts? Empirically revisiting the social origins of democracy. *Journal of Politics* 81(4): 1494–99.

Dawson, D. 1922. The Archduke Ferdinand Maximilian and the crown of Greece, 1863. *English Historical Review* 37(145): 107–14.

DeFronzo, James. 2011. *Revolutions and Revolutionary Movements*. 4th ed. Boulder, CO: Westview Press.

Del Aguila, Juan M. 1984. *Cuba: Dilemmas of a Revolution*. Boulder, CO: Westview Press.

Dennis, Peter. 2006. A brief history of Liberia. Working paper, International Center for Transitional Justice.

de Onis, Juan. 1979. Bolivia ruler decrees martial law, sends jets against demonstrators. *New York Times*, November 5.

Derby, Lauren H. 2009. *The Dictator's Seduction: Politics and the Popular Imagination in the Era of Trujillo*. Durham: Duke University Press.

Derpanopoulos, George, Erica Frantz, Barbara Geddes, and Joseph Wright. 2015. Are coups good for democracy? *Research & Politics* 3(1).

de Schweinitz, Karl. 1964. *Industrialization and Democracy: Economic Necessities and Political Possibilities*. London: Free Press of Glencoe.

de Waal, Alex. 2013. Sudan's elusive democratisation: Civic mobilisation, provincial rebellion and chameleon dictatorships. *Journal of Contemporary African Studies* 31(2): 213–34.

Di Palma, Giuseppe. 1990. *To Craft Democracies: An Essay on Democratic Transitions*. Berkeley: University of California Press.

Diamandouros, P. Nikiforos. 1986. Regime change and the prospects for democracy in Greece: 1974–1983. In O'Donnell, Schmitter, and Whitehead 1986b, 138–64.

Diamond, Larry. 1999. *Developing Democracy: Toward Consolidation*. Baltimore: Johns Hopkins University Press.

———. 2019. *Ill Winds: Saving Democracy from Russian Rage, Chinese Ambition, and American Complacency*. New York: Penguin.

Diaz-Cayeros, Alberto, and Beatriz Magaloni. 2013. Mexico: International influences but "Made in Mexico." In Stoner and McFaul 2013, 244–65.

Dickson, Bruce J. 1997. *Democratization in China and Taiwan: The Adaptability of Leninist Parties*. Oxford: Oxford University Press.

Dietrich, Simone, and Joseph Wright. 2014. Foreign aid allocation tactics and democratic change in Africa. *Journal of Politics* 77(1): 216–34.

Dietz, Henry. 1992. Elites in an unconsolidated democracy: Peru during the 1980s. In Higley and Gunther 1992, 237–56.

Dix, Robert H. 1987. *The Politics of Colombia*. New York: Praeger.

Dobson, William. 2012. *The Dictator's Learning Curve: Inside the Global Battle for Democracy*. New York: Doubleday.

Domber, Gregory. 2013. Poland: International pressures for a negotiated transition, 1981–1989. In Stoner and McFaul 2013, 62–90.

Doorenspleet, Renske. 2000. Reassessing the three waves of democratization. *World Politics* 52: 384–406.

Dore, Ronald. 1959/2013. *Land Reform in Japan*. London: Bloomsbury.

Dower, John W. 1999. *Embracing Defeat: Japan in the Wake of World War II*. New York: W. W. Norton.

Downes, Alexander B., and Jonathan Monten. 2013. Forced to be free?: Why foreign-imposed regime change rarely leads to democratization. *International Security* 37(4): 90–131.

Downing, Brian. 1993. *The Military Revolution and Political Change: Origins of Democracy and Autocracy in Early Modern Europe*. Princeton: Princeton University Press.

Dragu, Tiberiu, and Yonatan Lupu. 2018. Collective action and constraints on repression at the endgame. *Comparative Political Studies* 51(8): 1042–73.

Duff, Ernest A. 1985. *Leader and Party in Latin America*. Boulder, CO: Westview Press.

Dugas, John. 2000. The Conservative Party and the crisis of political legitimacy in Colombia. In *Conservative Parties, the Right, and Democracy in Latin America*, ed. Kevin J. Middlebrook, 80–109. Baltimore: Johns Hopkins University Press.

Dulles, John W. F. 2014. *Vargas of Brazil: A Political Biography*. Austin: University of Texas Press.

Dunkerley, James. 1984. *Rebellion in the Veins: Political Struggle in Bolivia, 1952–1982*. London: Verso.

——. 1988. *Power in the Isthmus: A Political History of Modern Central America*. London: Verso.

Dunkerley, James, and Rachel Sieder. 1996. The military: The challenge of transition. In *Central America: Fragile Transition*, ed. Rachel Sieder, 55–102. London: Macmillan.

Dunning, Thad. 2008. *Crude Democracy: Natural Resource Wealth and Political Regimes*. Cambridge: Cambridge University Press.

Durham, William H. 1979. *Scarcity and Survival in Central America: Ecological Origins of the Soccer War*. Stanford: Stanford University Press.

Easterly, William, Shanker Satyanath, and Daniel Berger. 2008. Superpower interventions and their consequences for democracy: An empirical inquiry. NBER working paper #13992.

Ebel, Roland H. 1998. *Misunderstood Caudillo: Miguel Ydigoras Fuentes and the Failure of Democracy in Guatemala*. Lanham, MD: University Press of America.

Edgell, Amanda B., Valeriya Mechkova, David Altman, Michael Bernhard, and Staffan I. Lindberg. 2018. When and where do elections matter? A global test of the democratization by elections hypothesis, 1900–2010. *Democratization* 25(3): 422–44.

Edwards, Jeffrey R., and Lisa Schurer Lambert. 2007. Methods for integrating moderation and mediation: A general analytical framework using moderated path analysis. *Psychological Methods* 12(1): 1–22.

Eisenstadt, Todd A. 2004. *Courting Democracy in Mexico: Party Strategies and Electoral Institutions*. New York: Cambridge University Press.

Ekiert, Grzegorz, and Jan Kubik. 1998. Contentious politics in new democracies: East Germany, Hungary, Poland, and Slovakia, 1989–93. *World Politics* 50(4): 547–81.

El-Affendi, Abdelwahab. 2012. Revolutionary anatomy: The lessons of the Sudanese revolutions of October 1964 and April 1985. *Contemporary Arab Affairs* 5(2): 292–306.

Ellis, Geoffrey. 2000. The revolution of 1848–1849 in France. In *The Revolutions in Europe, 1848–1849: From Reform to Reaction*, ed. R.J.W. Evans and Hartmut Pogge von Strandmann, 27–54. Oxford: Oxford University Press.

Eprile, Cecil. 1974. *War and Peace in the Sudan, 1955–1972*. London: David & Charles.

Ertman, Thomas. 1997. *Birth of the Leviathan: Building States and Regimes in Medieval and Early Modern Europe*. Cambridge: Cambridge University Press.

Everitt, Anthony. 2016. *The Rise of Athens: The Story of the World's Greatest Civilisation*. New York: Random House.

Fairbanks, Charles H. 2004. Georgia's Rose Revolution. *Journal of Democracy* 15(2): 110–24.

Falch, Åshild, and Megan Becker. 2008. Power-sharing and peacebuilding in Burundi: Power-sharing agreements, negotiations and peace processes. Working paper, Center for the Study of Civil War, Oslo, Norway.

Falola, Toyin, and Julius Ihonvbere. 1985. *The Rise and Fall of Nigeria's Second Republic: 1979–84*. London: Zed Books.

Fausto, Boris, and Sergio Fausto. 2014. *A Concise History of Brazil*. 2nd ed. Cambridge: Cambridge University Press.

Feng, Yi. 1997. Democracy, political stability and economic growth. *British Journal of Political Science* 27: 391–418.

Ferejohn, John, and Frances McCall Rosenbluth. 2016. *Forged through Fire: War, Peace, and the Democratic Bargain*. New York: W. W. Norton.

Fernandes, Tiago, and Rui Branco. 2017. Long-term effects: Social revolution and civil society in Portugal, 1974–2010. *Comparative Politics* 49(3): 411–31.

Ferreira, Hugo Gil, and Michael W. Marshall. 1986. *Portugal's Revolution: Ten Years On.* Cambridge: Cambridge University Press.

Finer, Samuel. 1962. *The Man on Horseback: The Role of the Military in Politics.* New York: Routledge.

Finkel, Steven E., Aníbal Pérez-Liñán, and Mitchell A. Seligson. 2007. The effects of US foreign assistance on democracy building, 1990–2003. *World Politics* 59(3): 404–39.

Fishman, Robert M. 2018. What made the third wave possible? Historical contingency and meta-politics in the genesis of worldwide democratization. *Comparative Politics* 50(4): 607–26.

Florquin, Nicolas, and Stéphanie Pézard. 2005. Insurgency, disarmament, and insecurity in Northern Mali, 1990–2004. In *Armed and Aimless,* ed. Nicolas Florquin and Eric G. Berman, 46–77. Geneva: Small Arms Survey.

Foran, John. 2005. *Taking Power: On the Origins of Third World Revolutions.* Cambridge: Cambridge University Press.

Fortna, Virginia Page. 2004. *Peace Time: Cease-Fire Agreements and the Durability of Peace.* Princeton: Princeton University Press.

Fortna, Virginia Page, and Reyko Huang. 2012. Democratization after civil war: A brush-clearing exercise. *International Studies Quarterly* 56: 801–8.

Fosu, Augustin Kwasi. 2002. Political instability and economic growth: Implications of coup events in sub-Saharan Africa. *American Journal of Economics and Sociology* 61(1): 329–48.

Foweraker, Joe. 1989. *Making Democracy in Spain: Grass-Roots Struggle in the South, 1955–1975.* New York: Cambridge University Press.

Francisco, Albertino, and Nujoma Agostinho. 2011. *Exorcising Devils from the Throne: São Tomé and Príncipe in the Chaos of Democratization.* New York: Algora Publishing.

Franco, Jennifer C. 2001. *Elections and Democratization in the Philippines.* New York: Routledge.

Frant, Howard, Frances Stokes Berry, and William D. Berry. 1991. Specifying a model of state policy innovation. *American Political Science Review* 85(2): 571–79.

Fraser, K. Michael. 1982. Brazil vote a step toward democracy. *Globe and Mail,* November 15.

Freedom House. 2016. *Freedom in the World 2016: The Annual Survey of Political Rights and Civil Liberties.* Lanham, MD: Rowman & Littlefield.

French, Howard W. 1990. Island's hushed scandals, unhushed. *New York Times,* June 16.

Friedman, Edward, and Joseph Wong, eds. 2008. *Political Transitions in Dominant Party Systems: Learning to Lose.* New York: Routledge.

Friedman, Steven. 2015. South Africa. In Bitar and Lowenthal 2015, 293–300.

Fukuoka, Yuki. 2015. Who brought down the dictator? A critical reassessment of so-called "people power" revolutions in the Philippines and Indonesia. *Pacific Review* 28(3): 411–33.

Fukuyama, Francis. 2015. Why is democracy performing so poorly? *Journal of Democracy* 26(1): 11–20.

Funk, Arthur Layton. 1944. Robert le Coq and Etienne Marcel. *Speculum* 19(4): 470–87.

Furlong, William L. 1993. Panama: The difficult transition towards democracy. *Journal of Interamerican Studies and World Affairs* 35(3): 19–64.

Galbraith, James K., and Hyunsub Kum. 2003. Inequality and economic growth: A global view based on measures of pay. *CESifo Economic Studies* 49(4): 527–56.

Gallagher, Tom. 1983. *Portugal: A Twentieth-Century Interpretation*. Manchester: Manchester University Press.

Gandhi, Jennifer. 2008. *Political Institutions under Dictatorship*. Cambridge: Cambridge University Press.

Gandhi, Jennifer, and Ellen Lust-Okar. 2009. Elections under authoritarianism. *Annual Review of Political Science* 12: 403–22.

Gapminder. 2018. Gapminder dataset. www.gapminder.org/data.

Gasiorowski, Mark J. 1995. Economic crisis and political regime change: An event history analysis. *American Political Science Review* 89(4): 882–97.

Gates, Scott, Benjamin A. T. Graham, Yonatan Lupu, Håvard Strand, and Kaare Strøm. 2016. Powersharing, protection, and peace. *Journal of Politics* 78(2): 512–26.

Gberie, Lansana. 2005. *A Dirty War in West Africa: The RUF and the Destruction of Sierra Leone*. Bloomington: Indiana University Press.

Geddes, Barbara. 1999. What do we know about democratization after twenty years? *Annual Review of Political Science* 2: 115–44.

Geddes, Barbara, Joseph Wright, and Erica Frantz. 2014. Authoritarian breakdown and regime transitions: A new data set. *Perspectives on Politics* 12(2): 313–31.

———. 2018. *How Dictatorships Work: Power, Personalization, and Collapse*. Cambridge: Cambridge University Press.

Gelb, Leslie H. 1983. U.S. officials say anti-Sandinistas are growing stronger by the day. *New York Times*, June 14.

Gervais, Myriam. 1997. Niger: Regime change, economic crisis, and perpetuation of privilege. In *Political Reform in Francophone Africa*, ed. John F. Clark and David Gardinier, 86–108. Boulder, CO: Westview Press.

Ghoshal, Baladas. 1982. *Indonesian Politics, 1955–59: The Emergence of Guided Democracy*. Calcutta: KP Bagchi & Company.

Ginsburg, Tom, and Aziz Z. Huq. 2018. *How to Save a Constitutional Democracy*. Chicago: University of Chicago Press.

Girling, John Lawrence Scott. 1981. *Thailand: Society and Politics*. Ithaca: Cornell University Press.

Gleditsch, Kristian S. 2000. International dimensions of democratization. Working paper.

Gleditsch, Kristian S., and Michael D. Ward. 2006. Diffusion and the international context of democratization. *International Organization* 60: 911–33.

Gleijeses, Piero. 1991. *Shattered Hope: The Guatemalan Revolution and the United States, 1944–1954*. Princeton: Princeton University Press.

Glynn, Adam N. 2012. The product and difference fallacies for indirect effects. *American Journal of Political Science* 56(1): 257–69.

Goemans, H. E., Kristian Skrede Gleditsch, and Giacomo Chiozza. 2016. *Archigos: A Data Set on Leaders, 1875–2015, Version 4.1*.

Goldsmith, Arthur A. 2008. Making the world safe for partial democracy? Questioning the premises of democracy promotion. *International Security* 33(2):120–47.

Goldstone, Jack A. 2001. Toward a fourth generation of revolutionary theory. *Annual Review of Political Science* 4: 139–87.

———. 2014. *Revolutions: A Very Short Introduction*. Oxford: Oxford University Press.

Goodsell, James Nelson. 1983. Nicaragua. In *Latin America and Caribbean Contemporary Record, Volume 1: 1981–1982*, ed. Jack W. Hopkins, 471–86. New York: Holmes & Meier.

Goodson, Larry P. 2008. The 2008 elections. *Journal of Democracy* 19(4): 5–15.

Goodwin, Jeff. 2001. *No Other Way Out: States and Revolutionary Movements, 1945–1991*. Cambridge: Cambridge University Press.

Goodwyn, Lawrence. 1991. *Breaking the Barrier: The Rise of Solidarity in Poland*. New York: Oxford University Press.

Gorman, Stephen M. 1984. Social change and political revolution: The case of Nicaragua. In *Central America: Crisis and Adaptation*, ed. Steve C. Ropp and James A. Morris, 33–66. Albuquerque: University of New Mexico Press.

Gow, Bonar A. 1997. Admiral Didier Ratsiraka and the Malagasy socialist revolution. *Journal of Modern African Studies* 35(3): 409–39.

Graham, Benjamin A. T., Michael K. Miller, and Kaare W. Strøm. 2017. Safeguarding democracy: Powersharing and democratic survival. *American Political Science Review* 111(4): 686–704.

Graham, Lawrence S. 1992. Redefining the Portuguese transition to democracy. In Higley and Gunther 1992, 282–99.

Grandin, Greg. 2004. *The Last Colonial Massacre: Latin America in the Cold War*. Chicago: University of Chicago Press.

Greene, Kenneth F. 2002. Opposition party strategy and spatial competition in dominant party regimes: A theory and the case of Mexico. *Comparative Political Studies* 35(7): 755–83.

———. 2007. *Why Dominant Parties Lose: Mexico's Democratization in Comparative Perspective*. Cambridge: Cambridge University Press.

———. 2010. The political economy of authoritarian single-party dominance. *Comparative Political Studies* 43(7): 807–34.

Greitens, Sheena Chestnut. 2016. *Dictators and Their Secret Police: Coercive Institutions and State Violence*. New York: Cambridge University Press.

Grewal, Sharan, and Yasser Kureshi. 2019. How to sell a coup: Elections as coup legitimation. *Journal of Conflict Resolution* 63(4): 1001–31.

Grimm, Sonja. 2008. External democratization after war: Success and failure. *Democratization* 15: 525–49.

Grugel, Jean, and Tim Rees. 1997. *Franco's Spain*. London: Arnold Press.

Grzymala-Busse, Anna M. 2002. *Redeeming the Communist Past: The Regeneration of Communist Parties in East Central Europe*. Cambridge: Cambridge University Press.

Gunitsky, Seva. 2017. *Aftershocks: Great Powers and Domestic Reforms in the Twentieth Century*. Princeton: Princeton University Press.

Gunther, Richard, Giacomo Sani, and Goldie Shabad. 1988. *Spain after Franco: The Making of a Competitive Party System*. Berkeley: University of California Press.

Guo, Sujian, and Gary A. Stradiotto. 2014. *Democratic Transitions: Modes and Outcomes*. New York: Routledge.

Gurr, Ted Robert. 1988. War, revolution, and the growth of the coercive state. *Comparative Political Studies* 21(1): 45–65.

Gurses, Mehmet, and T. David Mason. 2008. Democracy out of anarchy: The prospects for post-civil-war democracy. *Social Science Quarterly* 89(2): 315–36.

Haber, Stephen, and Victor Menaldo. 2011. Do natural resources fuel authoritarianism? A reappraisal of the resource curse. *American Political Science Review* 105(1): 1–26.

Haggard, Stephan, and Robert R. Kaufman. 1995. *The Political Economy of Democratic Transitions*. Princeton: Princeton University Press.

———. 2008. *Development, Democracy, and Welfare States: Latin America, East Asia, and Eastern Europe*. Princeton: Princeton University Press.

———. 2012. Inequality and regime change: Democratic transitions and the stability of democratic rule. *American Political Science Review* 106(3): 495–516.

———. 2016. *Dictators and Democrats: Masses, Elites, and Regime Change*. Princeton: Princeton University Press.

Hagopian, Frances. 1996. *Traditional Politics and Regime Change in Brazil*. Cambridge: Cambridge University Press.

Hale, Henry E. 2005. Regime cycles: Democracy, autocracy, and revolution in post-Soviet Eurasia. *World Politics* 58: 133–65.

———. 2013. Regime change cascades: What we have learned from the 1848 revolutions to the 2011 Arab uprisings. *Annual Review of Political Science* 16: 331–53.

Halperin, Ernst. 1970. *Fidel Castro's Road to Power*. Boston: Center for International Studies.

Han, Sungjoo. 1974. *The Failure of Democracy in South Korea*. Berkeley: University of California Press.

———. 1988. South Korea in 1987: The politics of democratization. *Asian Survey* 28(1): 52–61.

Handley, Antoinette. 2013. Ghana: Democratic transition, presidential power, and the World Bank. In Stoner and McFaul 2013, 221–43.

Hanratty, Dennis M., and Sandra W. Meditz, eds. 1988. *Colombia: A Country Study*. Washington, DC: Library of Congress.

Hanson, Jonathan K., and Rachel Sigman. 2013. Leviathan's latent dimensions: Measuring state capacity for comparative political research. Working paper.

Harding, Robert C. 2006. *The History of Panama*. Westport, CT: Greenwood Press.

Harris, David. 2012. *Civil War and Democracy in West Africa: Conflict Resolution, Elections and Justice in Sierra Leone and Liberia*. London: I. B. Tauris.

Harris, George S. 1970. The causes of the 1960 revolution in Turkey. *Middle East Journal* 24(4): 438–54.

Hartlyn, Jonathan. 1984. Military governments and the transition to civilian rule: The Colombian experience of 1957–1958. *Journal of Interamerican Studies and World Affairs* 26(2): 245–81.

———. 1998. *The Struggle for Democratic Politics in the Dominican Republic*. Chapel Hill: University of North Carolina Press.

Hartzell, Caroline, and Matthew Hoddie. 2003. Institutionalizing peace: Power sharing and post–civil war conflict management. *American Journal of Political Science* 47(2): 318–32.

———. 2015. The art of the possible: Power sharing and post–civil war democracy. *World Politics* 67(1): 37–71.

Havel, Václav. 1991. *Open Letters: Selected Writings, 1967–1990*, ed. Paul Wilson. New York: Alfred A. Knopf.

Henderson, James D. 1985. *When Colombia Bled: A History of the "Violencia" in Tolima*. Tuscaloosa: University of Alabama Press.

Hermet, Guy, Richard Rose, and Alain Rouquié, eds. 1978. *Elections without Choice*. New York: John Wiley & Sons.

Heston, Alan, Robert Summers, and Bettina Aten. 2011. *Penn World Table, Version 7.0*. Center for International Comparisons of Production, Income and Prices, University of Pennsylvania.

Higley, John, and Michael Burton. 2006. *Elite Foundations of Liberal Democracy*. Oxford: Rowman & Littlefield.

Higley, John, and Richard Gunther, eds. 1992. *Elites and Democratic Consolidation in Latin America and Southern Europe*. Cambridge: Cambridge University Press.

Hilton, Stanley E. 1987. The overthrow of Getúlio Vargas in 1945: Diplomatic intervention, defense of democracy, or political retribution? *Hispanic American Historical Review* 67(1): 1–37.

Hinds, David. 2005. Problems of democratic transition in Guyana: Mistakes and miscalculations in 1992. *Social and Economic Studies* 54(1): 67–82.

——. 2011. *Ethno-politics and Power Sharing in Guyana: History and Discourse*. Washington, DC: New Academia Publishing.

Hirsch, John L. 2001. *Sierra Leone: Diamonds and the Struggle for Democracy*. Boulder, CO: Lynne Rienner.

Hitchens, Christopher. 1997. *Hostage to History: Cyprus from the Ottomans to Kissinger*. London: Verso.

Hoge, Warren. 1981. A general loosens the reins in Brazil. *New York Times Magazine*, December 5.

——. 1982. Brazil elections bring victories for opposition. *New York Times*, November 25.

Holt, Peter M., and Martin W. Daly. 2014. *A History of the Sudan: From the Coming of Islam to the Present Day*. London: Routledge.

Hood, Steven J. 1997. *The Kuomintang and the Democratization of Taiwan*. Boulder, CO: Westview Press.

Horne, Alistair. 2007. *The Fall of Paris: The Siege and the Commune, 1870–71*. New York: Penguin.

Houle, Christian. 2009. Inequality and democracy: Why inequality harms consolidation but does not affect democratization. *World Politics* 61(4): 589–622.

Houle, Christian, Mark A. Kayser, and Jun Xiang. 2016. Diffusion or confusion? Clustered shocks and the conditional diffusion of democracy. *International Organization* 70: 687–726.

Howard, Marc Morje, and Philip G. Roessler. 2006. Liberalizing electoral outcomes in competitive authoritarian regimes. *American Journal of Political Science* 50(2): 365–81.

Howard, Michael. 2013. *The Franco-Prussian War: The German Invasion of France, 1870–1871*. New York: Routledge.

Huang, Reyko. 2016. *The Wartime Origins of Democratization: Civil War, Rebel Governance, and Political Regimes*. Cambridge: Cambridge University Press.

Hudson, Rex A., and Dennis M. Hanratty, eds. 1989. *Bolivia: A Country Study*. Washington, DC: Library of Congress.

Huneeus, Carlos. 2007. *The Pinochet Regime*. Boulder, CO: Lynne Rienner.

Hunefeldt, Christine. 2004. *A Brief History of Peru*. New York: Facts on File.

Hunt, Chris. 1976. *Portuguese Revolution 1974–76*. New York: Facts on File.

Hunter, Wendy. 1997. *Eroding Military Influence in Brazil: Politicians against Soldiers*. Chapel Hill: University of North Carolina Press.

Huntington, Samuel P. 1968. *Political Order in Changing Societies*. New Haven: Yale University Press.

——. 1991. *The Third Wave: Democratization in the Late Twentieth Century*. Norman: University of Oklahoma Press.

Hutchful, Eboe. 1973. Military Rule and the Politics of Demilitarisation in Ghana, 1966–1969. PhD diss., University of Toronto.

Hyde, Susan D., and Nikolay Marinov. 2012. Which elections can be lost? *Political Analysis* 20(2): 191–201.

——. 2014. Information and self-enforcing democracy: The role of international election observation. *International Organization* 68(2): 329–59.

Hyman, Anthony, Muhammed Ghayur, and Naresh Kaushik. 1989. *Pakistan, Zia and After . . .* New Delhi: Abhinav Publications.

Ibrahim, Jibrin, and Abdoylaye Niandou Souley. 1998. The rise to power of an opposition party: The MNSD in Niger Republic. In *The Politics of Opposition in Contemporary Africa*, ed. Adebayo O. Olukoshi, 144–70. Stockholm: Nordiska Afrikainstitutet.

Ikenberry, G. John, and Charles A. Kupchan. 1990. Socialization and hegemonic power. *International Organization* 44(3): 283–315.

Imai, Kosuke, Luke Keele, Dustin Tingley, and Teppei Yamamoto. 2011. Unpacking the black box of causality: Learning about causal mechanisms from experimental and observational studies. *American Political Science Review* 105(4): 765–89.

Inglehart, Ronald, and Christian Welzel. 2005. *Modernization, Cultural Change and Democracy: The Human Development Sequence*. Cambridge: Cambridge University Press.

International Crisis Group. 2011. The Communist insurgency in the Philippines: Tactics and talks. Asia Report #202.

International News Service (INS). 1951. Panama ousts, arrests Arias. *Lima Times*, May 11.

Iqbal, Zaryab, and Christopher Zorn. 2006. Sic semper tyrannis? Power, repression, and assassination since the Second World War. *Journal of Politics* 68(3): 489–501.

———. 2008. The political consequences of assassination. *Journal of Conflict Resolution* 52(3): 385–400.

Isbester, Katherine. 2001. *Still Fighting: The Nicaraguan Women's Movement, 1977-2000*. Pittsburgh: University of Pittsburgh Press.

Ishiyama, John. 2008. Learning to lose (and sometimes win): The neocommunist parties in post-Soviet politics. In Friedman and Wong 2008, 148–68.

Ishiyama, John, and John James Quinn. 2006. African phoenix? Explaining the electoral performance of the formerly dominant parties in Africa. *Party Politics* 12(3): 317–40.

Jackman, Robert W. 1978. The predictability of coups d'état: A model with African data. *American Political Science Review* 72(4): 1262–75.

Jakobsen, Jo, and Indra De Soysa. 2006. Do foreign investors punish democracy? Theory and empirics, 1984-2001. *Kyklos* 59(3): 383–410.

Jennings, Ray Salvatore. 2013. Serbia: Evaluating the Bulldozer Revolution. In Stoner and McFaul 2013, 91–119.

Jensen, Nathan. 2008. Political risk, democratic institutions, and foreign direct investment. *Journal of Politics* 70(4): 1040–52.

Jespersen, Knud J. V. 2004. *A History of Denmark*. London: Palgrave Macmillan.

Johnson, Jaclyn, and Clayton L. Thyne. 2018. Squeaky wheels and troop loyalty: How domestic protests influence coups d'état, 1951–2005. *Journal of Conflict Resolution* 62(3): 597–625.

Jones, Andrew. 1972. *The Politics of Reform 1884*. Cambridge: Cambridge University Press.

Jones, Benjamin F., and Benjamin A. Olken. 2009. Hit or miss? The effect of assassinations on institutions and war. *American Economic Journal: Macroeconomics* 1(2): 55–87.

Jones, Dan. 2012. *The Plantagenets: The Warrior Kings and Queens Who Made England*. New York: Penguin.

———. 2015. *Magna Carta: The Birth of Liberty*. New York: Penguin.

Joshi, Madhav. 2010. Post-civil war democratization: Promotion of democracy in post–civil war states, 1946-2005. *Democratization* 17(5): 826–55.

Jung, Courtney, and Ian Shapiro. 1995. South Africa's negotiated transition: Democracy, opposition, and the new constitutional order. *Politics and Society* 23(3): 269–308.

Kalck, Pierre. 2005. *Historical Dictionary of the Central African Republic*. Lanham, MD: Scarecrow Press.

Kantor, Harry. 1969a. The Dominican crisis. In *The Lingering Crisis: A Case Study of the Dominican Republic*, ed. Eugenio Chang Rodríguez, 1–19. New York: Las Americas Publishing.

———. 1969b. *Patterns of Politics and Political Systems in Latin America*. Chicago, Rand McNally.

Kaplan, Robert D. 1989. How Zia's death helped the U.S. *New York Times*, August 23.

Karl, Terry Lynn. 1990. Dilemmas of democratization in Latin America. *Comparative Politics* 23(1): 1–21.

Kasara, Kimuli, and Isabela Mares. 2017. Unfinished business: The democratization of electoral practices in Britain and Germany. *Comparative Political Studies* 50(5): 636–64.

Kawai, Kazuo. 1979. *Japan's American Interlude*. Chicago: University of Chicago Press.

Kaya, Ruchan, and Michael Bernhard. 2013. Are elections mechanisms of authoritarian stability or democratization? Evidence from postcommunist Eurasia. *Perspectives on Politics* 11(3): 734–52.

Keaten, Jamey. 2007. Denard, infamous mercenary and self-styled "pirate," dies at 78. *Associated Press*, October 15.

Kegley, Charles W., Jr., and Margaret G. Hermann. 1997. A peace dividend? Democracies' military interventions and their external political consequences. *Cooperation and Conflict* 32(4): 357–59.

Keita, Kalifa. 1998. Conflict and conflict resolution in the Sahel: The Tuareg insurgency in Mali. *Small Wars & Insurgencies* 9(3): 102–28.

Keller, Bill. 2011. Postscript: F. W. de Klerk responds. *New York Times*, March 4.

Kelley, Judith G. 2012. *Monitoring Democracy: When International Election Observation Works, and Why It Often Fails*. Princeton: Princeton University Press.

Kendall-Taylor, Andrea, and Erica Frantz. 2014. How autocracies fall. *Washington Quarterly* 37(1): 35–47.

———. 2016. When dictators die. *Journal of Democracy* 27(4): 159–71.

Keyserlingk, Robert H. 1988. *Austria in World War II: An Anglo-American Dilemma*. Montreal: McGill-Queen's University Press.

Keyssar, Alexander. 2000. *The Right to Vote: The Contested History of Democracy in the United States*. New York: Basic Books.

Khan, Sharief. 1992. October 5 is the day. *Stabroek News*, August 30.

Kier, Elizabeth, and Ronald R. Krebs, eds. 2010. *In War's Wake: International Conflict and the Fate of Liberal Democracy*. Cambridge: Cambridge University Press.

Kim, Quee-Young. 1996. From protest to change of regime: The 4–19 Revolt and the fall of the Rhee regime in South Korea. *Social Forces* 74(4): 1179–1208.

Kim, Sunhyuk. 2000. *The Politics of Democratization in Korea*. Pittsburgh: University of Pittsburgh Press.

King, Charles. 2001. Potemkin democracy: Four myths about post-Soviet Georgia. *National Interest* 64: 93–104.

Kinzer, Stephen. 1985. After 30 years, Guatemala tests democracy. *New York Times*, December 18.

———. 2006. *Overthrow: America's Century of Regime Change from Hawaii to Iraq*. New York: Times Books.

Klein, Herbert S. 2003/2011. *A Concise History of Bolivia*. 2nd ed. Cambridge: Cambridge University Press.

Kline, Harvey F. 1995. *Colombia: Democracy under Assault*. Boulder, CO: Westview Press.

Klopp, Jacqueline M., and Elke Zuern. 2007. The politics of violence in democratization: Lessons from Kenya and South Africa. *Comparative Politics* 39(2): 127–46.

Knack, Stephen. 2004. Does foreign aid promote democracy? *International Studies Quarterly* 48(1): 251–66.

Knutsen, Carl Henrik, Håvard Mokleiv Nygård, and Tore Wig. 2017. Autocratic elections: Stabilizing tool or force for change? *World Politics* 69(1): 98–143.

Kokole, Omari H., and Ali A. Mazrui. 1988. Uganda: The dual polity and the plural society. In *Democracy in Developing Countries: Africa*, ed. Larry Diamond, Juan J. Linz, and Seymour M. Lipset, 259–98. Boulder, CO: Lynne Rienner.

Kosack, Stephen. 2014. The logic of pro-poor policymaking: Political entrepreneurship and mass education. *British Journal of Political Science* 44(2): 409–44.

Krause, Krystin, and A. Pereira. 2003. Perón returns: Democratic transition in Argentina, 1969–1976. Working paper.

Kremaric, Daniel. 2018. Should I stay or should I go? Leaders, exile, and the dilemmas of international justice. *American Journal of Political Science* 62(2): 486–98.

Kryzanek, Michael J. 1977. Political party decline and the failure of liberal democracy: The PRD in Dominican politics. *Journal of Latin American Studies* 9(1): 115–43.

Kuehn, David. 2017. Midwives or gravediggers of democracy? The military's impact on democratic development. *Democratization* 24(5): 783–800.

Kuenzi, Michelle, and Gina Lambright. 2005. Party systems and democratic consolidation in Africa's electoral regimes. *Party Politics* 11(4): 423–46.

Kumar, Krishna, ed. 1998. *Postconflict Elections, Democratization and International Assistance*. Boulder, CO: Lynne Rienner.

Ladutke, Lawrence Michael. 2004. *Freedom of Expression in El Salvador: The Struggle for Human Rights and Democracy*. Jefferson, NC: McFarland & Company.

LaFeber, Walter. 1989. *The Panama Canal: The Crisis in Historical Perspective*. Updated ed. New York: Oxford University Press.

———. 1993. *Inevitable Revolutions: The United States in Central America*. 2nd ed. New York: Norton.

Langston, Joy K. 2017. *Democratization and Authoritarian Party Survival: Mexico's PRI*. Oxford: Oxford University Press.

Lawson, Chappell H. 2004. Introduction to *Mexico's Pivotal Democratic Election: Candidates, Voters, and the Presidential Campaign of 2000*, ed. Jorge I. Domínguez and Chappell H. Lawson, 1–22. Stanford: Stanford University Press.

Lawton, George A. 1987. Dynamic of missed opportunities. In Binnendijk 1987, 134–42.

Leamer, Edward E. 1985. Sensitivity analyses would help. *American Economic Review* 75(3): 308–13.

Lechner, Michael. 2011. The estimation of causal effects by difference-in-difference methods. *Foundations and Trends in Econometrics* 4(3): 165–224.

Lee, Hong Yung. 1993. South Korea in 1992: A turning point in democratization. *Asian Survey* 33(1): 32–42.

Lee, Jong-Wha, and Hanol Lee. 2016. Human capital in the long run. *Journal of Development Economics* 122: 147–69.

Lehoucq, Fabrice Edouard. 1991. Class conflict, political crisis and the breakdown of democratic practices in Costa Rica: Reassessing the origins of the 1948 Civil War. *Journal of Latin American Studies* 23(1): 37–60.

Lenin, Vladimir. 1920/1966. "Left-wing" Communism: An infantile disorder. In *Lenin: Collected Works, Volume 31*, 17–118. Moscow: Progress Publishers.

Lentz, Harris M. 1988. *Assassinations and Executions: An Encyclopedia of Political Violence, 1865–1986*. London: McFarland and Company.

———. 2013. *Heads of States and Governments*. London: Routledge.

Leonard, Thomas M. 1998. The quest for Central American democracy since 1945. In *Assessing Democracy in Latin America*, ed. Philip Kelly, 93–116. Boulder, CO: Westview Press.

Lerner, Daniel. 1958. *The Passing of Traditional Society*. New York: Free Press.

Levitsky, Steven, and Lucan A. Way. 2010. *Competitive Authoritarianism: Hybrid Regimes After the Cold War*. Cambridge: Cambridge University Press.

———. 2012. Beyond patronage: Violent struggle, ruling party cohesion, and authoritarian durability. *Perspectives on Politics* 10(4): 869–89.

———. 2013. The durability of revolutionary regimes. *Journal of Democracy* 24(3): 5–16.

Lewis, Daniel. K. 2014. *The History of Argentina*. Santa Barbara, CA: ABC-CLIO.

Lewis, Paul H. 2002. *Guerrillas and Generals: The "Dirty War" in Argentina*. Westport, CT: Praeger.

Lichbach, Mark I. 1987. Deterrence or escalation? The puzzle of aggregate studies of repression and dissent. *Journal of Conflict Resolution* 31(2): 266–97.

Lijphart, Arend. 2002. The wave of powersharing democracy. In *The Architecture of Democracy: Constitutional Design, Conflict Management, and Democracy*, ed. Andrew Reynolds, 37–54. Oxford: Oxford University Press.

Likhit, Dhiravegin. 1992. *Demi Democracy: The Evolution of the Thai Political System*. Singapore: Times Academic Press.

Lindberg, Staffan I. 2006. *Democracy and Elections in Africa*. Baltimore: Johns Hopkins University Press.

———, ed. 2009. *Democratization by Elections: A New Mode of Transition*. Baltimore: Johns Hopkins University Press.

Lindert, Peter H. 2004. *Growing Public: Social Spending and Economic Growth since the Eighteenth Century, Volume 1*. Cambridge: Cambridge University Press.

Linz, Juan J., and Alfred Stepan. 1996. *Problems of Democratic Transition and Consolidation: Southern Europe, South America, and Post-Communist Europe*. Baltimore: Johns Hopkins University Press.

Lipset, Seymour M. 1959. Some social requisites of democracy: Economic development and political legitimacy. *American Political Science Review* 53: 69–105.

———. 1960. *Political Man: The Social Bases of Politics*. New York: Doubleday.

———. 1994. The social requisites of democracy revisited: 1993 presidential address. *American Sociological Review* 59(1): 1–22.

Lizzeri, Allesandro, and Nicola Persico. 2004. Why did the West extend the franchise? Democracy and the scope of government with an application to Britain's Age of Reform. *Quarterly Journal of Economics* 119(2): 705–63.

Llavador, Humberto, and Robert J. Oxoby. 2005. Partisan competition, growth, and the franchise. *Quarterly Journal of Economics* 120(3): 1155–89.

Lobban, Richard A., Jr. 1995. *Cape Verde: Crioulo Colony to Independent Nation*. Boulder, CO: Westview Press.

Lohmann, Susanne. 1994. The dynamics of informational cascades: The Monday demonstrations in Leipzig, East Germany, 1989–91. *World Politics* 47(1): 42–101.

Lohr, Steve. 1984. Philippine army: Problems and possibilities. *New York Times*, November 6.

———. 1985. Manila says rebels gained in '84, killing 2,000. *New York Times*, January 10.

Londregan, John B., and Keith T. Poole. 1990. Poverty, the coup trap, and the seizure of executive power. *World Politics* 42(2): 151–83.

Longman, Jeré. 2011. Kim Jong-il, the sportsman. *New York Times*, December 20.

Loxton, James. 2018. Introduction: Authoritarian successor parties worldwide. In *Life after Dictatorship: Authoritarian Successor Parties Worldwide*, ed. James Loxton and Scott Mainwaring, 1–49. Cambridge: Cambridge University Press.

Luebbert, Gregory M. 1991. *Liberalism, Fascism, or Social Democracy: Social Classes and the Political Origins of Regimes in Interwar Europe*. Oxford: Oxford University Press.

Lust-Okar, Ellen. 2006. Elections under authoritarianism: Preliminary lessons from Jordan. *Democratization* 13(3): 456–71.

Lyons, Terrence. 2016. From victorious rebels to strong authoritarian parties: Prospects for post-war democratization. *Democratization* 23(6): 1026–41.

Machin, Ian. 2001. *The Rise of Democracy in Britain, 1830–1918*. London: Palgrave Macmillan.

Madrid, Raúl L. 2019. The partisan path to democracy: Argentina in comparative perspective. *Comparative Political Studies* 52(10): 1535–69.

Maeda, Ko. 2010. Two modes of democratic breakdown: A competing risks analysis of democratic durability. *Journal of Politics* 72(4): 1129–43.

Magaloni, Beatriz. 2006. *Voting for Autocracy: Hegemonic Party Survival and Its Demise in Mexico*. Cambridge: Cambridge University Press.

Mahoney, James. 2001. *The Legacies of Liberalism: Path Dependence and Political Regimes in Central America*. Baltimore: Johns Hopkins University Press.

Mahoney, James, and Richard Snyder. 1999. Rethinking agency and structure in the study of regime change. *Studies in Comparative International Development* 34(3): 3–32.

Mainwaring, Scott, and Aníbal Pérez-Liñán. 2013. *Democracies and Dictatorships in Latin America: Emergence, Survival, and Fall*. New York: Cambridge University Press.

Mainwaring, Scott, and Eduardo J. Viola. 1985. Transitions to democracy: Brazil and Argentina in the 1980s. *Journal of International Affairs* 38(2): 193–219.

Major, John. 1993. *Prize Possession: The United States and the Panama Canal, 1903–1979*. Cambridge: Cambridge University Press.

Major, Solomon. 2012. Timing is everything: Economic sanctions, regime type, and domestic instability. *International Interactions* 38(1): 79–110.

Malloy, James M., and Eduardo Gamarra. 1987. Transition to democracy in Bolivia. In *Authoritarians and Democrats: Regime Transition in Latin America*, ed. James M. Malloy and Mitchell A. Seligson, 93–120. Pittsburgh: University of Pittsburgh Press.

Manglapus, Raul S. 1987. A Philippine view of the U.S. role. In Binnendijk 1987, 308–12.

Manning, Carrie L. 2002. *The Politics of Peace in Mozambique: Post-conflict Democratization, 1992–2000*. Westport, CT: Greenwood Press.

Mansfield, Edward D., and Jack Snyder. 2010. Does war influence democratization? In Kier and Krebs 2010, 23–49.

Maoz, Zeev, and Errol A. Henderson. 2013. The World Religion Dataset, 1945–2010: Logic, estimates, and trends. *International Interactions* 39: 265–91.

Maravall, José María, and Julián Santamaría. 1986. Political change in Spain and the prospects for democracy. In O'Donnell, Schmitter, and Whitehead 1986b, 71–108.

Marcus, Richard R. 2004. Political change in Madagascar: Populist democracy or neopatrimonialism by another name? Institute for Security Studies Papers.

Marcus, Richard R., and Paul Razafindrakoto. 2003. Madagascar: A new democracy? *Current History* 102(664): 215–21.

Marinov, Nikolay, and Hein Goemans. 2014. Coups and democracy. *British Journal of Political Science* 44(4): 799–825.

Marks, Gary. 1992. Rational sources of chaos in democratic transition. *American Behavioral Scientist* 35(4/5): 397–421.

Marquez, Xavier. 2016. *Non-Democratic Politics: Authoritarianism, Dictatorship and Democratization*. London: Macmillan International Higher Education.

Marshall, Monty G., Ted Robert Gurr, and Barbara Harff. 2019. *PITF State Failure Problem Set, 1955–2018*. Vienna, VA: Societal-Systems Research Inc.

Marshall, Monty G., and Keith Jaggers. 2017. Polity IV Project: Political Regime Characteristics and Transitions, 1800–2016. Center for Systemic Peace, George Mason University.

Marshall, Monty G., and Donna Ramsey Marshall. 2018. Coup D'État Events, 1946–2017. Center for Systemic Peace, George Mason University.

Martin, Brian. 2007. *Justice Ignited: The Dynamics of Backfire*. Lanham, MD: Rowman & Littlefield.

Masterson, Daniel M. 1991. *Militarism and Politics in Latin America: Peru from Sanchez Cerro to Sendero Luminoso*. Westport, CT: Greenwood Press.

Mattes, Michaela, Brett Ashley Leeds, and Naoko Matsumura. 2016. Measuring change in source of leader support: The CHISOLS dataset. *Journal of Peace Research* 53(2): 259–67.

Mattlin, Mikael. 2011. *Politicized Society: The Long Shadow of Taiwan's One-Party Legacy.* Copenhagen: NIAS Press.

Mauceri, Philip. 1989. Nine cases of transitions and consolidations. In *Democracy in the Americas: Stopping the Pendulum*, ed. Robert A. Pastor, 204–44. New York: Holmes & Meier.

Maxwell, Kenneth. 1986. Regime overthrow and the prospects for democratic transition in Portugal. In O'Donnell, Schmitter, and Whitehead 1986b, 109–37.

——. 1987. Forces moving the transition. In Binnendijk 1987, 198–203.

——. 1995. *The Making of Portuguese Democracy.* Cambridge: Cambridge University Press.

Mazower, Mark. 1998. *Dark Continent: Europe's Twentieth Century.* New York: Random House.

McClintock, Cynthia. 1999. Peru: Precarious regimes, authoritarian and democratic. In *Democracy in Developing Countries, Volume 4: Latin America*, 2nd ed., ed. Larry Diamond, Juan J. Linz, and Seymour M. Lipset, 309–65. Boulder, CO: Lynne Rienner.

McClintock, Cynthia, and Fabián Vallas. 2003. *The United States and Peru: Cooperation at a Cost.* New York: Routledge.

McFaul, Michael. 2002. The fourth wave of democracy and dictatorship: Noncooperative transitions in the postcommunist world. *World Politics* 54: 212–44.

——. 2010. The missing variable: The "international system" as the link between Third and Fourth Wave models of democratization. In Bunce, McFaul, and Stoner-Weiss 2010, 3–29.

McGrath, Allen. 1996. *The Destruction of Pakistan's Democracy.* Oxford: Oxford University Press.

McKoy, Michael K., and Michael K. Miller. 2012. The patron's dilemma: The dynamics of foreign-supported democratization. *Journal of Conflict Resolution* 56(5): 904–32.

Meiselas, Susan. 1978. National mutiny in Nicaragua. *New York Times*, July 30.

Meyer, David. 2004. Protest and political opportunities. *Annual Review of Sociology* 30: 125–45.

Meyns, Peter. 2002. Cape Verde: An African exception. *Journal of Democracy* 13(3): 153–65.

Miller, Andrew C. 2011. Debunking the myth of the "good" coup d'état in Africa. *African Studies Quarterly* 12(2): 45–70.

Miller, James E. 1983. Taking off the gloves: The United States and the Italian elections of 1948. *Diplomatic History* 7(1): 35–56.

Miller, Michael K. 2012. Economic development, violent leader removal, and democratization. *American Journal of Political Science* 56(4): 1002–20.

——. 2015a. Democratic pieces: Autocratic elections and democratic development since 1815. *British Journal of Political Science* 45: 501–30.

——. 2015b. Elections, information, and policy responsiveness in autocratic regimes. *Comparative Political Studies* 48(6): 691–727.

——. 2016. Democracy by example? Why democracy spreads when the world's democracies prosper. *Comparative Politics* 49(1): 83–116.

——. 2020a. The Autocratic Ruling Parties Dataset: Origins, durability, and death. *Journal of Conflict Resolution* 64(4): 756–82.

——. 2020b. The strategic origins of electoral authoritarianism. *British Journal of Political Science* 50(1): 17–44.

——. 2021. Don't call it a comeback: Autocratic ruling parties after democratization. *British Journal of Political Science* 51(2): 559–83.

Miller, Michael K., Michael Joseph, and Dorothy Ohl. 2018. Are coups really contagious? An extreme bounds analysis of political diffusion. *Journal of Conflict Resolution* 62(2): 410–41.

Millett, Allan Reed. 1968. *The Politics of Intervention: The Military Occupation of Cuba, 1906–1909.* Athens: Ohio State University Press.

Mitchell, Sara McLaughlin, Scott Gates, and Håvard Hegre. 1999. Evolution in democracy-war dynamics. *Journal of Conflict Resolution* 43: 771–92.

Moore, Barrington, Jr. 1966. *Social Origins of Dictatorship and Democracy.* New York: Beacon Press.

Morgan, T. Clifton, Navin Bapat, and Yoshi Kobayashi. 2014. The threat and imposition of sanctions: Updating the TIES dataset. *Conflict Management and Peace Science* 31(5): 541–58.

Morgenbesser, Lee. 2016. *Behind the Façade: Elections under Authoritarianism in Southeast Asia.* Albany: SUNY Press.

Morton, Ella. 2014. Golden statues and mother bread: The bizarre legacy of Turkmenistan's former dictator. *Slate Magazine*, February 6.

Mousseau, Michael, and Yuhang Shi. 1999. A test for reverse causality in the democratic peace relationship. *Journal of Peace Research* 36(6): 639–63.

Mueller, John. 1999. *Capitalism, Democracy, and Ralph's Pretty Good Grocery.* Princeton: Princeton University Press.

Munck, Gerardo L. 1998. *Authoritarianism and Democratization: Soldiers and Workers in Argentina, 1976–1983.* University Park: Pennsylvania State University Press.

———. 2001. The regime question: Theory building in democracy studies. *World Politics* 54(1): 119–44.

Munck, Gerardo L., and Carol Skalnik Leff. 1997. Modes of transition and democratization: South America and Eastern Europe in comparative perspective. *Comparative Politics* 29(3): 343–62.

Mydans, Seth. 2003. Foes of Georgian leader storm into parliament building. *New York Times*, November 23.

Nardulli, Peter F., Michael Martin, Michael Slana, Sina Toosi, and Joseph Bajjalieh. 2013. The Coup D'Etat Project. Cline Center for Democracy, UIUC.

Newitt, Malyn. 2002. Mozambique. In *A History of Postcolonial Lusophone Africa*, ed. Patrick Chabal and David Birmingham, 185–235. Bloomington: Indiana University Press.

Nilsson, Marcus. 2012. Reaping what was sown: Conflict outcome and post–civil war democratization. *Cooperation and Conflict* 47(3): 350–67.

Nomikos, William G., Alexander B. Downes, and Jonathan Monten. 2014. Reevaluating foreign-imposed regime change. *International Security* 38(3): 184–95.

North, Douglass, and Barry Weingast. 1989. Constitutions and commitment: The evolution of institutions governing public choice in seventeenth century England. *Journal of Economic History* 49(4): 803–32.

Nunley, Albert C. 2012. *African Elections Database.* africanelections.tripod.com.

Nzouankeu, Jacques Mariel. 1993. The role of the national conference in the transition to democracy in Africa: The cases of Benin and Mali. *African Issues* 21(1–2): 44–50.

Ober, Josiah. 1993. The Athenian Revolution of 508/7 BC: Violence, authority, and the origins of democracy. In *Cultural Poetics in Archaic Greece*, ed. Leslie Kurke and Carol Dougherty. Cambridge: Cambridge University Press.

O'Donnell, Guillermo A. 1973. *Modernization and Bureaucratic-Authoritarianism: Studies in South American Politics.* Berkeley: University of California Press.

O'Donnell, Guillermo, and Philippe Schmitter. 1986. *Transitions from Authoritarian Rule: Tentative Conclusions about Uncertain Democracies.* Baltimore: Johns Hopkins University Press.

O'Donnell, Guillermo, Philippe Schmitter, and Laurence Whitehead, eds. 1986a. *Transitions from Authoritarian Rule: Latin America*. Baltimore: Johns Hopkins University Press.

———. 1986b. *Transitions from Authoritarian Rule: Southern Europe*. Baltimore: Johns Hopkins University Press.

Oquist, Paul. 1980. *Violence, Conflict, and Politics in Colombia*. New York: Academic Press.

Orenstein, Mitchell. 1998. A genealogy of Communist successor parties in East-Central Europe and the determinants of their success. *East European Politics and Societies* 12: 472–99.

O'Toole, Thomas. 2018. The Central African Republic: Political reform and social malaise. In *Political Reform in Francophone Africa*, ed. John F. Clark and David E. Gardinier, 109–24. London: Routledge.

Owen, John M., IV 2010. *The Clash of Ideas in World Politics: Transnational Networks, States, and Regime Change, 1510–2010*. Princeton: Princeton University Press.

Pace, Eric. 1999. Ernesto Melo Antunes, 66; led 1974 Portuguese coup. *New York Times*, August 16.

Pagan, Adrian. 1984. Econometric issues in the analysis of regressions with generated regressors. *International Economic Review* 25(1): 221–47.

Paige, Jeffery M. 1997. *Coffee and Power: Revolution and the Rise of Democracy in Central America*. Cambridge, MA: Harvard University Press.

Panama City ACAN. 1980. Exiles criticize García Meza government. FBIS-LAM-80-202, October 13.

Parajulee, Ramjee P. 2000. *The Democratic Transition in Nepal*. Lanham, MD: Rowman & Littlefield.

Pasquino, Gianfranco. 1986. The demise of the first fascist regime and Italy's transition to democracy: 1943–1948. In O'Donnell, Schmitter, and Whitehead 1986b, 45–70.

Patterson, Samuel C. 1971. Political leaders and the assassination of President Kennedy. In *Assassination*, ed. Harold Zellner, 269–97. Cambridge: Schenkman.

Paxton, Pamela, Kenneth A. Bollen, Deborah M. Lee, and HyoJoung Kim. 2003. A half-century of suffrage: New data and a comparative analysis. *Studies in Comparative International Development* 38(1): 93–122.

Paxton, Robert O. 2004. *The Anatomy of Fascism*. New York: Random House.

Payne, Anthony, Paul K. Sutton, and Tony Thorndike. 1984. *Grenada: Revolution and Invasion*. London: Croom Helm.

Payne, James L. 1968. *Patterns of Conflict in Colombia*. New Haven: Yale University Press.

Pearcy, Thomas L. 1998. *We Answer Only to God: Politics and the Military in Panama, 1903–1947*. Albuquerque: University of New Mexico Press.

Peceny, Mark. 1999. *Democracy at the Point of Bayonets*. University Park: Pennsylvania State University Press.

Peeler, John A. 1977. *Urbanization and Politics*. Beverly Hills, CA: Sage.

———. 1985. *Latin American Democracies: Colombia, Costa Rica, Venezuela*. Chapel Hill: University of North Carolina Press.

Pei, Minxin. 2013. China: The doomed transitional moment of 1989. In Stoner and McFaul 2013, 378–99.

Pepinsky, Thomas B. 2009. *Economic Crises and the Breakdown of Authoritarian Regimes: Indonesia and Malaysia in Comparative Perspective*. New York: Cambridge University Press.

———. 2014. The institutional turn in comparative authoritarianism. *British Journal of Political Science* 44(3): 631–53.

Peters, Jimi. 1997. *The Nigerian Military and the State*. London: I. B. Tauris.

Pevehouse, Jon C. 2005. *Democracy from Above: Regional Organizations and Democratization.* Cambridge: Cambridge University Press.

Pevsner, Lucille W. 1984. *Turkey's Political Crisis: Background, Perspectives, Prospects.* New York: Praeger.

Phillips, William D., Jr., and Carla Rahn Phillips. 2015. *A Concise History of Spain.* Cambridge: Cambridge University Press.

Phiri, Kings M. 2000. A case of revolutionary change in contemporary Malawi: The Malawi army and the disarming of the Malawi young pioneers. *Journal of Peace, Conflict and Military Studies* 1(1).

Pike, John. 2017. Albanian civil war (1997). www.globalsecurity.org/military/ world/war /albania.htm.

Pimlott, Ben. 1977. Parties and voters in the Portuguese revolution: The elections of 1975 and 1976. *Parliamentary Affairs* 30(1): 35–58.

Pinkney, Robert. 1972. *Ghana under Military Rule, 1966–1969.* London: Methuen.

Pion-Berlin, David, Diego Esparza, and Kevin Grisham. 2014. Staying quartered: Civilian uprisings and military disobedience in the twenty-first century. *Comparative Political Studies* 47(2): 230–59.

Poe, Steven. 2004. The decision to repress: An integrative theoretical approach to the research on human rights and repression. In *Understanding Human Rights Violations: New Systematic Studies,* ed. Sabine Carey and Steven Poe, 16–42. Farnham: Ashgate Press.

Polasky, Janet L. 1992. A revolution for socialist reforms: The Belgian general strike for universal suffrage. *Journal of Contemporary History* 27(3): 449–66.

Pope, Nicole, and Hugh Pope. 2000. *Turkey Unveiled: A History of Modern Turkey.* Woodstock, NY: Overlook Books.

Pop-Eleches, Grigore, and Graeme B. Robertson. 2015. Information, elections, and political change. *Comparative Politics* 47(4): 459–78.

Posada-Carbó, Eduardo, ed. 1996. *Elections before Democracy: The History of Elections in Europe and Latin America.* New York: St. Martin's Press.

Potash, Robert A. 1996. *The Army and Politics in Argentina, 1962–1973: From Frondizi's Fall to the Peronist Restoration.* Stanford: Stanford University Press.

Powell, Charles. 2015. Spain. In Bitar and Lowenthal 2015, 345–52.

Powell, Jonathan. 2012. Determinants of the attempting and outcome of coups d'état. *Journal of Conflict Resolution* 56(6): 1017–40.

———. 2014. An assessment of the "democratic" coup theory: Democratic trajectories in Africa, 1952–2012. *African Security Review* 23(3): 213–24.

Powell, Jonathan M., and Clayton L. Thyne. 2011. Global instances of coups from 1950 to 2010: A new dataset. *Journal of Peace Research* 48(2): 249–59.

Premdas, Ralph R. 1995. *Ethnic Conflict and Development: The Case of Guyana.* Aldershot: Avebury Press.

———. 1999. Recovering democracy: Problems and solutions to the Guyana quagmire. *Pouvoirs dans la Caraïbe* 11: 135–73.

Preston, Paul. 2004. *Juan Carlos: Steering Spain from Dictatorship to Democracy.* New York: W. W. Norton.

Przeworski, Adam. 1988. Democracy as a contingent outcome of conflicts. In *Constitutionalism and Democracy,* ed. Jon Elster and Rune Slagstad, 59–81. Cambridge: Cambridge University Press.

———. 1991. *Democracy and the Market: Political and Economic Reforms in Eastern Europe and Latin America.* Cambridge: Cambridge University Press.

——. 2009a. Conquered or granted? A history of suffrage extensions. *British Journal of Political Science* 39(2): 291–321.

——. 2009b. Constraints and choices: Electoral participation in historical perspective. *Comparative Political Studies* 42(1): 4–30.

——. 2013. *Political Institutions and Political Events (PIPE) Data Set*. sites.google.com/a /nyu.edu/adam-przeworski/home/data.

——. 2015. Acquiring the habit of changing governments through elections. *Comparative Political Studies* 48(1): 101–29.

Przeworski, Adam, José Antonio Cheibub, Michael E. Alvarez, and Fernando Limongi. 2000. *Democracy and Development: Political Institutions and Material Well-being in the World, 1950–1990*. Cambridge: Cambridge University Press.

Przeworski, Adam, and Fernado Limongi. 1997. Modernization: Theories and facts. *World Politics* 49: 155–83.

Raby, David L. 1988. *Fascism and Resistance in Portugal: Communists, Liberals and Military Dissidents in the Opposition to Salazar, 1941–1974*. Manchester: Manchester University Press.

Raeper, William, and Martin Hoftun. 1992. *Spring Awakening: An Account of the 1990 Revolution in Nepal*. New Delhi: Viking Press.

Rakner, Lise, and Nicolas van de Walle. 2009. Democratization by elections? Opposition weakness in Africa. *Journal of Democracy* 20(3): 108–21.

Ramos Pinto, Pedro. 2013. *Lisbon Rising: Urban Social Movements in the Portuguese Revolution, 1974–75*. Manchester: Manchester University Press.

Rapport, Mike. 2009. *1848: Year of Revolution*. New York: Basic Books.

Reilly, Benjamin. 2008. Post-war elections: Uncertain turning points of transition. In *From War to Democracy: Dilemmas of Peacebuilding*, ed. Anna K. Jarstad and Timothy D. Sisk, 157–81. Cambridge: Cambridge University Press.

Reinhart, Carmen M., and Kenneth S. Rogoff. 2011. From financial crash to debt crisis. *American Economic Review* 101(5): 1676–1706.

Reiter, Dan. 2001. Does peace nurture democracy? *Journal of Politics* 63(3): 935–48.

Remmer, Karen L. 1991. Review: New wine or old bottlenecks? The study of Latin American democracy. *Comparative Politics* 23(4): 479–95.

——. 1995. Review: New theoretical perspectives on democratization. *Comparative Politics* 28(1): 103–22.

Remnick, David. 1993. *Lenin's Tomb: The Last Days of the Soviet Empire*. New York: Random House.

Reuter, Ora John, and Jennifer Gandhi. 2010. Economic performance and elite defection from hegemonic parties. *British Journal of Political Science* 41: 83–110.

Reuters. 2013. Mozambique: 1992 peace pact collapses. October 22.

Reyntjens, Filip. 1991. The winds of change. Political and constitutional evolution in Francophone Africa, 1990–1991. *Journal of African Law* 35(1/2): 44–55.

——. 2005. Briefing: Burundi: A peaceful transition after a decade of war? *African Affairs* 105(418): 117–35.

Riding, Alan. 1984. Pastora vows to keep fighting Sandinistas even without U.S. aid. *New York Times*, June 14.

Riedl, Rachel B. 2014. *Authoritarian Origins of Democracy Party Systems in Africa*. Cambridge: Cambridge University Press.

Rigger, Shelley. 2001. *From Opposition to Power: Taiwan's Democratic Progressive Party*. Boulder, CO: Lynne Rienner.

Ring, Trudy, ed. 1995. *International Dictionary of Historic Places: Southern Europe*. Chicago: Fitzroy Dearborn.

Robinson, William Francis. 2012. Panama for the Panamanians: The populism of Arnulfo Arias Madrid. In *Populism in Latin America*, ed. Michael L. Conniff, 184–200. Tuscaloosa: University of Alabama Press.

Rock, David. 1975. *Politics in Argentina, 1890–1930: The Rise and Fall of Radicalism*. Cambridge: Cambridge University Press.

———. 1987. *Argentina, 1516–1987: From Spanish Colonization to Alphonsín*. Berkeley: University of California Press.

Roeder, Philip G. 2001. *Ethnolinguistic Fractionalization (ELF) Indices, 1961 and 1985*. weber.ucsd.edu/~roeder/elf.htm.

Roeder, Philip G., and Donald S. Rothchild, eds. 2005. *Sustainable Peace: Power and Democracy after Civil Wars*. Ithaca: Cornell University Press.

Roessler, Philip G. 2005. Donor-induced democratization and the privatization of state violence in Kenya and Rwanda. *Comparative Politics* 37(2): 207–27.

Roldán, Mary. 2002. *Blood and Fire: La Violencia in Antioquia, Colombia, 1946–1953*. Durham: Duke University Press.

Ropp, Steve C. 1982. *Panamanian Politics: From Guarded Nation to National Guard*. Stanford: Hoover Institution Press.

———. 2000. Panama: Militarism and imposed transition. In Walker and Armony 2000, 111–30.

Ross, Michael L. 2013. *Oil and Gas Data, 1932–2011*. thedata.harvard.edu/dvn/dv/mlross.

Rueschemeyer, Dietrich, Evelyne Huber Stephens, and John D. Stephens. 1992. *Capitalist Development and Democracy*. Cambridge: Polity Press.

Ruhl, J. Mark. 1996. Redefining civil-military relations in Honduras. *Journal of Interamerican Studies and World Affairs* 38(1): 33–66.

Rustow, Dankwart A. 1970. Transitions to democracy: Toward a dynamic model. *Comparative Politics* 2(3): 337–63.

Sala-i-Martin, Xavier X. 1997. I just ran two million regressions. *American Economic Review* 87(2): 178–83.

Sanborn, Howard, and Clayton L. Thyne. 2014. Learning democracy: Education and the fall of authoritarian regimes. *British Journal of Political Science* 44(4): 773–97.

Sanchez, Peter M. 1992. The Dominican case. In Higley and Gunther 1992, 300–22.

Sandbrook, Richard, and Jay Oelbaum. 1999. Reforming the political kingdom: Governance and development in Ghana's Fourth Republic. Working paper, Center for Democracy & Development.

Savada, Andrea Matles, and William Shaw, eds. 1990. *South Korea: A Country Study*. Washington, DC: Library of Congress.

Sawyer, Amos. 2005. *Beyond Plunder: Toward Democratic Governance in Liberia*. Boulder, CO: Lynne Rienner.

Saxer, Carl. 2013. *From Transition to Power Alternation: Democracy in South Korea, 1987–1997*. London: Routledge.

Schedler, Andreas, ed. 2006. *Electoral Authoritarianism: The Dynamics of Unfree Competition*. Boulder, CO: Lynne Rienner.

Scheve, Kenneth, and David Stasavage. 2010. The conscription of wealth: Mass warfare and the demand for progressive taxation. *International Organization* 64(4): 529–61.

Schlaudeman, Harry W. 1987. Fragmentation of power. In Binnendijk 1987, 234–40.

Schlesinger, Stephen, and Stephen Kinzer. 1982. *Bitter Fruit: The Untold Story of the American Coup in Guatemala*. New York: Doubleday.

Schlewitz, Andrew James. 1999. The Rise of a Military State in Guatemala, 1931–1966. PhD diss., New School University.

Schmitt, Reinhold. 2004. Interview with Mr. Lester Bryant Bird, former Prime Minister of Antigua. ISA-GUIDE. www.isa-guide.de/english-news/articles/7540.html.

Schmitter, Philippe C. 1996. The influence of the international context upon the choice of national institutions and policies in neo-democracies. In Whitehead 1996, 26–54.

———. 2010. Twenty-five years, fifteen findings. *Journal of Democracy* 21(1): 17–28.

Schock, Kurt. 2005. *Unarmed Insurrections: People Power Movements in Nondemocracies.* Minneapolis: University of Minnesota Press.

Schoenhals, Kai P., and Richard A. Melanson. 1985. *Revolution and Intervention in Grenada: The New Jewel Movement, the United States, and the Caribbean.* Boulder, CO: Westview Press.

Schulz, Donald E., and Deborah Sundloff Schulz. 1994. *The United States, Honduras, and the Crisis in Central America.* Boulder, CO: Westview Press.

Schumacher, Edward. 1985. Sudan chief announces talks to form a cabinet. *New York Times,* April 11.

Scranton, Margaret E. 1991. *The Noriega Years: U.S.-Panamanian Relations, 1981–1990.* Boulder, CO: Lynne Rienner.

Sebestyen, Victor. 2009. *Revolution 1989: The Fall of the Soviet Empire.* New York: Pantheon Books.

Seeberg, Merete Bech. 2014. State capacity and the paradox of authoritarian elections. *Democratization* 21(7): 1265–85.

———. 2018. Electoral authoritarianism and economic control. *International Political Science Review* 39(1): 33–48.

Seibert, Gerhard. 2002. São Tomé e Príncipe. In *A History of Postcolonial Lusophone Africa,* ed. Patrick Chabal and David Birmingham, 291–315. Bloomington: Indiana University Press.

Seligson, Amber L., and Joshua A. Tucker. 2005. Feeding the hand that bit you: Voting for ex-authoritarian rulers in Russia and Bolivia. *Demokratizatsiya* 13(1): 11–42.

Sengupta, Somini. 2005. Where Maoists still matter. *New York Times,* October 30.

———. 2008. Nepal reborn as a republic. *New York Times,* May 29.

Serra, Gilles. 2013. Demise and resurrection of a dominant party: Understanding the PRI's comeback in Mexico. *Journal of Politics in Latin America* 3: 133–54.

Shannon, Megan, Clayton L. Thyne, Amanda Dugan, and Sarah Hayden. 2015. The international community's reaction to coups. *Foreign Policy Analysis* 11(4): 363–76.

Sharp, Gene. 1973. *The Politics of Nonviolent Action.* Boston: Porter Sargent.

Silverstein, Josef. 1966. Burma: Ne Win's revolution considered. *Asian Survey* 6(2): 95–102.

Singh, Chaitram. 2008. Re-democratization in Guyana and Suriname: Critical comparisons. *European Review of Latin American and Caribbean Studies* 84: 71–85.

Singh, Naunihal. 2014. *Seizing Power: The Strategic Logic of Military Coups.* Baltimore: Johns Hopkins University Press.

Skaaning, Svend-Erik, John Gerring, and Henrikas Bartusevicius. 2015. A lexical index of electoral democracy. *Comparative Political Studies* 48(12): 1491–1525.

Skocpol, Theda. 1979. *States and Social Revolutions: A Comparative Analysis of France, Russia, and China.* Cambridge: Cambridge University Press.

Slater, Dan. 2006. The architecture of authoritarianism: Southeast Asia and the regeneration of democratization theory. *Taiwan Journal of Democracy* 2(2): 1–22.

———. 2010. *Ordering Power: Contentious Politics and Authoritarian Leviathans in Southeast Asia.* Cambridge: Cambridge University Press.

Slater, Dan, and Nicholas Rush Smith. 2016. The power of counterrevolution: Elitist origins of political order in postcolonial Asia and Africa. *American Journal of Sociology* 121(5): 1472–1516.

Slater, Dan, and Joseph Wong. 2013. The strength to concede: Ruling parties and democratization in developmental Asia. *Perspectives on Politics* 11(3): 717–33.

Smith, Benjamin. 2005. Life of the party: The origins of regime breakdown and persistence under single-party rule. *World Politics* 57: 421–51.

Snyder, Richard. 1992. Explaining transitions from neopatrimonial dictatorships. *Comparative Politics* 24(4): 379–99.

Solsten, Eric, ed. 1993. *Portugal: A Country Study*. Washington, DC: Library of Congress.

Sparks, Allister. 1996. *Tomorrow Is Another Country: The Inside Story of South Africa's Road to Change*. Chicago: University of Chicago Press.

Spatz, Benjamin J., and Kai M. Thaler. 2018. Has Liberia turned a corner? *Journal of Democracy* 29(3): 156–70.

Stahler-Sholk, Richard. 1987. Building democracy in Nicaragua. In *Liberalization and Redemocratization in Latin America*, ed. George A. Lopez and Michael Stohl, 57–103. Westport, CT: Greenwood Press.

Starr, Harvey. 1991. Democratic dominoes: Diffusion approaches to the spread of democracy in the international system. *Journal of Conflict Resolution* 35(2): 356–81.

Stepan, Alfred C. 1971. *The Military in Politics: Changing Patterns in Brazil*. Princeton: Princeton University Press.

———. 1988. *Rethinking Military Politics: Brazil and the Southern Cone*. Princeton: Princeton University Press.

———, ed. 1989. *Democratizing Brazil: Problems of Transition and Consolidation*. New York: Oxford University Press.

Stohl, Michael. 1987. *Liberalization and Redemocratization in Latin America*. Westport, CT: Greenwood Press.

Stoner, Kathryn, and Michael McFaul, eds. 2013. *Transitions to Democracy: A Comparative Perspective*. Baltimore: Johns Hopkins University Press.

Streeter, Stephen M. 2000. *Managing the Counterrevolution: The United States and Guatemala, 1954–1961*. Athens: Ohio University Center for International Studies.

Sullivan, John L. 2015. *ETA and Basque Nationalism: The Fight for Euskadi, 1890–1986*. London: Routledge.

Sunar, Ilkay, and Sabri Sayari. 1986. Democracy in Turkey: Problems and prospects. In O'Donnell et al. 1986b, 165–86.

Sundhaussen, Ulf. 2003. Peasants and the process of building democratic polities: Lessons from San Marino. *Australian Journal of Politics & History* 49(2): 211–21.

Sun-Sentinel Wires. 1985. Brazil elects first civilian president in 21 years. *Sun Sentinel*, January 16.

Svolik, Milan. 2012. *The Politics of Authoritarian Rule*. Cambridge: Cambridge University Press.

———. 2015. Which democracies will last? Coups, incumbent takeovers, and the dynamic of democratic consolidation. *British Journal of Political Science* 45(4): 715–38.

Tang, Min, and Dwayne Woods. 2014. Conditional effect of economic development on democracy: The relevance of the state. *Democratization* 21(3): 411–33.

Tansey, Oisín. 2016. The limits of the "democratic coup" thesis: International politics and post-coup authoritarianism. *Journal of Global Security Studies* 1(3): 220–34.

Teele, Dawn L. 2018. How the West was won: Competition, mobilization, and women's enfranchisement in the United States. *Journal of Politics* 80(2): 442–61.

Teorell, Jan. 2010. *Determinants of Democratization: Explaining Regime Change in the World, 1972–2006*. Cambridge: Cambridge University Press.

Teorell, Jan, and Axel Hadenius. 2009. Elections as levers of democratization: A global inquiry. In Lindberg 2009, 77–100.

Thank you Jimmy! 1990. Editorial, *The Mirror*, October 21.

Thomas, Robert. 1999. *The Politics of Serbia in the 1990s*. New York: Columbia University Press.

Thompson, Mark R. 2002. *The Anti-Marcos Struggle: Personalistic Rule and Democratic Transition in the Philippines*. New Haven: Yale University Press.

Thompson, Matthew. 2016. The Smoking Snakes. Mariners' Museum and Park blog. www .marinersmuseum.org/blog/2016/03/the-smoking-snakes.

Thyne, Clayton L., and Jonathan M. Powell. 2016. Coup d'état or coup d'autocracy? How coups impact democratization, 1950–2008. *Foreign Policy Analysis* 12(2): 192–213.

Thyne, Clayton, Jonathan Powell, Sarah Parrott, and Emily VanMeter. 2018. Even generals need friends: How domestic and international reactions to coups influence regime survival. *Journal of Conflict Resolution* 62(7): 1406–32.

Ticchi, Davide, and Andrea Vindigni. 2008. War and endogenous democracy. Working paper.

Tilly, Charles. 1978. *From Mobilization to Revolution*. Reading, MA: Addison-Wesley.

———. 1990. *Coercion, Capital and European States, AD 990–1992*. Cambridge: Blackwell.

———. 2004. *Contention and Democracy in Europe, 1650–2000*. Cambridge: Cambridge University Press.

Toft, Monica Duffy. 2010. Ending civil wars: A case for rebel victory? *International Security* 34(4): 7–36.

Toland, John. 2003. *The Rising Sun: The Decline and Fall of the Japanese Empire, 1936–1945*. New York: Modern Library.

Traore, Amadou. 1991. A mudança—change. *The Courier* 127: 10–11.

Treisman, Daniel. 2015. Income, democracy, and leader turnover. *American Journal of Political Science* 59(4): 927–42.

Trejo, Guillermo. 2012. *Popular Movements in Autocracies: Religion, Repression, and Indigenous Collective Action in Mexico*. New York: Cambridge University Press.

Trinkunas, Harold A. 2011. *Crafting Civilian Control of the Military in Venezuela: A Comparative Perspective*. Chapel Hill: University of North Carolina Press.

Tripp, Ali Mari. 2010. *Museveni's Uganda: Paradoxes of Power in a Hybrid Regime*. Boulder, CO: Lynne Rienner.

Trithart, Albert. 2013. Democratic coups? Regional responses to the constitutional crises in Honduras and Niger. *Journal of Public and International Affairs* 24: 112–33.

Trumbull, Robert. 1960. Korea city in grip of fear and fury. *New York Times*, April 14.

Tuchman, Barbara W. 1978. *A Distant Mirror: The Calamitous 14th Century*. New York: Alfred A. Knopf.

Tucker, Joshua A. 2007. Enough! Electoral fraud, collective action problems, and post-communist colored revolutions. *Perspectives on Politics* 5(3): 535–51.

Tusalem, Rollin F. 2014. Bringing the military back in: The politicisation of the military and its effect on democratic consolidation. *International Political Science Review* 35(4): 482–501.

Tzortzis, Ioannis. 2003. The Metapolitefsi that never was: A re-evaluation of the 1973 "Markezinis experiment." Working paper, Hellenic Observatory, London School of Economics.

UCDP. 2017. *UCDP/PRIO Armed Conflict Dataset, Version 18.1*. Oslo: Centre for the Study of Civil Wars, International Peace Research Institute.

Ulfelder, Jay. 2005. Contentious collective action and the breakdown of authoritarian regimes. *International Political Science Review* 26(3): 311–34.

UN. 1992. General peace agreement for Mozambique. peacemaker.un.org/mozambique -general-peace-agreement92.

———. 2006. Comprehensive peace agreement between the government of Nepal and the Communist Party of Nepal (Maoist). peacemaker.un.org/nepal-comprehensive agreement2006.

UNESCO. 2015. *UNESCO Institute for Statistics*. uis.unesco.org.

UNU-WIDER. 2005. *World Income Inequality Database, Version 2.0a*. www.wider.unu.edu.

UPI. 1985. Abdul Rahman Swar Al-Dahab Sudan's new military leader. *United Press International Archives*, April 6.

U.S. aides see Sudan coup as "pre-emptive" move. 1985. *New York Times*, April 9.

Vandeginste, Stef. 2009. Power-sharing, conflict and transition in Burundi: Twenty years of trial and error. *Africa Spectrum* 44(3): 63–86.

van der Laarse, Robert. 2000. Bearing the stamp of history: The elitist route to democracy in the Netherlands. In *European Democratization since 1800*, ed. John Garrard, Vera Tolz, and Ralph White, 50–75. New York: St. Martin's Press.

Vander Linden, Herman. 1920. *Belgium: The Making of a Nation*. Oxford: Clarendon Press.

VanderWeele, Tyler. 2015. *Explanation in Causal Inference: Methods for Mediation and Interaction*. Oxford: Oxford University Press.

van de Walle, Nicolas. 2006. Tipping games: When do opposition parties coalesce? In *Electoral Authoritarianism: The Dynamics of Unfree Competition*, ed. Andreas Schedler, 77–92. Boulder, CO: Lynne Rienner.

Varol, Ozan O. 2012. The democratic coup d'état. *Harvard International Law Journal* 53: 291–356.

———. 2017. *The Democratic Coup D'État*. New York: Oxford University Press.

Veenendaal, Wouter. 2015. *Politics and Democracy in Microstates*. London: Routledge.

Veigel, Klaus Friedrich. 2010. *Dictatorship, Democracy, and Globalization: Argentina and the Cost of Paralysis, 1973–2001*. State College: Pennsylvania State University Press.

Villalón, Leonardo A., and Abdourahmane Idrissa. 2005. Repetitive breakdowns and a decade of experimentation: Institutional choices and unstable democracy in Niger. In *The Fate of Africa's Democratic Experiments: Elites and Institutions*, ed. Leonardo A. Villalón and Peter VonDoepp, 27–48. Bloomington: Indiana University Press.

von Borzyskowski, Inken, and Felicity Vabulas. 2019. Credible commitments? Explaining IGO suspensions to sanction political backsliding. *International Studies Quarterly* 63(1): 139–52.

von Soest, Christian, and Michael Wahman. 2015. Not all dictators are equal: Coups, fraudulent elections, and the selective targeting of democratic sanctions. *Journal of Peace Research* 52(1): 17–31.

Waldner, David, and Ellen Lust. 2018. Unwelcome change: Coming to terms with democratic backsliding. *Annual Review of Political Science* 21: 5.1–5.21.

Walesa, Lech. 1994. *The Struggle and the Triumph: An Autobiography*. New York: Arcade.

Walker, Thomas W. 2000. Nicaragua: Transition through revolution. In Walker and Armony 2000, 67–88.

Walker, Thomas W., and Ariel C. Armony, eds. 2000. *Repression, Resistance, and Democratic Transition in Central America*. Wilmington, DE: Scholarly Resources.

Wantchekon, Leonard. 2004. The paradox of "warlord" democracy: A theoretical investigation. *American Political Science Review* 98(1): 17–33.

Wantchekon, Leonard, and Zvika Neeman. 2002. A theory of post–civil war democratization. *Journal of Theoretical Politics* 14(4): 439–64.

Way, Lucan A. 2008. The real causes of the Color Revolutions. *Journal of Democracy* 19(3): 55–69.

———. 2015. *Pluralism by Default: Weak Autocrats and the Rise of Competitive Politics*. Baltimore: Johns Hopkins University Press.

Weaver, Frederick Stirton. 1994. *Inside the Volcano: The History and Political Economy of Central America*. Boulder, CO: Westview Press.

Wedeen, Lisa. 1999. *Ambiguities of Domination: Politics, Rhetoric, and Symbols in Contemporary Syria*. Chicago: University of Chicago Press.

Weinberg, Samantha. 1994. *Last of the Pirates: The Search for Bob Denard*. London: Random House.

Wejnert, Barbara. 2005. Diffusion, development, and democracy, 1800–1999. *American Sociological Review* 70(1): 53–81.

Wells, Henry. 1966. Turmoil in the Dominican Republic. *Current History* 50(293): 14–21.

Welt, Cory. 2010. Georgia's Rose Revolution: From regime weakness to regime collapse. In Bunce et al. 2010, 155–88.

Werlich, David P. 1978. *Peru: A Short History*. Carbondale: Southern Illinois University Press.

Weyland, Kurt. 2010. The diffusion of regime contention in European democratization, 1830–1940. *Comparative Political Studies* 43(8/9): 1148–76.

———. 2014. *Making Waves: Democratic Contention in Europe and Latin America since the Revolutions of 1848*. Cambridge: Cambridge University Press.

Wheeler, Douglas L. 1972. The Portuguese Revolution of 1910. *Journal of Modern History* 44(2): 172–94.

———. 1978. *Republican Portugal: A Political History, 1910–1926*. Madison: University of Wisconsin Press.

Whitehead, Laurence. 1986. Bolivia's failed democratization, 1977–1980. In O'Donnell, Schmitter, and Whitehead 1986a, 49–71.

———. 1996. Three international dimensions of democratization. In *The International Dimensions of Democratization: Europe and the Americas*, ed. Laurence Whitehead, 3–25. Oxford: Oxford University Press.

Wiarda, Howard J., and Michael J. Kryzanek. 1992. *The Dominican Republic: A Caribbean Crucible*. 2nd ed. Boulder, CO: Westview Press.

Wig, Tore, and Espen Geelmuyden Rød. 2016. Cues to coup plotters: Elections as coup triggers in dictatorships. *Journal of Conflict Resolution* 60(5): 787–812.

Williams, Philip J. 1994. Dual transitions from authoritarian rule: Popular and electoral democracy in Nicaragua. *Comparative Politics* 26(2): 169–85.

Witte, Els, Jan Craeybeckx, and Alain Meynen. 2009. *Political History of Belgium: From 1830 Onwards*. Brussels: Academic and Scientific Publishers NV.

Wittig, Katrin. 2016. Politics in the shadow of the gun: Revisiting the literature on "Rebel-to-party transformations" through the case of Burundi. *Civil Wars* 18(2): 137–59.

Wobig, Jacob. 2015. Defending democracy with international law: Preventing coup attempts with democracy clauses. *Democratization* 22(4): 631–54.

Wong, Joseph. 2008. Maintaining KMT dominance: Party adaptation in authoritarian and democratic Taiwan. In Friedman and Wong 2008, 57–74.

Woo, Jongseok. 2017. South Korean democratization. In *Politics in North and South Korea: Political Development, Economy, and Foreign Relations*, ed. Yangmo Ku, Inyeop Lee, and Jongseok Woo, 29–48. London: Routledge.

Wood, Elizabeth Jean. 2000. *Forging Democracy from Below: Insurgent Transitions in South Africa and El Salvador*. Cambridge: Cambridge University Press.

———. 2003. *Insurgent Collective Action and Civil War in El Salvador*. Cambridge: Cambridge University Press.

Woodberry, Robert D. 2012. The missionary roots of liberal democracy. *American Political Science Review* 106(2): 244–74.

Woodward, Peter. 1990. *Sudan, 1898–1989: The Unstable State*. Boulder, CO: Lynne Rienner.

World Bank. 2017. *World Development Indicators (WDI)*. www.worldbank.org/data.

Wright, Joseph, and Abel Escribà-Folch. 2012. Authoritarian institutions and regime survival: Transitions to democracy and subsequent autocracies. *British Journal of Political Science* 42(2): 283–309.

Wu, Jaushieh Joseph. 1995. *Taiwan's Democratization: Forces behind the New Momentum.* Oxford: Oxford University Press.

Wurfel, David. 1988. *Filipino Politics: Development and Decay.* Ithaca: Cornell University Press.

Yashar, Deborah J. 1997. *Demanding Democracy: Reform and Reaction in Costa Rica and Guatemala, 1870s–1950s.* Stanford: Stanford University Press.

Yates, Lawrence A. 1988. *Power Pack: U.S. Intervention in the Dominican Republic, 1965–1966.* Fort Leavenworth, KS: Combat Studies Institute, U.S. Army Command and General Staff College.

Yukawa, Taku, Kaori Kushima, and Kaoru Hidaka. 2019. Coups, justification, and democracy. OSIPP Discussion Paper DP-2019-E-03.

Zak, Paul J., and Yi Feng. 2003. A dynamic theory of the transition to democracy. *Journal of Economic Behavior & Organization* 52: 1–25.

Zeldin, Theodore. 1958. *The Political System of Napoleon III.* London: MacMillan.

Ziblatt, Daniel. 2017. *Conservative Political Parties and the Birth of Modern Democracy in Europe.* Cambridge: Cambridge University Press.

Zimbalist, Andrew, and John Weeks. 1991. *Panama at the Crossroads: Economic Development and Political Change in the Twentieth Century.* Berkeley: University of California Press.

Zin, Min. 2016. Burma votes for change: The new configuration of power. *Journal of Democracy* 27(2): 116–31.

1848 revolutions, 3, 18, 44, 182, 215, 243, 251. *See also* France

1989 revolutions. *See* Soviet Union, collapse of; Soviet Union, and withdrawal from Eastern Europe

actor-based school. *See* agency

Afghanistan, 101, 122, 129, 137, 185

agency: and democratization, 12, 23, 71, 80, 145, 231, 247; versus structure, 2, 13–14, 245

Albania, 261–62; civil conflict in, 96, 98, 102, 109n, 262; Communism in, 137n

Algeria, 57, 158, 185–86, 251

Antigua and Barbuda, 153, 262; elections in, 153, 166n34

Arab Spring, ix, 18, 44, 182, 215, 243, 245, 251. *See also* Egypt; Tunisia

Argentina, 35n14, 53, 86–87, 162, 220, 263–64; coups in, 82–85; elections in, 153, 162; and Falklands War, 3, 30, 124; military, 45, 60–61, 86–87, 131; political violence in, 61, 84, 98, 112n53

Armenia, 42, 186, 228, 251

assassinations, 19, 34, 47, 51–52, 61, 192n3, 234, 243, 248; coding of, 31, 35, 191, 258; and democratization, 114–21, 189, 196

Athens. *See* Greece, ancient

Austria, 264–65; and World War I, 123, 129, 131n; and World War II, 134, 139

autocracy: beliefs in, 40–41, 43–44, 52–53, 75, 117, 157–74; elections in (*see* electoral authoritarianism); stability of, 4–5, 39–47, 62–63, 182–87, 203–7

autogolpes. *See* coups, self-coups

Bangladesh, 265–66; coups in, 67n7, 80–83; democratic potential of, 228, 249n; elections in, 83, 169; military, 41, 57, 75–76, 172; protest in, 56, 75–76; repression in, 56

Belgium, 266; elections in, 162; protest in, 154, 156

Benin, 33, 34n, 266; elections in, 33, 166n34; protest in, 154

Bolivia, 3, 57, 88–90; coups in, 54, 61, 73, 88–90, 247; former dictators in, 146, 169; military, 73–74; MNR, 88–89

Brazil, 78, 169–70, 176, 178, 249; coups in, 67n7, 78, 80; democracy literature and, 19, 179; elections in, 33, 40, 57, 159, 169–70, 180; military, 169; protest in, 3, 43, 56–57; and World War II, 124

Bulgaria, 134, 137, 162n28, 267

Burma, 184, 268; civil war in, 98, 108n48, 111; coups in, 70n12, 82–83, 111; elections in, 158, 184; failed liberalization in, 184, 187; military, 43, 57, 184; protest in, ix, 43, 215

Burundi, 110–11; civil war in, 98, 100, 109–11

Cameroon, 42, 185

Cape Verde, 19, 165; Soviet collapse and, 48, 151

causal inference, 21–23, 191–93, 195–203, 210–11, 217

Central African Republic, 172, 176, 179–80, 184

Chad, 185–86

Chile, 178–80, 255, 257, 268–70; elections in, 148n

China, 184, 228; Chinese Revolution, 108, 123, 131; repression in, 42, 135; stability of, 108, 184, 215, 249n; Tiananmen Square protests, 18, 184, 245

civil wars, 17, 20, 31, 65, 68, 96, 126n8, 156, 171, 186, 232n, 243, 247, 250; coding of, 31, 35, 103, 191, 258–59; and democratization, 14, 24, 96–114, 189, 196–97; effects of, 21, 47, 49–52, 54, 100–103, 124, 234–35; motives for, 98, 144, 158; settlements, 82, 99–100, 109–11, 121

coercion. *See* repression

Cold War, 19, 28, 38, 40n20, 76, 96, 110, 128, 142, 150–52, 201–4. *See also* Soviet Union; United States

Colombia, 85–86, 270; civil war in, 98, 109; coups in, 70n12, 85–86, 101; elections in, 153, 162; protest in, 75

Color Revolutions, 154, 182. *See also* Georgia; Serbia

Communism. *See* Marxism

Comoros, 84, 87–88; civil war in, 98, 109

Costa Rica, 107, 271; civil war in, 68, 80, 98, 107

coups, 1–3, 30–31, 35–38, 40, 43, 51n28, 61, 114–15, 184, 186–87, 209, 230, 250; coding of, 30–31, 35, 66–68, 77, 191, 258; and democratization, 14, 17–18, 20, 48, 66–96, 195–96, 246–48; effects of, 47, 52–54, 57, 62–63, 70–77, 181, 189, 232n, 233–35, 243; motives for, 41, 50–51, 53, 69–70, 77, 80, 82–85, 101, 111, 144; self-coups, 30–31, 66n5, 68, 81, 84, 88, 107, 121, 231, 265, 274, 277, 284, 286, 294, 297, 304, 308

Croatia, 220, 271; civil war in, 98, 103; elections in, 152, 156; natural death of dictator in, 152, 181

Cuba, 168–69, 272; American intervention in, 67, 83; coups in, 73, 82, 168

Cyprus, 35n14, 255, 272–73; coup in, 67n8, 131; war in, 98, 123–24, 131, 280

Czechoslovakia, 56, 62n, 273; Communism in, 43, 134; elections in, 169n39

de Klerk, F. W., 59, 152n

democracy, 3–4, 26–28, 251; coding of, 26–28, 39, 203, 255–56; erosion of, 231, 233, 249, 251; future of, 249–51; quality of, 231–34, 236–40; trends in, 28–29, 249–50 (*see also* waves)

democracy promotion, 18, 100, 109, 122, 155, 200, 247–49, 257–58, 261; as foreign aid conditionality, 44–45, 54, 76, 101–2, 106, 122, 155, 167, 172, 185, 257; sanctions, 211–14

democratic survival, 3, 12, 230–40, 247–51

democratization: cases of, 2–3, 18–19, 26–29, 39, 179–80, 249–51, 253–56, 261–309; empirical testing of, 18–23, 190–93, 199–201, 210–11, 215–17, 246–47; international influence on, 122–23, 245 (*see also* democracy promotion; foreign-imposed regime change; hegemons; wars); theories on, 3–4, 13–18, 178–80, 241–44

Denmark, 255, 273; coding of, 33n, 134n, 255; electoral reform in, 148, 153, 160n

dictatorship. *See* autocracy

Dominican Republic, 22, 49, 71, 118; assassination of Rafael Trujillo, 22, 71, 115–18; political instability in, 52, 57, 73, 186

Eanes, António Ramalho, 2, 61, 95–96

East Germany, 134

economic crisis, 10–11, 15, 17, 48, 51–52, 100–102, 131, 150–53, 157, 179–82, 192, 198–99, 221–24, 233, 240

economic development, 11, 13, 62, 191, 204, 217–18, 237, 238n, 260; contingent effects of, 69, 130, 181n6, 209, 217–23, 227–28, 243

Ecuador, 172, 274–75; coups in, 54, 57, 76, 85; protest in, 84, 121; war in, 124

education, 13, 200, 210, 221–23, 226, 240, 251, 261

Egypt, 71, 118, 157, 186–87

electoral authoritarianism, 18, 45, 57, 141–47, 231–34, 248–51; effect on democratization, 144–45, 149, 157–71, 180, 197–98; history of, 141–43; protest in, 154–55, 164–65, 172–73, 209, 211–15; triggers in, 48, 150–54; violent opposition in, 156–57. *See also* electoral continuity; ruling parties

electoral continuity, 1–2, 6–8, 20, 23, 33–39, 141–74, 184–85, 190, 193–95, 201–7, 209–15, 225–27, 234–40, 248–51; coding of, 32–33, 35, 259; definition of, 32–33, 147–48; theory on, 48–49, 60–62, 150–59, 232–34. *See also* electoral authoritarianism; ruling parties

El Salvador, 44, 131–33, 158n21, 275–76; civil war in, 54, 98, 100–102, 111–12; coups in, 84–85; elections in, 168; foreign intervention in, 129; protest in, 33, 54, 102

England, 65, 125–26. *See also* United Kingdom

European Union, 76, 234, 294

Fiji, 28, 169, 276; coups in, 84–85

foreign-imposed regime change (FIRCs), 122, 128, 186, 199. *See also* United States, interventions by

France, 28, 65, 132, 173, 179–80, 182, 276–77; coding of, 27n3, 255; Franco-Prussian

War, 24, 123–24, 124n4, 132; French Revolution, 65, 108n47, 123, 131; medieval era, 126–27; protest in, 179–80; and World War II, 123, 129, 134, 136, 139

Fujimori, Alberto, 146n7, 179, 297–98. *See also* Peru

Gambia, 300; coding of, 39, 256

Georgia, 176–77; elections in, 40, 154, 157; elite disagreement in, 40–41, 176–77, 181; protest in, 154, 177, 180, 182

Germany, 39, 123n2, 158n21, 256, 265, 277–78; East Germany, 134; and World War I, 54, 123, 124n4, 128, 131n, 132, 264; and World War II, 32, 122, 133, 139–40, 280

Ghana, 163–64, 278–79; coups in, 82–83; elections in, 152, 158, 162–64; international influence on, 155, 163–64. *See also* Rawlings, Jerry

Gorbachev, Mikhail, 137–39

Greece, 3, 181, 272, 279–80; ancient, 64, 142n; coups in, 61, 67n7, 82–85, 85nn31 and 33; protest in, 84; war in, 124, 279–80; and World War II, 123, 129, 280

Grenada, 123–24, 129

Guatemala, 57, 59n, 247, 281–83; assassinations in, 114–15, 117; civil wars in, 98, 101, 111–12; coups in, 67, 71, 73, 75, 80, 85; protest in, 84; ruling party in, 168–69

Guinea-Bissau, 185–86, 283; revolution in, 91; ruling party in, 162–63; and Soviet collapse, 48, 151

Guyana, 152, 167; coding of, 33, 147; natural death of dictator in, 152, 181

Haiti, 142, 184–86, 249n

Havel, Václav, 43, 273

hegemons, 24, 32, 47, 51–52, 122, 235, 243; coding of, 32, 35, 133, 191, 259; withdrawal and democratization, 133–40, 189, 196. *See also* Germany; Soviet Union

Honduras, 132–33, 283–85; coups in, 54, 66n5, 67n7, 76, 82–83, 85, 182; military in, 169n38; natural death of dictator in, 181; ruling party in, 145; war in, 122–24, 128, 131–33

Hungary, 134, 137, 220, 249, 285; Soviet period in, 134, 136–37, 187

Indonesia, 59, 61, 108, 152, 285–87; civil wars in, 98, 108–9, 156; protest in, 154, 156; ruling party in, 57, 145, 159, 162n28, 165; stability in, 43, 71, 186

Iran, ix, 186, 215, 249n

Iraq, 101, 122, 129, 184, 186, 247

Ireland, 108, 114; coding of, 39, 256

Italy: and World War I, 123, 128, 132, 287; and World War II, 30, 32, 123, 129–30, 136, 139–40

Japan, 130–31; elections in, 141; occupations by, 122, 298; and World War II, 32, 38n, 123, 129–31, 140

Kenya, 179, 287–88; ruling party in, 40, 169n39, 176, 179–81

Kim, Jong-il, 43

King Juan Carlos I, 61, 119–20

Latvia, 133, 136, 288; coding of, 27n4

Lebanon, 249n, 288–89; civil war in, 98

Lesotho, 73, 289; ruling party in, 145, 168n36

Liberia, 185, 246, 289; civil war in, 31, 98, 107, 289; elections in, 142

Libya, 101, 186

Lithuania, 133, 136, 289–90; coding of, 27n4; ruling party in, 162n28

Luxembourg: coding of, 39, 256n4

Madagascar, 172–74; protest in, 154, 156, 172; repression in, 56, 156; ruling party in, 57, 166, 172–74

Malawi, 56, 290; ruling party in, 152, 158, 166n34

Malaysia, 246, 251

Maldives, 152, 169, 290–91; ruling party in, 158, 162n28, 182

Mali, 52, 56, 75, 78; civil war in, 98, 111–12; coup in, 78–80

Marcos, Ferdinand, 51, 53n, 112–14, 169. *See also* Philippines

Marxism, 92–95, 129, 133–36, 171n40, 234, 266, 269; parties, 48, 52, 110, 142, 150–52, 159, 262, 267, 273, 277, 285, 288, 290–91, 299 (*see also* ruling parties); rebel movements, 51, 98, 101, 104–8, 112–14, 178–79, 278, 280, 285–86, 292–93, 302, 304–5. *See also* Soviet Union

mediation analysis, 210–27

Mexico, 7, 19, 150, 152, 156–57, 246; opposition in, 40, 156–57; ruling party in, 57, 147, 150, 157, 165–66, 203n

migration, 91, 132

military dictatorships, 30, 44–46, 66–67, 69n11, 71–74, 84–85, 112–14, 117–20, 130–31, 168–70, 184, 192n2, 193, 204, 221–24, 234, 259–60

modernization theory, 217–8; contingent effects of, 11, 210, 220–23, 226, 251. *See also* economic development; education

monarchies, 33n, 65n4, 78–79, 107, 117, 119, 121, 125–27, 132, 139, 154, 183–84, 249n, 259

Mongolia, 133, 137–38, 291; ruling party in, 162n28; Soviet period in, 134, 136, 137n

Mozambique, 91, 100, 110, 152; civil war in, 24, 96, 98, 102, 109–10, 156; ruling party in, 162n28, 233

Myanmar. *See* Burma

Namibia, 185

NATO, 54, 96, 102, 124, 234

natural disasters, 152, 182

Nazi Germany. *See* Germany, and World War II

Nepal, 35n14, 179, 182, 184, 246, 292–93; assassination in, 114–17, 121; civil war in, 98, 100, 102, 104, 107–9

Netherlands, 108, 293, 304; ruling party in, 148, 153, 162, 174

Nicaragua, 22, 52, 104–7, 121, 182; civil war in, 31, 54, 98, 102, 104–6; ruling party in, 168n36, 233, 249

Niger, ix, 293–94; assassination in, 114–15, 117; coups in, 54, 66n5, 84; natural death of dictator in, 154, 181; ruling parties in, 156, 165–66

Nigeria, 35n14, 109, 120, 251; assassination in, 114–17, 120; civil war in, 98, 108n48; coding of, 27, 256; coups in, 82–83

oil dependence, 200, 217, 221–23, 226–28, 240, 246, 251, 260

Pakistan, 62n, 117–18, 295; assassination in, 24, 35n15, 114–15, 117–18; civil war in, 98, 101, 111, 112n52; coding of, 39, 256; ruling party in, 112n52, 169n39

Panama, 81–82, 129; coding of, 28n6, 82n29, 114n, 255; coups in, 30, 66, 80–82, 84; natural death of dictator in, 81, 181; ruling party in, 168n36; war in, 123–24, 129

Paraguay, 152, 154, 186, 296; ruling party in, 162, 296

paths, 2–3, 6–8, 19–21, 29–39, 47–62, 188–90, 209–10, 224–28, 232–34, 242–43, 249–51. *See also* electoral continuity; shocks

Peru, 176–81, 274, 296–98; coups in, 45n, 75, 80–81, 85, 177; ruling party in, 146n7, 169n39, 176

Philippines, 112–14, 249, 298; civil war in, 24, 51, 98, 101–2, 111–14; protest in, 41, 53n, 54, 57, 112–14, 154; ruling party in, 146n6, 157, 159, 169, 172; and World War II, 123, 129–30, 298

Poland, 19, 137–39, 249; protest in, 100, 138; ruling party in, 147, 159, 165n32, 166; and Soviet collapse, 24, 136–39; Soviet period in, 59, 134, 138

Portugal, 1–2, 22, 59, 62n, 65, 78–79, 90–96; assassination in, 114–15, 117; coups in, 29, 77–80, 85, 90–91, 95–96, 247; military in, 74, 231; protest in, 79, 84, 93–94; significance to theory, 19, 85, 90

protest, 19, 34n10, 40–43, 183–84, 228, 240, 260; and democratization, 2, 11, 14–15, 18, 59, 179–80, 198, 209, 213–15, 243, 245, 247, 257–58; electoral, 48, 144, 152–55, 163–65, 170–74, 211–13, 233; failed cases of, ix, 5, 10, 39, 44, 182, 215, 243; shocks and, 53–55, 71, 75–76, 80, 84, 101–2, 111–12, 209, 211–13; waves of, 152, 182

Qatar, 186

Rawlings, Jerry, 155, 164

regime strength, 4–5, 16–17, 23, 40–44, 62–63, 183–87, 203–7; as confounder, 22, 199–201; effect of shocks, 49–63, 71–74, 100–101, 116–18, 131–32, 135–36, 233–34

repression: capacity for, 16–17, 41–44, 100–103, 131–32, 136, 183–84, 199–200, 223–24; dangers of, 51–53, 56–57, 75–76, 157–58 revolutions, 5, 8, 15, 40–41, 43, 46, 54–55, 62, 65, 88, 103–8, 122, 129, 131–32, 156, 186, 190, 198, 243, 260, 285, 292. *See also* civil wars

Romania, 57, 134, 299; and Soviet collapse, 137, 151

ruling parties, 6–7, 10, 45, 48–49, 57, 142–45, 150–52, 157–74, 184–85, 189–90, 193–95, 198–207, 209, 219–28; coding of, 32–33, 35, 259–60; after democratization, 45, 61–62, 145–47, 232–40, 249–51. *See also* electoral authoritarianism; electoral continuity; Marxism, parties

Russia, 144, 176–77, 186, 228, 256; Russian Revolution, 108n47, 122, 131, 156. *See also* Soviet Union

Sandinistas. *See* Nicaragua, civil war in

San Marino, 19, 123, 128, 130, 134, 139–40

São Tomé and Príncipe, 151, 166–67

Saudi Arabia, 59, 183, 186

self-coups. *See* coups, self-coups

Senegal, 62n, 300; civil war in, 98, 111–12; ruling party in, 169n39, 171n42, 203n

Serbia, 41, 52, 101–2, 124, 172, 186; civil war in, 98, 101–3; protest in, 54, 102, 154, 171, 177; ruling party in, 169n39, 184

shocks, 2–3, 6–8, 10–11, 16–23, 33–39, 47–49, 185–87, 233–35, 237–40, 246–49; coding of, 34–35, 191–92, 258–59; definitions of, 30–32, 180–82; and democratization, 49–63, 189–90, 193–203, 209, 211–28, 242–44, 249–51. *See also* assassinations; civil wars; coups; hegemons; wars

Sierra Leone, 108–9, 168n36, 186, 246; civil war in, 96, 98, 102, 108–9

Singapore, ix, 144, 185, 228, 246

Skocpol, Theda, 15, 54–55

Solidarity, 100, 138–39, 159

Solomon Islands, 98, 301

South Africa, 15, 19, 45, 102, 109–10, 152, 170–71, 182; elite split in, 178–81; opposition in, 15, 101, 176n2; ruling party in, 169n39, 170–71, 176, 184. *See also* de Klerk, F. W.

South Korea, 71, 114n, 155, 164–65, 176, 181; military in, 45, 172, 187; protest in, 56, 154, 164–65, 171, 180; repression in, 56–57; ruling parties in, 145, 152, 162, 164

Soviet Union: collapse of, 3, 8, 11, 17, 24, 29, 35, 38, 48, 52, 133–34, 136, 150–52, 157, 179–80, 185, 234, 247, 251; interventions in client states, 32, 122, 128, 137; and withdrawal from Eastern Europe, 136–39, 182. *See also* Russia

Spain, 22, 59n, 65, 76, 79, 118–21, 171n41, 181, 184, 186, 220, 301–2; assassination in, 24, 114–20; civil war in, 98, 111; coups in, 84, 302. *See also* King Juan Carlos I

Sri Lanka, 165n32, 302; civil war in, 98, 102, 111n, 156, 302; coding of, 114n, 255

state collapse, 8, 48, 52, 122, 185–86, 259–60

structure: versus agency, 2, 13–14, 245; contingent effects of, 11, 13–14, 20–21, 127–28, 130, 187, 209–10, 217–28, 243, 245, 251; empirical testing of, 215–28, 246–47. *See also* economic development; modernization theory

Sudan, 83, 121, 185, 246, 303; civil war in, 96, 98, 102; coups in, 82–83, 102; protest in, 83, 102, 111

suffrage, 27–28, 79, 142, 203n; extensions of, 24, 38, 107, 127, 145, 148, 156, 160–62

Suriname, 19, 146, 168n36, 303–4; civil war in, 31, 82, 98, 102, 111–12, 303–4; coups in, 67n7, 83, 111, 303–4

Sweden, 7, 126n6, 153, 186, 304; ruling party in, 148, 160, 165

Taiwan, 1–2, 24, 57, 152, 163; ruling party in, 1–2, 145, 147, 158, 162–63, 203n

Thailand, 56, 98, 304–6; coups in, 21n8, 67n7, 68, 75, 80, 82–83, 247, 304–6; protest in, ix, 56, 68, 75

transitional theory, 16, 178–79

Tunisia, 27, 41, 59, 186, 198, 256

Turkey, 124, 131, 142, 169n38, 231, 234n, 273, 279–80, 306–7; civil conflict in, 84, 98, 108n48; coups in, 67n7, 77–78, 80, 82–84

Turkmenbashi, 43

Uganda, 53, 307; war in, 123–24, 128, 131–32, 307

United Kingdom, 7, 24, 153, 158n21, 160–61; interventions by, 109, 140, 279; ruling parties in, 153, 160–61. *See also* England

United Nations, 109–10, 262, 272

United States, 27n2, 108n47, 118, 168, 249, 282; foreign policy of, 1, 76, 88–89, 102, 106, 112–14, 152, 155, 163, 165, 167, 176, 262, 269, 274–76, 282–84, 294, 298, 304; interventions by, 49, 67, 71, 75, 107, 128–29, 271–72, 275, 282, 305; and World War II, 38n, 130–31, 257, 298

Uruguay, 19, 156n18, 178–81, 307–9; coding of, 255; ruling parties in, 153, 162, 307–8

Venezuela, ix, 56, 76, 309; coups in, 73, 85, 309; opposition in, 54, 75, 215

Wałęsa, Lech, 138–39

wars, 47–48, 51–52, 54–57, 64–65, 186, 234–39; coding of, 31–32, 35, 191, 258–59; defeat and democratization, 122–33, 189, 195–97. *See also* World War I; World War II

waves, 28–29, 38, 85, 133–34, 182, 201, 246–47

West Germany, 39, 123n2, 256

World War I, 38, 54, 117, 123, 128, 131, 143, 278–79

World War II, 28, 32, 122–23, 128–31, 133–34, 139–40

Zaire, 42–43

Zambia, ix, 152, 181, 309; ruling party in, 162n28, 163, 233

Zimbabwe, 42, 108

## A NOTE ON THE TYPE

THIS BOOK has been composed in Miller, a Scotch Roman typeface designed by Matthew Carter and first released by Font Bureau in 1997. It resembles Monticello, the typeface developed for The Papers of Thomas Jefferson in the 1940s by C. H. Griffith and P. J. Conkwright and reinterpreted in digital form by Carter in 2003.

Pleasant Jefferson ("P. J.") Conkwright (1905–1986) was Typographer at Princeton University Press from 1939 to 1970. He was an acclaimed book designer and AIGA Medalist.

The ornament used throughout this book was designed by Pierre Simon Fournier (1712–1768) and was a favorite of Conkwright's, used in his design of the *Princeton University Library Chronicle.*

CPSIA information can be obtained
at www.ICGtesting.com
Printed in the USA
JSHW021607240621
16212JS00004B/17